SECURITY AND CONTROL IN INFORMATION SYSTEMS

'Andrew Hawker has produced a very practical text on a subject which is ever growing in importance, with a primary focus on the security of computer data, and with theoretical reflections which will stimulate further study. The material is at a level which makes it accessible to a wide readership, and will be of interest to both students and practitioners. Illustrations, tables and case examples are used effectively to bring the subject to life.'

Dr Steve Clarke, Luton Business School, UK

'The book is an excellent contribution to the important field of computer security as it provides a comprehensive and authoritative account of critical issues which concern contemporary business managers.'

Dr Ray Hackney, Manchester Metropolitan University, UK

With the advent of electronic commerce, and the increasing sophistication of the information systems used in business organisations, control and security have become key management issues. Responsibility for ensuring that controls are well designed and properly managed can no longer simply be delegated to the technical experts. It has become an area in which the whole management team needs to be involved.

This is a comprehensive review written for the business reader. It includes coverage of recent developments in electronic commerce, as well as the more traditional systems found in many organisations, both large and small.

The text is intended for any manager whose work depends on financial or other business information. It includes case studies, summaries and review questions, making it suitable as a source text for students of business studies at postgraduate or advanced level.

Andrew Hawker worked for 15 years in the computer industry, and has written numerous articles on privacy and security issues. He is currently Lecturer in Information Systems at the Birmingham Business School.

ROUTLEDGE INFORMATION SYSTEMS TEXTBOOKS
Series Editors: Steve Clarke, Brian Lehaney *both of Luton Business School* and D. Rajan Anketell, *Anketell Management Services*

This major new series in information systems consists of a range of texts which provide the core material required in the study of IS at undergraduate, post-graduate and post-experience levels. Authors have been chosen carefully for the scope of their knowledge and experience, providing a series designed for a range of abilities and levels. Students studying for an HND, BA, BSc, DMS, MA, MBA, or MSc in information systems, business or management will find these texts particularly useful.

1. **Security and Control in Information Systems**
   A guide for business and accounting
   Andrew Hawker

2. **Information Systems Strategic Management**
   An integrated approach
   Steve Clarke

SECURITY AND CONTROL IN INFORMATION SYSTEMS

A guide for business and accounting

Andrew Hawker

LONDON & NEW YORK

First published 2000 by Routledge
11 New Fetter Lane, London EC4P 4EE

Simultaneously published in the USA and Canada
by Routledge
29 West 35th Street, New York, NY 10001

Routledge is an imprint of the Taylor & Francis Group

Typeset in Plantin by Wearset, Boldon, Tyne and Wear
Printed and bound in Great Britain by
T J International Ltd, Padstow, Cornwall

British Library Cataloguing in Publication Data
A catalogue record for this book is available from the British Library

Library of Congress Cataloging in Publication Data
Hawker, Andrew.
 Security and control in information systems: a guide for business and
 accounting/Andrew Hawker.
  p. cm. – (Routledge information systems textbooks)
 Includes index.
  1. Electronic data processing departments–Auditing. 2. Computer security.
 3. Information technology–Security measures. I. Title. II. Series.

 HF5548.35 .H39 2001
 005.8–dc21
                                                                00–032838

ISBN 0-415-20534-4 (hbk)
ISBN 0-415-20535-2 (pbk)

Contents

Acknowledgements

Information Systems (IS) security and control is a rapidly changing field, and one where there can be strong disincentives to making information public. I am indebted to many people who have provided information, often informally, which has helped to guide the writing of this book. In particular, I should like to thank the members of specialist groups in the British Computer Society, including Tony Ball, Fleur Fisher, Mary Hawking, Glyn Hayes, Brian Layzell, Willie List, John Pike, and Mark Treleaven. The BCS Computer Audit Specialist Group has also provided invaluable information through its meetings. I have also benefited from the many challenges and ideas thrown up by postgraduate and final-year students, particularly Olivier Massart and Jog Dhody.

Ray Hackney and Steve Clarke provided very thorough and helpful reviews of early drafts of the text, and Andrew Thomas gave sound practical advice about the stresses of writing a book. Despite their best efforts, there are no doubt many deficiencies which remain, and these are the responsibility of the author.

Publisher's acknowledgements

The authors and publishers would like to thank the following for granting permission to reproduce material in this work:

Biometric Identification Inc for the use of the Veriprint 2100 image (Figure 4.4).

Sage Software Ltd for the use of Sage Line 50® screen images (Figures 4.11 and 5.2). Depictions of the Sage names and trademarks are included with the consent of The Sage Group plc, whose property they are and remain.

Every effort has been made to contact copyright holders for their permission to reprint material in this book. The publishers would be grateful to hear from any copyright holder who is not here acknowledged and will undertake to rectify any errors or omissions in future editions of this book.

Introduction

1 AIMS OF THIS BOOK

Businesses are accustomed to dealing with risks, but this is not to say that they welcome having to face new ones. Information technology (IT), having blazed a trail through most areas of business activity, has turned out to be surprisingly fragile. It has introduced new uncertainties into the world of business, since it seems to be vulnerable to errors, accidents, fraud, and various kinds of malicious attack. It is hardly surprising, therefore, if business organisations have mixed feelings about their dependence on information systems (IS). The arrival of electronic trading, in particular, has caused many to wonder about whether the new technology is completely trustworthy.

In response to these anxieties, a wide range of authoritative publications has become available. Many of these are aimed primarily at practitioners in computer auditing. Others offer in-depth technical explanations of security methods and principles. Much attention is currently being given to the security of the Internet, which has captured the popular imagination, and is proving to be one of the most anarchic technological developments of all time. Security and control are also receiving greater prominence in more orthodox quarters, such as the standard texts on information systems. What, then, does this book hope to contribute?

Its starting point is an assumption that IS security and control should have a place among the core skills of *everyone* who is concerned in the management and financial oversight of a business. It suggests that this is an area in which we need a great many more general practitioners, as well as expert consultants. The book attempts to describe principles and practice in a way which is accessible to the business reader, using examples drawn from both the private and the public sectors.

There is no intention to suggest that the experts can be dispensed with. Indeed, with information systems proliferating at a rapid pace around the world, it is probable that we need more of them. When consulting with experts, however, it is hoped that the information in this book will help to give non-specialists a head start. They will already know where weaknesses in control can be expected, and the kind of remedies which are available. They will not need background briefings on matters such as what encryption can achieve, how access controls should work, or the techniques commonly used in computer auditing. They should also feel more confident about taking an active part in optimising the controls in the systems they themselves use, and in demanding appropriate security features from suppliers. Even more usefully, they should be able to challenge the mechanistic approach which often dominates in IS security, where the answers are assumed to be mainly technological. This rests on a view that clear boundaries can be drawn between what is to be permitted, and what is not. In most organisations, life is simply not that tidy.

A recurring message from the UK Audit Commission is that much misuse of information systems results from failure to take very elementary precautions. For example, in one of its triennial surveys of computer fraud and abuse the Audit Commission (1994) observed:

> All the reasons cited for computer fraud and abuse could be found in any textbook on control mechanisms and a lack of basic controls caused most incidents.

This belief in a need to 'get back to basics' is one which is shared by many working in the field of computer audit. They complain of staff who not only omit to take simple precautions, but seem unaware of the need for them. Perhaps even more frustratingly, they find that it is widely assumed that security and control are the responsibility of senior management, of technicians, of the internal audit team – anyone, it seems, apart from those who are actually using the computer system on a daily basis.

All this seems to point to a need for more people to become actively involved in dealing with security and control problems. This book tries to encourage this broader involvement, by concentrating on underlying principles, providing plenty of practical examples, and stopping short of providing in-depth technical analysis. Much of the book is, inevitably, concerned with technical matters, but where possible the simplest possible examples are shown, and references to other books and articles are provided for the reader who wishes to get to grips with the more difficult cases.

It has to be acknowledged that several factors conspire to discourage people from becoming involved in IS security and control. For example, the vendors of technical solutions rely on playing on people's fears. Their aim, naturally enough, is to sow the seeds of doubt, and then to move discussion on to their technical remedies. The prospective purchaser is put in a no-win position. Investing nothing at all raises the prospects of endless inquests if things *do* go wrong, yet almost any level of investment which is actually chosen will be challenged by colleagues as being excessive. Many decide to play safe, and end up with an information system which fairly bristles with monitors, filters and checkers. Unfortunately, they may have only the haziest ideas about what they are all meant to achieve.

Another deterrent is the 'check list' approach of some guides. Check lists are much loved by consultants who, like vendors, have a vested interest in inducing worry. They can spark useful ideas, but they are of little help in deciding which issues are really important. The result? Still more anxiety, since the check list invariably throws up more problems and issues than anyone can possibly find time to deal with.

Finally, there is the alarming effect, not always intended, of some of the technical output on security. Through a desire to demonstrate their professional competence, or perhaps because of a love of the many puzzles and paradoxes of security, technical authors are eager to explore every imaginable threat and weakness. The result is rather like reading through a medical encyclopaedia. Before long, you begin to suspect that all the symptoms and ailments described must apply to your own system. This modern form of hypochondria can quickly lead to security measures which are badly thought out and expensive.

When a company's computer systems are running smoothly, there is every temptation to sit back with fingers crossed, and hope that this happy state of affairs will continue. A busy manager, in particular, will always have many other more urgent matters in the in-tray. Even in educational institutions, teachers are constantly seeking to avoid curriculum overload. For them security and control represent yet another topic, to compete with many others in the business curriculum. However, at a time when information technology is transforming the business world faster than ever before, all of us need to be investing time in this subject area, and seeking a properly balanced position, somewhere between complacency and panic.

The commitment of this book is therefore to cover as many as possible of the major issues in IS security and control, and to try to do so in a way which makes sense to the average reader. Referencing has been kept unobtrusive, but it is hoped that it will be rigorous enough for academic readers, and others who want to follow up on points of particular interest. Case studies and examples have been used to illustrate points wherever possible. The review questions at the end of each chapter are intended primarily for those who are following a course of study. However, many of the questions are intended to provoke further ideas, and some suggest practical observations in the workplace, so it is hoped that they will also interest other types of reader.

Before offering any further explanation of the aims and structure of the book, it will be helpful first to take a brief look at some of the simple pictures and models which have been applied to IS security and control.

2   MODELS OF SECURITY IN A BUSINESS SETTING

'Computer security' was originally the preserve of the military, whose main concern was to ensure the secrecy of information which might be helpful to an enemy. As a result, it was assumed that the key requirements were to build strong defences around the information system, and to keep the release of information to a minimum. It has taken some time for the commercial world to shake off these assumptions, and develop new ones of its own. Although businesses do not want their information systems, as a general rule, to be open to outsiders, they have some other equally important concerns. For example, they will want to be confident that their systems provide information which is accurate and reliable, that electronic records can be used in evidence, if need be, and that those who enter or use information can be readily identified.

Military models of information system security, on the other hand, assume that secrecy is paramount, and that there is a hierarchy of users, with the extent of a user's security clearance reflecting his or her seniority. A formal model along these lines was proposed by Bell and La Padula (1973) (see Figure I.1), and in 1983 this was enshrined in the US Department of Defense's 'Trusted Computer System Evaluation Criteria'. (This became better known as the 'Orange Book', and has been regularly revised as a guide for security levels ever since).

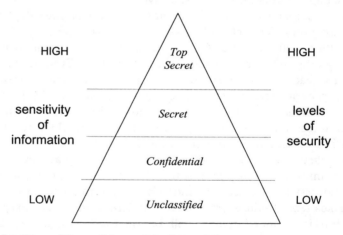

Figure I.1 **The military (hierarchical) model**

The military concerns about data security led to considerable investment in software built around the Bell–La Padula model, and in due course adaptations of this began to find their way onto the commercial market. At this point, however, some began to question whether the military model was entirely appropriate for business. Clark and Wilson (1987: 185) noted that:

> In the commercial environment, preventing disclosure is often important, but preventing unauthorized data modification is usually paramount.

Clark and Wilson went on to suggest that businesses were not, by and large, concerned with preventing the 'leakage' of information to the wrong people. They were far more concerned with being able to depend on the information provided by their systems, particularly where accounting was concerned. To this end, businesses would want to prevent errors occurring, and to make it as difficult as possible for employees to commit fraud. Clark and Wilson therefore borrowed two ideas from accounting practice, of *well-formed transactions* and *separation of duties*, and suggested how these might be applied in computer systems. Well-formed transactions are those for which a body of corroborative evidence is constantly being built up. The modification or erasure of information is not allowed: instead, changes are always made through additional 'correcting' entries. Separation of duties involves assigning tasks in ways which are intended to make it difficult for people to collude and commit fraud. Neither of these ideas is concerned particularly with whether information should or should not be *released*. The concern is centred much more on the information's *accuracy* and *integrity*.

With these priorities in mind, a wider view needs to be taken of the way in which commercial IS security should operate. Clark and Wilson began with secrecy, and added accuracy and protection against tampering. In the age of electronic commerce, there are at least five other objectives which need to be added, and these are listed here.

EIGHT OBJECTIVES OF COMMERCIAL IS SECURITY AND CONTROL

- Protect secrets
- Promote accuracy
- Prevent tampering
- Prove authorship
- Challenge repudiation
- Authenticate over time
- Ensure survival
- Maximise auditability

The chapters which follow develop ideas for achieving *all* these objectives. They are examined in the context of all kinds of administrative and financial records, in both the private and the public sector. All organisations are assumed to have security and control among their 'business' objectives, although there will inevitably be major differences in emphasis, particularly when it comes to areas such as privacy protection for personal data, or the need for long-term retention of records.

In implementing any security model (whether military or commercial) it is important to identify where controls are to be applied which are fully or partially *automated*. This implies the setting of an *automated control boundary* around certain system components and activities. Ideally, all the information systems in the organisation will be collected together inside one boundary. In practice, there may have to be a number of separate 'containers'. Each one can be depicted as in Figure I.2.

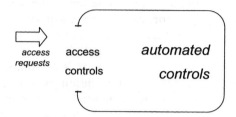

Figure I.2

Note that everyone wishing to use the information services inside the container must first be authorised to do so, by passing through the 'doorway' of access controls. Inside the container, restrictions are enforced by the system to ensure that each user is confined to those activities he or she actually needs (how this is done is discussed in Part 2).

In Figure I.3, the container is shown as being surrounded by another boundary (shown with a dotted line) which encloses everyone working for the organisation.

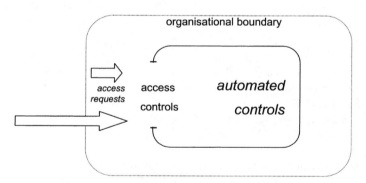

Figure I.3

Because the organisation may wish to give access to selected outsiders (such as customers and suppliers), two arrows are now shown for access: one representing *internal* access by those inside the organisation, and the other showing *external* access by those outside it. If the security or integrity of the system is threatened, these threats too can be regarded as being generally either *internal* or *external* in origin.

3 THE STRUCTURE OF THE BOOK

Part 1 of the book introduces some concepts which are relevant mainly to the first three objectives listed above. It considers how information may be valued, and how different types of threats against information systems can be classified. Two topics are then presented in which managers have to make difficult judgements: first, in estimating levels of risk and, second, in acknowledging some of the human factors which have to be taken into account when designing controls.

The setting up of automated control boundaries is covered in **Part 2**. Much of Part 2 is concerned with the creation and management of the access control 'doorways', by which all traffic across the boundaries should be regulated. Attention is also given to controls which need to be applied to business transactions *inside* the automated control boundary, and the kind of organisational structures and procedures which should complement and support them. Up to this point, the emphasis is still on the first three security and control objectives (secrecy, accuracy, and tamper-proofing).

In **Part 3**, attention switches to situations where systems are linked to one another. The situation can now be viewed as in Figure I.4. Managers are now faced with judgements about the extent to which trust can be extended over the links in a network.

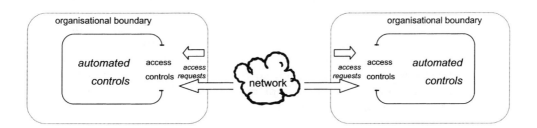

Figure I.4

Some of the same issues arise even if different systems which are nominally within the same organisational boundary are linked via a network. Such situations (with a special emphasis on Local Area Networks) are covered in Chapter 8.

Up to this point, the book is concerned with routine controls over everyday transactions in the typical information system. **Part 4** moves on to some of the more strategic and long-term issues, particularly in connection with making business survival possible in the event of a disaster, and creating archives which will remain operational well into the future. A common theme is the preservation of data over time. Today's organisations are conscious that data, in all its various forms, is an asset with considerable value. A failure of the computer systems may mean the loss of the records on which the business depends, and in extreme cases, will cause the business to collapse. Dependence of a different kind is growing as more and more historical data goes into electronic stores. It cannot be taken for granted that this data will be intelligible, and still have evidential value, after the passage of years.

Part 5 is concerned with issues of compliance. The role of the Computer Auditor is described, and compared with that of others such as IS Security Officers. These are important functions for all organisations using IS, although the responsibilities are not always assigned very formally. Good computer audit looks beyond the here-and-now, and is involved in planning security into new systems, and in helping to build in controls at the design and testing stages. A chapter on computer forensics is also included. Although 'detective' work is only required relatively infrequently, it is helpful to know about the techniques which are available (and the threat of using them can sometimes be a useful deterrent).

Consideration of the industry standards and legal provisions relating to IS controls is kept until **Part 6**. This gives a number of examples, and plenty of reference points for those who wish to check up on the latest situation. The section can be used in conjunction with the list of web sites provided in Appendix 2. Finally, some 'rules of thumb' pick out themes from the book, and attempts to present them in a way which managers will find easy to bring to mind (Appendix 1).

Table I.1 shows how the eight security and control objectives are addressed in different parts of the book. (Part 6 is not included in the table: standards and legislation can be assumed to relate to *all* the objectives). Table I.1 is only intended to give a very approximate guide to the part of the book in which the various objectives are *introduced*. By the beginning of Part 5, the aim is that most of the objectives will have been covered in some detail, so that attention can be switched to the role of those who have to implement them. More detailed guidance on chapter content is given in the summary information at the start of each chapter.

Table I.1

	PART 1 Threats and risks	PART 2 Internal systems	PART 3 Networked systems	PART 4 Continuity and archive	PART 5 Computer audit
Protect secrets	•	•			
Promote accuracy	•	•			
Prevent tampering	•	•	•	•	
Prove authorship			•	•	
Challenge repudiation			•		
Authenticate over time				•	
Ensure survival				•	
Maximise auditability					•

The table reflects the way in which attention in IS control and security is gradually shifting away from the more traditional objectives (in **Parts 1 and 2**) to the newer objectives covered in **Parts 3 to 5**. The latter are growing in importance with the emergence of the 'wired society'. The growth of electronic commerce over the Internet, and increased dependence on magnetic and optical media for storing records, mean that even organisations with well-developed security and control policies must keep them under constant revision.

4   THE OBJECTIVES OF THE BOOK

It is hoped that the reader will find that the book offers the following:

- Analysis and recommendations which acknowledge the untidy and imperfect state of systems in most organisations. This is an inevitable result of acquiring different hardware and software products over the years, and having to run these alongside one another.
- Basic principles which apply across all types of system, from ageing 'legacy' software to modern client-server applications, as well as the exciting prospects now opening up in electronic commerce.
- An emphasis on the way techniques should be applied, rather than on detailed expositions of how they work. Cryptography, for example, is presented as a means of creating a 'kit of tools', rather than as a scientific topic in its own right.
- Insights into the human and organisational aspects of security and controls, so that managers can make themselves more effective in these areas, and know what help they can expect from specialists, particularly in the field of computer audit.
- Enough background to equip the reader to take part in the kind of IS security review which may be required in all organisations from time to time, and to understand requirements such as those of the BS 7799 standard in the UK.
- Realistic suggestions for ways of evaluating the costs and benefits of security measures. These seek to avoid the situation where idealised and comprehensive solutions are proposed, even where they are likely to be unaffordable.
- Illustrations and case studies wherever possible, drawing from the experience of organisations both large and small, from different parts of the world, and from both the public and private sector.

Above all, the text strives to present the field of IS security and control as one which calls, at different times, for ingenuity, initiative, imagination, attention to detail, and foresight. In short, it is bound to stretch the capability of even the best of managers to get it right. It should not be seen as simply a nuisance associated with information systems. This is exciting territory, and deserves to be explored with enthusiasm by anyone who is pursuing a business career.

Part 1

THREATS AND
RISKS

INTRODUCTION TO PART 1

Risk is a part of everyday life for all of us. We make decisions about whether or not to drive fast along the highway. We consider the implications of eating food which has passed the sell-by date on the label, and try to avoid walking down badly lit streets. It is only by understanding and dealing with these risks that we survive.

In the same way, business survival depends on successful responses to risk, and an increasing number of these risks are associated with information systems. Unfortunately, they are often hard to see. Software and data are completely invisible, and one piece of computer hardware looks very like another. Warning signs may be few and far between and, by the time they are noticed, it may be too late.

Part 1 begins by examining the kind of threats which apply to information systems. It points out that these threats will not always result from actions which are malicious, or even deliberate. As well as considering their capacity to cause harm, it is important to decide how likely they are to happen. This enables calculations to be made of the *size* of the risks involved, and comparisons can then be made between them.

It should not be assumed that protection against risk is achieved by throwing up massive fortifications around the IS installation. It is more important to select exactly the *right* countermeasures, targeted at the risks which matter most. Some methodologies for estimating the seriousness of risks are described, and suggestions are made for ways of ensuring that all the countermeasures which are introduced are appropriate and cost-effective.

chapter
one

INFORMATION
UNDER THREAT

SOME TOPICS ADDRESSED IN THIS CHAPTER

- How organisations can assess the *value* of the information held in their systems
- Why businesses have come to be *more dependent* on information systems
- Changes in the ways in which information systems are used and configured, and how these have given rise to *new types of threat*
- Defining and *classifying* the different types of threat

SECURITY AND CONTROL OBJECTIVES

- Protect secrets
- Promote accuracy
- Prevent tampering

1.1 PLACING A VALUE ON INFORMATION

The desire to control and protect information is rooted in the notion that information has a value. But how can this value be assessed? Clearly it is more than the medium on which the information is stored, as evidenced by the high prices consumers are willing to pay for commercial 'information products', such as CDs containing music or computer games.

When information is traded in this way, it is possible to test out its market value. But this cannot be done for the bulk of the information which is held by business organisations, which they keep for their own internal use, and which is not subject to any kind of pricing. Of course, some trade secrets may have an obvious value to competitors. Equally, business systems contain a lot of information which has little intrinsic value (such as advertising copy which has been widely published) but which it is useful to keep on file.

The value of business information has been the subject of theoretical analysis by economists. Marschak, for example, points to the value of *quality* in information, which will enable the business to make sound decisions. Conversely, the presence of errors will undermine the credibility and therefore the value of the information (Marschak 1968). Writers on information systems have built on some of the economists' ideas. Monk points out that merely *searching* for information amounts to an economic transaction, and that 'acts of communication are necessarily economic events'. Thus value is to be obtained not just from holding information, but in being able to communicate it easily across networks (Monk 1993: 16).

A more pragmatic approach has been described by Keen, who cites the case of a bank which drew up an 'IT Asset Balance Sheet'. Somewhat to the bank's surprise, it found that the amount it had invested in developing software and collecting data came to three times the amount spent on its Information Technology (IT) hardware (Keen 1991: ch. 6). Notwithstanding the large numbers involved, the calculations still only indicated the *costs* of acquiring the information assets. Their actual *value* to the bank could have been quite unrelated to these costs.

In a study of twelve manufacturing companies in North America, McKinnon and Bruns (1992) asked managers what *they* felt made information valuable. The researchers found that there was general agreement that it should be trustworthy, timely, relevant and accurate. However, the same information might be perceived to have different value by different managers. Those with accounting degrees, for example, valued financial reports much more than those whose accounting background was limited.

Perhaps the most ambitious attempt to provide a general framework for valuing information has been provided by Boisot. Boisot (1998) describes a 'knowledge asset' as having three dimensions. *Codification* organises information into classes or categories, so that it becomes easier to search. *Abstraction* helps to reveal the shape and meaning of information, and *diffusion* determines the availability of information for those who want to use it. Each of these dimensions has an effect on the value of the information. For example, a database may have high codification, increasing its value to interested individuals. At the same time, the diffusion might be kept low, giving it a scarcity value and justifying a premium rate for access. Boisot concedes that using these three dimensions does not eliminate the need for subjective judgements, but suggests that it can provide a useful framework for discussion, to help members of an organisation arrive at a better consensus about the value of the information they are using.

Rather than trying to value the information itself, it may be more practicable to set about valuing the information system as a whole. This is the approach taken when reviewing proposals to buy a new system, or to extend an old one. Unless some value can be placed on the benefits expected from the upgrade, there is no basis for judging whether the investment is going to be worthwhile. A number of guides are available to help with decision-making in this area, most of which focus mainly on the cost side of the equation. Unfortunately, detailed and accurate costings are not much help if the figures for the benefits have all been arrived at by fudges and guesswork. Nor is it common for predictions of benefits to be checked against actual outcomes. As Hares and Royle point out, it is rare for organisations to do any kind of analysis after implementation to see whether the expected benefits from a new system have actually been delivered. Consequently they do not learn from the experience of what Hares and Royle (1994: Ch. 8) term *benefits realisation*.

Valuing IS assets is also a problem for accountants. Although intangible assets are regularly included on Balance Sheets, no precise methods are available for valuing them. A draft standard from the US Financial Accounting Standards Board (FASB 1999) has a classification of 'technology-based assets', including software, databases and information systems. It distinguishes these from assets whose value is protected for a set period of time by law, such as patents, trademarks and copyright, where the value will fall sharply when the legal protection expires. However, the determination of the actual values remains a matter for professional custom and practice.

In summary, exact valuations of information systems and their contents are difficult because:

- value is not necessarily related to acquisition or development costs;
- perceptions of value will vary widely among different users of the same system;
- value often depends on transient qualities, such as timeliness and relevance;
- for information internal to the firm, values cannot be 'market-tested'.

In order to compare the severity of risks (Chapter 2) and to plan for business continuity (Chapter 9), it is necessary to assess at least the *relative* value of different IS resources. Methods of doing this are discussed in the chapters concerned. In general, however, businesses do not need to know the exact values of their IS services in order to appreciate that they tend to be very high. In fact, in many cases the information systems are so integral to the functioning of the organisation that its very survival depends on them.

1.2 BUSINESS DEPENDENCE ON INFORMATION SYSTEMS

In the late 1950s, the London-based food manufacturer J. Lyons & Co was a pioneer in new business methods using an electronic computer. The computer in question – which the company built and programmed itself – depended on electrical valves and moving parts, and in today's terms was extremely unreliable. It was also not without its hazards, as the case study shows.

THE LEO BUSINESS COMPUTER

J. Lyons & Co ran a chain of 200 tea shops, each of which submitted daily orders to the central bakery. This process was automated using the LEO ('Lyons Electronic Office') computer. It was found to give better control of the catering operations (among other things, the computer could be used to check the *expected* revenue from each shop, based on the items supplied to it), and provided useful statistics for manufacturing and marketing. Because of frequent computer failures, an alternative system based on the manual processing of forms was on permanent stand-by.

Lyons then experimented with optical mark reading. A printer capable of producing the necessary forms (the 'Xeronic') was acquired, and the completed forms were read by an 'Autolector' reader. Both these products used new and relatively untried technology. The Autolector reader was inclined to misinterpret smudges from the printing process. This was welcomed by some of the staff, since smudges occurring in some positions on the payroll input forms resulted in the system giving them extra pay. (The internal audit department, understandably, took a rather different view.) The Xeronic printer also gave problems, as it required toner to be heated to a very high temperature, and the paper had to be run through the machine very quickly to avoid burning it. In July 1967 one of these printers caught fire, causing considerable damage to the machine room and destroying two of the LEO computers.

Based on Bird, P. J., *Leo: The First Business Computer*, Hasler Publishing, London 1994

J. Lyons & Co was in a position to take advantage of IT, *without* becoming completely dependent on it, and this experience was reflected in many other companies as they automated many of their clerical and manufacturing processes for the first time.

Today, it would be hard to find any manufacturer who does not use information technology, but the technology is now expected to be completely reliable, and underpins all kinds of activities which are crucial to the business. Computers are expected to schedule the requirements for raw materials, to take control of the processes on production lines, and to support the distribution of the products on to the retailers. Modern supermarket chains, in turn, use their systems to keep goods moving as quickly as possible through the warehouses, onto the store shelves, and through the check-outs. The movement of goods through supply chains has been speeded up dramatically over the years, and mistakes or failures at any point can have severe knock-on effects.

The prospect of a sudden computer failure has now become a worst nightmare for many managers: a supermarket packed with Saturday morning shoppers, with no check-outs working; or a warehouse in which the tracking system has failed, so no-one knows where anything is; or a production line requiring speed and temperature to be kept within precise limits, where the controls have failed. This heavy dependence on IT has also spread inexorably through other sectors of business, most noticeably bureaucracies, particularly in the administrative arms of government and the military. Small businesses, too, have begun to move on from their traditional computing applications such as word-processing and account-ing, and now use computers in a much wider variety of situations. Examples range from hotels keeping track of their room bookings and occupancy, to sellers of books and music CDs operating via web sites on the Internet.

Just *how* dependent each business is on its IT facilities varies from busi-ness to business, and from day to day. Some factors likely to indicate higher than average dependence include:

- services based on an *immediate response* to the customer (such as booking airline seats or telephone banking);
- reliance on a *centralised database* (for example, a vehicle manufacturer with a national database of components and spares);
- use of IS in processes connected with *health or safety* (for example, in a hospital, or a manufacturing process involving dangerous chemicals);
- working in a market where decisions have to be based on *up-to-the-minute* information (for example, day trading in bonds and shares);
- dependence on IS for the organisation's *core activity* (for example, running a lottery, or air traffic control).

Many organisations have a high dependence for more than one of these reasons. Their vulnerability may also be greater at some times than at others: for example, a computer failure over a summer weekend might have a negligible effect on a manufacturing company whose factory is closed, but could be disastrous for a theme park on its peak visiting day.

1.3   NEW SOURCES OF THREATS TO INFORMATION SYSTEMS

As the dependence of businesses on IS increases, so does the range and severity of the threats which can arise. This can happen for a number of reasons:

- *Scale.* Systems increasingly operate on a national or international scale. For example, a failure in a bank's computer centre can put all its auto-mated teller machines offline.
- *Speed.* Previously, it could take some time for fire, flood or malicious damage to destroy records. Large computer files, on the other hand, can be deleted or corrupted electronically in a matter of seconds. Sim-ilarly, unauthorised transmission or copying of data can be carried out almost instantaneously.
- *Technical innovation.* New technology changes all the ground-rules, and

many people do not understand it very well. Previously, it was reasonable to rely to a large extent on employees' good sense (for example, in not leaving filing cabinets unlocked). With IT-based systems, they may not even realise that they are taking unacceptable risks. At the opposite end of the skills spectrum, on the other hand, there are highly talented technicians who regard it as a challenge to invade and disrupt systems. They can conduct their attacks from the other end of a network – without needing to go anywhere near the premises they are attacking.

- *Hidden causes.* Sometimes, it is difficult to trace back to the cause of a problem in a complex system. For example, on 1 January 1985, customers trying to use the cash machines of two major clearing banks, which normally accepted each others' cards, found themselves getting unpredictable results. The problem was eventually traced to erroneous updating of the magnetic strips on the cards by one of the banks. It seems that some of the bank's software had failed to recognise that 1984 was a leap year, and entered date information on the cards which then confused other parts of the system.

In summary: new threats can:

- have a far-reaching potential impact;
- be very rapid in their effects;
- arise from both absence and misuse of technical skills; and
- prove difficult to trace back to their source.

1.4   OUTSOURCING AND RE-ENGINEERING: TWO DECADES OF CHANGE

At the same time that businesses have grown more dependent on information systems, they have had to accept some quite radical shifts in ideas about how these systems should be managed and organised. During the 1980s, many organisations began to see advantages in distancing themselves from the everyday business of running computer systems. Their aim was usually to reduce or contain costs, as their internal data centres required ever more expensive equipment, and small armies of programmers and operators, to keep them going. Handing responsibility for information systems to an outside organisation would, it was felt, enable management to concentrate on the core aspects of their business. If outsiders could take over functions like transporting finished products around the country, or managing the employee pension scheme, why not IT?

This became known as *outsourcing*, and some major players swiftly moved into this rapidly expanding business. Some (like IBM) were computer suppliers who saw it as a logical extension of the IT products and services they were already offering. Others (like Andersen Consulting) moved in from their original base in accountancy. One of the most successful transnational outsourcing companies has been Electronic Data Systems (EDS). EDS began as a provider of outsourced services to its parent company, General Motors, and gradually broadened its operations until it now provides outsourcing to companies around the world. Outsourcing acquired respectability when it was adopted by heavily IS-dependent companies like the Continental Bank in the USA (Huber 1993). The experiences of other US companies which outsourced have been extensively documented by Lacity and Hirschheim (1993 and 1995).

In theory, handing over responsibility for running IT to an outsider ensured that management could forget all its worries about dependence on IT. If a round-the-clock service was required, this would be specified in the contract with the service provider, who would be held liable for any failures. In practice, however, outsourcers were reluctant to give any such absolute guarantees. Instead, management had to place their confidence in the technical skills and integrity of an organisation, aware that there were many aspects of computer operations over which they now had no direct input or control.

As with all major organisational changes, staff have often felt threatened by outsourcing plans. For example, in 1996 the Community and Public Sector Union in Australia campaigned vigorously against a number of government outsourcing initiatives. The charged atmosphere which results from such confrontations is not conducive to securing co-operation and compliance from staff, on which good security practice very much depends.

Hard on the heels of outsourcing came the new fashion at the start of the 1990s, known as *Business Process Re-engineering* (BPR). Up to this time, information systems had largely been used to automate the existing way of doing things. Michael Hammer dismissed this as just 'paving the cow paths'. Instead, businesses should look at radically new ways of organising their activities, taking advantage of the power and flexibility of information technology (Hammer 1990). Hammer later developed a 'manifesto' for re-engineering (Hammer and Champy 1993), which, as one critic pointed out, drew heavily on the ideas of socio-technical systems design developed in the 1950s (Mumford 1995).

BPR was taken up enthusiastically by a number of organisations, particularly those competing on quality and speed of service to customers. Banks, for example, found ways of shortening the cycle time for approving loans, and integrated their systems so that customers could enquire about various services without the frustration of having to be passed around between departments. Some companies chose to attack the accounting function, with Ford in the USA being one of the first to re-engineer the way it handled payments to suppliers. Others, like the German optical equipment manufacturer Zeiss, applied BPR to their warehousing and distribution network.

BPR projects met with mixed success, particularly where too much emphasis was placed on trying to make cost savings (Hall *et al* 1993). Even in the successful implementations, it has not always been easy to anticipate some of the security risks created by the new methods of working. For example, the BPR philosophy includes 'empowerment' of those who serve the customer. Unless this is planned carefully, it can mean that staff will be given a mix of responsibilities which should, in the interests of control and audit, be kept separate.

As with outsourcing, the prevailing mood of staff may be hostile, as they wonder whether their jobs will change for the worse, or even disappear. Unlike outsourcing, this concern extends to anyone involved in the processes which are being 're-designed', and not just those employed to run the information systems.

In summary: the new approaches of outsourcing and BPR:

- shifted control and influence over IT operations;
- generated anxieties among staff affected by the changes;
- were not always accompanied by a corresponding updating of security measures.

The pattern of continuing innovation in the way information systems are used looks likely to continue well into the twenty-first century. For example, companies selling goods via the Internet will have to develop new and more versatile methods for handling orders and distributing goods, and in some industries manufacturers are already exploring ways of leapfrogging the retailer, and dealing directly with consumers (Bridge 1999).

1.5   THE NATURE AND SOURCES OF THREATS

An organisation cannot hope to develop effective data security measures unless it first of all has a clear idea of what it is trying to protect itself against. It should be stressed that 'threats' to data do not necessarily arise from a *deliberate* intention to cause damage. A threat in this context is defined as *any potential source of harm to the reliability or integrity of the IT system*. The threat may originate through ignorance, incompetence, carelessness, malice, or a combination of these factors. It is also important to anticipate potential failures due to weaknesses built into the system, which can be triggered quite innocently – in other words, the system itself is in a state which safety analysts would regard as constituting a *hazard*.

Various approaches to categorising threats have been proposed. The UK Audit Commission, for example, uses *nine* categories for its analysis of computer abuse incidents (Audit Commission 1998). As a basis for management response to the different types of threat, it is proposed that some of these should be combined, to give *five* main headings, as follows.

1.5.1   Theft

Theft is directed at removing assets from the organisation. Fraud (discussed below) can therefore be regarded as one particular form of theft. However, some useful distinctions may be made: in theft, there is little or no attempt to conceal the disappearance of the assets, while someone committing a fraud may go to great lengths to hide his or her activities by making all the records look consistent and 'normal'. Thefts may, of course, also be difficult to detect, and take some time to come to light, so the difference between fraud and theft is not always clear-cut. A particular example is the theft of *intangible* assets such as data and software, which can be 'stolen' by taking unauthorised copies. Since the originals are left unchanged and unmarked, the thief may leave no tell-tale signs at the scene of the crime. This is perhaps best regarded as a surreptitious form of theft, rather than fraud, because the thief has not had to arrange some kind of 'cover-up' in order to hide the crime.

If an employee misuses the organisation's resources, this too may amount to theft in a strictly technical sense (for example, in respect of the stationery or electricity consumed). In some cases, however, there will be separate grounds for action under specific rules or legislation, for example, if the misuse involves material which is offensive or pornographic.

CASES OF THEFT

Police in Sweden monitored an Internet site operated by two students in Stockholm. Over a period of 3 weeks, they noted that around 150 copies of software packages were being sent out over the Internet each day, including several 'market leader' products for use on PCs. It was estimated that £1 million worth of software had been copied illegally. Both the instigators and those receiving the software faced prosecution for software theft.

Computing, 22 June 1995: 3

An employee of 22 years' standing used the company's IT equipment to set up a printing business to compete with his employer. He stole software and used equipment to create and print private work in the office. He also stole office equipment to set up a system at home, duplicating the one he used at work.

Audit Commission, *Ghost in the Machine*, 1998: 14

1.5.2　Fraud

Fraud involves the taking of assets, aided by some form of deception. This will usually involve outwitting controls designed to protect the system from just such an attack. Not surprisingly, fraud is a major preoccupation of those who design and audit system controls.

Fraud can be committed by people working within the organisation, or by outsiders. In some cases, both are involved. The perpetrators may be at quite a low level in the organisation, in which case the aim is usually to siphon off relatively small amounts over a long period. Fraud can also occur at very senior levels in the organisation, where the aim is usually to achieve more indirect benefits, such as boosting a company's share price, or persuading a client to place a lucrative contract.

The UK Law Commission has reviewed the law relating to fraud, and has suggested ways in which offences involving dishonesty and deception could be better defined. In particular, the Commission notes that:

'As a result of technological change, particularly the development of the Internet, it is becoming possible to fraudulently obtain services of significant value without deceiving a human mind. Such conduct is not currently criminal. We therefore provisionally conclude:

(1) that it should be criminal to obtain a service without the permission of the person providing it, albeit without the deception of a human mind . . .'

Law Commission 1999

CASES OF FRAUD

In 1993 the US supermarket chain King Soopers moved its computing onto IBM PCs. The manager in charge of the system migration, aided by two senior clerks, took advantage of the situation to manipulate the data on the system, and create a large number of sales 'voids'. The team then pocketed payments associated with the 'void' transactions. They also adjusted the bar-code systems to over-charge customers, and kept the surplus payments. Managers in the company did not understand the new system very well, and relied heavily on guidance from the manager who was running the fraud. The crimes eventually came to light when the expensive life styles of the fraudsters attracted suspicion.

Computerworld, 30 March 1998: 1

A local authority issued housing benefits via a decentralised system of 'Neighbour-hood Offices'. An assessment officer in one of these local offices set up false benefit cases, with fictitious details for the tenants. Cheques generated by the system were either sent to addresses where the officer knew he could intercept them, or directly to friends of the officer who were assisting him with the fraud. The fraud was detected by chance, when a batch of cheques was examined closely, following problems with printing some of them.

Audit Commission, *Survey of Computer Fraud and Abuse Supplement*, 1990: 20

The chief accountant for a car sales firm kept two sets of management accounts. One recorded the true position, and was shown only to the directors. The other showed a much healthier financial position, and was used in support of an application for £6 million-worth of investment from a major bank. At the trial, the accountant was quoted as saying: 'The investors didn't have total control in checking our accounts . . . They were definitely misled by the accounts presented to them'.

Birmingham Post, 10 October 1996

1.5.3 Malicious damage

The 'damage' in this case may be physical, for example, setting fire to a machine room or destroying a diskette containing vital data. However, organisations increasingly need to protect themselves against more subtle and devious types of damage. They may be singled out as a target for this, or find that they are the victim of indiscriminate attacks by rogue programs such as computer viruses. In either case data can be altered or erased surreptitiously, without leaving any obvious traces. The damage may not come to light until a legitimate user next tries to access the data, only to find that the enquiry program cannot function, or starts to give strange error messages.

CASES OF MALICIOUS DAMAGE

Internet web sites have become a common target for malicious attack. In the run up to the UK General Election in 1997, the web pages of both the major political parties were altered by hackers. The Labour Party's page featured a caricature of the party leader and a list of items including 'The Budget Response: More of those lies all parties feed you close to an election'. A few weeks later it was the turn of the Conservative Party's page. This featured its leader against a background of a swastika, above a long tirade which asked (among other things): 'Are we putting our country in the hands of these parties, who can't even secure a web page?'

The US airline AirTran found its site hacked in September 1997, following its change of name from Valujet. The hacked version was a malicious spoof of the original site, accusing the company of wishing to change its name because it had an unsatisfactory safety record, and carrying a picture of a burning jet falling out of the sky next to a headline 'AirTran introduces new services, begins strategy to kill all Americans'.

Source: files of hacked web sites at the Hacker Quarterly site, **http://www.2600.com**

A schoolboy in West Yorkshire, England, gained access to a computer run by the *Financial Times*. This contained a database of share prices used in the production of the newspaper. He deleted a password file, and introduced a program which generated a constant stream of outgoing calls from the computer. The computer had to be withdrawn from service in order to track down and remove all the changes which had been introduced. This cost the *Financial Times* an estimated £25,000.

Independent, 26 February 1993

1.5.4 Incompetence and mistakes

If routine users of a system are careless, or simply do not understand what they are doing, they may unwittingly cause errors or failures in the system. However, the aim of good system design is to stop them before they can cause any serious or lasting damage. This is done by restricting their access to the system, and putting checks and limits on their ability to use some of the more powerful facilities in the system. However, there have been instances where mistakes have slipped through the net, as the cases of incompetence show.

Those who are more intimately involved with the running of the system, and who are therefore given more powerful access to it, generally represent a more serious threat. They have the potential to cause extremely serious problems if they do not understand what they are doing. People in this position include mainframe operators, systems programmers, and those who have access rights to enable them to investigate what is going on in the system (including computer auditors).

CASES OF INCOMPETENCE

A junior employee of a German financial institution made a mistake during a training exercise. Instead of simulating a deal in German bond futures, he unwittingly created a *real* transaction worth £11.5 billion. His employers lost an estimated £10 million in extricating themselves from the confusion which followed.

Daily Telegraph, 19 November 1998: 1

In September 1989, Citibank sent out payments via the UK Clearing House Automated Payments system, to the value of approximately £2 billion. Unfortunately, these were all duplicates of payments which had been made the day before. A subsequent comment from Citibank read: 'The error was discovered almost immediately as a result of other operating controls. All payments were interbank payments and as convention dictates duplicate payments were reversed.'

Computer Weekly, 26 October 1989: 9

A student who bought a second-hand computer from an army surplus store found that the hard disk contained sensitive files relating to the Royal Signals and Research Establishment of the Ministry of Defence. The files included details of staff and the projects they were working on. The computers had been sent for auction following a replacement programme, but the need to erase the files had been overlooked.

BIS Computer Disaster Casebook, 1987: 201

1.5.5   Accidents and disasters

However well an organisation tries to anticipate threats under the above four categories, there will always be a residual category of events which are very unlikely, but which cannot be entirely ruled out. Examples include the effects of severe weather conditions, the accidental release of toxic materials from a factory or tanker, or a fire in the office. Terrorist actions – although these represent the ultimate in malicious damage – are usually included in this category, because their effects are usually similar to those of natural disasters. All such events can paralyse or destroy computer systems, and in many instances the only solution will be to fall back onto stand-by arrangements which have been planned in advance.

CASES OF ACCIDENTS AND DISASTERS

In April 1992, 250 million gallons of water from the Chicago River poured through a break in the walls of a tunnel under Chicago's business district. Many basement offices were flooded. Shortly afterwards, the city authorities ordered that the power supplies to the area should be disconnected. Altogether 30 data centres suffered disruption to their activities.

EDP Audit, Control & Security Newsletter, July 1992: 13

A rented truck containing a home-made bomb made from ammonium nitrate fertiliser and fuel oil was detonated outside the Alfred P. Murrah Federal Building in downtown Oklahoma in April 1995. The building housed several federal offices, including Customs and Social Security. One third of the building was destroyed, and 168 people (most of them employees of organisations located in the building) were killed. At least 2,000 businesses suffered economic loss.

Disaster Recovery Information Exchange, **www.drie.org**

1.5.6 Categories of threat: conclusions

The first three types of threat (i.e. theft, fraud and malicious damage, where the threat is a deliberate one) are sometimes grouped together under the general heading of *computer abuse*. This is a useful catch-all term, which can be used to encompass various activities which do not fit neatly into the categories provided so far. For example, if an employee intends to send an offensive message to a colleague by electronic mail, but sends it off to a supplier by mistake, it seems hardly worth arguing over exactly which category this belongs to. What is abundantly obvious is that the employee has abused the system.

'Abuse' is, in turn, often used interchangeably with 'misuse'. *Misuse* is in some ways a gentler term, but it is difficult to draw a line between the two meanings. In the UK, *misuse* is increasingly used with a specific meaning, to denote unauthorised use of a computer in ways which are offences under the Computer Misuse Act, 1990.

Different *motivations* lie behind each of the threats. The first two (theft and fraud) are driven by hopes of *personal enrichment*. This may be through acquisition of money, services, or goods directly (in the case of theft), or through more devious means (as in the case of a director who issues accounts which misrepresent the company's position). Since the aim is to make use of someone else's assets, the latter will be left undamaged, unless this happens to be unavoidable in furtherance of the crime.

This motivation may lie dormant until there is a gap in security measures, such as discovering a password on a scrap of paper lying on a desk, or noticing that a control procedure is not being followed correctly. Alternatively, someone may drift into wrong-doing in a more gradual way. Some will take a systematic approach; they will set about building up knowledge about weaknesses in the system, and experimenting (perhaps quite innocuously at first) to find out how to take advantage of them.

Probably the most difficult motives to discern are those associated with malicious damage. These can be divided between two main headings: *grievance* (including retaliation against a person or organisation, furtherance of an ideology, or some kind of unfocused disenchantment with the world at large) and *vanity* (proving one's skills to oneself, or to a wider community of hackers). Often the motives are mixed, as in the case of talented hackers, who want to demonstrate their skills, but at the same time wish to inconvenience organisations with whose aims or values they disagree. Hackers will usually take a systematic approach in probing for weaknesses which they can exploit.

Mistakes and incompetence create particular problems for management. It may be that they can be traced back to a general lack of motivation, in the sense that employees are not committed to their work and so do not give of their best. Equally, the lack of skill or knowledge which gives rise to the damage may be due to inadequate training, and therefore not altogether the employee's fault.

Finally, natural disasters can be classified as 'Acts of God', in the sense used by insurers. They will be due to freak weather conditions or other circumstances over which the organisation cannot hope to have any control, and there is no point in considering questions of motivation. There may be strong motivation behind terrorist attacks, but such resentment is often of a general kind; the organisation may simply be unfortunate in being in the wrong premises at the wrong time.

The motives and outcomes associated with each of the types of threat are summarised in Table 1.1.

Table 1.1

	Motive			Outcome		
	Personal gain	Vanity, malice, revenge, idealism	No motive applies	Assets mis-appropriated (directly or indirectly)	Loss concealed	Assets destroyed
Fraud	✔			✔	✔	
Theft	✔			✔		
Malicious damage		✔				✔
Incompetence			✔			✔
Accidents and disasters			✔			✔

Motives and outcomes for the five types of threat.

1.6 INTERNAL VERSUS EXTERNAL THREATS

Where do threats originate? The cases highlighted in the previous section suggest that they can come from all directions. In the previous chapter, the idea was introduced that threats should be regarded as either *internal* or *external*, depending on whether they came from inside or outside the *organisational boundary*. This implies that there are two groups of people: those inside the boundary, over whom the organisation has some influence, and those outside the boundary, in respect of whom the organisation is relatively powerless.

In practice, life is not quite this simple, and the nature of the boundary is difficult to define. It is easy enough to identify the set of people who are directly employed by the organisation, and who are therefore obliged to follow management instructions, under the terms of their employment. However, most organisations hire in assistance under a variety of other agreements, for example using agency staff, contractors for services, and consultants. This has become increasingly common under the kind of outsourcing and contracting arrangements described in section 1.4, both in IT and elsewhere. These contractors may be allowed full access to the organisation's premises and facilities, and be treated in many respects just like the regular employees. The contracts for these staff typically insist that they must comply with the organisation's everyday rules, including those relating to data security. Ultimately, however, there will be aspects of their training and working practice which remain outside the direct control of the organisation, and in which they are answerable to their own management. If such people misbehave, should they be regarded as operating 'internally' or 'externally'?

One solution is to replace the model based on a *single* boundary with one which recognises a *series* of boundaries. As each boundary is crossed, the extent of the influence exercised by the organisation becomes weaker. The situation is illustrated in Figure 1.1.

From the perspective of the individual manager, there is an additional boundary around the work group for which he or she has direct responsibility. In a well-run organisation, this should be of little significance; however, if the organisation is not so harmonious, there may be problems in establishing influence in other parts of it.

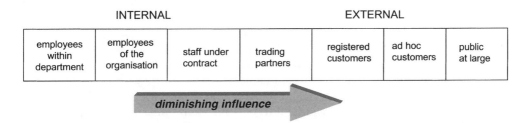

INTERNAL				EXTERNAL		
employees within department	employees of the organisation	staff under contract	trading partners	registered customers	ad hoc customers	public at large

diminishing influence

Figure 1.1 **Influence across the 'organisational boundary'**

Contractors, even if they are subject to the same terms and conditions in theory, can be harder to influence in practice. Trading partners have still more independence; nevertheless pressure can be brought to bear, perhaps through legally binding agreements, or because they value the business relationship and do not want to jeopardise it.

Probably the biggest changes occur when considering the organisation's customers (or clients). There is no reason for them to feel beholden to the organisation. Even though they may be given direct access to the organisation's systems (such as web sites or on-line banking services) they may choose to treat directives or warnings with disdain. This is particularly likely if they know they have the option of transferring their custom to a competitor.

In some cases (as with credit cards or on-line information services) the customer will have to register with the service provider, which makes it possible for conditions to be attached to the use of the service and formally imposed. This is simply not feasible, however, in respect of a first-time Internet enquirer or shopper. Finally, in addition to those who have dealings with the organisation in all these different capacities, a vast mass of people is left who have had no contact with it whatsoever, but who could potentially gain access to its computer systems.

The more 'external' the threat, the more rigorous one is likely to need to be in applying automated controls *within* the computer system. This is because other options for influencing users' behaviour become increasingly limited; even where they exist, they can be cumbersome to use. For example, as one moves from the left to the right of Figure 1.1, the following will generally apply:

- *Appeals have to be made to the jurisdiction of authorities outside the organisation.* Typically such an authority will be a law enforcement agency. Other bodies may also become involved, for example those charged with regulating an industry sector or profession.
- *It takes longer to invoke sanctions* against those suspected of being responsible for security threats. Evidence will be less accessible, building a case will be more complicated.
- *More reliance has to be placed on mandatory rather than advisory controls.* Advisory controls depend on the goodwill and compliance of those who are subject to them. These cannot be presumed in the case of someone whose relationship with the organisation is remote or non-existent.

The 'spectrum' of influence in Figure 1.1 is particularly important in respect of those threats in the general area of computer *abuse* (covering fraud, theft, and malicious damage). These threats may originate internally, externally, and at all points in between. In the case of threats which are unintended (negligence, accidents and disasters) the position is a little different. Negligence will tend to be a problem *inside* the organisation, and disasters will generally originate *externally*. The distribution of threats is therefore as shown in Figure 1.2.

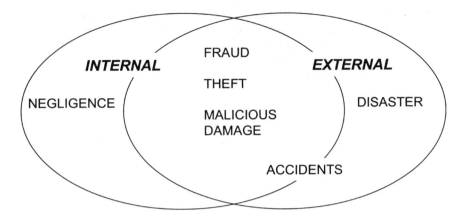

Figure 1.2 **Internal versus external threats**

Accidents raise some special questions (hence their position on the chart). Within the organisation's own sphere of influence, it should be possible to prevent, or at least to minimise, accidents. For this reason, they ought not to feature very often on the 'internal' side, and are shown as belonging more to the 'external' side of the chart. This issue is discussed further in chapter 9.

1.7 QUESTIONS

1 Decide which category of threat (as defined in section 1.5) applies to each of the following incidents.
   • A secretary re-formats a diskette (thereby deleting all the data on it), believing that it contains old memos which nobody needs. In fact it contains the only copy of an important report for the chief executive.
   • A debtors clerk accepts cash payments from customers outside normal business hours, issuing hand-written receipts and keeping no records. He keeps the money.
   • A secretary decides that the graphics package used in the office would be useful for her son's homework, and so copies it onto a diskette in order to take it home for use on her own computer.
   • A company rents space in a large office block. One of the other tenants tampers with the gas heating system, causing a large explosion which puts the company's local network server out of action.
   • An employee who has just been made redundant spends his last few minutes at his desk deleting vital electronic mail records, and substituting a series of unflattering messages about the management.

2 Analyse the following questions in the same way as in Question 1. Note, however, that these cases are intended to be more difficult to categorise (e.g. more than one category of threat may be involved).

- Employee A has legitimate access to the accounting system. While A is away from her desk, employee B, from another department, uses her terminal to increase the amount he will be paid that month.
- A newspaper reporter bribes a nurse, in order to obtain information from a patient administration system about a show business personality who is being treated in hospital.
- An employee downloads what is advertised as a 'cure-all anti-virus package' from a shareware Internet site. The software actually contains a dangerous virus, which quickly puts several of the office PCs out of action.
- A junior employee rings the secretary of a senior manager, claiming to be an internal auditor checking on passwords. He asks for and obtains the manager's password. He then logs on as the manager, sends a hoax email message to all staff, and makes alterations to the month's sales figures.

3 What influence might you, as a manager, be able to bring to bear in the following situations?
- A self-employed consultant is on a one-month contract to produce a cost-benefit analysis, which is required urgently. The consultant has been given full access to the company's accounting and production systems. She frequently downloads data onto her portable PC to work on at home. The PC appears to lack any security features, and one of your staff has just brought it to you, having found it left on a chair in the staff canteen.
- You are the manager of a local branch of a High Street bank. An irate customer has sent back a newly issued card for the cash dispenser machines, saying it does not work. It turns out that the customer has written his personal information number (PIN) on the back of the card. How would you handle this if:
  (a) the card had been damaged by the process of writing the PIN number on it?
  (b) the card was wrongly encoded in the first place, so the malfunction was actually the bank's fault and had nothing to do with writing the PIN number?
- You receive an electronic mail message from a source on the Internet which you have never heard of. It invites you to visit a 'red hot' pornographic web site, and indicates that the same invitation has gone to other people in your organisation.

4 Classify the following threats as 'Internal' or 'External' (or, if appropriate, indicate that the threat has features of both).
- The System Manager sends you a new sign-on password via email. Your secretary duly prints out the message and leaves it on your desk in an open-plan office.
- You issue magnetic-stripe cards to your customers to identify them. One such card is borrowed, copied, and used to impersonate the owner.

- An unknown telephone caller rings up the senior secretary in charge of the operation of your local area network (LAN) server. The caller tells a plausible story, as a result of which the secretary reveals your password onto the LAN.
- Regular reports from your accounting system show that three of your suppliers are apparently based at the same location, which is actually an accommodation address. Nobody has noticed this.

chapter *two*

RISK APPRAISAL AND MANAGEMENT

SOME TOPICS ADDRESSED IN THIS CHAPTER

- Why risk appraisal is an important *first step* in selecting appropriate remedies and controls
- Differences between individuals in the way they *perceive* risks
- The pros and cons of using *check lists* when reviewing risks
- *Expected Utility* and *Annual Loss Expectancy*
- Formal methodologies for risk appraisal in *large organisations*
- Less formal approaches which can be used in *smaller organisations*
- Some ways of looking at *costs and benefits* of risk reduction

SECURITY AND CONTROL OBJECTIVES

- Protect secrets
- Promote accuracy
- Prevent tampering

2.1   WHY APPRAISE RISK?

It is relatively easy to list all the possible threats which *might* apply to information systems. However, some of these could be ridiculously improbable, or result in little or no damage. They can safely be ignored, on the grounds that it would waste everyone's time to worry about them.

On the other hand, the list could include threats which were much more frequent, or less frequent but potentially devastating. In such cases, management is bound to demand action to deal with them. Most threats fall somewhere in between these two extremes. The problem then is to find some way of weighing up the seriousness of the threat, before deciding what is to be done about it.

The situation can be compared to that faced by householders in deciding how to protect their homes. It is possible to imagine all kinds of dangers, including fire, flood, debris falling out of the sky, gas explosions, burglaries, structural collapse and storm damage. While householders aim to make themselves as safe as possible from such threats, they stop short of trying to eliminate every possible risk. To do so would involved reinforcing the house with blast-proof walls, installing electronic gadgets in every room to detect intruders, and installing a missile battery on the roof with a view to pulverising any debris which might fall from aircraft. The cost and inconvenience of such measures would be seen as unreasonable, except perhaps by someone in a state of advanced paranoia. At the same time, most householders would expect to take precautions against more commonplace threats, for example by fitting smoke detectors, window locks, and a burglar alarm.

Risk is a helpful concept in evaluating and comparing threats, and putting them in some kind of context. Risk enables us to take account of the damage potential of a threat, *and* the probability of it occurring. So, for example, while our householder might accept that landslips can cause huge amounts of damage, he or she could still treat this as a zero risk if the house in question has been built on a plateau of solid rock. In the same way, even if burglaries occur frequently in the neighbourhood, it may still not be worth fitting security locks on the garden shed, because it contains only items which no-one in their right mind would want to steal.

Above all, risk assessment provides a way of *quantifying* the expected level of impact or damage. This opens the way to estimating risks on a basis which everyone can agree on, thus making it much easier for the management team to compare one risk with another, and decide which ones need to be given priority. In the simplest possible approach, all the risks would be listed in order of priority, and management would decide how far down the list they were prepared to go. The 'cut-off' point could be decided in one of two ways. They could either decide to work their way down the list until they had spent all they could afford, or they could aim to eliminate all risks which exceeded a certain level of seriousness, regardless of the cost. These choices are illustrated in Figure 2.1.

Both these approaches presuppose that the risks can be put in some kind of order, depending on how seriously the organisation rates them. Much effort has gone into developing methodologies designed to compare and prioritise risks, and some of these are described in section 2.5. Defining a universal, general-purpose methodology has become in some ways the 'holy grail' of IS security. However, it is always likely to remain elusive, and some reasons for this are set out in the next two sections.

Rather than looking for a 'universal' risk appraisal tool, which can be

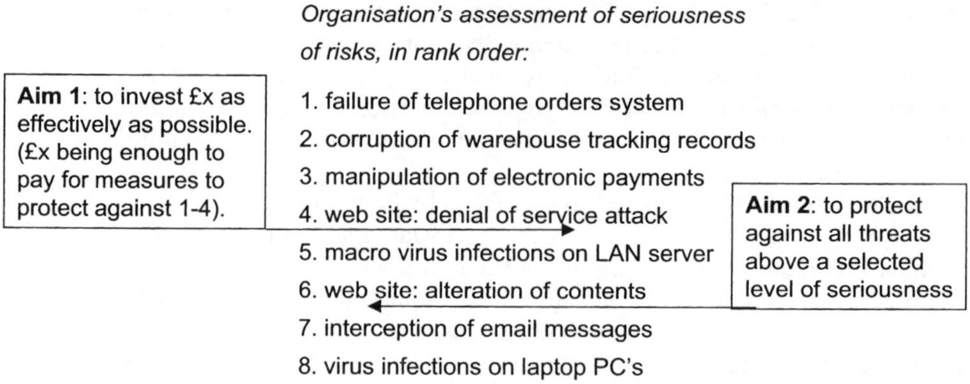

Organisation's assessment of seriousness
of risks, in rank order:

Aim 1: to invest £x as effectively as possible. (£x being enough to pay for measures to protect against 1-4).

1. failure of telephone orders system
2. corruption of warehouse tracking records
3. manipulation of electronic payments
4. web site: denial of service attack
5. macro virus infections on LAN server
6. web site: alteration of contents
7. interception of email messages
8. virus infections on laptop PC's

Aim 2: to protect against all threats above a selected level of seriousness

Figure 2.1

turned to on every occasion, it is preferable to seek out a suitable methodology for each particular case. Major situations will merit a thorough review, perhaps taking several weeks and requiring a highly formalised investigation. Minor ones will need to be dealt with much more quickly and less formally. In either case, the appraisal will still only provide a 'snap-shot' of the risks at one particular moment in time. There will be a need for periodic reviews and follow-up. This process of monitoring risks on an ongoing basis, and taking corrective action where necessary, forms the basis of *risk management*.

The later sections of this chapter set out some ways in which risk management can be applied in the context of IS security. Risk management is not something which can take place in a vacuum. The desirability of seeing risk management as part of a wider management role is put strongly in a NASA (1993) Guideline:

> Risk management is not an independent function distinct from other management functions. Instead, risk management is an inherent part of normal planning, organising, controlling, directing and coordinating. In other words, risk management is just part of good management.

2.2 PERCEPTIONS OF RISK

For anyone to take action in relation to a risk, he or she must first be persuaded to accept that it is serious. Unfortunately, each of us tends to hold our own individual view on how to weigh up the seriousness of risks. This is because our perceptions of risk are strongly influenced by experience and temperament, as well as more rational analysis of facts and figures. Although many techniques exist for calculating risks, often in ways which are very sophisticated mathematically, the results may still be challenged by people when their instincts tell them that the conclusions do not *feel* right.

Management scientists have long been intrigued by this area. Numerous studies have sought to establish how managers make decisions involving risk, but have found it difficult to pin down consistent patterns in their behaviour. For example, it is reasonable to assume that people will tend towards being either *risk-averse* or *risk-seeking* by nature. These terms are defined further in section 2.4, but can be defined in general terms as follows:

- *Risk-averse* people are cautious, reluctant to accept risks (certainly those they do not fully understand) and sceptical about any claims or assurances about the absence of risk.
- *Risk-seeking* people are, on the other hand, more inclined to accept that some risks are inevitable, and may even feel that accepting some risks is desirable. This does not mean that they take decisions any less carefully or seriously. Being risk-seeking means taking a generally more optimistic view about outcomes, but *not* necessarily to an extent which is silly and irresponsible.

As with many human characteristics, such labels are not infallible, simply because people do not always behave in a consistent way. They may confuse the issue by being risk-averse in some areas of their lives, and risk-seeking in others. For example, a security officer may behave in a risk-averse way while at work, stopping anyone who looks the least bit suspicious, and summoning help at the first sign of trouble. Out of hours, he may compensate for this by rock-climbing or visiting casinos. All that can safely be assumed is that if someone is cast in a role concerned with eliminating risks (such as a computer auditor), he or she will always try to take a risk-averse point of view, at least in the workplace.

Attitudes to risk can also alter very rapidly, if and when a risk actually materialises. For example, if the office's local network is crippled by a virus, it is likely that, once the network service is restored, everyone will become very risk-averse. There will be a sudden enthusiasm for using the virus checker, and obeying rules about not downloading programs from the Internet. Unfortunately this enthusiasm may not last long, as memories of the disaster start to fade. Once the risk no longer *seems* so real, people will drift back to taking short cuts, and ignoring office guidelines about viruses. In doing so, they become steadily more risk-seeking in their behaviour. This kind of human response is understandable, but in terms of risk analysis it is completely illogical, since the nature of the threat has not changed at any stage. Just as dangerous is the opposite reaction which sometimes occurs, where people assume that, because a threat has materialised recently, there is a very low probability that it will reappear for a while.

Risk-taking behaviour is also likely to change if staff are under pressure. This can be related to the kind of effect observed by McGothlin (1956) at the race track. McGothlin noted that people who were running up a string of losses from their bets would, as the day wore on, increasingly choose to put their money on 'long shots'. It seemed that their determination to win back their losses made them throw caution to the winds, and become more and more risk-seeking in their behaviour. The same kind of effect can sometimes be seen if a sense of crisis develops during efforts to get a failed system 'back on the air'. If moderate efforts to restore the system do not bring results, people may begin to try increasingly reckless measures. This results in additional damage to whatever it was that crippled the system in the first place.

Some researchers have attempted to identify *cultural* forces influencing the way people view risk. They suggest that the background and temperament of individuals will affect the way in which they try to make sense of uncertainty. Four different cultural types are described by Adams (1995). *Individualists* feel that the world is essentially benign, and can absorb quite a lot of risk-taking behaviour, whereas *egalitarians* are instinctively more cautious. *Fatalists* are indifferent to outcomes, and see little point in efforts aimed at trying to change them, while *hierarchists* believe that it is important that all risks are properly investigated and managed. These world views particularly affect people's attitudes towards any relevant evidence. For example, they will express deeply held views on threats such as carcinogens in food or global warming, despite having little acquaintance with any of the relevant scientific data. Similarly, most individuals will register some emotional reactions to information technology. In extreme cases, they may feel that it is anti-social, de-humanising, and inclined to lurch from one problem to the next; or they may regard it as an exciting and beneficial force, working to the greater good of humankind. This will owe more to 'gut feeling' than to extensive scientific study. Unfortunately it is extremely difficult to set such feelings aside when approaching information systems used in the workplace. In an ideal world, we would perhaps ensure that all employees were hierarchists, in favour of measuring and controlling risks. However, the cultural theorists suggest that these are attitudes of mind which are buried deep within ourselves. They develop over long periods of time, and are not going to be changed quickly or easily by management.

There is also a dilemma here for the managers themselves. Generally, the success of an organisation will depend on managers being optimistic about their ability to overcome obstacles, and being willing to take risks accordingly. Nevertheless, they need always to beware of going too far – and certainly not as far as believing that they have found an option which is entirely risk-free. Stephen Fay described such a situation in connection with Barings Bank. Fay (1996: 186) refers to the state of mind of Barings management early in 1995, not long before the bank collapsed with massive debts caused by the dishonest and reckless actions of Nick Leeson in Singapore:

> At Barings in London, everyone thought Leeson's operation was risk-free. The executive committee believed it: Andrew Tuckey [the Deputy Chairman of Barings]…told friends that the top men at Barings knew

Leeson's profits were bound to fall rapidly once other banks discovered how he was making so much money. However, for the time being, Tuckey insisted, they were risk-free.

The Barings managers, it seems, *preferred* to believe that Leeson had found a new way of playing the system, with no serious risks involved. A handful of people in the bank had their suspicions, but found it difficult to follow them up against the prevailing climate of opinion. In the same way, if IS security is to be maintained, it is important to beware of any unduly optimistic inclinations or beliefs which seem to be taking hold among the management team, and to ensure there is always some scope for more sceptical points of view to be heard.

2.3 DECISIONS ABOUT RISK: THE NEED FOR ANTICIPATION

Even if management resolves to be as objective and impartial as it can when assessing risks, it may quickly run into a further problem. Let us assume that our model managers are predisposed to reviewing evidence in as impartial a way as possible. Unfortunately the evidence may be in short supply. Since the role and nature of information technology is constantly changing, there may be a lack of relevant past experience to provide a reliable guide. A consequence of this is that management must assume that entirely new risks may appear at any time.

An illustration of some of the problems of doing this can be found in a case study from the early days of computing. Today, the idea that someone could wander in and out of the main computer area in this way seems a little quaint. But we have the benefit of hindsight applied over

---

THE HANDYMAN IGNORED

A computer operator, posing as a handyman, appeared every day for 2 weeks in the data processing centre of a major insurance company. He replaced a cracked glass in a partition, touched up scratched paint surfaces, remounted fluorescent ceiling lights, and among other chores gave the ladies' rest room a fresh wallcovering of paper in a delightful floral pattern.

Everybody saw him doing these jobs. But what they did not see him doing was giving commands to the computer to issue cheques to his order amounting to a total of $56,000. That did not come to light until three months after he had gone.

Who had hired him to do the odd jobs? No one knew. Why hadn't he been challenged, asked about the authorisation for the work he did? No one knew. How could a stranger intrude on the computer centre for 10 consecutive work days and arouse no suspicion? Because everybody on the staff though he was the responsibility of some other staff member.

Farr 1977: 165

many years. At the time these events happened, the risks of letting people roam around the machine room were not nearly so well recognised. The kind of questions raised towards the end of the extract might well have been seen as being trivial or alarmist. Anyone pushing for tighter security policies would have had to show a certain amount of determination and persistence.

Once particular risks *have* become more widely recognised, they pass into the general pool of knowledge, and it becomes much more clearly negligent to disregard them. A common way of transmitting this knowledge is through *checklists*. In today's world, there are plenty of checklists covering the physical security of a machine room, for example. While checklists are a good way of accumulating ideas about sources of risk, they do not, as we have seen, help to distinguish the significant from the trivial. They may also end up being altogether too wide-ranging, so that many of the questions raised have no relevance to the situation in hand.

Finally, it also has to be recognised that a checklist, however extensive, cannot cover *every* possibility. It must be expected that new forms of risk may emerge, which can only be identified through *anticipation*. If one were to go back to 1977, one would enter a world where the security risks associated with machine rooms had not been widely experienced, and so it was up to enlightened managers to apply their foresight as to what *might* happen. In today's world, where IT is used more widely, and continues to change at a hectic pace, a willingness and ability to anticipate new sources of risk remains equally important.

Anticipation depends on the ability to ask 'what if' questions about all aspects of the equipment, software, and working environment. It calls for a combination of initiative and imagination. It requires a close look at the implications of what may be quite minor changes in technology and procedures – even if at first sight they seem to have nothing to do with security. (In some cases, indeed, changes may have been intended to *improve* security, but unexpected side effects followed). Two examples are given, drawn from the field of system safety, where similar problems of risk anticipation have been evident for some time.

EXAMPLE 1. THERAC-25

In 1985, Atomic Energy of Canada Limited (AECL) introduced a new radiation therapy machine, the Therac-25, for the treatment of cancer. AECL had more than a decade of experience of building such machines, and during this time the company had developed a good understanding of all the safety mechanisms required. The Therac machines delivered doses of high-energy radiation under precisely controlled conditions. If patients received too large a dose, this could cause them very serious harm. Those operating the machines were therefore accustomed to following the operating procedures meticulously, to ensure that exactly the right doses were given.

Previous Therac machines had a good safety record, and AECL incorporated many of the old safety features into the new Therac-25. However, this was the first time the company had designed a machine which would be controlled entirely by a computer. An error in the program logic had the unfortunate result that if the operator entered one particular sequence of commands, the machine would deliver a dangerously high overdose. This 'bug' in the program meant that the operator could cause this malfunction quite innocently. Because the sequence only occurred very rarely, the cause of the problem was extremely difficult to track down and resolve. At least six patients received potentially lethal doses of radiation in the meantime.

In her analysis of the Therac-25 failures, Leveson notes that (a) AECL had tended to assume that safety was primarily a 'hardware' issue, and so did not consider the software as a likely source of error. This assumption was backed up by second one, (b) that since much of the software used in the Therac-25 had been used in an earlier product, it could be relied on, even though the hardware had been completely redesigned.

Both these assumptions were wrong, and arose from preconceived ideas about the sources of risk in the new product.

Based on Leveson 1995

EXAMPLE 2. THE DRIVERLESS TRAIN

A safety system for use on passenger trains was designed as follows. (1) The passenger doors could not be open while the train was in motion and (2) the train would move only so long as the driver maintained pressure on a spring-loaded 'drive' button. Thus the safety of passengers would be assured: they could not fall out of a moving train and, in the event of the driver losing consciousness, the train would come to a halt.

What the safety analysts did not anticipate was the reaction of drivers when they realised how the system worked. In order to leave the station quickly, they would tape the 'drive' button down. While the train was standing in the station, the safety system ensured that the train would not move because the doors were still open. But immediately the doors closed, the safety protection would no longer apply, and the train would move forward without any further delay.

In normal circumstances, this was not dangerous. However, on one occasion the closing of one set of doors was prevented when a child's pushchair got jammed between them. Realising the problem, the driver left his cab to help the mother free the pushchair. The mother and child climbed aboard, and the doors closed. At that point, the train moved off, leaving the driver on the platform.

Measures intended to improve safety had, therefore, given rise to an extremely dangerous situation. The problem was that the way the drivers abused the safety mechanism, and the sequence of events which could lead to an accident, were difficult to anticipate.

Based on Neumann 1995: 53

It is not hard to see how comparable situations can arise when information technology is put to use in novel ways. For example, lottery systems have traditionally been based on the use of paper tickets and counterfoils. Nowadays, most large state or national lotteries are run using networks of computer terminals. This is in effect a complete 're-engineering' of the business process, and requires a fresh appraisal of all the possible risks from counterfeiting and fraud. In other instances the changes may be much more minor, but a re-assessment of risk is still needed. Some typical examples follow.

- All the equipment in the main computer room is to be moved to a new site. Even if the aim is to move everything exactly 'as it is' to the new premises, there will inevitably be some changes in the working environment and the provision of services, such as telecommunications. Risks are also likely to arise in the course of the move itself.
- A company uses PC-based software to calculate quotations for customers. This software is of great interest to competitors. Up to now, the software has been run on desk-top machines. It is now proposed that some staff should be given the same software on portable PCs. In technical terms, this is a trivial change, but the new methods of working will create new risks of theft and loss.
- A company announces to its employees that it has installed a 'firewall' to protect its systems against attack from outside networks. Although the aim of this is to improve security, an unwanted outcome is that employees become less vigilant, because they assume that now the firewall is there, it will take care of all the security risks for them.
- An organisation has not experienced any hacking attacks over the past few years, and has become complacent. In fact it has been fortunate in not being the subject of any serious attacks, and its defences have been sufficiently strong to deter the few hacking attempts which have been made – up to now. Unbeknown to anyone in the organisation, the next day's newspapers will be full of adverse publicity about the company, which will suddenly become a target for attacks by hackers who are angered by the news items.

Unfortunately, as the examples suggest, there are no obvious rules about what should alert management to the appearance of new risks. It is common for risks to be created when new technologies or working methods are adopted. At the same time, some risks will creep up, quite unexpectedly, because of events external to the organisation, and completely outside its control. When considering systematic methods of appraising risk, therefore, it is important to bear in mind that there will always be certain risks which lie outside their scope: methodologies (like every other technique in security and control) should never be assumed to be able to deliver complete answers.

2.4   SYSTEMATIC APPRAISAL OF RISK: AN INTRODUCTION

One way of trying to make analysis of risk more precise is to express it in numerical terms. A simple case is describing a risk as 'one per cent' rather than 'low'. It is tempting to assume that this means that the risk has been assessed more accurately. However, this is not always the case, for the following reasons.

- Some professions (such as scientists and engineers) feel more comfortable if they can express things as numbers; but this does not mean that the numbers in question are based on any hard evidence. There can be temptation to use numbers from force of habit, or simply because they *sound* more authoritative. Accountants, it seems, are also inclined to express probabilities as numbers – except when it comes to putting them in audit reports, when they have been found to revert to rather more vague forms of expression (Sullivan *et al* 1985).
- People often fail to use numbers consistently. An interesting experiment was conducted by Fischhoff and MacGregor (1983), in which subjects were asked to estimate 'death rates' and 'survival rates' for a range of diseases. In theory, you should be able to work out one figure from the other (for example, if 1 out of 10 people dies, this implies that 9 out of 10 will survive). However, the results showed that people generally responded with survival rates which were too high, when compared with the numbers implied by their answers for death rates.
- Numbers can develop their own special meanings in a particular workplace. Thus a sales force may be asked to estimate the probability that they will secure certain contracts in the next sales period. They know that if the probability is rated at more than 50% they will qualify for extra sales support, and so they will choose a number which is a bit above this. On the other hand, even if a sale is more or less 'in the bag', they may still rate it as being only 70% probable, in order to make their achievement seem more impressive when the sale eventually goes through. This 'tactical' use of numbers is quite common, and can spread across into all kinds of discussions and negotiations.

Notwithstanding these reservations about using numbers, quantitative risk assessment is a useful tool, if used with care in the right circumstances. In order to make calculations about risk, it is helpful first to divide the 'risk' into two components:

- the *scale* or *impact* of an outcome; and
- the *probability* of that outcome occurring.

Generally, organisations are not concerned about risks which have a low impact and low probability; and if they are faced with risks with high impact and high probability, they have probably already had to apply some method of eliminating the risk altogether, simply to survive. This situation is illustrated in Figure 2.2. Generally, as we shall see, risks towards the bottom right hand corner of the chart are the easiest ones to assess and deal with.

Scale and *impact* are most easily expressed in terms of financial loss or

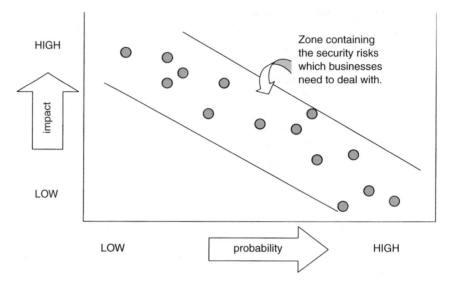

HIGH

LOW

impact

LOW   probability   HIGH

Zone containing
the security risks
which businesses
need to deal with.

Figure 2.2

gain, and this is often appropriate for business situations. However, there are cases where it is difficult to make a purely financial assessment. Suppose we are concerned with information about a trade visit to a politically unstable country which, if it fell into the wrong hands, would put lives at risk. What if the records contain details of a patient's health, and release of the information would cause that person great distress? Some would argue that not only is it inappropriate to set a cash value on possible outcomes of this kind, it is morally wrong to do so (Kelman 1995).

Probability can be even more elusive. Ideally, one would wish to look at a sizeable set of statistics, and see what has happened in the past. One can then assume that, if circumstances remain the same, certain events will carry on happening with the same frequency in the future. This approach works well in areas such as health, safety, and insurance, where relevant statistics are available going back over many years. However, IS security has a much shorter 'track record', and moreover the circumstances keep changing. If the problem under consideration is new it is impossible to base probability estimates on the past. All that can be said honestly is that the levels of *uncertainty* are so high that probabilities cannot be estimated. This was very much the situation many companies found themselves in when first confronting the 'Year 2000' problem. Faced with programs of doubtful provenance and lacking any documentation, they could only guess at the risks of failure due to the incorrect handling of Year 2000 dates. Here, one option was to try and reduce the uncertainty, by under-taking analysis of how dates were handled in the programs: this might eventually lead them to a position where they *could* estimate probabilities more reliably. Alternatively, the company could make a qualitative (and very risk-averse) judgement that the risks were so great that it should replace all the suspect programs with brand new software. (In the event, this proved to be a situation in which those who took a highly risk-averse stance did not see many benefits compared with those who did not).

Let us assume for the moment that credible values for both the scale and the probability of the outcome can be agreed upon. The seriousness with which a risk is viewed is a function of *both* of these. In other words, the worst situations are going to be those where the potential damage is very heavy *and* the probability of it happening is very high. A measure of 'risk' can therefore be provided by combining the scale and probability: in the simplest case, by multiplying one by the other. The result of combining them in this way is sometimes known as the *Expected Utility*. Expected Utility provides a useful way of comparing risks with one another, and for comparing a risky alternative with a certain one. For example, if you have a lottery ticket which has a 50% chance of winning £100, how much would you sell it for? If you were relying solely on logic and arithmetic, you would price the ticket at 0.5 times £100, or £50.

However, if you were averse to taking risks, you might be willing to sell the ticket for less than this, knowing that if you took a smaller sum (say £40) you could be sure of ending up with this cash in hand. On the other hand, a risk-seeker might price the ticket at £60, because he or she is attracted by the thought that the ticket could actually turn out to be worth £100. The situation is illustrated in Figure 2.3, based on Keeney and Raiffa (1976).

Figure 2.3 shows that the risk-averse person is always willing to accept a lower value in return for certainty. The risk-seeking person prefers to take a chance, and the 'safe' alternative on offer therefore needs to be higher. The straight line represents 'risk-neutral' choices.

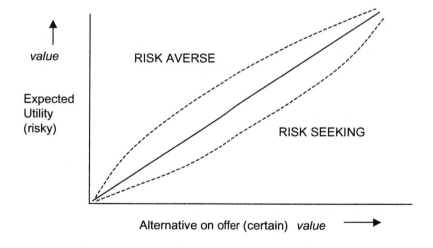

Figure 2.3

Clearly one could not set about devising an equivalent of Figure 2.3 for every decision: it would be immensely time-consuming. However, it can help to understand the kind of behaviour which is seen routinely when people confront IS security risks. For example, if you install a virus checking program on your PC, you may have to spend 2 minutes every morning waiting while the checker goes through all the files. This creates a minor and predictable level of nuisance, which you may prefer to the kind of major and unpredictable nuisance which will happen from time to time if viruses attack your PC. (For some other examples to consider, see the Questions at the end of the chapter).

A general-purpose method for assessing and comparing risks, based on Expected Utility, is *Annual Loss Expectancy* (ALE). An ALE is calculated as:

(COST OF THE OUTCOME IN £s) × (PROBABILITY OF THIS OUTCOME OCCURRING IN 1 YEAR)

An ALE in this case would be quoted in pounds sterling per year. For example, if the average loss due to an error in handling an invoice is estimated to be £5, and errors are expected to occur 1,000 times each year, the ALE for invoice errors will be **£5,000 per year**.

ALEs offer a quick and simple way of reducing a number of different risks to a single numerical value, so that they can be compared with each other. If, in the example just given, the ALE associated with errors in customer letters was calculated in the same way and found to be **£250 per year**, this would help in deciding to focus attention on invoices rather than letters.

The ALE figure can also be used to help assess how much it will be worth investing in order to *reduce* the risk. Let us suppose that by spending a fixed sum of £9,000 on improving the error checking in the invoice software, we can reduce the incidence of errors to 100 times per year. The ALE will now fall to **£500 per year**, a drop of £4,500. This suggests that, by virtue of the annual 'savings' in the ALE, the software improvement should pay for itself in about 2 years.

When using a simple measure of this kind, it is important to recognise its limitations, which include the following.

- Much depends on the *quality of the estimates* used in the ALE calculations. For example, it may be *known* that around 1,000 errors have been occurring in invoices each year, with the losses associated with each error being carefully researched and then averaged. Alternatively, both figures may be rough estimates. Even more searching questions will need to be asked about the claim that software improvements will reduce errors from 1,000 to 100 per year. Is this based on the experience of other users of the same software, or is it just an informed guess? Note that it only takes one 'rogue' figure in all the ALE calculations to throw the whole basis for comparison into disarray.

- When comparing ALEs with one another, great caution is needed in cases involving *very high costs and very low probabilities*. (Such cases are found towards the top left hand corner of Figure 2.2). Suppose, for example, that the probability of an aircraft falling on the main computer centre in any given year is rated at once in a million years. The cost (assuming the crash wipes out the centre) is estimated at ten million pounds. The ALE will be quite low – just £10 per year. Now consider the risk that a portable PC will be stolen from the office. In this case the probability is put at once in a hundred years, and the value of the PC at around £1,000. This gives the *same* ALE of £10 per year. Few would regard the risks as being in any way equivalent. Furthermore, any payback calculations in respect of the computer centre, based on £10 per year, will be quite meaningless.

- ALE assumes that there is a *predictable* amount of *direct financial* loss. However this is not always the case. What, for example, if a hacker manages to get into an organisation's web site? We could perhaps estimate the probability of this happening. But suppose the outcomes could range from leaving a trivial message, to sabotaging everything on the site. Do we use the 'worst case' scenario? Unfortunately this is not very sound, since the worst case is inherently less likely than hacking events in general – on which we originally based our probability estimate.

In the late 1970s, Robert Courtney Jr developed a revised version of ALE. His ideas were incorporated in a document issued by the US National Institute of Standards and Technology in 1979, known as Federal Information Processing Standards Publication Number 65 (or 'FIPS 65'). Instead of simply multiplying the costs and probability per year, Courtney suggested putting both of these on 'rating' scales, going up in powers of ten (see Table 2.1). This is sometimes referred to as an *Order of Magnitude* method.

The 'impacts' were originally envisaged as being measured in US dollars, but any roughly equivalent local currency unit could be used. The

Table 2.1 **FIPS 65 Ratings**

Impact	Impact Rating, i	Frequency	Frequency Rating, f
10	1	Once in 300 years	1
100	2	Once in 30 years	2
1000	3	Once in 3 years	3
10000	4	Once in 100 days	4
100000	5	Once in 10 days	5
1000000	6	Once per day	6
10000000	7	10 times per day	7
100000000	8	100 times per day	8

ALE was calculated from a specially devised formula: $(10^{(f+i-3)}/3)$. Unfortunately this attempt to make ALE a little more systematic did nothing to address its underlying weaknesses as a general measure of risk. Despite enjoying quite wide popularity at the time, FIPS 65 is now comparatively little used.

ALE techniques in general are only likely to be helpful if:

- incidents are sufficiently frequent for probabilities to be readily *observable*, preferably both before and after any remedial measures are taken. (This means that the frequencies will need to be somewhere in the range between levels 5 and 8 in the Order of Magnitude table in Table 2.1). In the example earlier in this section, the assumption was that if an investment in error checking software was made, the incidence of errors would be reduced from 1,000 to 100 per year. Assuming the new software *was* successful, its effectiveness should be evident within a month or two, since there should be a marked fall, from around twenty errors per week to just one or two. Thus the predicted cost savings could be demonstrated in practice, and this means that there is some way to *calibrate* the probabilities, by comparing the earlier estimates with the observed values.
- financial loss must be a practical and appropriate measure of the (undesired) outcome. Ideally, it will be a fixed amount of direct cost, for example, the expenditure required to replace equipment or software. Any indirect costs (for example from loss of files) or intangible costs (such as loss of customer goodwill) will involve 'softer' estimates, which are bound to undermine the accuracy and reliability of the ALE calculations.

Used within its limitations, ALE can be a useful decision aid for any organisation. However, it is dangerous to try and stretch it beyond its capabilities, particularly in attempting comprehensive reviews of *every* type of risk.

2.5   RISK ASSESSMENT: LARGE ORGANISATIONS

2.5.1   Risk assessment methodologies: an overview

One UK consultancy offers to probe network security risks with a service which it describes as an 'IT Security Health Check' (DERA 1997). Asking for a 'health check' implies that the management has looked at the systems in place and found no particularly worrying symptoms, but has still decided that it wants to be reassured that all is well. Other circumstances where risk assessment may be thought necessary include the introduction of a completely new system, the addition of extensions to an old one, or as a response to a bad experience in IS security.

Generally speaking, risk assessment should be commenced as early as possible in the development of a system (an issue which is returned to in Chapter 11). This section, however, is confined to risk assessment for systems which are already in operation. Furthermore, it is mainly concerned with the kind of extensive and systematic analysis which is affordable only in larger organisations.

A project to assess IS security risks should deliver at least two main outcomes:

- it should provide a *comprehensive list of all the possible threats* which may apply to the information systems;
- it should enable the *magnitude of the risk* associated with each threat to be estimated in a consistent fashion, so that reliable comparisons can be made between the different risks.

These outcomes should be presented in a way which facilitates the preparation of strategies for *reducing or eliminating* the risks, and *improving risk management*. An assessment which covers a wide range of the systems in the organisation and is initiated by senior management is described as taking a *top-down* approach. Smaller initiatives taken by individuals or departments represent a *bottom-up* approach.

It should be noted that IS security risk assessment differs in many respects from risk assessments carried out in other areas, such as by external auditors (in planning a programme for auditing the accounts) or by corporate treasurers (when analysing risk exposures in financial markets). Experience in these other fields is a source of useful thoughts and ideas, but the skill set should not be assumed to be directly transferable.

One way of 'buying in' some of the expertise required for risk assessment is to apply a *methodology*, perhaps in conjunction with consultancy services to help in applying it. A risk assessment methodology offers a ready-made 'kit of parts', and enables the organisation to get started quickly, without having to invent all the necessary procedures and techniques for itself. Most methodologies are in some way proprietary, and will usually be subject to a licensing fee, plus charges for advice and consultation. The 'product' will consist of a set of documentation, including guidance on how to apply the methodology, and a range of forms (paper or electronic) which have to be filled in. Much of the actual processing and analysis of data will be done with the help of computer programs, which can normally be handled quite comfortably on an ordinary PC.

Although adopting a standard methodology can save the organisation a lot of time initially, it should be stressed that any project to *apply a methodology* will nevertheless be very time-consuming, because of the extensive fact-finding and analysis involved. These may take weeks or months to complete – one reason why this approach will rarely be cost-effective for small organisations. (In their case, reliance will have to be placed on less formal methods, as discussed in section 2.6).

At any early stage in any methodology, fact-finding will be required in three main areas.

- *Assets to be protected.* These will vary considerably, depending on the nature of the organisation. 'Assets' here are not just those which would be listed as such in the Balance Sheet, but any element of the information system which has value, including software and any extensions made to it, the information assets of the organisation, and any features of the system in which staff time has been invested, such as setting up account codes or compiling email distribution lists for various purposes.
- *The nature and source of threats.* Again, it is important to identify every possible threat, and to record how and where it might arise. The threats will need to be grouped together according to factors such as those discussed in Chapter 1: for example, where does this threat originate? What are the motives of those causing it?
- *The vulnerabilities of assets.* This involves a process of deciding which assets are vulnerable to which threats. The connections may not always be obvious, and detailed consultations with staff may be needed to find them. The situation may also be complicated by the existence of possible 'knock-on' effects: for example, if there are circumstances where the failure of one network server could disable other servers on the same network.

Besides offering a systematic approach to identifying and recording all the above, a good methodology will offer practical guidance on how to set up and manage the assessment project. This should include help with determining exactly which systems should be included in the scope of the project, making an estimate of the number of staff-hours required, and putting together the project plan.

The key benefit which a methodology should provide is the ability to *exploit other people's previous experience* in making appraisals. This experience is transferred in four main ways.

- By use of a *catalogue of known risks* (which should be continually updated by the providers of the methodology). This will work best if the methodology is directed *solely* at IS security. Methodologies which look at 'security' in general, or which claim to be applicable across other fields such as safety or finance, are unlikely to have a sufficiently extensive or focused database of security risks.
- By creating *standardised approaches to data gathering.* Ideally, these will be backed up by documentation which is comprehensive and well-written, and an appropriate set of forms and check-lists. Those involved in the data gathering should be able to set about their work with minimal training, confident in the knowledge that they will all collect the information in the same way, making their results comparable with each other.
- By providing *tools for analysing the data*, preferably supported by computer processing. Managers should be able to ascertain the key principles behind the analysis, which should not be something which is

simply fed through a 'black box' process. (Indeed, managers should be suspicious of any methodology where complexity or a capacity to mystify are held out as virtues.)

- By generating *informative reports* of findings and recommendations. These should be concise, and framed in terms which managers can understand. (A criticism of some methodologies is that they produce dense and copious reports, which make it difficult when it comes to homing in on the salient points and using them to frame action plans).

Ideally, the methodology will score well on all these counts, but this alone will not guarantee a good *match with the needs* of the organisation. Some methodologies, for example, have their roots in the old centrally organised and mainframe-dominated days of computing, and are relatively weak when it comes to new types of threat involving PC's or the Internet. Others are much more up to the minute, but specialised, so that they only deal with risks in one area, such as networking. Methodologies also vary in the degree of detail and accuracy which they require. If results are required quickly, or if limited funding is available, it makes no sense to embark on an ultra-rigorous methodology which will take months to complete. The most likely outcome is that a few small areas will be analysed properly, and it will be impossible to arrive at any firm conclusions.

There is also a balance to be struck between buying in the entire process, with a team from the supplier taking responsibility for the whole project, and the opposite extreme where reliance is placed wholly on the efforts of the organisation's own staff. It is important that staff *should* be actively involved in data gathering and analysis, as this encourages them to think about security issues, and their involvement will make them more likely to support any proposals for change. At the same time, they will resent being asked to take on significant extra workloads, or carry out investigations using methods they do not understand. One way of making it easier to get staff involved is to invite them to submit their data and run analyses on a PC, using software based on Expert Systems. Software of this kind can avoid asking unnecessary questions, and offer more 'intelligent' guidance to the users, making it much friendlier for them to use.

If the appraisal is of a crucial nature, or if the methodology is to be used on several different occasions, it may be worthwhile drawing up a short-list, and comparing two or three methodologies in some detail. This was done, for example, by the Californian Employment Development Department, in deciding which product to use in the state's employment agencies (State of California 1995).

Some examples of risk appraisal methodologies which have been marketed commercially are given in Table 2.2.

Table 2.2 shows only a small sample of methodologies which have been developed. A review of a range of products can be found in Moses (1992). Before deciding to adopt any particular methodology, it is important to obtain current information about as many products as possible, and then consider the questions listed.

Table 2.2

Product	Name/source	Place of origin
CRAMM v3	CCTA Risk Analysis and Management Methodology	Norwich, UK
HAWK	Hankuk risk Analysis Watch-out Kit	Seoul, Korea
IST/RAMP	International Security Technology, Risk Analysis Management Program	New York, USA
LAVA	Los Alamos Vulnerability and Risk Assessment	Los Alamos, USA
MARION	Méthode d'Analyse de Risques Informatiques et d'Optimisation par Niveau	France
RiskPAC	Computer Security Consultants, Inc	Connecticut, USA
RiskWatch	Expert Systems Software, Inc	Maryland, USA

IS THE RISK ASSESSMENT METHODOLOGY SUITABLE?

- Is it *tried and tested*? (How many other organisations have used it up to now?)
- Has it been kept thoroughly *up to date* (particularly in respect of lists of possible assets and threats)?
- Is it *too general* (covers many kinds of risk) or *too specialised* (only covers some specialised areas of IS security)?
- Is it *too vague* (not many quantified measurements) or *too precise* (requires a great many measurements)?
- Is the *documentation and support* of good quality?
- Does it produce the kind of *results and reports* which managers will need?
- Does it take advantage of *personal computing* (for example, using a PC to help collect and process data, maybe based on Expert System software)?

2.5.2 Risk assessment methodologies: the theoretical basis

As risk assessment methodologies have grown and multiplied, they have developed mainly in terms of the range and volume of data they handle, and the sophistication with which they present their results. The principles underlying them have not, however, developed very far.

A recurring problem facing the designer of any methodology is that of finding ways of assigning values to all the items being measured. There is usually an element of cheating, since assessors are asked to provide ratings in numerical form, even though the valuations they are making are subjective. For example, assessors may be told to rate the impact of a threat on a scale between 0 and 5, as a part of what is sometimes termed *impact analysis*. If (as in one case) the bottom of the scale is 'negligible' and the top of the scale is 'catastrophic', this begs many questions about how one should assign values for the threats which lie somewhere in between. Another possibility is to use terms such as 'high', 'medium' and 'low', but this still amounts to rating threats subjectively on a three-point scale. However conscientiously the assessor approaches this task, it will involve making choices based on experience, intuition, and other inputs of a not very exact nature.

Similar problems arise in deciding how to define assets, threats and vulnerabilities. A workable methodology must bundle these into a manageable number of categories. This necessarily involves many compromises. For example, are physical threats to a computer installation put all together as one type of threat, or divided into different types (fire, flooding, bombs, etc)? The latter will enable risk analysis to be more discriminating, but will add tremendously to the workload.

A great deal, therefore, depends on the skill of the methodology designer in devising appropriate categories and scales. The first step will be to collect data in a consistent fashion according to the designer's definitions. Then the process of analysis will begin, based on two further steps, as shown in Figures 2.4 and 2.5.

Figure 2.4 illustrates the kind of relationships which have to be defined. In reality, they would be even more complex, and the task of recording and analysing them would be given to a computer. In Figure 2.4 it is assumed that a list of threats has been reviewed, and that every instance where a threat applies to an asset has been identified. Threat T4 is used as an example. It has been found to apply to two assets, A3 and A6. It has been estimated that the severity of the possible *impact* of T4 on A3 is $i(4,3)$, and that the *probability* of the threat T4 occurring is $p(4)$. This

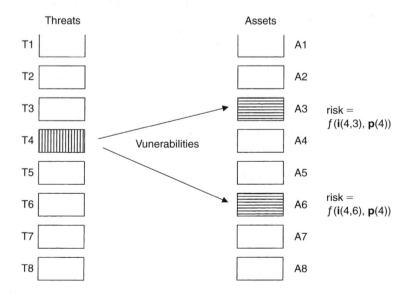

Figure 2.4

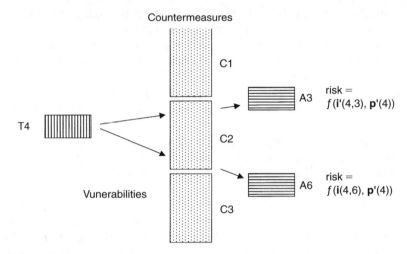

Figure 2.5

particular risk is then calculated using a function based on $i(4,3)$ and $p(4)$. This might be expressed as an ALE, as described earlier, but other forms of loss expectancy calculation could be used.

Having examined each risk in this way, the second stage in the analysis looks at the effect of possible *countermeasures*. The methodology should provide an extensive list of countermeasures, C1, C2. ... Figure 2.5 shows just three countermeasures, with C2 being effective against threat T4. Countermeasure C2 is shown as being used to reduce the risks which threat T4 creates for the two assets A3 and A6. In the case of A3, it has done this by reducing *both* the impact and the probability elements of the risk (so that there are new values for i and p, represented by i' and p'). In the case of A6, only the probability has changed. In some cases, it may be desirable to use more than one countermeasure. Once this level of complexity is reached, it is again essential that computer analysis is available to assist.

If two or more countermeasures are used, they should *complement* rather than *duplicate* one another. For example, suppose that fraud is a key threat in respect of a system for making welfare payments. Three possible countermeasures have been identified as:

A. Stricter procedures for adding new clients to the system;
B. Keeping better logs of activities on the system, such as cheque production;
C. New stationery to make it easier to control the printing of cheques.

It is likely that (B) will add very little to (C), and vice versa. However, *either* of them in conjunction with (A) will result in two different methods of attacking fraud, which complement each other. If a choice is to be made between (B) and (C), then further analysis may well reveal that (B), being a more general countermeasure, helps to reduce risks in several other areas, whereas (C) is more specialised. If so, (B) is likely to be a better investment.

In a real risk assessment, there would be dozens, maybe even hundreds, of decisions of this kind to consider. Each involves referring to least six items of data (viz. asset, threat, vulnerability, impact, probability and countermeasure). Furthermore, in many cases the situation will be much more complex than the ones mentioned (e.g. with several threats affecting one asset, or multiple countermeasures). A vital role of the PC software supporting the methodology is to keep track of the huge amounts of data which all this implies, and provide intelligible reports based on it.

2.6 RISK ASSESSMENT: SMALLER ORGANISATIONS

Risk assessment, as so far described, is very much the province of larger organisations, which can afford to staff and equip projects of this kind. Anyone contemplating a risk assessment in a small business, or a department initiating its own 'bottom-up' security review, will be looking for an altogether cheaper and quicker approach. Can risk assessment be made feasible and worthwhile in these settings?

A manager in a small unit can claim to start with one or two advantages. Not least is a first-hand knowledge of the business processes which take place at the local level, and insights into how they work. Identifying and listing assets is also relatively easy, particularly if this is a small business run by an entrepreneur who acquired or created most of them.

However, the corresponding list of disadvantages facing the manager is much longer. The number and variety of threats, particularly from external sources, is likely to be much the same as for a larger organisation. If the unit is a small business or partnership, rather than a department with access to corporate resources, there will be no prospect of help from specialists in computer audit. The unit may even lack anyone in the role of computer manager: instead, it is more common for individuals to take on the job of looking after the systems which are of concern to them. This means that knowledge of how systems have been set up, and how they are operated, is not documented, and resides in several people's heads. Perhaps most problematic of all, the working style of many small enterprises is highly idiosyncratic and informal. Those running small businesses do so, primarily, because they enjoy being independent (Gray 1992). This almost guarantees a mismatch between the general culture of the workplace, and the culture of investigations based on bureaucratic procedures and checklists.

In these circumstances, there is little point in trying to devise 'miniaturised' versions of MARION or CRAMM. Instead, more open-ended enquiries will need to be substituted, with employees being invited to contribute whatever knowledge and insights they can. There is still some merit, however, in following the same three basic steps laid down in the formal methodologies.

1 Gather information about as many assets, threats and vulnerabilities as possible.
2 Decide which vulnerabilities the business needs to take particularly seriously.
3 Ascertain which countermeasures will work best in reducing these vulnerabilities.

It is particularly important that step (1) is carried out without too many preconceptions. This includes aspects of the daily routine of the business which everyone assumes to be well understood. For example, it may *appear* that the accounts clerk has been following a certain control procedure, but it may be that she has been quietly ignoring it, and concealing this from everyone, because she does not really see the point of it. Similarly, if systems are all being managed on an ad hoc basis by different individuals, it is quite likely that A is erroneously assuming that B is looking after issues such as backing up all the system files. Simply opening up such questions can bring important vulnerabilities to light, and it may be possible to find solutions for some of them very quickly.

For step (2), lack of time and resources will preclude many quantitative measures on which to base comparisons. However, this is a familiar predicament for most small businesses. The main concern at this stage should be to make sure the assessment has highlighted all the vulnerabilities capable of proving truly devastating to the business. External advice may need to be sought at this stage, particularly where threats of a more technical nature are involved.

Finally, in selecting the countermeasures (step (3)), it will be a good idea to check whether there are some simple solutions, and to ignore some of the blandishments of vendors of security products. Maybe a particular link to the Internet is not necessary, or some systems could be switched off altogether at certain times, or it simply is not necessary for certain files to be available 'on-line'.

All the above assumes that risk assessment is something the business has undertaken of its own volition, but on occasions there will be pressure from outside. For example, if a site in the UK is registered for the purposes of data protection, it will need to show that it has taken appropriate security measures, and that these are based on some kind of risk assessment (Data Protection Registrar 1997). Pressure may also be applied indirectly, by trading partners. For example, a retail chain may specify certain security standards to be met by suppliers, before they will be permitted to link in electronically to the retailer's systems.

In all such cases, it is vital to treat the risk assessment as if it were the organisation's *own* idea. Otherwise it will risk developing into a 'ticks in boxes' approach, with the over-riding objective being to obtain the necessary approval or certification. There is then a danger that awkward issues are not investigated properly, because of the possibility that they will delay things, or cause approval to be withheld. Power (1997) has described the results which flow from turning procedures into a 'ritual' in this way.

Some of the wider issues raised by official certification programmes, such as BS 7799 in the UK, are discussed further in Chapter 14.

2.7 COSTS AND BENEFITS OF RISK REDUCTION

Whatever methods are used for selecting countermeasures – whether formal or informal – minds will become concentrated when the costs begin to emerge. Up to now, it has been assumed that a single cost can be identified, which can be offset against the expected benefits from reducing the loss expectancy. Unfortunately, security costs are rarely as simple as this. There are just a few situations where it is possible to buy equipment which can be installed and then operate without further intervention. Everyday security situations perhaps provide a misleading comparison, since it is possible to invest in a front door lock, or a car alarm, and then use them free of any further charges. With most IS security measures, some costs will be ongoing.

Costs to be considered fall under four headings:

1 *Start-up costs*. The expenditure needed to purchase any equipment, software, consultancy or staff time needed to set up the countermeasure and ensure that it is working correctly.
2 *Fixed operating costs*. Recurring costs arising from such things as line rentals, service agreements, or software updates. An example would be the charges made by some vendors of virus protection software for providing regular updates to the list of viruses which the software can recognise.
3 *Variable operating costs*. These costs vary with changes in the scale or use of computer services. For example, a security device may need to be purchased for each new PC acquired by the organisation, or a fee may have to be paid to register an encryption key with a Certification Authority (as described in section 7.3).
4 *Indirect costs*. Quite apart from all the costs above, the organisation pays for security in a number of ways which will not show up in the accounting ledgers. For example, staff spend time following security procedures (e.g. running virus checks, making back-up copies and changing passwords). Security software may cause some processes to be slower than they would be otherwise. Costs also arise if controls need to be tested or audited periodically.

Some simple cost models are suggested to help in decision-making. It is not suggested that actual graphs should be drawn, except perhaps for very substantial investments. However, such models can be helpful in creating a mental picture of how costs are likely to behave.

Suppose for example that a business is faced with two possible countermeasures on its network, both of which will address the same vulnerabilities. Measure A requires a complex and expensive piece of software to be installed at the heart of the network, but from then on it is very cheap to

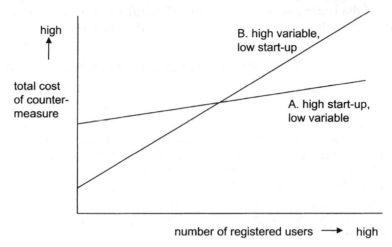

Figure 2.6

operate. Method B, on the other hand, has low set-up costs, but requires every user of the network to be issued with a smart card costing £5. The respective cost lines are shown in Figure 2.6. In such a situation, the choice between A and B will depend very heavily on the number of users expected on the system. Furthermore, if the costs per user *recur,* the difference between the two schemes could become even more marked. This might arise, for example, because the smart cards need to be updated or reissued periodically.

In other cases, the level of investment may not be geared to the price of products, but to staff costs. An example would be the time and effort to be spent in investigating fraud. Generally speaking, one would expect the benefits from uncovering and deterring fraud to rise in proportion to the effort committed to this by the internal auditing team, as shown by line C in Figure 2.7. However, the ideal position (and one which auditors try hard to achieve) is one in which (limited) efforts are directed at the most likely targets. This, one hopes, will yield results more like those shown by line D. Here, the initial investment gives the most benefit, and subsequent investment yields diminishing returns.

Finally, a similar analysis can be attempted of costs arising from inconvenience to users. Life for staff will be easiest if controls are light or non-existent. This situation is shown at the left-hand end of curve E in Figure 2.8. Indirect costs will be low, but security will suffer. As the curve moves to the right, security is improved, but staff will experience more interruptions and delays. An example would be the setting of time-outs on office terminals. If applications shut themselves down after 2 hours of non-use, users will hardly ever need to log themselves back in. However, this also makes life easy for intruders. If the time-out is reduced to 5 minutes, logging in will become a regular and irritating occurrence, but security will be much improved.

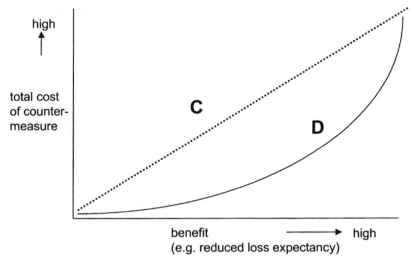

Figure 2.7

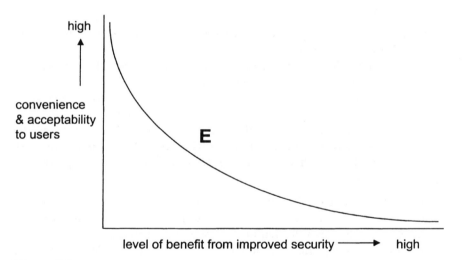

Figure 2.8

If precise figures for costs are elusive, figures for *benefits* are even more so. Primarily, organisations will be looking for loss avoidance, related to the elimination of individual threats. However, there are a number of more general benefits which can be obtained:

1 *Efficiency gains*. Having systems which are reliable and deliver accurate information enables staff to work with speed and confidence. Good controls play their part in delivering these benefits, just as much as more obvious features such as rapid response times or well-designed screen lay-outs.

2 *Competitive advantage*. Evidence of the reliability and accuracy of systems will filter through to customers. Indeed, in the case of Internet-based services they will be able to judge directly for themselves. Customers who are impressed and reassured by their experiences with the business are likely to stay loyal.

3 *Increased value of information assets*. By maintaining good controls over information as it is collected and stored, the business ensures that it is constantly adding to the value of its 'information capital'. Managers basing judgements on historical information can be sure that it will not be misleading because of errors or omissions. If early signs are picked up of something going adrift, everyone can be sure that this is genuine, and not just 'noise in the system'.

4 *Corporate privacy*. Sometimes an organisation will need to make crucial decisions, but without any hint of this reaching the outside world. The quality of decision-making will be much improved if those involved know that they can exchange information freely via the IS infrastructure, without worrying about leakage or interception.

2.8   QUESTIONS

1 In what ways might you see 'risk-seeking' or 'risk-averse' behaviour in the following situations?
   • Someone is installing a 'screen saver', obtained by taking a copy on diskette from a friend, on their PC in the office.
   • An Internet user at home is purchasing a music CD from a web site.
   • A computer operator is about to print out 200 payroll cheques.
   • On 1 April, a message which *appears* to be official, is sent to all the computer screens in the office. It advises everyone to save their work and log off immediately, because the system will be closing down in 5 minutes.

2 A retailing company has five large stores, each of which operates in much the same way. It has built up extensive electronic links with its suppliers, and uses information technology in processing payments at the point of sale, and in managing all the inventory. Managers have recently become suspicious that frauds are being perpetrated in some of the computer systems.

   The manager of one of the stores has asked you to write a report (not more than 600 words) on how an IS security risk appraisal might be undertaken. Indicate the kind of approach which you feel would be appropriate in this situation, and give your reasons.

3 A risk assessment has produced the following list of vulnerabilities for the server which controls the office's Local Area Network.
   A. Unauthorised copying of licensed program materials onto hard drives of individual PCs, or onto diskettes.
   B. Using Internet access via the server to 'surf the Net' for pornographic sites.

C. Corruption or destruction of word processing files by macro viruses.
D. Users with passwords for the accounting system exchange and share their passwords.

For each vulnerability, select what you feel to be the *most* effective countermeasures from the list below. Give reasons for each of your choices.

T. Access to server facilities to be available only during normal office hours.
U. Disable the ability of individual PCs to read or write diskettes.
V. All passwords to be changed at least once per month.
W. Only permit access to Internet sites on an approved list.
X. Bar access to Internet sites on a *not*-approved list.
Y. Make a daily back-up of all files on the server.
Z. Details of all activities on the server to be logged electronically.

4 If you have access to the Internet, you may like to test out your *own* perceptions of risk. Find one or two sites which offer online services (preferably those which can involve substantial payments by the customer, such as booking holidays, or opening an investment account). Put yourself in the position of a customer about to do business with the company concerned. Give particular attention to the arrangements for making payments, and any assurances which are given (many sites, for instance, have pages of 'small print' about matters such as the law, security, and privacy).

   Now compile two brief lists. One should indicate the reasons you would be *reluctant* to become a customer of the web site, and the other should give reasons why you would feel *reassured and confident* about being a customer.

Part 2

CONTROLS FOR INTERNAL SERVICES

INTRODUCTION TO PART 2

The internal information systems within an organisation have often become 'part of the furniture', and so are not expected to reveal many security and control problems. Some of them may be 'legacy' systems which have been around for as long as anyone can remember. Others may have caused a few headaches when they were first put in, but now seem to be running quite happily. Concerns about controls may be attributed to auditors justifying their existence, or pointless anxieties being raised by people with nothing better to do. Surely the really tough problems of control arise with the use of the Internet and other networks (as discussed in Part 3)?

Such views need to be contested for at least two reasons. First, complacency in whatever form helps to create an ideal atmosphere for fraud, carelessness and the irresponsible use of systems. Second, if connections are made out on to networks, they will often link back into these very same internal systems, and at this point the controls in those systems may be tested as never before. Thus, while organisations should take particular care when setting up new outside services, they must also keep a close eye on what is happening in their own backyard. Many of the foundations of good control are based there.

Part 2 is concerned with ways in which controls are applied *within* the organisation's own internal IT infrastructure. It begins by looking at a number of aspects of the relationship between systems and their users, and between managers and the people they manage. (These are sometimes described as the 'soft' issues, but this should not be taken to imply that they are easy to deal with.) The final two chapters describe some of the many automated techniques available for basic security and control, looking first at methods of identifying users and restricting their access, and then at the checks and balances which can be built into the individual transactions which they carry out on the computer.

chapter three

COMPUTERISED CONTROLS: THE ORGANISATIONAL CONTEXT

SOME TOPICS ADDRESSED IN THIS CHAPTER

- Why IS security and control are increasingly a responsibility of general, as well as IS, management
- The importance of good *alignment* (or *fit*) between the information system and the organisation, and how this can be extended to measures for security and control
- How *trust* may be a factor in selecting and implementing controls
- Internal policies and conventions, such as *Chinese Walls*
- The impact of *professional codes*, and the *ethical dilemmas* which can arise

SECURITY AND CONTROL OBJECTIVES

- Protect secrets
- Promote accuracy
- Prevent tampering

3.1 INTRODUCTION

Chapter 2 suggested some principles which can be applied to the assessment of risk, and the selection of countermeasures to reduce it. However, it side-stepped many of the human and practical problems which confront a manager who is trying to improve security. For example, the jurisdiction or competence of the manager to intervene over the security aspects of information systems may be challenged, perhaps because others feel that their territory is being invaded. Success will also depend on a good understanding of the way responsibilities for implementing and operating information systems have been assigned within the organisation.

This chapter explores the cultural and organisational background against which decisions about security and control have to be made. It concentrates on matters which are internal to the organisation and ignores, for the moment, some of the wider issues which are raised by inter-organisational links through data networks (Part 3 of the book returns to these issues). It looks particularly at the consequences which can arise if mismatches develop between information systems and the strategic aims of an organisation. Such mismatches can easily arise when the organisation embarks on a series of rapid and radical changes, perhaps because it needs to cut costs, or is striving to introduce new services in order to beat its competitors. Whatever their cause, mismatches invariably increase the tensions surrounding the use of the system, and this is not conducive to good security practice.

It is equally important to understand some of the everyday pressures which arise from the effects of information systems on people's working lives, even when the systems are well established and stable. People's responses will be shaped both by their individual attitudes, and by the general culture of the workplace. For this reason, the later sections of the chapter consider how employees' actions may be influenced by feelings of trust or loyalty, and the conflicts which can arise when disagreements arise about the ethics of certain forms of control.

Managers also need to have well tuned antennae when it comes to the pursuit of apparently attractive and quick-acting technological 'fixes'. Such fixes may be advertised by vendors, or canvassed by those who merely insist that 'something must be done' about a situation. It is not just that procurements along these lines can easily proceed without even the most elementary form of risk analysis and a full exploration of all the available alternative remedies. The 'knee-jerk' solution may not align at all well with the way employees work, and could turn out to be a source of resentment amongst them. Thus the organisational context can be important in even the simplest and smallest of security decisions.

3.2 INFORMATION SECURITY AND CONTROL AS A RESPONSIBILITY OF GENERAL MANAGEMENT

In the earliest days of commercial computing, almost every responsibility for the development and management of information systems rested with a large 'data processing' department. Any questions of security and control would be picked up quite naturally as part of the activities of this department. Most of the staff in the data processing department were very technically minded, and understood the innermost workings of 'their' systems in some detail.

The user departments, for their part, were only too happy to leave someone else to wrestle with the technicalities of controls, which were frequently incomprehensible to anyone without programming or engineering skills.

Many useful ideas for techniques for auditing and controlling systems were developed during these formative years. However, the business of implementing controls was quite simple in many respects, because all the computer services were kept firmly under the control of one department. Furthermore, the services on offer, particularly those which worked on an interactive basis, were very primitive by today's standards. This meant that users did not hold high expectations about the range of functions and data which were going to be made available to them. Some types of threats (such as hacking and viruses) were as yet largely unknown. This all added up to a situation in which the threats and remedies to be considered were far fewer than they are today.

In the final analysis, the data processing manager was also in a very strong bargaining position, being in charge of what was often a monopoly service within the organisation. He or she could foreshorten any debate about the appropriateness or acceptability of security measures simply by taking a unilateral decision, or (perhaps more deviously) by claiming that technical considerations ruled out any alternative solutions.

During the 1980s, this centralised model came under increasing strain, and many organisations began to seek out new approaches to the management of their IS infrastructure and services. This was driven chiefly by advances in technology, which could now deliver much smaller, cheaper and resilient systems. Suppliers seized the opportunity to bypass the data processing department, and started to sell their products directly to the users. At the same time, there was a growing realisation at board level that IT had come of age. It was no longer just another tool in the factory or the office, and now had to be seen as a potentially vital factor in determining business success. This in turn led to a debate about the kind of people who should be responsible for managing the information systems, with a view to taking organisations forward into the new era. Calls were made for more people with 'hybrid' skills, spanning IT and other aspects of the business (Dixon and John 1989), or for 'well-rounded' managers who would feel comfortable with the broader strategic issues raised by IT (Meiklejohn 1989). Much attention was given to the way organisations ought to be shaped and managed in order to exploit information systems effectively, for example by Keen (1991) and Scott Morton (1991).

For most organisations today, these issues continue to be a matter of concern for senior management. Within the more general debate about IS management, questions of IS security and control represent an increasingly common thread. In particular, there are three aspects of security and control which frequently come to the surface.

- *Security and control are no longer exclusively, or even primarily, the preserve of central technicians.* In the world of ready-to-use software packages and 'plug and play' hardware everyone can be a 'do-it-yourself' system builder. This new breed of DIY enthusiast is primarily concerned with getting the system up and running, and does not necessarily pay much attention to issues of security and integrity. As a result, new vulnerabilities are created, perhaps quite unwittingly. Because all this can now happen without the central IT department having to be involved or consulted, a useful safety net has been removed. Threats which would previously have been identified by experienced technicians at the centre now pass unnoticed.

Organisations have therefore had to become more proactive in monitoring how and where new information systems are introduced. This has sometimes led to the restoration of powers to the IT department, particularly in respect of tracking the IT equipment installed throughout the organisation, and enforcing standards in respect of commonly used items of packaged software.

- *Security and control issues cut across normal demarcation lines.* The issues may not fit neatly inside normal departmental boundaries, for example, a user in department A may wish to be allowed access to some data files maintained by department B. This will require appropriate security measures to be agreed jointly by *both* departments. Demands for such cross-border arrangements are inevitable if individual departments are all engaged in running their own autonomous systems. If the requirements for cross-linkages are only occasional it may be easy to resolve them amicably and securely, but if any data exchanges on a larger scale are contemplated, security and control may become entangled in much bigger political issues surrounding the status and ownership of information. Davenport (1994) puts the position succinctly: 'If information is power and money, people won't share it easily'.

- *The costs and benefits of security and control fall unevenly.* Very few security measures come at zero cost. Even instilling 'good practice' requires training, and one probable outcome will be that staff have to spend additional time on the processing of each transaction. Unfortunately, the costs of security can fall particularly heavily on certain departments, such as those responsible for a lot of data entry, or where there are frequent dealings with customers. The benefits, meanwhile, do not usually accrue to that department but to the organisation as a whole. In many instances the benefits will, in any case, be largely invisible, certainly to those who are being subjected to all the extra pressures and overheads. All this makes for further political tensions, particularly if requirements for high standards of security and control are handed down from the top of the organisation, leaving individual departments to find the resources to implement them.

For all these reasons, few managers can avoid being drawn into discussions, at some time or another, about the way information is to be controlled, vetted, or stored. To arrive at workable solutions, they will need to consider not just the security-related aspects of information systems, but some more general questions about the purpose of the systems, and how well they fit in with the objectives of the organisation. If there is a good match between the functions provided by the systems, and the business objectives which the organisation has set for itself, it will be much easier to establish good controls. Conversely, it can be extremely difficult to agree and impose controls on systems which are not perceived as being particularly useful, or whose mode of operation 'runs against the grain'.

3.3 MATCHING CONTROL SYSTEMS TO THE ORGANISATION'S STRUCTURE AND CULTURE

How should information systems be tailored to fit the needs of the organisations they serve? This question has been subjected to a good deal of research and analysis. Generally, it is agreed that there must be, in some sense, a good *fit* or *alignment* between IT and the business. Raymond *et al* (1995) have shown that there are business incentives for getting the alignment right, since a firm can then expect to achieve better results, as measured by a range of financial and other indicators. However, there are differing ideas about how to achieve good alignment, or even how to tell whether it has actually been accomplished.

McKersie and Walton (1991), for example, draw attention to the different ways in which the alignment can be brought about: for example, does the organisation pull the technology into place to correspond with its existing ways of working, or does it adjust some of its working practices to fit *around* the technology? The idea of technological versus organisational 'pull' has been further developed into a model by Burn (1996), who suggests that the introduction of IT can be stifled in rigid and heavily bureaucratised organisations, with the result that IS strategies are reduced to being 'pseudo-innovative'. Equally, an organisation which is more flexible in its outlook and working methods may still be held back, because it lacks any real vision of the potential applications of IT. Keen (1993) suggests that the ultimate aim should be a situation where IT is *fused* into the organisation. Organisations which achieve this state of fusion will find that whenever they plan and implement changes in their operations, technology becomes an issue like any other, and is seen as being completely intertwined with everything else they do.

In the same way, there are differing schools of thought about the best way to set about designing an organisation, in order to optimise the use of IT. A comprehensive review of these is provided in Stebbins *et al* (1995). An empirical study of organisational design by Broadbent and Weill (1993) looked at the way IT implementation and strategy were related in four Australian banks. One of their conclusions was that strategy-formation worked best if it was taking place concurrently at a number of different levels of the organisation, and that 'the most effective management of IS occurred when these resources were managed by those closest to business needs'.

The factors which predispose firms towards central versus local decision-making about IT have been investigated by Sambamurthy and

Zmud (1999). Eight corporations were studied, of which only one made all its key IT decisions centrally. The rest were found to work with either decentralised or 'federal' structures. In a federal arrangement, some decisions (for example, on IT infrastructure) would be made centrally, and others (for example, concerning the implementation of individual projects) would be made at a more local level. The researchers suggest that federalism tends to happen when centralising forces (such as an emphasis on cost-reduction through resource sharing) are in conflict with decentralising forces (such as the users being geographically dispersed).

However well a 'federal' approach may suit the organisation, it is probably the least promising from the point of view of IS security. There will be a constant danger that security and control issues will 'fall into the cracks' between local and central decision-making. Alternatively, the centre may seek to impose controls without a sufficient understanding of how activities are managed at the local level, or local users may regard controls as being connected with other policy initiatives, which are being resisted because the centre is promoting them in an insensitive manner. All these factors were found to be at work in a study by Dhillon (1997), who looked at the way controls were being managed in a UK local council. The council had adopted an essentially federalist approach to IT management, and Dhillon's researches found a number of instances where conflicts and confusions over management responsibilities meant that controls were either absent or ineffectual.

Problems of alignment can also be detected within quite small working groups, such as a small business, or in semi-autonomous units within a large organisation.

The misalignment can often be traced back to a decision to hand over the management of computer systems to someone who is relatively junior. Such decisions are based on expediency rather than careful thought. A member of staff is seen to be enthusiastic about computing, or appears to have some previous knowledge of the relevant software. Perhaps because of a shortage of alternative candidates, these are treated as sufficient qualifications for entrusting systems into this person's care (Hawker 1996). The problem is that this person's status may be wholly inappropriate when it comes to questions of security. Having overall responsibility for the system implies setting up access controls, ensuring that back-ups are taken, and maintaining appropriate logs and trails. Meanwhile, the person concerned is also armed with a master password, and so potentially has the run of everyone's data files. Such powers do not rest easily with someone who may be in all other respects a junior member of the organisation.

There are many reported cases which suggest just how easy it can be to misjudge how responsibilities within the working group should be assigned. The example on page 69 is taken from a UK Audit Commission report. In this case, it seems unlikely that the teller was ever *supposed* to use any discretion in setting the exchange rates. Such matters are usually determined in Head Office. An ideal solution, therefore, is one where the

Head Office decision is made and enforced from the centre, perhaps through down-loading of exchange rate values via a secure network link each morning. The functions which are accessible locally, meanwhile, must be restricted by automated access controls, as described in chapter 4.

FOREIGN EXCHANGE FRAUD

The teller in charge of a foreign exchange currency desk fed false exchange rates into the system. This resulted in a false excess cash position each day, which the teller removed from the till. The resulting offset was a debit to the bank's foreign exchange profit and loss account. This account was only reconciled weekly, and 30 days elapsed before the losses debited to the account were detected and reconciled. The system has now been changed, and tellers cannot access the computer and alter or set exchange rate tables.

Based on Audit Commission, *Survey of Computer Fraud and Abuse: Supplement*, 1990: 34

As Barings Bank discovered, even more disastrous failures of control can result if there are no restraints on the ability of local staff to modify the computer systems for themselves. The reporting system operated by Barings required the Singapore office, where Nick Leeson was a settlements clerk, to submit daily reports to London, giving summary figures for all the active accounts in Singapore. In July 1992, Leeson gave instructions to one of the local Barings staff, Dr Wong, to alter the programming of the local accounting system, so that key figures for one of the accounts (the '88888' account) would be excluded from the daily reports. No-one appears to have documented or questioned this change. The subsequent use of this account was crucial to the frauds which Leeson perpetrated against the bank. The official inquiry into the Barings collapse noted:

It appears . . . that Leeson intended to use account '88888' for unauthorised activity from the outset, and that the action [of Dr Wong] . . . was designed to exclude the account from the books and records of Barings. In London, Barings' management and other personnel have said that at no time until Thursday 25th February 1995 were they aware of the existence of account '88888'.

Board of Inquiry 1995: 78

That a local programmer could modify the central reporting system in this way owed much to the free-wheeling style of the Singapore office, where reporting lines were unclear, and staff were split between two offices ten floors apart. Meanwhile, in the London office there was a prevailing (and misplaced) assumption that Singapore was following corporate procedures properly. So, for example, no attempt was made to reconcile certain of the figures reaching London, because it was assumed that a reconciliation had already been done in Singapore (Fay 1996).

The eagerness of Barings to expand into new markets caused some of the pressures leading to its institutional carelessness. Over the past two decades, it has been commonplace for banks around the world to go through major upheavals, causing constant problems in aligning their organisation, technology, and controls. In developed economies, there have been numerous acquisitions and mergers, as local or regional banks seek to establish themselves in the global market. Thus, for example, in 1998 two major bank mergers were initiated in Canada, with a claim from one of the chief executives involved that the outcome would be 'the most advanced electronic bank in Canada, if not North America' (Middlemiss 1998). American banks, spurred on by the prospect of a rapid growth in cross-border trading, have been making overseas acquisitions, and consolidating their services in a way which is 'enough to overwhelm even the most energetic IT professionals' (Caldwell 1998). In less developed economies, banks have been able to leap-frog some of the earlier steps involved in computerisation, but now find themselves caught up in the same whirlwind of rapid change, with many implications for organisational integrity and security (as for example in the case of banks in China (Hood and Yang 1998)). Set against the background of all this frenetic activity in the banking sector, the calamity at Barings is no less excusable, but perhaps a bit less surprising.

Other sectors have not had to face the same pace of change as banking, but have nevertheless moved to new ways of using and configuring their information systems. For example, they have pushed selected activities out to *client* PCs, which work jointly with a central *server*, to create so-called 'client-server' systems. They have also totally redesigned business processes, to improve services to customers. These innovations are frequently technology-led, and the organisational implications may not be fully thought through. Even in cases where the new system and the organisational structure *have* been successfully matched, there is a danger that some forms of control will disappear, unnoticed, in the course of the changeover. This is particularly likely to happen if, for example, a layer of management has been stripped away, or responsibilities are regrouped in a way which happens to be conducive to fraud. These unwanted side-effects have been analysed extensively by Marcella (1995), and Sia and Boon (1996).

3.4   BALANCING TRUST AND ENFORCEMENT

Attitudes towards information systems are often ambivalent. Staff welcome the idea of not having to trawl through filing cabinets, and being able to rely on the system to do complicated calculations. However, antipathy can be triggered by quite minor design defects, or by a badly managed system implementation. In the worst cases, staff may exhibit what Marakas and Hornik (1996) dub 'passive resistance misuse'. This occurs when misgivings about a system are not resolved in open discussion, and staff resort to more devious ways of making their point. Marakas and Hornik cite a case involving a patient administration system in a hospital. Implementation coincided with a hiring freeze, so that very high workloads had to be imposed on staff during the changeover period. This overload was especially bad in the parallel running phase, during which the staff had to keep both the old and the new systems going. Shortly after this phase, it was found that serious errors were appearing in the data being fed into the new system. No technical explanation could be found, and when eventually the management announced a crackdown to find the cause of the problem, it immediately disappeared.

Resentment can also develop because those who are charged with installing a system tend to have an outlook and approach which is predominantly technical. In the case of a project in an architectural firm, one researcher noted: 'There's a poor fit between the system installed and the interaction between the people who use it, because there's *a cultural difference between the people who install the technology and the users*' (italics added) (Purcell 1993: 56). A similar cultural conflict has also been observed by Backhouse and Dhillon (1996), specifically in respect of IS security controls. As a result of observations of controls in a UK hospital, they concluded that problems were bound to arise because '. . . a rigid rule based structure of the formal system (the computer-based IS) is imposed onto a predominantly informal norm based environment'. The informal norms in this case are those adhered to by groups such as doctors, nurses and managers. Each of these groups has its own ideas about what is a 'proper' approach to work, and the groups do not always share the same outlook. In such situations, it is bound to be difficult to design controls which everyone finds acceptable.

An early casualty in all such conflicts is the level of mutual trust. Some degree of trust is required in every personal or commercial relationship. It is a quality which most of us can recognise in our interactions with others, and yet it is difficult to define or measure. Often we rely on it without realising that we are doing so. It takes time to build up, and can easily and quickly be destroyed. It cancels out more selfish calculations of personal risk and gain, at least in the short term. Francis Fukuyama (1995: 152) observes:

> We often take a minimal level of trust and honesty for granted and forget that they pervade everyday economic life and are crucial to its smooth functioning. Why, for example, do people not walk out of restaurants or taxicabs without paying their bills more often? . . . if they were intent, as economists assert, simply on maximising their incomes unconstrained by noneconomic factors like convention or moral considerations, then they ought to calculate every time they go into a restaurant or cab whether they could get away without paying. If the cost of cheating (in terms of embarrassment or, at worst, a minor legal run-in) were higher than the expected gain (a free meal), then a person

would stay honest; if not he or she would walk out. Were this kind of cheating to become more prevalent, businesses would have to bear higher costs, perhaps by stationing someone at the door to make sure customers did not leave before they paid or by demanding a cash deposit in advance.

In place of Fukuyama's example of the customer in the restaurant, one can substitute an employee who is faced with an opportunity to defraud his employer. The employee, too, can make a purely utilitarian judgement. Will the cost of cheating (which in this case, presumably, would involve dismissal from his job and everything which that entails) be outweighed by the gain from the money or goods received? (If the employee is being particularly rigorous, he may of course include some risk analysis to help with this comparison). However, most employees do not approach ethical decisions in this cold and calculating way. They will be motivated by a personal moral code, a desire to retain a good reputation, or a belief that business ought to be conducted according to certain minimum standards.

An idea put forward by Jacobs (1992) is that systems based on trust evolve naturally when people start to form trading relationships. She argues that evidence for this can be found in trading communities throughout history, and that it remains a hallmark of business culture today. She describes this as the 'commercial moral syndrome'. Jacobs contrasts these 'commercial' attitudes with those shown by 'guardians', who work in organisations where their role is to administer or regulate, such as government departments or the legal system. Here, a higher value is set on loyalty to the institution, and a willingness to abide by the rules. Proper adherence to procedures may actually require that trust should *not* be shown. Organisations, particularly larger ones, contain groups representing both of the Jacobs 'moral syndromes'. The 'commercial' departments look after the manufacturing, trading, and generation of revenue, and a 'guardian' role is taken by corporate functions such as accounting and human resources, which regulate the affairs of the organisation, and concern themselves with questions of probity and fairness.

Whether or not they fall neatly on either side of the commercial/ guardian divide, different working groups within an organisation will inevitably hold varying attitudes about trust – or perhaps more specifically, about any imputation that they are *not* to be trusted. These variations will depend not just on the nature and function of the working group, but on the staff's status and seniority, their degree of professional independence, and the effects of personal 'networking'. To complicate matters, some groups will regard bluffing and deceit as normal business tactics. Bluffing is a complex game, since the bluffer presents a partial or distorted version of the facts, but only within bounds which it is believed will be accepted and understood by the listener. Overstepping the mark will result in the complete collapse of trust between the parties. It is normally used in negotiations between businesses, but can also be a tactic in the course of an internal fight for influence or resources (both of which, as we have seen, loom large in control and security decisions). The legitimacy of bluff as a business tactic has exercised the minds of a number of business ethicists, including Carr (1993) and Bowie (1993).

Ultimately, intuition will have to be the main guide assessing how trust is working in any given situation. However, it can never be ignored when implementing controls because of two factors.

- *Staff attitudes and sensitivities*. Controls which appear to send signals of distrust will be resented, particularly by staff who are used to working in a highly trusting environment. Equally, if the working atmosphere is of the opposite kind, where scepticism prevails and few people take anything at face value, it will be unwise to presume that all users can be trusted. This will simply be interpreted as a sign of management weakness, or incompetence.
- *Minimising costs*. Trust can be regarded as an asset, with a real value in monetary terms. If staff *can* be trusted, any investment in elaborate and expensive controls is going to be wasted (besides being potentially counter-productive). However, this can be an extremely difficult position for a manager to take and defend, since it requires a high level of faith in other employees, and a willingness to forego the 'safer' option of relying on the more predictable protection afforded by explicit controls. Yet the resulting savings to the organisation in both start-up and recurring costs can be substantial.

3.5 THE LIMITS OF TRUST: THE RISE OF 'SOCIAL ENGINEERING'

If organisations can reap benefits from cultivating a culture of trust, they can also find themselves seriously at risk if their employees are both trusting *and* naïve. Staff must be made aware of the threats presented by confidence tricksters of various kinds, who will try to impersonate legitimate users, and then exploit the trusted status which this provides. This has become a popular technique with those embarking on schemes for computer misuse, and the term *social engineering* has been coined to describe their activities. The simplest example is the use of some ploy to persuade someone to reveal their password. Being able to type in a valid user identifier and password is always a good deal easier than having to resort to technical trickery to get into a system.

Social engineering can be a useful starting point for those interested in committing fraud or theft, but it is mostly associated with malicious intrusion by hackers. Kevin Mitnick is a hacker who developed his social engineering skills as a youth in Los Angeles, as the incident described shows.

A CASE OF SOCIAL ENGINEERING

If the guard thought there was anything peculiar about a Pacific Bell employee arriving at 1.00 a.m. on a Sunday to give a guided tour to two friends, he didn't show it. Kevin appeared far older than his seventeen years, and he talked a convincing line. As Roscoe and Mark stood by, Kevin chatted up the guard. First came idle chit-chat: Kevin had a report due on Monday, he said, and was upset that he had to come in to work on Memorial Day weekend. Apparently welcoming the distraction from his nighttime vigil, the guard didn't ask to see Kevin's company ID, nor did he ask which department the pudgy young man worked for. In a friendly and inquisitive manner, Kevin strolled over to a television monitor that wasn't working and asked the guard about it. They both shrugged. 'Just on the blink, I guess', Kevin suggested. Then, as if he had done it a thousand times, he signed the name Fred Weiner in the logbook, and Sam Holliday for Roscoe. His imagination apparently spent, he entered M. Ross for M. Ross.

Hafner and Markoff 1993: 62–3

Having talked their way into the building, the trio helped themselves to manuals for software used by telephone companies in running and maintaining their services. They walked out with these in the same nonchalant style. The venture was not entirely successful, since the disappearance of the manuals was soon noticed, and the intruders were tracked down on the strength of the guard's description, and other clues they had left.

The episode illustrates the three basic principles of social engineering:

- Invent a plausible identity for yourself, and a justification for what you are doing.
- Divert attention from your true motives and intentions.
- Play on people's susceptibilities and weaknesses.

The third principle was applied by Mitnick in taking advantage of the fact the guard was bored. Social engineers may also exploit people's eagerness to please, their feelings of insecurity, and their reluctance to become involved in wrangles over what may seem very minor points of procedure.

While social engineering can be used to gain access to buildings, or to charm information out of people in face-to-face conversations, the social engineer's preferred medium is the telephone. Freed from the need to put in an actual appearance, the imposter can adopt a number of different roles. Gordon (1995) suggests that these fall into five basic categories:

1 *The clueless newbie.* The imposter plays the part of a new employee, or somebody whose PC has just been connected to the network, and rings the computer centre for help. Playing dumb in this way enlists sympathy, and encourages people to spell out every detail.

2 *The technical person.* Here the roles are reversed, for example, the

imposter rings a secretary, claiming to be involved in some deeply technical work for the company, and asks if he could have someone's password to help carry out a test.

3 *The VIP.* This person pulls rank, pretending to be a senior manager or official. There will be some vital and urgent reason for revealing the information, and serious consequences if it is not revealed.

4 *The person with an angry boss.* In this case a play is made for the listener's sympathy: 'The sales manager is giving me a really hard time over this. Could you help me out?'

5 *The security person.* A risky option, but if successful this combines the authority of a VIP with the intimidating use of jargon of a technical person. Impersonating a security officer allows all kinds of questions to be asked about procedures, passwords, and system facilities.

Countermeasures against social engineering depend on constant vigilance, and a willingness to respond with pertinent questions. If staff have doubts about the identity of a caller, they should be encouraged to seek as much corroborative information as they can, in a calm and persistent manner. Their training should cover the dangers of giving out even apparently innocuous details, such as a person's working hours, or the systems for which she has access rights, to anyone whose identity is in doubt. Above all, staff should be encouraged *never* to take it for granted that a telephone caller is actually the person he or she claims to be.

3.6 LEGITIMACY OF CONTROLS: SOME ISSUES OF PROBITY AND SURVEILLANCE

In theory, every organisation aspires to make all of its data perfectly accurate and reliable, with access restricted according to legitimate 'need to know'. There are of course technical limits to these ambitions (which are explored in later chapters), but limits are also imposed by the social and ethical framework within which the company has to function.

Take, for example, the transnational company which tries to apply a unified accounting system across all its operations. It trades in a country where customs officers expect to receive substantial bribes before goods can be moved from the dockside, or where politicians expect to receive substantial inducements to lubricate business deals. How are these payments to be recorded? Does someone make a ledger entry showing, with complete accuracy, that X dollars were paid out in bribes on such-and-such a date? Even if this were to be recorded in the ledgers, it is highly unlikely that a sum would later appear under 'bribes and inducements' in the corporate accounts. Somewhere along the line, the accounting system must be fudged so that these payments are buried alongside other, more legitimate, costs of sales.

Kelly (1984) describes a predicament of this kind faced by an American bank in Italy:

[The bank] was advised by its Italian attorneys to file a tax return that misstated income and expenses and consequently grossly underestimated actual taxes due. The bank learned, however, that most other Italian companies regarded the practice as standard operating procedure and merely the first move in a complex negotiating process with the Italian Internal Revenue Service. The bank initially refused to file a fallacious return ... but because the resulting tax bill was many times higher than what comparable Italian companies were asked to pay, the bank changed policy in later years to agree with 'Italian style'.

Such scenarios are not confined to businesses operating internationally. In some industries it is an accepted convention that the price on the invoice will routinely exceed the value of the goods supplied (for example, in respect of raw materials which will be billed to a customer further down the supply chain). In others, payments are made for work which is known to be unnecessary or non-existent. All these payments nevertheless have to be accommodated in accounting systems which purport to maintain a full and accurate record.

Similar problems arise when local custom and practice condones the use or removal of assets by employees. Most organisations tolerate this at the trivial level of making occasional private photocopies or phone calls. However, in some industries it is recognised that a certain amount of stock, particularly in the form of off-cuts or substandard components, will find its way out through the factory gates. Other employers turn a blind eye to moderate amounts of private use of the firm's premises, vehicles or equipment.

Tolerance of 'grey area' transgressions of this kind can be the only available option when they are difficult or impossible to detect. It is convenient to regard them as 'flying below the radar' of the organisation's controls. However, the introduction of a new IT system can quickly transform this situation, by providing measurement and tracking which is much more rigorous and detailed. The outcomes, in terms of monitoring, can be both deliberate and unintended. For example, in the case of a components warehouse known to the author, a new computerised inventory system was introduced to record the location of each stock item. It was then realised that the system could be used to analyse the activities of the fork lift truck drivers working in the warehouse. The trucks constantly on the move about the warehouse appeared to be very fully occupied, but it transpired that quite a few of the journeys were completely unnecessary. The drivers were driving about simply in order keep themselves looking busy.

Alternatively, a new system may be introduced with the express intention of monitoring employees. The computerised cash register systems used in bars and restaurants are an example. Previously, bar staff would serve drinks, put money in the cash register, and at the end of the day a very approximate reconciliation could be done between the cash received and the drinks sold. Informal 'perks', such as the ability to give occasional free drinks to friends, were likely to pass undetected. But if staff are made to identify themselves and the details of each item sold via a special keypad, a much more precise record can be kept. Management can then use the data in various ways. As the advertising material for one software package developed for use in restaurants explains:

> Managers can track sales activity, customer order histories and employee efficiency, as well as communicate critical store data to a remote office quickly and easily.

Cashiers at supermarket check-out points and clerks dealing with telephone orders and enquiries are similarly aware that computer systems can monitor the rate at which they work. Staff tied to a system throughout their working day are particularly susceptible to monitoring; the stresses this can cause are documented by Picard (1994). Picard quotes an employees' representative as saying that monitoring should be used only to train staff, evaluate trends, or to check up on employees where there are already grounds for suspecting that they are underperforming. Otherwise, 'it's just a stick to beat people over the head with'.

Negative reactions from staff will not only sour industrial relations, but can have unintended effects on the way they approach record-keeping. This was illustrated in a study of a UK electronics company, described by Walton. The company introduced a computer-based system to track the work of its field technicians, who installed and repaired electrical appliances in people's homes. The system monitored the time taken, and the outcome, for all their home visits. The technicians were particularly upset by 'effectiveness ratings' calculated by the system, since these failed to take account of *unproductive* time which was not the technician's fault (such as occasions when the householder was not at home). Walton (1989: 170) quotes the following reactions from technicians:

> 'It's a spy in the camp' said one; 'it knows exactly what you do.' A field technician admitted that he kept a manual diary of his activities as a protection against management enquiries. 'I've started to write a diary of what I do every hour. That way when they ask I'll be able to defend myself'.

Similar problems can arise with 'groupware', where a clerical staff have PCs all linked in to the same office system, and the office manager can direct tasks to different individuals. The problems of introducing such a system were described to the author by the head of a unit responsible for a company pension scheme. Staff were wary of the idea that the manager could monitor what they were doing, and impose a sequence of doing things via the electronic 'in-tray'. This had to be the subject of extensive consultation before the system was introduced (Westcott and Hawker 1994: 15).

The greater detail and accuracy provided by computer systems may also give the lie to certain forms of bluffing. Sproull and Kiesler (1992) describe a 'phantom' head office procedure, which was invented in order to persuade sales representatives to make their returns earlier than was really necessary. Such ruses cannot easily survive in a more transparent world based on electronic communications. However, Sproull and Kiesler suggest that adjustments are constantly being made by all concerned, so that if one method of manipulation is eliminated, new methods will be invented to take its place. For example, people will bias the information they put into the system:

> Technology and technology policies that assume everyone shares or wants to share accurate information can generate new problems that did not arise with more organizational ignorance. Other things equal, if groups send and receive accurate and complete information, they potentially compromise their strategic positions and threaten the balance of control in the organization. Senders, knowing this, misrepresent information. Recipients, knowing this, discount information. Simply increasing the rate and scope of information sharing might only increase the number of misleading and discounted communications.
>
> Sproull, Kiesler 1992: 117

Even where inaccurate information is entered with *good* intentions, this can lead to bizarre results. In a case reported by the UK Data Protection Registrar, a Building Society customer complained that she had been upset to discover that the Society's files recorded her as being 52 years old, when she was actually only 42. The staff's efforts to avoid offence went spectacularly awry, since the customer was clearly less than flattered by their estimate of how old she was.

A MISTAKEN ESTIMATE

The Building Society explained that from 1982 onwards it began to ask customers for their ages (but not their dates of birth) and, because a number of customers objected to this practice, some branches took it upon themselves to estimate the customer's age to avoid causing offence. By 1988 the financial market place had become increasingly competitive and date of birth information was perceived as a valuable piece of marketing data, so the Society decided to collect dates of birth on all its new customers. At this time the Society decided to convert the age information it already held into 'assumed dates of birth' on its computerised customer records.

DP Registrar 1994: 40

The foregoing illustrations show that imposing controls to make data 'accurate' is not always as straightforward as it seems. Sometimes it may be prudent to allow a certain amount of ambiguity, or to give assurances that restrictions will apply to the ways in which data can be used and analysed.

3.7 CONFLICTS OF LOYALTY AND OBLIGATION

An employer is entitled to expect loyalty from employees, but cannot expect this loyalty to be completely unconditional. For example, employees may feel entitled to 'blow the whistle' on corporate misbehaviour, or to refuse to accept instructions which they regard as dishonest or unsafe. Such conflicts of loyalty have been extensively discussed by writers on business ethics (Hoffman and Frederick 1995).

More commonly, however, conflicts of loyalty arise where employees wish to abide by a formal *code of ethical behaviour* which originates outside the organisation. This is usually because their work is governed by a professional body, as in the case of the caring professions in medicine and social work, or the business professions of law and accounting. In such cases, the employee may be faced with dilemmas over the proper exercise and use of controls. Some examples include:

- Those responsible for areas such as *staff welfare* and *occupational health* may feel obliged to protect confidentiality in respect of some of the information they receive from employees. This could be because it concerns family matters and therefore mentions people outside the organisation, or because it is part of a health record, which the individual concerned wishes to keep private. This may entail barring access to the relevant data fields to senior managers, who would normally expect to have complete access to the personnel records of employees (for example to examine their hours worked, or their latest appraisal ratings).
- Employees of an agency of *government*, at local or national level, may have similar concerns about making certain items of information accessible to elected representatives. This could be, for example, because they suspect that it is being sought primarily as a way of bringing pressure to bear on political opponents. The most famous proponent of this technique was probably US President Richard Nixon, who sought information about the tax affairs of his political enemies (Watergate Hearings 1973; Impeachment Report 1974).
- Staff may want reassurances about controls over material with future *evidential value*. Sometimes a finding or opinion is to be put 'on the record'. This could include statements made in a professional capacity, or in connection with an internal investigation or inquiry. In such cases, it is reasonable to expect that special safeguards should apply to any electronic versions of the statements. For example, a safety officer might record some observations or measurements which pointed to failings in the safety regime, and wish to be sure that these could not be changed or deleted subsequently.

If loyalty is owed to clients, it may be necessary to set up *Chinese walls*. These are typically used where organisation has clients A and B, who are competitors in the same market. The team assigned to client A must be able to reassure their client that commercially sensitive information will not be accessible to the team for client B. The other team must be able to give similar assurances to *their* client. Yet both teams may be storing files and documents on the same system.

A Chinese wall is created by extending the normal security controls, to make sure that no undesirable cross-flows of information can occur, even unintentionally. Chinese walls are also used if a client requires work to be done in complete secrecy for other (legitimate) reasons, for example, if the circulation of information could give rise to allegations of insider trading, or the client is in the process of preparing a surprise take-over bid. In these cases the requirement for additional, tailor-made, security will need to go beyond the basic client files, and include electronic messages, and any documents being transmitted to and from the client.

In some instances, customers may expect Chinese walls to apply, even for quite routine services. This applies particularly in the financial services industry, where banking, insurance, credit and investment services may all be offered by the same company. Customers will expect that some trans-actions – especially through the bank account – will be kept confidential to just one service centre. The pressure on companies *not* to impose restrictions arises from the commercial value of the data they hold. The American Institute of Certified Public Accountants (AICPA 1999) has noted:

> As more company and individual transactions are processed electronically, it will be possible to accurately and intimately profile individuals and companies based upon the pattern and content of their transactions. There will be a tremendous appetite among commercial enterprises, government agencies, and unscrupulous individuals for this information. There will be both legitimate and illegitimate markets for the collection and resale of this information. Companies and individuals within companies will be tempted to sell information captured in the context of confidentiality. Many companies will claim to have constructed Chinese walls to prevent unauthorized distribution of information. Users will require assurance that effective procedures are in place.

A similar 'appetite' for information can be expected if company X undertakes data processing services on behalf of a competitor. In 1993, a furious row erupted between the Virgin airline and British Airways, with Virgin alleging that a 'dirty tricks' campaign had been pursued by British Airways, based on passenger information which it processed for Virgin under an outsourcing contract (Hawker 1993). More recently, a similar dispute between two online booksellers ended in a court case, when Alibris, owners of the company providing Internet services for Amazon, admitted to snooping on Amazon's email traffic (Silicon 1999).

3.8 QUESTIONS

1 You are senior partner in a law firm. You have invested heavily in a new IT system for your offices, in which over 50 people are employed. The senior administrator, who has been a loyal and very effective member of the firm for 25 years, is less than enthusiastic about the changes which IT has brought. The selection and implementation of the system has been led by a young, newly qualified solicitor who joined the firm 2 years ago.

What problems might arise in managing the security of the new system? Suggest how some of the key responsibilities might best be assigned in this situation.

2 A directive has been sent to all managers by Head Office, stating that in no circumstances is the company's electronic mail service to be used for personal communications. It indicates that managers will be held responsible for any abuses of the system within their departments.

You are a manager responsible for a team of twenty clerical workers, who all use electronic mail regularly. Draft a memo for circulation to your team, explaining and justifying the policy, and describing the kind of checks you intend to make.

3 You are alone in your company's London office, working late in the evening, when the telephone rings. You do not recognise the caller, who claims to be an accountant working in the Toronto office of your company. You are aware that the company has a substantial workforce based in Canada, but know little about it. The caller has a Canadian accent.

The caller apologises for calling so late in the day, but states that he is under great pressure to produce some analysis for the Canadian national manager, for a deadline which is only 3 hours away. To download the necessary information, the only practicable method would seem to be to borrow your password, and use the extensive access which this allows to the company's international accounting system. The caller suggests you could change your password immediately he has finished.

How would you respond to this request? How would you justify your response to your own manager the following day?

4 'It is important to align information systems and their controls carefully with the organisation they serve.' Comment critically on this statement.

chapter four

ACCESS CONTROLS

SOME TOPICS ADDRESSED IN THIS CHAPTER

- The methods available for checking on the *identity* of users when they log on to a system
- The implications of *'false positive'* and *'false negative'* results at log-in time
- Distinctions between *general* and *application* controls
- The role of *access control tables*, and how these should be set up and maintained
- Controls over access to individual details in *aggregated databases*

SECURITY AND CONTROL OBJECTIVES

- Protect secrets
- Promote accuracy
- Prevent tampering

4.1   INTRODUCTION

If someone calls at your home and asks to be allowed in, your immediate response will be to apply access controls. You will first of all want to check on the person's identity. You may deem it prudent to do this by taking a look through the window, to see if you recognise your visitor *before* you open the door. If it is someone on official business, you may ask to see an identity card, or cross-examine them to find out whether they seem to be genuine.

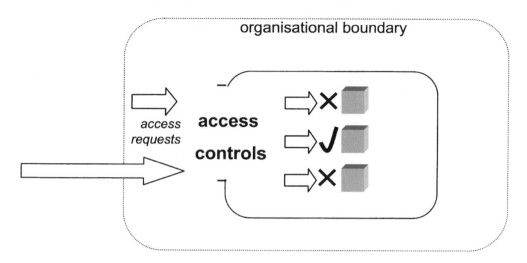

organisational boundary

access requests

access controls

Figure 4.1

Once inside your home, you will expect to place some restrictions on your visitor's behaviour. For example, someone who wishes to read the electricity meter will be taken to the cupboard under the stairs where it is located, and will not be expected to wander freely around the house. A good friend, on the other hand, may be trusted to roam anywhere.

The same basic ideas apply to access controls in information systems. Figure 4.1 is developed from a diagram used in the introduction to this book (Figure I.3). Note that even if the user *is* permitted access to the system, restrictions will be placed on the facilities which can be used (marked with a tick or a cross in the diagram). The pattern of access which is enforced in this way will be specially tailored for each user.

This chapter is concerned with what happens at the system equivalent of the front door. In the example, a brief description is provided of an early implementation of an access control system, and the reasons which led to its adoption. The objectives which were set for the system at IBM in 1973 remain just as relevant today.

AN EARLY ACCESS CONTROL SYSTEM

In 1973, the IBM Research Laboratory at San Jose was facing increasing difficulties in managing its internal computer services. In the space of 5 years, the number of users had leapt from 50 to 800. These users had been busily creating files (10,000 of them), occupying 4,000 megabytes (a massive amount of disk space in those days). Yet access to the facilities and the files was not being controlled in any systematic way.

Clearly, the Laboratory needed an access control system. Since nothing was available 'off the shelf', it would be necessary to design one. A number of key objectives were agreed among the computer support team. These included:

- There should be a centralised inventory of the resources of the system, and the privileges allowed to each user.
- All data should be included, even if it had been archived (and was therefore not currently 'on-line' to users).
- All access controls should be pre-set, so that their operation would be completely automated.
- The access controls should create minimal system overheads, and users should not be inconvenienced.

Gladney et al 1975

4.2   CHARACTERISTICS OF METHODS OF USER IDENTIFICATION

The starting point for all access control is to make a check on the identity of absolutely anyone who is trying to get into the system. Since this has to be done by automated means, the process will generally be more impersonal than in the case of the householder at the front door (although the technology to scan and recognise human faces is now commercially available). After that, there are other types of access restrictions which may be brought into play, which are described later in this chapter.

Crucially, if someone manages to deceive the system at the outset, and impersonates an authorised user, all the subsequent lines of defence will be hopelessly compromised. Not surprisingly, therefore, a great deal of effort has been directed at devising reliable and foolproof ways of checking the credentials of people who claim they are entitled to system access.

4.2.1   Characteristics of identity checking systems

Some characteristics of a good method of identity checking are the following.

- It does not allow *false positives*. A false positive is where the system concludes that the user is authorised for access, when this is not actually the case. For example, the aim of someone hacking in to a system is usually to persuade the system that he or she is an authorised user, and so create a false positive.
- It does not allow *false negatives*. False negatives arise when an authorised user is mistaken for an *un*authorised one, and is excluded from the system. At first sight, this seems a less of a problem. It may be regarded as unfortunate if authorised users are occasionally excluded, but at least the security is not being compromised. However, users tend to take strong exception to false negatives, and this is one of a number of human factors which need to be taken into consideration (see below).

- It must not be time-consuming or awkward to use. Users do not want to be kept waiting while the system deliberates on whether their identity is genuine, nor do they want to be subjected to lengthy questions or tests. All they are really interested in is getting down to work on the computer system.
- It must be suited to the type and location of workstation for which it is being applied. This can be a particular problem for portable terminals and PCs, and for workstations in locations away from a normal office environment, such as those in factories or warehouses, or people dialling in from home.

Finding the best method of checking identification necessarily involves an element of compromise. If the screening is too extensive and demanding, it will irritate users, and create an increased risk of false negatives. If it is too relaxed, users may feel more comfortable, but there will be a higher risk of letting in some imposters.

The result can be pictured as shown in Figure 4.2. If an organisation is determined to keep false positives to an absolute minimum, it will tighten up its controls and move across to the left of the chart. By doing so, it will run the risk of there being more false negatives. If on the other hand, the organisation is applying security to transactions by people it is particularly keen not to upset (for example, customers of cash machines or home banking) it may be anxious to avoid false negatives, for fear of annoying them and losing their custom. It will therefore tend to move to the right of the chart. In this case, any costs which arise from occasional frauds may be felt worth accepting in the interests of good customer relations. The

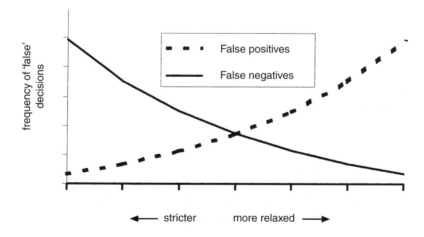

Figure 4.2

ideal access method will have curves which converge on a point where false positives and false negatives are both zero. In practice, it is difficult to get even close to this ideal without committing very high levels of expenditure (see section 4.7).

4.2.2 Methods of user identification

Methods of user identification can be classified into three main types, being based on:

- something you know (a password);
- something you possess (a token);
- one or more of your personal characteristics (biometrics).

In practice, these approaches are often used in combination. For example, to obtain cash from a cash machine you will need to use something you possess (a card) together with something you know (a Personal Identification Number). Such combinations are considerably stronger than each method on their own, providing that they are independent of one another: for example, it should not be possible to deduce your PIN number from anything, such as an account number, printed on the card (nor, of course, should the owner of the card ever write down the PIN number *on* the card

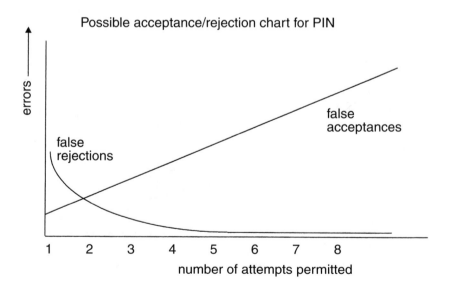

Figure 4.3

itself). If we apply Figure 4.2 to the use of a cash card, the result will look something like Figure 4.3.

Note that the probability of false positives climbs steadily as we increase the number of times the user is permitted to re-try entering the PIN. On the other hand, by reducing the number of re-tries permitted, we increase the chances that a legitimate user will be rejected (i.e. a false negative). Normally the bank will draw the line at three attempts, which allows one or two instances where the user simply has 'finger trouble'. After this it will treat the situation as suspicious, and abort the transaction (and the teller machine may swallow the card).

The three types of user identification will now be examined in more detail.

Something you know

Passwords remain by far the most widely used method of access control. This is not because passwords are a particularly strong method of controlling access (nor are they particularly popular with users, especially if they have to keep track of passwords for more than one system). However, passwords have the major advantage that no additional equipment needs to be installed in order to use them. All that is needed to enter the password is the existing keypad or keyboard. This compares with costs involved in giving everyone cards or tokens, and building special readers or recognition devices into the computer terminal.

Passwords can be relatively *strong* or *weak*. Ideally, a password should be as strong as possible. Strong passwords have the following characteristics:

- They are not based on any personal attributes of the owner (e.g. name of spouse, house number, date of birth, or star sign, or any other data which could be discovered by anyone who is inclined to make a few inquiries).
- They are as long as possible. Merely adding to the number of letters or numbers makes the password more difficult to guess.
- The range of characters used is as wide as possible (upper and lower case letters, numbers, and special characters such as ! or *).
- They are generated randomly (for example, 2$hP91j, rather than LETMEIN).

A weak password has properties directly opposite to those listed above. A password of 2301 will, if my birthday is 23 January, be a very weak password because it is short, consists only of numbers, and can easily be guessed. This problem of making access codes difficult to guess actually pre-dates computers, as Richard Feynman's experiments show.

RICHARD FEYNMAN AND THE SAFE COMBINATIONS AT LOS ALAMOS

In 1943, the physicist Richard Feynman was posted to the Los Alamos laboratory in New Mexico, to work on the wartime development of the atomic bomb. Feynman combined a very lively mind (he went on to win a Nobel Prize in 1965) with insatiable curiosity and a wicked sense of humour.

In his own account of his time at Los Alamos, he describes how he took up safe-cracking. All the top-secret files were stored in filing cabinets fitted with combination locks. Feynman regarded these as a challenge, and set about exposing some of their weaknesses.

From experiments on his own filing cabinet, Feynman was able to work out how the lock mechanisms worked. He taught himself how to find out the combinations of other people's locks, by going up to cabinets whose doors were open, and engaging the owners in idle conversation while he fiddled with the lock behind his back. He built up a dossier of the lock combinations around the site, and when there was a legitimate reason for breaking in to a safe (perhaps because the owner was away) he was able to help out. Feynman was always careful to surround his technique in mystery, and his reputation gradually spread around the laboratory.

If Feynman found himself faced with a filing cabinet where he had not been able to work his fiddling-with-the-dial trick in advance, he found there were always other ways of finding the combinations. These included:

- When the safes were shipped to the site, the combinations were set to one of two default values. Feynman found that in about one case in five, these were left unaltered.
- Feynman found that a secretary had written down the value of a physical constant on a scrap of paper in a desk drawer. This seemed an odd thing for a secretary to do, so he tried this as the combination. It did not work, but another commonly used constant (the constant e, equal to 2.718) did the trick.
- In another instance, the owner of the filing cabinet had used the date of birth of his young daughter.

As with some modern hackers, Feynman always used his skills in a way which was ultimately loyal to his employers (although there were inevitably some tense confrontations with the military officers who ran the labs, who felt he was undermining discipline). The dangers which he identified remain very much the same in an age when PCs have taken over from filing cabinets fitted with combination locks.

Based on Feynman 1985

Equally important is the *management* of passwords. Some rules can be imposed by the computer system, such as:

- Passwords must be changed at set intervals (say once a week or once a month).
- New passwords should always be different from ones which have been

used previously, i.e. a user should never be allowed to 'recycle' an old password.

The system can also give indirect support to the maintenance of a good password regime by:

- generating passwords for issuing to users to ensure that they have the 'strong' characteristics described previously, or vetting passwords for their suitability if users choose them for themselves;
- suppressing the display of passwords whenever they are typed in. One convention is to show a meaningless character (such as an asterisk) on the screen in place of each character of the password. This enables the user to judge when all the characters have been entered. A bystander watching the screen, meanwhile, cannot read the password. The bystander can, of course, see how long the password is, which may be helpful in trying to guess it. From the point of view of data security, it is best if nothing at all appears on the screen; however, users like to be able to see some reaction each time they enter a character. Even with suppression of the display, it is possible that someone may be able to find out the password by watching the keyboard rather than the screen, as described in the example of 'shoulder-surfing'.

SHOULDER-SURFING

While on a commuter flight in the United States, Sarah Gordon relieved the boredom by taking a look at what her neighbours were doing on their personal computers. To her surprise, she saw one of them type in a password (slowly enough for her to see each key being pressed) and begin work on a presentation clearly marked as 'confidential'.

To see how her fellow passengers would react, Sarah rose to her feet and peered over the seat back to get a better look. She was able to read details of the marketing and corporate restructuring plans of a well-known company. None of the other passengers was at all concerned by her behaviour.

Ms Gordon concludes: 'With no ingenuity at all, I acquired some rather juicy information, which could, I believe, have been of considerable commercial value were I a bad guy or a corporate spy.'

Gordon 1998: 587

Other rules should be enforced by management, including:

- Staff should never store passwords in written form in any location which other people have ready access to. (This applies particularly to obvious hiding places, like the top drawer of the desk, or a diskette box sitting alongside the computer.)
- Passwords should not be shared or 'loaned' to other people to enable them to gain temporary access to the system.

- Anyone suspecting that a password has been compromised should notify the management or, if the system allows this, change the password immediately.
- Ensure that new passwords are issued to staff by a secure route, for example by travelling from the password administrator to the staff member in a sealed and tamper-proof envelope.
- Make sure that a password is inoperative immediately it is no longer needed (for example, when an employee has left the company).

Something you possess

Passwords are error-prone, since people forget them, or memorise them with some of the figures transposed, or type them in incorrectly. These problems can be solved by incorporating the person's identity code into some kind of *token*. The most familiar form of token is the standard $3\frac{1}{8}$ by $2\frac{1}{8}$ inch plastic card, which carries the code on a magnetic strip running along the back of the card. This coded information can be much more extensive than anything an individual could reasonably be expected to remember in the form of a password. Furthermore, unless the card is damaged in some way, it will give an accurate and reliable read-out each time it is fed into an appropriate reading device.

New types of token are constantly being introduced. They come in a variety of shapes and forms, the primary requirement being for something which is small, light, and not easily damaged. It should be convenient to carry around in a pocket or handbag, or to be worn as part of a bracelet or necklace. Some have to be placed in contact with a reading device, while others can be detected at a distance, using infra-red or radio frequencies (in this respect, they are similar to the remote control devices used in car alarms).

The main weakness of tokens is the possibility that they will find their way into the wrong hands. The ease with which they can be carried around makes them particularly vulnerable to loss or theft. For this reason, tokens should always be used in conjunction with another, independent, form of identification such as a password or fingerprint.

Copying is also a problem. For example, it is not too difficult to build or acquire equipment which can make exact duplicates of standard magnetic cards. Even if the data on the card is made quite meaningless to the person making the copy (perhaps by encrypting it), this makes no difference. The fact that the copy is indistinguishable from the original is enough to ensure that the system will be fooled into permitting access.

A way of countering these vulnerabilities is to introduce some 'intelligence' into the token. This means incorporating a tiny processing chip, effectively turning the token into a miniature computer. This can be done with a $3\frac{1}{8}$ by $2\frac{1}{8}$ inch plastic card, producing a card which is only marginally thicker than an ordinary credit or debit card: these are usually known as *smart cards*. Smart cards can be used in a number of ways, for example:

- They may incorporate a small, flat keyboard, into which the user types a password in order to activate the card.
- They may have a display panel, which shows an access code which changes every minute or so. The user reads off the code and treats this as a temporary, one-time password. The program controlling access to the system, meanwhile, knows which code to expect from each user at any given time.
- The card itself may be interrogated by the card reader, and use its logic to compute the correct response. This logic cannot be copied in the same way as the data on a magnetic stripe. (Even if attempts are made to disassemble the card to try and work out the logic, it will be designed so this will result in irreversible internal damage, making the task impossible.)

One or more of your personal characteristics

The ideal method of identification is one which does not require users to remember passwords or carry tokens. Instead, they can simply present themselves to the computer system, and have themselves identified by some aspect of what they *are*. The system must of course have some information on record about all the possible users and the characteristics which are going to be checked.

Such approaches depend on *biometrics*, i.e. measurements of certain predefined, and permanent, identifying features of a person. Most commonly these measurements are based on the voice, hand, or eye. The idea is that the user should be identified by some quick and natural action such a speaking a short phrase, or placing a hand on a scanner. This removes many of the problems associated with distributing and storing passwords or tokens. However, biometric methods have only been introduced to a limited extent, because:

- Biometrics depends on complex pattern recognition being carried out on large amounts of data. It therefore needs a lot of computing power and data storage capacity to run the identity checks.
- The setting up of a biometric checking system tends to be more complex. The user must speak some sample phrases, or allow fingerprints to be taken, under controlled conditions. This may not be too difficult if the users are all employees of one firm working in the same building, but is much less feasible for a dispersed set of users, such as the customers of a bank.
- The system, like any other, must be adjusted to minimise false positives and false negatives. Some margin of error has to be allowed. For example, if voice recognition is being used, you cannot expect people always to speak a phrase in exactly the same way, and some characteristics of the voice will be changed by conditions such as hoarseness or a chest infection. In allowing for this, however, there is always a danger of moving too far to the right in Figure 4.2 and letting in false positives.

Another key factor in determining the application of biometrics is the acceptability of the approach to users. One potentially very accurate method of identifying people involves using a laser beam directed to the back of the eye to examine the pattern of blood capillaries in the retina. Although this can be done without any risk of damaging the eye, many people recoil at the idea of submitting to a retinal scan, partly because they fear that their eyesight will be damaged, and partly because of the awkwardness of staring into a special sensor.

For this reason, attention has shifted to the possibility of using the patterns in the iris as a basis for recognition. The iris is external to the eye, and can be scanned from some distance away. Ultimately researchers hope to enable the computer to scan a person's face, and recognise it in much the same way that a human can. This, however, will call for considerable sophistication if the machine is to be able to take account of different lighting conditions, the angle of the face, the use of make-up, and so on.

The idea of providing a fingerprint for checking purposes can, like the retinal scan, meet with some resistance, because fingerprints are associated in the popular mind with procedures followed by the police when a suspect is arrested. A more acceptable alternative is the use of hand geometry, where the hand is placed on a flat surface and its dimensions are measured. It is also possible to use a personal signature, written in the normal way but on a special sensitive pad. In this case, it is important to record the pattern of pen movements, and not just the shape of the signature, since otherwise the method is open to abuse through plain old-fashioned forgery.

Even using a conventional keyboard can give some indication of identity, although this is not very practicable for access control purposes. Because everyone develops certain styles and rhythms of working on a keyboard, it is possible to identify the user by analysing a recording of the keystrokes. This can be useful in checking to see whether someone who is already logged in is actually who they claim to be.

Figure 4.4 **Picture of fingerprint reader with keypad**

In summary, the following methods can be used in biometrics:

(a) passive testing (the user does not have to take any action):
   - retina pattern;
   - iris pattern;
   - face recognition;
(b) active testing (the user has to participate in some way):
   - hand geometry;
   - fingerprint;
   - voice pattern;
   - written signature;
   - keystroke pattern.

4.2.3 Supplementary measures applicable for all methods of identification

Regardless of the method (or combination of methods) used for identification, certain measures can be applied to reinforce protection against the misuse of user IDs. The emphasis can be on controls aimed at either *prevention* or *feedback* controls, which facilitate the detection of misuse after it has occurred.

Prevention

- *Terminal time-out.* If a user has logged in, but no activity has occurred for a set period of time, the system disconnects the user. This reduces the risk that someone else will find the terminal unattended, and read what is being displayed, or take advantage of the access rights associated with the terminal when it was left running. A similar effect can be achieved by using a 'screen saver', which works in much the same way: if no-one appears to be using the computer, the material on the screen is replaced by a pattern or a picture, which can only be removed by typing in the screen saver password.
- *Access tied to working patterns.* It is often the case that staff will only ever need to access the system during normal working hours, or from terminals in their own working area. If so, the system can be set to limit access to, say, the terminals in one particular office, between 8.00 a.m. and 6.00 p.m. on weekdays.

Feedback

- *Information about previous log-ins.* Whenever the user logs in, the system should respond with a message saying when that user's ID was last used. This allows the user to check whether the date and time accord with his recollection or his normal working patterns. An obvious example of a problem would be if the system asserted that the ID had been used in the early hours of the morning over a weekend, when the office was closed. The user should immediately alert the system administrator to the probability that the ID has been compromised.

- *Analysis of the use of IDs.* Certain occurrences are clearly suspicious, for example, if the same ID is used to log on in two different places at the same time. Analysis software can be used to go through the records of log-ins to the system, highlighting any situations which ought not to occur. Such analysis can also be done in 'real time', enabling suspect log-ons to be barred or queried as they happen, and turning this from a feedback into a preventive type of control.

Other forms of feedback and preventive controls are discussed in section 5.1.

4.3   SYSTEM-WIDE ACCESS CONTROLS

The IT landscape which is found in many organisations results from years of adding, extending and modifying a wide mixture of systems. As departments have had to merge, or have gone their own way in making IT purchases, or have struggled along using outdated software which they cannot afford to replace, an untidy patchwork of IT provision has resulted. (All that everyone can usually agree is that, if they were able to start afresh, they would almost certainly do things differently).

This legacy from the past can also make it difficult to align the IT systems very exactly with current organisational structures and boundaries. Some of the implications of this have already been touched on (compare sections 1.6 and 3.3). Unfortunately, the whole concept of access control depends on being able to make a clear distinction between the entities which are being protected, and those which are not. This forces the issue, by making it necessary to decide very precisely where the boundaries of systems lie, and who is to be permitted to use them. This can prove particularly difficult if it has been the practice hitherto for facilities to be shared on an informal basis, or if 'open access' has been the norm for some of the more elderly or infrequently used systems.

Traditionally, the boundaries for access control are set at two levels. The first marks the point at which *general controls* are applied. Ideally, these cover all the IT facilities used in the organisation. On occasions, it may be appropriate to consider a smaller unit, such as an individual office location or a division of a company. At the second level, *application controls* are used to regulate access and usage once people have started to use individual facilities (an 'application' in this case meaning a service based on a specific piece of software, such as accounting or computer aided design). The piecemeal evolution of IT in many organisations means that this model will often not fit very neatly in practice; however, it is helpful in exploring some of the questions of how and where access control should best be managed.

Access control at the general boundary can be compared to using the key to the outer door of a shared office building. It is the first step in gaining access to the facilities you would like to use. Giving you this 'general' access by no means implies that you are allowed to roam freely inside the building. Once admitted to the system, you will find yourself restricted to the range of applications which are regarded as relevant to your needs. This can be compared with being able to enter an office block, but being obliged to use a lift which will only stop at the floor where you work. This model of controls is depicted in Figure 4.5.

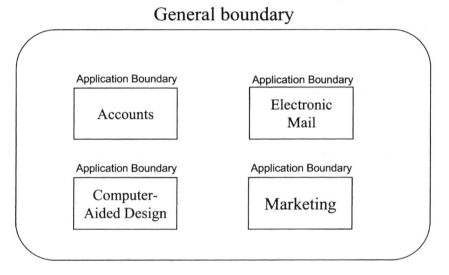

General boundary

Application Boundary

Accounts

Application Boundary

Electronic Mail

Application Boundary

Computer-Aided Design

Application Boundary

Marketing

Figure 4.5 **General and application controls**

In a business system, some of the applications (like Electronic Mail) will be made accessible to almost everybody. Others (such as databases used by Research and Development or Marketing) will contain data which is of considerable commercial value, and so their use will be much more restricted. Ideally, the general access controls should present each person with a 'logical' view of the system, which gives the impression that there are no applications other than those for which that user is authorised. Thus user A and user B may be presented with two quite different sets of options when they first log on (see Figure 4.6). Hiding applications in this way is quite convenient for users, since they will not waste time trying to get in to applications which are barred to them, and at the same time it makes life a little more difficult for aspiring hackers and fraudsters.

The access to be permitted to each user will need to be defined in an *Access Control Table (ACT)*. This is a table, created in software, which links users and applications. In its most basic form, the Access Control Table will list all the authorised users, and show the applications which are to be made accessible to each of them (as shown in Figure 4.7). It should preferably be an integral part of the central operating system or network management software; since access control is so fundamental to

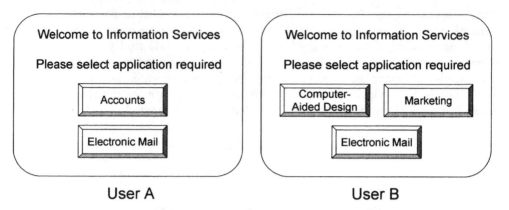

Figure 4.6 **Two versions of logons to applications**

	Email	Accounts	Marketing	R&D	C.A.D.
User A	☑	☑			
User B	☑		☑		☑
User C	☑				
User D	☑		☑	☑	

Figure 4.7 **Access Control Table**

security, it is best if it has been designed and built into the heart of the software. Special security software products can also be bought to tighten up control, if the basic operating system is felt to have weaknesses, or to help in day-to-day management of changes to the ACT.

Anyone who is in a position to modify the Access Control Table is in an extremely powerful position. It is therefore vital that the Table itself is subject to rigorous access control, with only one or two senior members of staff being authorised to make changes to it.

4.4 APPLICATION CONTROLS: MULTIPLE VERSUS SINGLE SIGN-ON

Once a user has gained legitimate access to an application, the need to impose some further access controls is dependent on the nature of the application. For example, every email user will need much the same set of standard functions; someone using the marketing database will want to be able to browse through all the data contained in it. In these cases, access to the application will imply the freedom to use it without any further restraints.

In other cases, there will be a need to introduce extra levels of control. For example, a junior clerk may be allowed access to the accounting system, but only to enter orders or invoices. His supervisor, on the other hand, will be allowed to carry out more sensitive tasks, such as entering new customers on the system and writing off bad debts. Similarly, in the case of an application which tracks the goods in a warehouse, certain people will be limited to enquiring about the stock position, while others will be permitted to record changes as the goods are shipped in or out. In a hospital, junior staff may be able to use the patient administration system to discover the whereabouts of a patient, but not to browse through any other patient details. The addition of this application level of control is illustrated in Figure 4.8.

In Figure 4.8, access within the application (in this case, accounting) is determined by an additional ACT, showing the functions to be made available to each user.

If a separate access control regime for an application is created in this way, there are some advantages and disadvantages, as follows.

1 *Advantages*
   • *Proximity*. If there is a department which is the primary user of the application, responsibility for access control can be assigned to one of its senior staff. This person will be well placed to know how the application is being used, and so can judge the kind of access likely to be needed by different members of the department.

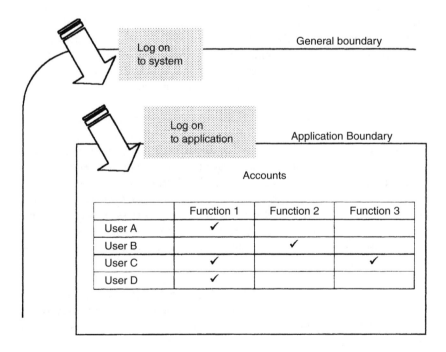

	Function 1	Function 2	Function 3
User A	✔		
User B		✔	
User C	✔		✔
User D	✔		

Figure 4.8

- *Responsiveness*. Handing over responsibility to someone based in the user department means that it should be easier for users to request updates and changes, and to report any concerns they may have about the way controls are working.

2 *Disadvantages*

- *Complexity of sign-on*. Taking the most common situation, where passwords are being used, the creation of a totally separate access control regime means that users will have to enter one password for their general access, followed by another one to get into the application. Users, understandably, resent having to use multiple passwords. It may be possible to arrange matters so that the same password can be used in both cases (a process known as *synchronising* the passwords). However, this implies constant liaison between the local password administrator and the centre. Additionally, it is not always possible to apply the same conventions about the format of the password and user ID across different software packages. If any token or biometric methods are being used, the complexities multiply.
- *Split responsibilities*. Responsibility for setting up and maintaining access controls now resides in two places, which users may find irritating and confusing, especially if they are trying to sort out an urgent problem.

One way of combating the 'multiple passwords' problem is to adopt an approach based on *single sign-on*. For this to work, secure linkages must be created between the software operating the two different levels of control. Once the user has passed through the general access control, information about him is forwarded automatically to the application software. The application software then relies on this as proof of identity.

Single sign-on can be achieved in two different ways:

- *Scripting*. The general access control software stores a user ID and password which the application software will recognise. These are fed across to the application software in a way which simulates the effect of the user typing in the appropriate log-on sequence on a screen.
- *Authentication server*. All access control is handed over to a specialised server machine. This makes an initial check on every user. Specially coded signals are exchanged with applications to pass on the user identities. For this approach to work, each application must have special code embedded in it, which can process and respond to the signals from the authentication server.

Scripting is much easier to implement, but is difficult to make completely secure. If the script is not quite right, unpredictable results may occur, and the application may respond by sending back baffling messages. An authentication server is a much better means of control, but requires considerably more effort to set up and manage. In either case, single sign-on should only ever be embarked upon as a well-coordinated effort covering the whole organisation (Hardy 1996).

4.5   CONSTRUCTING AND IMPLEMENTING RULES FOR ACCESS CONTROL

Access control facilities are often provided as a standard feature in software packages. As such, they should be reviewed with the same thoroughness as any other aspect of the package. When comparing products for accounting, for example, it would be regarded as naïve to accept suppliers' assurances that the handling of foreign currencies or the generation of reports was simply child's play. Requests would immediately be made for documentation and demonstrations to back up such claims.

Furthermore, purchasers usually expect to find that some packages are more suitable than others, simply because they offer a better 'fit' with the needs of the business. The same principle applies in respect of access controls. Some of the criteria likely to be relevant to this aspect of the assessment include:

- the degree of *granularity* which is needed in controls. In controlling access to data, for example, is it important to be able to discriminate down to the level of individual data items, or will more generalised controls suffice?
- *user-friendliness* in creating ACT entries. It is extremely time-consuming to try and build ACT's from scratch. The product should offer effective help and short-cuts.
- *sharing* and *delegation* of controls. For example, will owners of protected files want the discretion to grant access to other users, without having to refer back to the security administrator?
- consistency with *standards* in the organisation. Examples would be a company requirement that all passwords are to be changed after a set time interval, or if single sign-on is to be used.
- requirements *specific to the organisation*. Will there perhaps be a requirement to be able to link access rights to location, terminal identifier, or the time of day?

In an effort to make access control easy to operate, some suppliers reduce it to the bare essentials. For example, they may create a limited number of predetermined access 'levels'. This is reminiscent of the hierarchical/military approach to security. Each employee is assigned a number, say between one and nine: the higher the number, the greater the range of facilities which will be made accessible. The trouble is that the mix of facilities at a given level may not match very well with the job specification of any particular employee. Thus in one accounting package for small businesses, the level chosen will govern the employee's rights across *all* the facilities, ranging from the ledger, inventory and tax records to the setting of discounts, prices and report formats. This does not allow for the situation where, for example, an employee may require a high level of access to the sales ledger only. The system insists that a similarly high level of access must be granted across the whole range of facilities.

Reputable packages usually offer more flexibility than this in allocating access rights. For example, it should be possible to define a precise list of the types of tasks which a user will be permitted to carry out. Ideally, each task can be linked to a particular icon or menu option which is selected by a user in order to execute it. The effect is then to leave some of these as 'live' functions, while the others will refuse to execute, or simply vanish from the options presented on the screen.

To see how the process of setting up the ACT can be speeded up in this case, let us consider a hypothetical system which covers three main functional areas, F1, F2 and F3. In the case of an accounting system, for example, these might correspond to the activities surrounding the Sales, Purchase and Nominal Ledgers. If a clerk is only going to deal with routine customer transactions, no direct access will be needed to the Purchase and Nominal Ledgers. The access to these can therefore be barred en bloc, as shown in Figure 4.9.

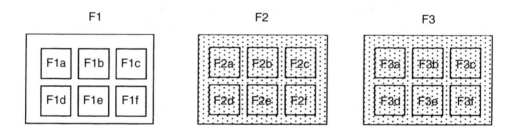

Figure 4.9

In the case of sales, however, we might wish to narrow down the definition of what the clerk is allowed to do. We would therefore go through the sub-functions within F1, switching some on and some off, as shown in Figure 4.10.

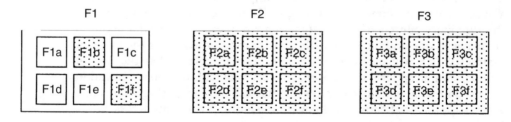

Figure 4.10

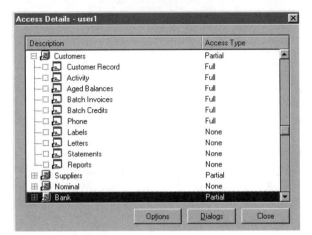

Figure 4.11

An example of the kind of screen which might be used to do this is shown in Figure 4.11 (taken from Sage Sterling).

Figure 4.11 shows the options being set for a user who is to be barred from the Nominal Ledger, but given partial access for customer and supplier transactions. To specify the access rights in more detail it is necessary to request the next level down, and flip the entries in the 'Access Type' column. In Figure 4.11, this is being done for tasks which come under 'Customers'.

Not all packages, however, lend themselves to controls which work in this way. Sometimes it is necessary to apply access control rather differently, by concentrating on rights which people have to read and write data. This is discussed in the following section.

4.6 ACCESS TO DATABASES AND AGGREGATED DATA

Databases were originally conceived as centrally managed repositories of data which could be used by everyone in the organisation. In a 'true' database, all the data is managed by one piece of software, called the *Database Management System (DBMS)*. Any data which is read from or written to the database must go via the DBMS, which enforces standard approaches to the way data is coded and organised. The aim is to ensure that there is a single, reliable source of data, which is independent of the applications which use it. This 'custodial' role of the DBMS makes it a useful place to enforce certain types of access control. The function of a DBMS is shown schematically in Figure 4.12.

Unfortunately, 'database' has proved a useful word to describe a large collection of data of any kind. Even when a database software product has been installed (and there are now several which will run on ordinary PCs) there is no guarantee that it is actually being used as a DBMS. It may just be a convenient way of holding a single large file which needs to be

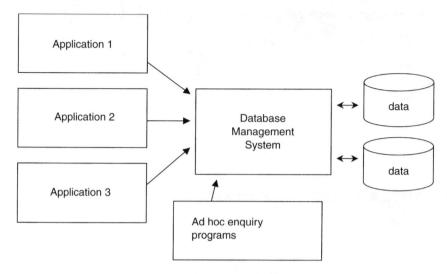

Figure 4.12

searched in all sorts of rather complex ways. In such circumstances, the database has no system-wide role, and is really no different from any other application.

If the database *does* have custody for data used across the whole organisation, however, the control of access rights becomes a crucial issue. Although certain applications may regularly feed data into the database, the data does not, strictly speaking, 'belong' to them. The data has now become a resource belonging to the organisation as a whole.

It is therefore necessary to look closely at exactly what each user of the database is permitted to do. Access rights to data can be put under five main headings:

- READ. The user can read the data, and make copies, but not change it in any way.
- WRITE. The user can enter new data. This is usually applied to data which is *expected*, i.e. an empty field has already been created for it.
- UPDATE. The user can change existing data. For example, a salary might be updated from £15,000 to £16,000 per year. Erasing an existing entry is also equivalent to updating, in this context.
- CREATE. The user can set up a new record or file. For example, a record might be created for a new employee, or a new file could be set up to contain sales information for the coming year.
- DELETE. The user can delete an existing record or file.

In each of these cases, the 'user' could be someone using an enquiry

Surname	First Name	D.O.B.	Job Title	Salary	Appraisal
Chang	Harold	12 Feb 1971	Technician	£17,200	

Figure 4.13

program (based on a search language such as Structured Query Language) or an application which depends on the database for its data. The application will ultimately, of course, also be responding to commands from a 'user'.

The ACT for a database tends to be complex, because it has to specify, for each user-application, the data which may be accessed, and the type of use which is to be permitted. In some cases, the access will need to be specified right down to the level of an individual data field.

For example, an employee record may contain several fields. Figure 4.13 shows just six fields for Mr Chang. The first three fields, showing name and date of birth, should not change, and should therefore be *read-only* for the majority of users. One or more users will however need to be able to *update* the next two fields, as Harold progresses in his career with the company. A grading will also need to be *written* into the appraisal field at some point in the future. Harold's record will be *created* when he joins the company, and *deleted* (at least from the current employee files) when he leaves.

All this must be specified in an ACT for the database. Setting this up requires an understanding of the intricacies of the database, and of the applications which are likely to use it. This is not therefore a task in which general management should expect to intervene directly. Instead, guidelines will need to be communicated to the technical team, and in particular to the Database Administrator. Since the resulting access rules cover all users of the database, they should be viewed as a *general* rather than *application* level of control.

Since a database is intended to be a widely used resource, it is common to find read-only access being made quite widely available. There is a danger of focusing attention on the more active access right where there are potential threats to the integrity of the data. For example, in the wrong hands, the ability to make updates or create records can be all too helpful in committing various kinds of fraud. However, even read-only access rights should be scrutinised with some care. This applies particularly if the database contains personal information about individuals (such as in H. Chang's record quoted above) or which is commercially sensitive (for example, because it shows details of sales by product and area).

A common requirement is that an overall picture should be available (for example, showing the number of employees at a given grade, or the number of sales for the whole country), while denying access to more specific details. This makes it possible for data to be made available for planning and administrative decisions, without risking breaches of confidentiality. General statistics of this kind can be provided by *aggregating* the data, so that everything is reduced to a form such as '25 employees in the northern office earn more than £20,000 p.a.'. Alternatively, the records can be *anonymised*, so that the details are retained, but cannot be related to individual names or places. This 'de-identification' may be a permanent feature of the data held in the database, or may be enforced by special protective routines used in generating the replies, whenever enquiries are made against records which are likely to be sensitive. Techniques to protect anonymity in these situations are sometimes known collectively as *Privacy Enhancing Technologies (PET)*. The threat which PETs are designed to resist is the *inference attack*. Inference attacks can be carried out in a number of ways (Hinke *et al* 1997), but all share the same objective. A number of (quite legitimate) queries are submitted to the database, each of which gives anonymised and apparently innocent results. These are then compared, in order to infer specific items of information. The simplest technique, first pointed out by Hoffman and Miller (1970), involves the use of a certain amount of cunning in comparing slightly different sets of aggregated figures. Suppose, for example, that the following statement can be retrieved from the database:

Average salary for 10 managers in the northern region = £28,000

This is an aggregated statement, which gives no information whatsoever about any individual manager.

However, suppose that the same query a week later gives the response:

Average salary for 11 managers in the northern region = £29,000

Simple arithmetic reveals that, if the average has increased by £1000, the new manager must be earning £39,000 p.a. If the enquirer knew the identity of a manager newly appointed to the northern region (from the database, or elsewhere) it would then be a simple matter to connect the person and the salary.

4.7   SOME RISK AND COST ISSUES

The possible weaknesses of access controls can, like any other control, be subjected to risk analysis. However, when it comes to estimating the severity of losses, organisations can be expected to take differing views about the kinds of failures which they see as particularly damaging. For example, if on-line services are being provided directly to the public, a false negative may be regarded as being extremely undesirable, since the customer is likely to be upset and might express this resentment by moving to a competitor. Indeed, many financial services companies would prefer to accept a certain number of false positives, and the frauds which go with them, rather than run this risk. Accordingly, they bias their acceptance criteria slightly towards the lenient side.

On the other hand, if the organisation needs to retain public trust in its ability to handle confidential data (such as an insurance company, or many agencies in the public sector), it will be much more concerned about false positives. The last thing such organisations want to see is newspaper coverage of claims that their files have been hacked in to, and details obtained about their clients' personal affairs.

Access controls should also be considered in terms of pay-back, and other measures of value for money (as outlined in section 2.7). For example, an access control mechanism which is cheap to buy (perhaps because it comprises a few basic options built into a cut-price package) may prove to have high recurring costs, due to the staff time spent subsequently in sorting out problems and wrestling with updates to the ACT. A successful single sign-on project, on the other hand, will involve a substantial initial investment, with the prospect of much reduced costs in the long run (for example, through centralised maintenance of all passwords, and reduced disruption and wasted time for staff).

Investments in access control are, unfortunately, usually tied up inextricably with other investment decisions. For example, if a company is running an old 'legacy' application which it plans to replace in a year or two, it will not welcome the thought of investing funds now in making upgrades to improve the access controls. In this case the problem is not that the access controls are unreasonably expensive, but that they have only a short or uncertain payback period.

Similarly, it may be that the organisation has made a commitment to use a particular type of token for access control across all its systems. Any new software which is purchased must therefore be capable of supporting this approach. The result may be that one or two products which would otherwise be promising candidates have to be excluded from the short list, and the product which is finally chosen may not therefore offer the best possible value for money. Here, the software purchaser is effectively paying a premium in order to stay in line with the organisation's broader security aims.

4.8 QUESTIONS

1 The service department of a garage uses a computer system which provides the following functions:
   - booking cars in for servicing and repairs;
   - ordering and tracking spare parts;
   - tracking work in progress, and the time spent on each job;
   - preparing itemised bills for customers;
   - sending customers reminder letters when services are due.

The system is used by the receptionist (who also deals with all telephone calls); the administrator (who looks after the accounts); and a supervisor and five mechanics, who comprise the servicing team.

Draw up a simple Access Control Table for the system. Show the access you would permit for each type of user for each function, indicating in each case if you would permit access to be 'full', 'partial' or 'none'.

2 You are in charge of a neighbourhood social work team, and several of your staff have been issued with portable PCs for recording information about clients. In the course of an informal discussion with the head of social services, she indicates that she has just been reading an article about voice recognition software. She feels this would provide a much more convenient means of identification for staff, compared with the existing system based on passwords. You suggest that there could be one or two drawbacks, and undertake to write a short memorandum on the subject.

Write a brief memo (not more than 400 words) explaining the advantages and disadvantages of using voice recognition for user identification in this kind of situation.

3 'Eventually, the use of passwords will die out completely.' Do you agree? Identify some of the possible drawbacks associated with trying to replace passwords with other identification methods based on tokens and biometrics.

4 Explain how single sign-on might have benefits for employees in a large corporation, and explain the difficulties which can arise in trying to implement such a scheme.

chapter
five

CONTROLS
WITHIN BUSINESS
PROCESSES

SOME TOPICS ADDRESSED IN THIS CHAPTER

- The controls which can be applied to everyday *transactions* handled by the information system
- The different kinds of checks which can be made on data *as it is entered*, in order to improve its accuracy and integrity
- Other controls which can be applied while data is being *processed* in the system, or sent as *output* to printers and displays
- The difference between controls which work by *prevention*, and those which work by *feedback*
- Considerations concerning controls over data used for the purposes of *management reporting*, and *decision support*

SECURITY AND CONTROL OBJECTIVES

- Protect secrets
- Promote accuracy
- Prevent tampering

5.1   INTRODUCTION: TRANSACTIONS AND PROCESSES

The previous chapter described how checks could be made on the credentials of those who are logging on to the information system, and decisions made about the facilities which are to be made accessible to them. This chapter looks at the next step, which is to control what happens once the user actually gets down to work. Checks may be needed on the kind of data which is being entered, or the way it is to be processed. Warning messages may need to be sent to the user, or records kept of certain types of activity. These checks are often concerned with the accuracy and integrity of the data itself, rather than just with questions of whether the action the user is taking is authorised.

Anyone who is working at a terminal or a PC is constantly engaging in *transactions* with the information system. Suppose, for example, that a user logs on, interrogates her email folders, looks up the latest production statistics, and instructs the accounting software to issue a purchase order. Each of these activities will be carried out by a different software *application*. Within an application, the transaction is the basic unit of activity, carrying out some task for the user which he or she has probably done many times before, and is part of the daily routine.

In Information Systems parlance, such applications are known collectively as *Transaction Processing Systems*. They can be contrasted with other types of software, such as spreadsheets and financial models, which allow the user much more freedom to manipulate figures and make assumptions. These are typically used to explore strategic options, and carry out ad hoc analysis. In these cases, the application is described as providing *Decision Support* facilities to the user.

The use of the term 'transaction' in this context can be confusing, because it often has a quite different meaning elsewhere (for example, a property deal which takes months to negotiate may be regarded as a single business 'transaction'). However, for the purposes of the analysis which follows, the much narrower definition, as normally applied in the context of computer systems, will be adopted.

Each transaction will involve one or more sequences of:

INPUT → PROCESSING → OUTPUT.

The *input* will normally be from a human operator, pressing keys or clicking on a mouse. Occasionally, activities will be started off automatically inside the computer system, when one transaction triggers another one, without requiring any further human intervention. An example would be where a warehouse is requested to despatch some goods, and the resulting fall in inventory takes it below a pre-selected re-order level. A transaction might then be started up automatically to order items to re-fill the shelves.

The *processing* of a transaction may be carried out on a big central computer, on the user's own PC, or on both of these working together (an arrangement known as *client-server*). The *output* will then be sent back to the user's display screen, to a printing device, or sent off to an interim destination, such as a disk file or a network.

Because transactions come in all shapes and sizes, it is not always easy to define exactly where each one begins and ends. For example, if the output is not sent to the user immediately, but is put in some kind of queue to be retrieved later, when exactly is the transaction completed? Such points of detail may be vital when designing controls into a system. However, for the moment all such complications will be ignored. A transaction will be assumed to be one simple task carried out by a user. It could entail looking up some details on a price list, changing a customer's credit limit, or having the system generate a standard monthly report.

Of course, in many cases a whole *series* of transactions is needed to achieve a particular end. These transactions may be carried out by a number of different people in different locations. This entire series is regarded as comprising a *business process*. Taking a loan application through all the necessary steps, between receiving the form and sending the customer an offer letter, is a business process. So is the sequence of issuing a lottery ticket, checking its number against the draw, and sending a cheque to a lucky winner. A formal definition, provided by Davenport (1993: 5), is:

> A structured, measured set of activities designed to produce a specified output for a particular customer or market. . . . A process is thus a specific ordering of work activities across time and place, with a beginning, an end, and clearly identified inputs and outputs: a structure for action.

Davenport mentions 'inputs' and 'outputs' as applying to the process as a whole. The situation may therefore be pictured as in Figure 5.1.

Usually the inputs and outputs for the entire *process* will be those which form the basis for interaction with a customer. Thus the applicant for a loan may fill in a form, and this becomes the *process input*. The *process output* might be a personalised standard letter offering the loan, and indicating the terms and conditions. All the transactions in between will be internal to the company. Some will involve operators interacting with screens, and dealing with one customer at a time. Others may involve 'batch' processes, where the same details are processed for several customers together, for example, to add all their names and addresses onto a mailing list.

←----------------------------- process ----------------------------- →

INPUT   PROCESSING   OUTPUT

← - - - transaction 1 - - - → ← - - - transaction 2 - - - → ← - - - transaction 3 - - - →

INPUT PROCESSING OUTPUT → INPUT PROCESSING OUTPUT → INPUT PROCESSING OUTPUT

Figure 5.1

This chapter concentrates mainly on the controls which should apply to the input, processing and output of a typical transaction. More wide-ranging controls, based on tracking the progress of individual cases from one end of a process to the other, are discussed in the connection with the role of auditors, whose role and function is described in Part 5.

Transaction controls may aim to work either through *prevention* or *feedback*. Preventive controls anticipate the potential problem situations, and cut in immediately it is suspected that something is amiss. Feedback controls work retrospectively, enabling the source of problems to be identified *after* the event. Thus, if a customer tries to place an order which is in excess of his credit limit, this can be detected immediately by a preventive control. If, on the other hand, a customer makes payment with an invalid cheque, it may be some time before the bad news is received from the bank, and this then acts as a feedback control.

Preventive controls may work in ways which are either *advisory* or *mandatory*. If the control is only advisory, it can be overruled. Our customer who has exceeded his credit limit could still be allowed to place his order, if it is decided that it is in the company's interests to let him do so. On the other hand, the company may have a firm (mandatory) rule that customers may never exceed their credit limits, and if so the system will be programmed to refuse to accept the order.

Feedback controls by their very nature are usually advisory, since they take the form of some kind of report or error message. Sometimes the feedback is available quite quickly, and it is possible to envisage situations where it would be useful to make it mandatory to react in a particular way. However, this can have its dangers. (For some examples to consider, the reader is referred to Question 1 at the end of the chapter).

5.2   INPUT: CHECKS APPLIED TO DATA CAPTURE

The entry of data into a commercial computer system needs to be controlled both to ensure that the data is of reasonable *quality* (that is, it is as accurate as possible) and to prevent the introduction of data capable of having any *adverse effects* on the system. Input checks should be seen as a first and best opportunity to filter out anything which could give rise to problems later.

Sometimes an application will be fairly flexible about the shape and form in which it will accept data. An everyday example is the word-processing package. This assumes that users should be allowed to key in more or less anything they want. Similarly, the general purpose functions in a spreadsheet or graphics package offer complete freedom to enter data without any regard to its accuracy, completeness or propriety. Increasingly these packages offer options to do certain types of checks, which are discussed in section 5.2.5. It can be made company policy to use these checks, or some degree of enforcement can be applied, using facilities such as templates and macros. However, the big attraction of the so-called

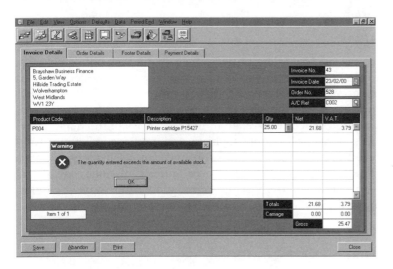

Figure 5.2 **Data capture screen for an invoice**

'generic' office packages is that they are cheap, quick to learn, and allow users to enter whatever data they want to with as little fuss as possible.

More specialised transaction processing systems, on the other hand, require data to be entered in a way which is strictly prescribed. An accounting package, for example, will require specified codes, dates, and amounts in order to deal with matters such as processing payments received. A local council's housing system will need tenants' names, addresses, and types of property entered in exactly the right way, with perhaps special codes to indicate if the property is suitable for the elderly or the disabled. These systems have a structure and predictability which make it possible to design quite precise checks on the data which is being fed in to them. In most cases, the entry of data can be controlled via *data capture screens* (Figure 5.2), which specify to the operator exactly what data is to be entered, and in which areas of the screen.

When data is being entered in this way, there are a number of different types of checks which can be made. Note that it is *not* essential that the data is actually being typed in through a keyboard. It could just as well be picked up from a bar code, a magnetic card, a smart card, or a scanner which can read numbers and letters. In the future, it is likely that operators will make greater use of voice recognition facilities, and simply dictate the contents of the different fields to the computer. In all these cases, similar processes are used to check the data before it is actually accepted and stored away by the system. Data can also be entered (or more strictly speaking, selected) by using a mouse. If all the permitted values can be predicted, and the list is not too long, this can be a good way of ensuring that only valid entries are made into the system.

Input checks are predominantly *preventive*, and usually combine both *advisory* and *mandatory* features. They can be used to control the entry of various types of unacceptable data.

5.2.1 Data with inconsistent or not permitted values

No system can provide complete protection against *all* possible errors. All it can do is to challenge entries which do not appear to make sense. Thus most accounting systems will refuse to process payments of £0.00, and a medical system may reject the idea that a patient aged 55 needs her pre-school immunisation. Such tests relate to the *consistency* of the data. These checks on consistency may be quite sophisticated, perhaps involving cross-referencing to other information. So, for example, a retailer's check on a credit card number may reveal that it is on a 'hot list' of stolen cards, and this will cause the retailer to abort the transaction. The value of consistency checking in preventing fraud is shown in the accompanying case.

THE NEED FOR CONSISTENCY CHECKING

A typical example of false data entry is the case of a timekeeping clerk who filled out data forms of hours worked by 3,000 employees in a railroad company department. He noticed that all data on the forms entered into the timekeeping and payroll system on the computer included both the name and the employee number of each worker. However, the computer used only employee numbers for processing and even for printing employee names and addresses on payroll cheques. He also noticed that outside the computer all manual processing and control was based only on employee names, because nobody identified people by their numbers. He took advantage of this dichotomy of controls by filling out forms for overtime hours worked, using the names of employees who frequently worked overtime but entering his own employee number. His false data entry was not discovered for years until by chance an auditor examining US W-2 files and data forms noticed the clerk's unusually high annual income. An examination of the timekeeping computer files and data forms and a discussion with the clerk's supervisor revealed the source of the increased income. The clerk was confronted with the evidence and admitted his fraudulent activities. Well-designed timekeeping and payroll systems use the first few letters of employees' names appended to their identification number to reduce the likelihood of this type of crime.

Based on Parker 1992: 452

Rules for judging the consistency of a particular value may either be pre-set by the providers of computer software, or be specified by the organisation operating the system. For example, many systems will be pre-set to refuse dates which are set some time in the future, since they deal with business activities which can only be recorded 'after the event'. Similarly, a reservation system will reject an illogical situation such as a holiday booking where the end date precedes the start date. In other instances custom-designed rules about dates may be appropriate. A hotel reservation system, for example, could be quite happy to process dates set a long way into the future, but if the hotel is offering special bargain breaks, it might incorporate its own automatic checks as to whether a date is one for which the cheap rate is actually available. In practice, many systems allow rules embedded in the basic software to be combined with other optional rules which can be set up and changed at will by the system manager.

Other checks which are commonly made involve *sequence* and *range*. Sequencing involves assigning a reference number to each transaction. This can be done by the person entering the data, but preferably it should be done by having the numbers assigned independently by the system. If the numbers are in ascending order, a cross-check can be made against the times at which the transactions were recorded as taking place. If the record then shows that transaction 73 apparently occurred before transaction 72, this will draw attention to the likelihood that something fraudulent has been going on.

Ranges are a useful way of preventing errors due to 'finger trouble'. It is obvious, for example, that if your are entering percentage marks for an examination, you will not expect any values to exceed 100. Similarly, you cannot have the 32nd day of a month. If an operator makes a mistake in typing in any of these values, it can be made mandatory to correct them immediately. Some range checks may be tailored specifically to the needs of the organisation. Thus while common sense says that 'weekly working hours' cannot possibly exceed 168, there may be provisions in the law or in company policy which set the limit at a lower level, perhaps 48 hours per week. Similarly, a company may be in the business of offering motor insurance policies which are only available to people above a certain age, or a company accepting orders over the telephone may insist that each order has to have a minimum value.

Sometimes the system will be asked to check the *reasonableness* of the data, which cannot always be specified in hard and fast rules. In such cases the control will usually be advisory. For example, although employees may normally be limited to 48 hours per week, the number of hours may be permitted to go higher in special circumstances. It is still helpful to highlight any cases which exceed the norm, as the operator can then check whether this is indeed a special case, or some kind of error. Reasonableness checks can be applied to anything which is possible but out of the ordinary, such as a booking for 44 theatre tickets: the aim is not to make it difficult for coach parties to book trips to the theatre, but to make sure that the operator has not intended to book 4 seats, and hit the same button twice by mistake.

5.2.2 Invalid or incorrectly formatted data

It is often useful to be able to specify that only certain values will be regarded as *valid*. This means defining an acceptable set of values. A simple example would be to insist that responses to a question must be 'Y' or 'N'. In some instances, the checking may be more sophisticated, as in the case of a reference number including one or more 'check digits', which are added on to the end of the number. Any number containing an incorrect check digit will be rejected. The data entry software needs to know in advance how many check digits to expect, and how they have been calculated. It then works out the check digits for itself, and compares its answer with the one which has been typed in. The calculation of the check digits in a VAT registration number is shown as an example. The method of calculation has, of course, to be chosen quite carefully, so that it will always deliver the right number of digits, and give all possible answers with more or less equal frequency.

THE CALCULATION OF CHECK DIGITS IN A VAT REGISTRATION NUMBER

A registration number for Value Added Tax (VAT) in the UK has a total of nine digits. The real number is only seven digits long – two extra digits are added as 'check digits'.

To work out the check digits, the first seven digits are used as a basis for calculation, as follows:

(a) multiply the first digit by 8, the second by 7, and so on until the seventh digit, which is multiplied by 2;
(b) add up all the numbers which have just been calculated;
(c) keep on subtracting 97 from the result, until the answer becomes a negative number;
(d) take this negative number, remove the sign, put a zero in front if it is only one digit, and use this as the check digit.

Take as an example the VAT number **198923209**

(a) Multiplying the different digits gives:
$1 \times 8 + 9 \times 7 + 8 \times 6 + 9 \times 5 + 2 \times 4 + 3 \times 3 + 2 \times 2$
(b) Add the result: $8 + 63 + 48 + 45 + 8 + 9 + 4 = 185$
(c) Subtracting 97 gives 88. Subtracting 97 again gives -9.
(d) Thus the check digits are **09**.

In other cases, data may be declared valid only if it adheres to a set *format* of letters and numbers. For example, a company might give each of its customers a reference number of the form CUST123. The data entry software will then check that anything being entered in the customer number field consists of four letters followed by three numbers. A format check may be more general than this, for example, it could ensure that a customer name consisted only of letters and punctuation, or that an amount of money was entered solely in figures. Formats may be specified for anything which follows a predictable pattern, such as dates and times. In the case of dates, people may be used to different conventions (so that 01/02 may fit in correctly with the required format, but mean 1 February to a European reader and 2 January to an American one). In such cases, one solution is to insist on an unambiguous format, such as a day-number followed by three letters indicating the month.

5.2.3 Incomplete data

Incompleteness may be detected by some of the format checks described in the preceding section, but these apply to just one value at a time. Thus the format check may reveal that the customer number is not long enough, but cannot check whether the operator has filled in all the other fields which may be needed for the transaction to proceed. In the simplest case, it may be required that something should be entered in *every* field on a data entry screen. In other cases, the amount of information required may be made conditional. For example, a telephone order-taking screen may allow customers either (a) to opt for an invoice or (b) to give their credit card number. The software may then regard the data provided as being complete in *either* of the following cases:

(a) the customer provides an order reference number; or
(b) the customer provides a credit card number *and* expiry date of the card.

Note that the software could also apply consistency tests, so that it could reject inappropriate mixtures, such as an order reference number and a credit card expiry being entered on the same screen.

Since testing for completeness implies some degree of predictability about the data being entered, some data items do not lend themselves very easily to this kind of test. Addresses can be a particular problem, especially if they are from a number of different countries (something which is increasingly common for vendors setting up store on the Internet). It is possible to test for completeness in including, for example, some kind of post code or zip code, but other elements such as the 'town', 'state' or 'province' may not always be relevant. In other instances, the number of entries required for completeness simply cannot be known, for example, when asked about 'qualifications' or 'disabilities', a person may list just one, or several.

5.2.4 Requirements for independent authorisation or verification not met

All the checks mentioned so far will be part of an automatic screening process, built in to the application software. For data which the business regards as particularly critical, and especially where there is threat of fraud, it can be useful to add in some additional controls, based on human interventions.

Three commonly used approaches are:

- *Dual entry* (sometimes known as *dual keying*). The same data is entered independently by two different people. The system compares the two versions, and highlights any differences. Someone then has to check through all the cases where a conflict has been found, and select the correct version. This is a good way of identifying and eliminating keying errors, but is very expensive in terms of staff time. If the intention is to protect against deliberate attempts to falsify the input data, it is important that the final stage (of reviewing the data and sorting out any discrepancies) is handled by someone senior and trustworthy.

- *Explicit authorisation.* If the data entry in question is of a kind which could facilitate fraud, the system can be programmed to require some kind of authorisation before the data is accepted. Most commonly this is done by requiring a supervisor to log in with a higher level of authorisation, and indicate approval of the transaction (the approval being given on the same terminal or, ideally, on another one, where there is less risk of the supervisor's password being detected). This procedure might be followed when a refund is to be made to a customer, or a debt is to be written off.

- *Control totals.* Control totals are mainly used for financial data, but can be applied to almost any transactions where a cumulative record is kept of items of value. The sequence of steps is as follows.

(a)　A number of similar transactions are batched together.

(b)　Person A goes through the source of data for the transactions (e.g. a pile of paper invoices) and calculates the total value of all the transactions (the total of the amounts due for all the invoices).

(c)　This total is entered into the computer. Person B now enters all the data for the transactions.

(d)　When B has finished entering the data, the computer makes its own calculation of the total value, and compares it with the value fed in at the beginning by A.

(e)　If the totals match, processing of the transactions goes ahead. If not, the system refuses to proceed, and the data entry must be checked until the discrepancy is accounted for.

Like check digits, control totals can be a useful way of showing up keying errors. They may also help to deter fraud, providing that A and B work completely independently of one another.

5.2.5　Non-standard syntax or vocabulary

Even where information is being entered in free form, as with word-processing and electronic mail, a business may wish to ensure that material complies with its own codes and standards. Office software packages now offer a range of options for checking text, either highlighting possible errors as they are typed in, or running checks subsequently. Most commonly the checker will compare the words in the text with a list of standard spellings, and query any words which are not in the list. The operator is left to make the final decision: since there are always occasions where names, acronyms, or quotations in another language will not be identifiable in the official list, this is a process which cannot be completely automated.

Some checkers go further, and look for lapses in grammar, punctuation or even style.

Although they can be helpful in picking up badly written or confusing phrases, they can only apply relatively simple rules and cannot take account of the context. Thus most checkers will ignore a phrase such as 'payment to be made in ponds sterling', because it conforms with all the rules of spelling and grammar, though not with common sense.

5.3 PROCESSING THE DATA

Once the data has been entered into the system, it will undergo processing in ways which are largely hidden from the view of the user. Indeed, it should not be assumed that the logic of the processing will be readily apparent even to highly skilled technical staff. This can be because the code in question is very old, and perhaps the documentation about it has been lost, or because it was written using languages which have since become obsolete. 'Packaged' programs can also cause problems, for different reasons. In this case it is because suppliers prefer to ship their products as *object* code. This is code which is ready to run on the machine, but does not contain any of the information from the original *source* program, which is needed in order to understand the program logic. Many organisations have been made uncomfortably familiar with problems of figuring out what is going on 'under the covers' of their systems, as they tried to establish whether or not their programs could handle dates correctly for the year 2000 and beyond.

The potential difficulties of detecting and identifying software anomalies are shown in two old cases, one featuring fraud and the other a logic error. In both these cases, it took external pressures to reveal what was going on. The aim in today's installations should be to build in measures which will ensure that aberrations of this kind are detected quickly, before they become a source of embarrassment. These measures could include:

A CASE OF SOFTWARE FRAUD

An accountant and systems analyst formed a company which developed and marketed a software package aimed at video recording hire shops. The packages gave shops a system for keeping stock records, monitoring the hiring of videos and also the hire income.

Within the program was a secret 'patch' which, when activated on the inputting of a special password, allowed a shopkeeper to hide a part of what he earned each day so that it reduced his statement of earnings for VAT purposes.

The software package had been sold to 120 retailers, though only 12 had been told of the VAT reductions routine by the salesman, and had defrauded Customs and Excise of £100,000.

Based on Audit Commission 1987: 58

AN ERROR IN THE LOGIC

An examination board used a computer to process the results of a chemistry examination taken by 12,000 schoolchildren. None of them obtained a grade higher than 'C'. After complaints from parents and teachers, the computer program was checked. It was found that there was an error in the logic dealing with the marks from an optional paper. Manual checking of the records showed that 1800 of the candidates should have been graded 'A' or 'B'.

Based on BIS 1987: 175

1 *Preventive controls*
   - *Dual processing.* Like dual keying (see 5.2.4) this depends on doing everything twice. Two computers are linked, and transactions are processed simultaneously on both of them. The results are continually compared. The primary aim of such an arrangement is usually to ensure system availability (for example, in a supermarket check-out system). However, the additional checks on accuracy are a useful by-product. Since both processors run the same software, there is still a danger that both will agree on an erroneous result, if this is due to a software flaw which has been replicated on both of them.
   - *Control totals.* Again, the principle used here is the same as in the case of input (see 5.2.4). The method can only be applied if a number of records are all to be processed in the same way (i.e. 'batch' processing is being used). If, for example, an electricity supplier is generating quarterly statements to be sent to its customers, a control total can be created for the number of statements which the program is expected to process. Alternatively, a total could be made of the number of units of electricity, or the total amount to be billed. This total must match up with a total calculated independently elsewhere in the batch processing.
2 *Feedback controls*
   - *Test transactions.* These can be selected 'real' transactions for which the expected outcomes have already been computed, or 'dummy' transactions may be fed into the system, using data specially chosen to probe whether the system is working to specification. Dummy transactions need to be cancelled or discounted afterwards – which will of course be a matter for careful control in itself.
   - *Transaction logs.* While the transaction is in progress, selected details are written to a computer file. Ideally, this file is on a 'write-once' medium, such as a write- once, read-many optical disk (or WORM). This ensures that even if someone succeeds in interfering with the transaction or its output, the log itself cannot be tampered with, and helpful clues or evidence are retained 'on the record'. From the transaction log it should be possible to ascertain the identity of the user, the time, and indications about the data which was entered, or

the files which were written to. Some software suppliers refer to this kind of log as providing the computer-based 'audit trail'. However, an audit trail should always include other corroborative evidence (see section 13.3).

5.4   OUTPUT: PRINTERS AND DISPLAYS

In most cases, output is returned directly to the user who initiated the transaction, in the form of a message on a screen. However, there may also be other outputs (for example, messages sent to other employees, or documents sent to a print queue). Once output is sent on to a network, it may be extremely difficult to keep control over its ultimate destination: this is a problem which is discussed further in Chapter 6. Within the organisation's internal systems, the threats to output can be grouped in three main categories.

1 *Threats from casual browsing.* Just as sensitive documents should not be left around on a desk, output devices ought to be kept out of view if they are likely to carry information which is not intended for general distribution. Particular care needs to be taken with positioning. It can be all too easy for passers-by to glance at a screen, or to read the contents of material coming off a printer. Locations for which this kind of risk is high include open-plan offices, or offices with glass partitions. Similar problems can arise in places where both staff and the public have ready access, such as hospital wards or reception areas.

   Sensitive printed output can be protected by using special envelope packs which have a carbon coating on their inner surface. Stationery of this kind is widely used for payslips. The printer (which must be one using an impact technology, such as daisy wheel or dot matrix) does not mark the outer surface, but the carbon coating ensures that the information is transferred onto a blank sheet inside. The result is that even those operating the printer will be unable to tell what has been printed.

2 *Opportunities for fraud and theft.* If the output involves the creation of something of value, such as a cheque or a certificate, safeguards are needed against attempts to create forgeries. Typically, a set of blank forms will be preprinted, usually with anti-fraud features such as watermarks, or the use of special inks which reveal attempts to erase information which is printed over them. Clearly, every effort must be made to ensure that these forms do not fall into the wrong hands. A useful precaution is to number the forms sequentially, so that a specified number can be assigned to a batch run (thereby providing, in effect, a control total). Further control information may also be added to the details printed onto the form, for example, a reference number which can be used later as a check on authenticity.

3 *Onward communication of output.* When output is transmitted back to a user, it is easy to assume that it will simply be displayed on a screen for

perhaps a few seconds. However, the technology has now advanced to the point where it is easy to convert output into other forms. For example:

- The screen output can be captured as an image (on the Windows keyboard, this simply requires the use of the Print Screen key), and it can then be pasted into a document and sent via email, or printed out.
- The output text may be 'read' by a voice synthesiser. Such software is now routinely installed to help those with poor sight or other disabilities.
- The 'client' software in the user's PC may enable output to be diverted to disk storage, on this or some other machine.

Given the ease with which output can be converted and copied, the following rules should be applied as rigorously as possible.

- If sensitive information is being sent as output, it should be 'labelled' as such, preferably by including warning messages *within the information itself*. This may mean departing from some of the conventions adopted by the organisation in respect of paper documents. For example, many companies use stationery which includes headers or banners such as 'draft' or 'company confidential'. It is possible to devise equivalent electronic templates for word-processed documents, but these are by no means as easy to use as the paper equivalents. Word-processing documents can in any case easily be converted into plain text versions, which will not carry any of the warning information created by the template.
- Staff should be advised to be cautious about assuming that electronic output has been 'deleted'. Software very often declares that data has been deleted, when it has in fact merely declared that the file space in question is now available for over-writing. Until the space is actually over-written, the original material will remain readable by anyone willing to take the trouble to examine the storage medium directly, or to use a command such as the DOS 'undelete' or the Windows 'recycle bin'.

Care should also be taken in disposing of media on which output has previously been recorded. Just as confidential paper documents should be made illegible by feeding them through a shredder, magnetic and optical disks should be systematically wiped or destroyed. Output should not be assumed to be unimportant simply because its meaning is not immediately apparent: for example, print-outs of two-dimensional bar codes may be unintelligible to the human eye, but will contain useful information, and data may be stored 'invisibly' in plastic cards and other tokens.

Where output is subject to proprietary rights (for example, licensed software or text subject to copyright) other, more specialised, controls may be needed to prevent possible infringements. These are discussed further in section 13.5.

5.5 INFORMATION DERIVED FROM TRANSACTIONS

The records which are routinely stored away by routine transactions accumulate over time, and become a valuable source of information for management. For example, sales and marketing may want to know how well products have been selling, or the production department may want to check whether they have met their targets. General managers, too, depend on a regular flow of reports and briefings derived from computer data. It is tempting to regard this acquisition of management information as simply a useful 'by-product' of transaction processing. The extraction of this kind of data ought not, it would seem, to raise too many questions of security, since it will be done by a limited number of people, under conditions which are relatively easy to control.

There are, however, other aspects of derived information which need to be considered. These can be illustrated by considering the particular case of information collected by and for management accountants. The role of management accountants (sometimes called 'managerial accountants') varies from organisation to organisation, but their work has two key characteristics:

(a) it depends very heavily on derived information (from almost all sectors of activity, not just accounting), and
(b) it affects all managers in some way, because it determines how costs and resources are to be allocated within the organisation.

In acquiring and using 'by-product' data, management accountants have to consider the following factors. These affect both the reliance which can be placed on the data, and the security measures which should be built around it.

5.5.1 Integrity of data input

The way employees record data during transactions can be influenced by their perceptions of how the data is going to be used. If they suspect that it will provide a basis for making assessments of themselves or their organisation, elements of selectivity and bias can creep in. A case in point concerns the logging of the time taken for activities. If time is to be billed to a client, the length of the task may be exaggerated. If the object is to appear very productive, it may shrink. Staff quickly develop a sense of the 'appropriate' way to record such data. This does not unduly mislead management, so long as everyone concerned is aware of the forces which are at work. However, the trouble with 'by-product' data is that it may eventually find its way into all manner of assessments and calculations, where the underlying distortions remain hidden and unrecognised.

These problems are exacerbated by the growing fashion for using 'performance indicators'. These have been adopted particularly in connection with the provision of public services, where it is not always easy to find indicators which are both measurable and meaningful. Often, the easiest option is to base them on whatever can be made available as output from transaction processing. The indicators can then be used in 'benchmarks', whereby the achievements of different organisations are compared. This may be through comparisons with 'industry norms', as calculated by consulting firms, or through the publication of 'league tables' for public sector institutions such as hospitals. Examples of performance indicators include waiting list lengths, costs per client, and service response times. The pressure to achieve good indicators can result in under- or over-recording, or the adoption of quite fundamental changes in recording methods. For example, an episode of activity may be broken down into two or three separate parts, in order to give an appearance of greater throughput and productivity.

Staff may also be conscious that they will be appraised personally on the basis of the transaction data. This will be particularly important to them if incentives and rewards are being linked to measurements of their productivity (Moizer 1991).

This raises some delicate questions when considering the security objective 'to ensure accuracy'. If the data being recorded is known to be inaccurate from the outset, why protect it as it makes its way through the system? The answer is that in many cases organisations will live with data which is consistently biased, since this can be recognised and allowed for. Other kinds of deviations, such as those caused by input errors or tampering with individual records, cause more serious problems, because the information can no longer be trusted to provide an accurate indication about anything.

Management should always be conscious of the risk that controls are actually doing no more than providing a secure conduit for bad information. It is a variation on the old theme of 'garbage in–garbage out'. It should never be assumed that the controls, however well designed, can *guarantee* the accuracy or validity of what comes out of the information system.

5.5.2   Informal information systems

People will only use information derived from computer systems if the latter can deliver what they need in a timely manner. Otherwise, they will resort to their own methods of collecting and reporting what they need. McKinnon and Bruns studied twelve manufacturing companies in North America, and discovered a high degree of reliance on informal reporting mechanisms. They report one plant manager as saying:

> The accountants could probably get me a report on yesterday's output by 1 p.m. each day. By that time, we only have 2 or $2\frac{1}{2}$ hours of production time left on the first shift. So instead of relying on accounting, I have my shift supervisors write up our daily input and downtime figures

at the end of each shift. That way they are available when we open the plant each morning.

McKinnon and Bruns 1992: 220

This unofficial data gathering may be carried out for the best of reasons, but it will not be covered by controls designed into the 'official' information system. If the data in question is commercially sensitive, or if the informality of approach extends to the way the data is passed on to others, then security can all too easily be compromised.

5.5.3 Data used in analysis

Once derived data has become separated from transaction data, it can find its way into all kinds of stores of information, both official and unofficial, and it can be difficult to maintain control over its use and dissemination. On the one hand, it may be fed into formal reports, which are issued and stored according to set rules. It may also be held in a Decision Support System (DSS), for analysis using tools such as spreadsheets and statistical packages. If the DSS is well organised, it will include a data management facility which tracks and indexes all the data held in store.

However, the data may also find its way into more 'private' stores which are held by individuals as part of their own file allocation on a mainframe, or on the disk drives of their own PCs. These may be acquired and developed for the best of motives. The management accountant, for example, may feel it is useful to build up a small archive in order to be able to look at longer-term trends in costs or profitability.

Such stores are problematic, because the owners are unlikely to bother with setting up access controls for individual files, while some of them may contain quite sensitive material. The best solution may be to take a blanket approach, and to treat *all* the files as if they are potentially sensitive. If they are on a PC, the machine should have strong security protection (with, for example, a power-on password, and password protection covering all the derived data). If they are on a mainframe, there may be a case for making the controls mandatory rather than discretionary.

5.5.4 Internal versus external reporting

Data which is collected and analysed internally provides the basis for reports which are passed to people *outside* the organisation. These may be covered by conditions of confidentiality (for example, in furnishing information to tax authorities or regulatory bodies) or be available for anyone to read, in print or on the Internet.

In the case of the management accountant, information which has been acquired on costs and activity levels now becomes a starting point for statements in the annual report and accounts. Material which was previously used only for internal decision-making is converted into a picture of the financial health of the company, which is then published. The numbers themselves may not change, but by issuing them into the public domain they are given an entirely new status.

Responsibility for ensuring that published accounts comply with all the relevant standards, laws and regulations rests with the organisation's financial accountants, aided by the external auditors. Until the form of the accounts has been agreed, however, any 'leakage' of financial information may be damaging. Particular sensitivity surrounds information which will be of concern to shareholders, prior to its official release, such as the prospects of a merger with a rival, or the issue of a profits warning. Some of the practical and ethical issues which arise in ensuring that information is passed to investors appropriately are analysed by Mayer (1995).

In theory, an organisation could make all its information systems completely transparent to outsiders. The advent of the Internet creates the possibility that shareholders, or any other interested party, could browse through the firm's up-to-the-minute data, and there would be no need to issue annual reports. Although technically feasible, such arrangements would deny organisations the commercial privacy they need in order to compete and survive. It would also make it difficult to know exactly which figures should be regarded as fully 'audited'. The internal barriers described in this section of the book should be expected to survive for quite a long time.

Information technology has, nevertheless, opened a Pandora's box in terms of the ease with which data can now be accessed and transferred across electronic links. This inevitably complicates the task of restricting any information to purely 'internal' use. Methods available for dealing with the challenges presented by networks are described in the next three chapters.

5.6   CASE STUDY: THE FAO MICROBANKING SYSTEM – SELLING SECURE SYSTEMS IN THE THIRD WORLD

The following case study describes how one supplier has attempted to address some of the issues discussed in the preceding chapters. In many countries of the world, the information revolution is still progressing very slowly. These are territories where telephone lines are in short supply, and are not always reliable. Power supplies may be erratic, and computer technology is not well supported because few people have the necessary training and experience.

There is little incentive to use automation to reduce labour costs, since these are low-wage economies. However, the absence of information technology in banking can put the country at a disadvantage in various ways. It means that information cannot easily be gathered on economic activity, and it can be time consuming to set up funding for new projects, and ensure that expenditure is properly directed and supervised. Additionally, countries find themselves unable to offer the kind of services which are taken for granted by visitors on business or vacation.

In 1988, the Food and Agriculture Organisation of the United Nations set about trying to help such countries to take their first steps into automated banking. It initiated the development of a banking software package, known as the FAO MicroBanking System (or 'MicroBanker' for short). The aim was to address the needs of the small indigenous banks found in many developing countries. The package is now in use in some 30 different countries around the world. It supports all the routine activities of a typical retail bank, such as loan and savings accounts, and provides for the use of more sophisticated technology if required, such as teller machines and smart cards.

The designers of 'MicroBanker' recognised that they had to make the package flexible and adaptable, so that it could meet the standards and conventions of all its different customers world-wide. Providing lots of options for customers, however, would inevitably make the programming in the product more complex, with extra facilities having to be added in to tailor it to the needs of each new market. The challenge was to achieve this without leaving any gaps or weaknesses in the coding which could weaken security.

'MicroBanker' addresses these problems by ensuring that, wherever possible, the variations are introduced in separate software modules. This way, the basic accounting code can be left unchanged. For example, an international product like this needs to be available in different languages (currently, ten languages are catered for, including some, such as Russian and Thai, which use a different script). All the messages and menu lists for each language are kept in separate, independent files. If a new language is to be added, new versions of these files are created – there is no need to modify any of the basic programming logic. This reduces the risk that any inappropriate changes can be made. Even in the 'developers'' version, designed to allow users to add on their own extra features to the software, around 80% of the code remains in execute-only form, and thus firmly under the control of the FAO's own coding team.

The designers have also had to assume that many banks will use the software in locations where working conditions are less than ideal. Power supplies, for example, may be erratic. (Sophisticated Uninterruptible Power Supply systems will simply not be affordable for most clients.) The software must therefore provide clients with a 'soft landing' in the event of failures. For example, it must be possible to move quickly from computerised operations to back-up procedures based on more traditional paper-based methods. This requires that the system should routinely create plenty of paper records, which can be consulted if and when the system goes down. The routines for starting up and closing down are also designed in such a way that they can be re-run without any risk of error, in the event of their being disrupted by power or equipment faults.

Emphasis is also placed on facilitating recovery following a system failure, with automated procedures to prompt operators to re-enter any transactions which have not completed properly. The software enforces the taking of regular data back-ups: one generation of data for every day of the week, plus end-of-month copies.

The need to keep system costs low means that the software cannot rely on any sophisticated hardware, such as token or biometric readers for user identification. Indeed, the aim is that the system should never need more than modestly specified PCs and printers, which can be obtained 'off-the-shelf' from suppliers around the world. This some-times calls for changes in working methods: for example, pass books are a popular way of recording details of savings accounts, but it is not practical to print updates in these using a standard A4 paper printer. The idea of a single-sheet document, or 'passcard', has been intro-duced instead, calling for a different approach to the way the entries are made and controlled.

Similarly, telecommunications facilities may be of poor quality, ruling out any reliance on round-the-clock connections or high-grade digital links. In really remote areas, there may be no telephone lines at all, so that electronic communication is only possible by sending diskettes, or by installing up-links to satellites.

The software can, nevertheless, take advantage of advanced tech-niques to protect its own security, and to provide access controls. Hash algorithms are used to provide checks against any attempts to tamper with the record entries. The access controls, based on passwords, enable access rights to be set at seven different levels.

'Microbanker' has had to strike a difficult balance. It must be afford-able, and relatively simple to operate. However, it must provide strict protection of the personal and financial data collected by the bank, and ensure that the integrity of transactions is enforced at all times. The success of the product owes a great deal to the implementation of a 'no-frills' approach to security, which makes it easy for clients to build and maintain a secure system.

FAO 1999

5.7   QUESTIONS

1 Decide whether each of the following controls is a *preventive* or *feedback* control. Would you recommend that its effects be made advisory or mandatory?

   (a)   A hospital system for prescribing drugs detects that the dosage being specified on the label exceeds a level which is usually fatal.

   (b)   Your monthly credit card statement contains several items you do not recognise.

   (c)   A virus checking program scans all your files, and produces a report indicating that it has detected and removed a dangerous virus.

   (d)   Some 'intelligent' software monitors all debit card transactions as they occur, and detects what it regards as a suspicious pattern of usage for one particular card. It immediately puts the card on a black list so that it is no longer valid.

   (e)   A leisure centre requires membership cards, containing a bar code, to be produced whenever bookings are made. A member wishes to book a tennis court but left her membership card at home.

2. What kind of input check(s) might be desirable in each of the following cases?

   (a)   Entering the date of birth of a child in a travel booking (assume that a half-price fare is available for children under 14).

   (b)   Entering the part number for a component being issued from a warehouse.

   (c)   Entering the amount received as payment for the balance payable on a holiday booking.

3 Explain how a *control total* might be used in connection with entering a batch of invoices received from suppliers.

Part 3

CONTROLS FOR NETWORKED SERVICES

INTRODUCTION TO PART 3

In 1845, Henry Thoreau built himself a wooden shack by Walden pond near Concord, Massachussets, and spent two years pondering life, nature, and the follies of modern technology. He railed particularly against people's obsessions with railroads and the telegraph, observing famously that 'we are in great haste to construct a magnetic telegraph from Maine to Texas; but Maine and Texas, it may be, have nothing important to communicate' (Thoreau 1910). One can only imagine what he would have made of mobile phones, and the Internet.

Businesses today need to be connected. Their customers and suppliers want to communicate by electronic mail. Their competitors will be setting up shop on the Internet, and opening up new markets. More traditional forms of electronic commerce, such as Electronic Data Interchange (EDI), continue to flourish and grow. There is really no option of cutting oneself off, and retreating to the calm of Walden pond.

Part 3 explains how organisations can set up protective barriers between themselves and outside networks, and how they should set about communicating securely with their customers and business partners. This necessarily takes discussion into some rather esoteric areas, such as asymmetric cryptography and public key infrastructures. Such techniques do not need to be understood in detail, but it is important to know exactly what they can and cannot be expected to achieve.

Part 3 begins with descriptions of some of the technology used in networking, and suggests where some of the main threats can be expected.

Discussion then moves on to ways of implementing and managing security measures. Finally, attention is turned to some of the smaller-scale problems of networking. Most of these centre on Local Area Networks in the office, which are actually a part of the internal infrastructure. However, they have been included as 'networking' rather than 'internal' topics, since they are rarely completely isolated from wider networks, and some network-related problems have to be seen as a whole. It is impossible, for example, to consider virus protection on the office cluster without reference to the propagation of viruses via the Internet. At this point, the opportunity is also taken to look more closely at other aspects of control related to small-group working.

chapter
six

CONTROLS FOR
NETWORK
COMMUNICATIONS

SOME TOPICS ADDRESSED IN THIS CHAPTER

- The main *threats* which are encountered when using networked communications
- How threats may apply to the different *layers* of software used in a typical network transmission
- An introduction to some of the techniques of *cryptography* which have been developed to support control and security in networks
- How these cryptographic techniques can be used to *check on the identities* of the parties to an electronic transaction over a network, and to ensure that *no-one can tamper* with the messages they exchange
- Some implications for businesses who trade on the Internet, and the use of *Virtual Private Networks and Firewalls*

SECURITY AND CONTROL OBJECTIVES

- Protect secrets
- Prevent tampering
- Prove authorship
- Challenge repudiation

6.1 INTRODUCTION

The expectation that the future belongs to 'e-commerce' has led to a flurry of investment in networking technology around the world. One example is Singapore, which has made IT investment a priority for many years, but which has recently diverted much of this into its networking infrastructure (Donovan 1991). In the same region, Malaysia has launched a Multimedia Supercorridor, and the new federal capital at Putrajaya has been designed as a fully 'wired city'. Not to be outdone, Hong Kong has a scheme to turn part of the island into a networked 'Cyberport'. Similar initiatives can be found in many other countries, and this in turn has led to an upsurge in business for companies selling network equipment and services (Anon 1999).

Cairncross (1997: xiv) has identified some 30 consequences of this telecommunications revolution. Some of these, such as erosion of individual privacy, and competition between tax regimes, have been evident for some time. The validity of some of the others has yet to be proven, for example, that 'services will become more reliable and people will be more likely to trust each other to keep their word'. One certainty is that every aspect of data security has to be re-appraised as electronic trading pervades more and more aspects of business.

Many businesses are now totally dependent on networks, just as they originally became dependent on their mainframes. Many of them rely on Electronic Data Interchange for their everyday trading, and make their routine payments through electronic systems such as BACS in the UK and the ACH Network in the USA. They exploit the new breed of Internet-based systems and services, which are widely accessible and friendly enough to be used by just about anyone. To do this, they are obliged to undertake some radical re-thinking about security. For example, ways have to be found of checking the credentials of trading partners on the other side of the world, of making services easily accessible to customers (but not hackers), and auditing electronic exchanges between several different organisations which are now keeping fewer, if any, paper-based records of the transactions.

6.2 COMMERCIAL NETWORKS: FUNCTIONS AND ORIGINS

In the 1960s, an engineer at the RAND Corporation, Paul Baran, had visionary ideas for a network which would enable computers in different research institutions to communicate more easily with each other. He envisaged connecting the computers via a giant lattice arrangement – a novel idea for the time. The telephone companies at first declared Baran's ideas were unworkable and declined to help in testing them out, but with the backing of the US Department of Defense and its Advanced Research Projects Agency, a prototype network was eventually built and began operating in 1969 (Hafner and Lyon 1998). ARPANET divided messages into 'packets' of data, which could travel via a number of alternative routes across the network. These ideas were rapidly taken up in the business world, and new 'packet-switching' standards were developed (such as CCITT X25 in Europe). It now became possible for companies to buy terminals running the X25 standard, and to connect themselves to a variety of commercial network services.

During the 1970s, business networks tended to be one of two kinds. Larger companies preferred to create their own private networks, based on proprietary software such as IBM's Systems Network Architecture (SNA). These software products kept tight control over everything that was happening on the network, which radiated out from a powerful mainframe in the corporate data centre. This enabled companies to feel confident that security issues were being monitored, and kept under their control. At the same time, an alternative approach was being advocated by the proponents of Open Systems, who distrusted the motives of suppliers promoting SNA and other proprietary software, since these often had the effect of 'locking in' the customer to the supplier's own products. The alternative approach of 'open' standards centred on the UNIX operating system for running the computers, and X25 and a related set of protocols for telecommunications. Open Systems were promoted particularly strongly in the public sector, where it was felt they reduced dependence on any one supplier and created a fairer 'playing field' for systems procurement.

The security of the Open Systems approach was not, unfortunately, one of its strong points. UNIX was originally developed by AT&T Bell Laboratories to provide a general-purpose operating system which would run on hardware from various manufacturers. It could then be a standard in all its research establishments, making it easier for them to work together. UNIX's popularity was boosted by Bell's decision to place it in the public domain. A free version developed by the University of Berkeley became widely used, especially in universities. This ensured a regular flow of computer science graduates who knew and liked UNIX. UNIX also appealed to software developers, because they could modify and extend the functions of the operating system relatively easily. This meant that a large number of people became familiar with the details of UNIX's internal operations. Unfortunately, it also created a substantial community of those who were inclined to find ways of subverting it, using their skill to alter or bypass parts of the code. Putting security *back in* to UNIX became an uphill battle over the years which followed.

The 1980s saw two developments which were to have a major impact on the subsequent development of the Internet. The first was the development of two communications protocols for the ARPANET: Transmission Control Protocol and Internet Protocol. These are generally used in combination, and referred to as TCP/IP. When the ARPANET later evolved into the Internet as we now know it, the TCP/IP standards continued to be used. The second development was the arrival of the IBM personal computer in 1981. The architecture of the IBM PC quickly became a world-wide standard. It was seen as being an ideal 'client' machine, powerful enough to carry out tasks on its own, while also acting as an access point for networks. The architecture effectively became an 'open' standard (despite efforts by IBM to prevent this) and manufacturers around the world moved in to supply the rapidly growing customer base. Unfortunately neither TCP/IP nor the DOS operating system used by PCs were designed particularly with security in mind.

Businesses began to see the advantages of linking their office PCs together into *local area networks*. Initially, these were sold as a way of keeping costs down, for example by enabling several PC users to share the use of a single high-quality printer. However, it quickly became clear that the 'server' machine which took charge of the LAN could take on other roles. It could act as a repository for many kinds of commonly used files, and provide a library of programs for users to download as and when they needed them. This in turn made the security of LANs, and particularly of the LAN servers, a key issue. LAN server security became still more important when servers began to be used as gateways to and from other networks outside the business. Security now needed to take account of all the possible ways in which users might try to link themselves to and from the outside world.

The 1990s saw the maturing of the Internet as the ultimate public data network. The lattice approach to networking proved ideal for a service which needed to expand rapidly around the world. Many aspects of information technology had by now changed beyond all recognition since the days of the original ARPANET. In particular, the typical PC on the office desk or in the home could cope with sound and graphics to an extent way beyond the capabilities of anything available in the 1960s. This powerful technology made it possible to give Internet access to anyone with a PC, a telephone line, and a willingness to learn the basic commands of a browser, such as Netscape or Explorer. Even the most IT-sceptical person could now buy all the necessary software and equipment as a package, and be surfing the Net within a few minutes. But despite the much improved sophistication of the services, as seen by the user, the Internet continued to depend on the operating systems and transmission protocols it had grown up with. In security terms, it became increasingly apparent that these were less than ideal for the task.

6.3   EAVESDROPPING ON DATA TRANSMISSIONS

Anxieties about the possibility that others may listen in on networked messages go back a long way. In 1845 the Great Western Railway launched its new electric telegraph service between London and Slough, advertising that its customers could have 'despatches instantaneously sent to and fro with the most confiding secrecy'. Even at the time, the claim was a highly dubious one, since it has always been easy to detect the changes in electric current at any point along a telegraph line, and to use this to work out the contents of the message.

In the event, the market for telegraph services developed quite slowly. The real growth in demand was for voice-based telephony. This has led to a situation where, in most developed countries, the ratio of telephone lines to inhabitants is now 50% or more. In some areas, such as North America and Scandinavia, the ratio has climbed to around 70%. In the Third World, on the other hand, many of the ratios remain extremely low: in Africa, for example, the average for the whole continent is just over 2% (ITU 1999). Wherever extensive telephone networks are already in place, they offer a cheap and immediate means of connecting up to data services. This is notwithstanding the fact that telephone cables are not particularly well suited to carrying data 'digits', rather than the analogue voice signals for which they were originally designed.

Ingenious methods have been devised for getting round the limitations of telephone cables, for example by using intelligent modem devices or by transmitting along two lines at once (Anon 1998). In the longer term, however, more radical solutions are required, if users are to be able to transmit and receive large volumes of data at reasonable speeds. Accordingly, many countries have introduced Integrated Services Digital Networks (ISDN), designed specifically to handle data. ISDN is essentially a digital version of the old voice-based telephone system, with subscribers dialling up each other to create connections as and when they need them. ISDN eliminates the need for modems, and provides higher transfer speeds with much lower error rates.

In telephony, the most rapidly growing sector at present is mobile phones. Mobile subscribers are already in the majority in Finland, and this is expected to be the norm in many countries within the first few years of the twenty-first century (Black 1999).

As in the early days of wire-based telephony, the voice-based services have been the initial driving force behind the expansion of networks. However, the data services are close behind and moving up fast. The Groupe Spéciale Mobile (GSM) standard, widely used in Europe, supports data traffic at 9,600 bits per second, matching the rate available with cheaper modems on a conventional telephone line. GSM also includes Short Message Service, supporting messages of up to 160 characters. GSM has been adopted in many countries, but differing standards have evolved, particularly in Japan and the USA. Strenuous efforts are being made within the telecommunications industry to secure world-wide agreement for a new and more advanced standard, the Universal Mobile Telecommunications System (UMTS). This will not only ensure that an individual's phone will work in any country, but will support much faster data transmissions (Holley and Costello 1998; Emmerson 1998).

Radio can also be used in a localised way to connect up conventional-style telephones within a building, or in any area of high population density (Anon 1996). In today's world, therefore, it must be expected that most messages will end up being routed across a variety of different media. They may be sent through land lines, beamed to a mobile computer by radio, or bounced to and from telecommunications satellites. The increasing reliance on radio for many of these communications links inevitably increases the opportunities for outsiders to locate and intercept the data traffic.

A distinction should be drawn between the deliberate use of radio to carry data messages (which can then, by definition, be intercepted by anyone tuning in to the appropriate frequency), and the emission of radio signals as an unwanted by-product. All computer and telecommunications equipment sends out a jumble of low-intensity signals, which can be picked up and interpreted, albeit with some difficulty and only by getting quite close to the equipment. This is only worthwhile if the stakes are high, and the eavesdroppers need to be skilled and determined. Protection against this kind of leakage of signals is mainly confined to top-secret military installations. A range of measures which can be taken to combat this problem have been defined by the TEMPEST programme in the United States (Russell and Gangemi 1991).

The different types of cable-based transmission media each have their vulnerabilities, which are summarised as follows.

- *Unshielded Twisted Pair.* UTP has traditionally been widely used in telephone networks, especially in providing the final link from the local distribution point into the home or office. Being unshielded, it gives off weak signals, which can be used to listen in on the traffic flowing along it. UTP is also used in many Local Area Networks.
- *Coaxial Cable.* LANs based on the idea of connecting everyone onto a single 'bus' (as in Ethernets) tend to use coaxial cable. This has an outer layer, added primarily to prevent outside signals from interfering with those travelling inside the cable. However, this also works the other way round, making it difficult to pick up signals from outside. Nevertheless, it is relatively easy to insert a probe into a coaxial cable, without disturbing its operation, and read off the signals this way.
- *Electrical Mains Circuits.* Electricity utilities have explored various ways of sending data signals over the circuits used to provide power supplies. Providing the correct equipment is used, this is not as dangerous as it sounds, and of course there is a big advantage in that power cable is already in place throughout most buildings. However, the data security of this method of transmission is poor. In particular, if signals are travelling through vertical lengths of wire (as in street lights) these act as very effective radio transmitters (Ward 1998).
- *Optical Fibre.* Optical fibre cables rely on light waves which carry signals along very thin filaments of glass. The cable is surrounded by an opaque plastic coating, which makes it impossible for anyone to 'read' the signals without first tampering with the cable. It is extremely difficult to intercept the signals without causing them to be distorted, thus giving the game away.

6.4 COMMUNICATION LAYERS

Wiretapping and eavesdropping tend to capture the popular imagination, but they are by no means the best or only way of finding out what is being sent over networks. If security measures are directed solely at preventing these direct methods of interception, some other serious security exposures are likely to be overlooked.

Data communications can be regarded as depending on a series of 'layers'. The lower layers concentrate on the business of sending data between different points in the network, and ensuring that every data packet is accounted for and has no errors. The higher layers deal with the data as it is actually created and worked on by the computer users. Data being transmitted from a user's computer application is usually broken up into smaller packets, with special codes being added to indicate the destination of the data and other control information. For incoming data the same process is carried out in reverse. The individual data packets are recombined and presented back to the user as intelligible messages and images.

An analogy can be made with conventional mail services: a manager dictates a letter to a secretary which is typed up, put in an envelope, and put in the mail 'out' tray. These activities, which all take place in the office, can be equated with the *top* layers. The letter is subsequently routed between sorting offices, depending on the address information on the envelope. This activity, which requires no knowledge of what is actually *inside* the envelope, is equivalent to the work of the *lower* layers.

In 1978 the International Standards Organisation established a Reference Model for Open Systems Interconnection, defining a total of seven different communications layers. These layers have been widely used as guidance for those designing communications software, and have been extensively described and documented (Halsall 1996; Judge 1988). However, for the purposes of analysing security risks in general, it is sufficient to simplify this to just three layers, as shown in Figure 6.1.

Eavesdroppers are concerned with the *lowest* layer, since they hope to obtain a read-out of the data as it passes through the physical links (i.e. along a wire, or broadcast through the air-waves). Because the data will

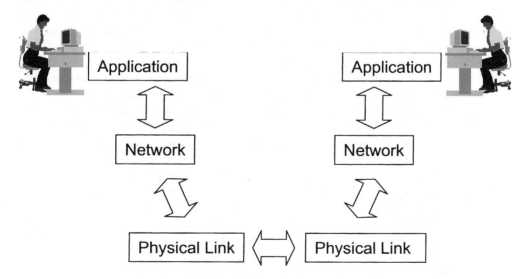

Figure 6.1

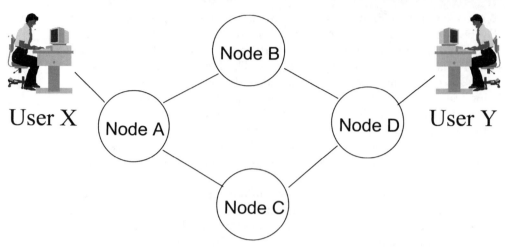

Figure 6.2

have been chopped up into packets and have control codes mixed in with it, they face the challenge of sorting through the resulting jumble and stripping out the meaningful bits relating to a particular message. It is possible that several messages will all be carried across a link at the same time, giving the eavesdropper still more of a problem.

The attacker may therefore prefer to target the middle (network) layer, which determines how messages are to be routed over the network. For example, there could be two possible routes between users X and Y, as shown in Figure 6.2.

The routing software will expect to find header information in each packet, which includes the sender's address (in this case, User X) and the destination address (User Y). The role of the Network Layer is to decide which route would best be used, given the prevailing traffic levels and other relevant conditions on the network. It will therefore make a decision as to whether the message goes via Node B or Node C.

If an intruder can find some way of subverting the addressing system or the routing process, this opens up all kinds of possibilities for diverting messages. It also avoids a problem which could otherwise arise from eavesdropping on one particular link such as that between Node A and Node B. The message being sought could, after all, end up being routed via Node C instead. Successful interference with the routing mechanisms will enable the attacker to send messages to a different destination, create bogus messages, or simply facilitate eavesdropping at a more convenient location. Information about the routing of messages may also be of interest simply to establish whether traffic is flowing between X and Y; in some circumstances, this can be enough to reveal valuable information in itself.

Finally, an attacker could focus on the top (application) layer, which interacts with the application programs being run in the computer. This layer is invoked whenever an application needs to send or receive data

Table 6.1

Layer	Data	Threats arise from:
Application	Complete, and close to form actually seen by users	Interference with software on the user's computer
Network	Divided up, with control information added	Interference with the network routing software
Link	Divided up (may also be incomplete, if multiple routes are used)	Eavesdropping on individual nodes or links

across the network. The fact that the data is still in a form very close to that seen by the application users means that it will be much easier to interpret. The threats for each type of layer are summarised in Table 6.1.

6.5 THE ROLE OF CRYPTOGRAPHY

It is simply not practicable to make every cable tamper-proof, or to prevent unauthorised people from listening in to radio transmissions if they wish to. However, it is possible to thwart them by sending the messages in a form which has deliberately been rendered completely unintelligible. This is one of the major roles of cryptography. Cryptography has a number of advantages, since it can be applied to data while it is still in the Application Layer. This automatically provides protection against interception as the data moves through all the other layers. This use of cryptography is sometimes described as 'end-to-end' (see Figure 6.3).

The use of cryptography to keep messages secret can be traced back to Greek and Roman times (Beutelspacher 1994). One of the first methods was devised by Spartan generals around the fifth century BC. A long thin strip of paper was wrapped around a stick in a spiral fashion. The message was then written on the paper, along the length of the stick. When the paper was unwound, it contained a string of meaningless letters. However, by wrapping the paper around another stick of the same diameter, a recipient could immediately decode the message. If the paper strip fell into enemy hands, it would appear to contain complete nonsense.

Throughout most of the twentieth century, governments and the military have continued to apply cryptography in much the same way as the Spartans. The techniques have steadily improved, but the main preoccupation has been with preventing hostile states from spying on internal communications (Andrew 1996). In recent years, however, the arrival of cheap and plentiful computing power has facilitated the development of new cryptographic techniques which can be used for other purposes. For example, they can be used to 'sign and seal' messages. These techniques

END-TO-END CRYPTOGRAPHY

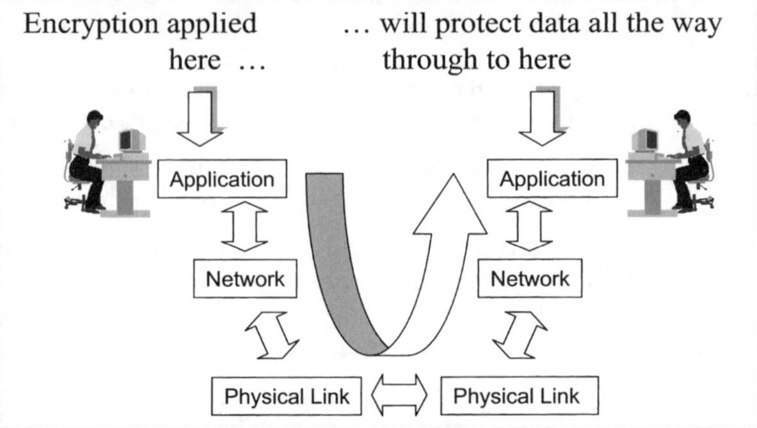

Encryption applied here …   … will protect data all the way through to here

Figure 6.3

Cryptography can be introduced into *any* of the layers, but the best security is provided by encrypting data as close as possible to the user, i.e. within the Application Layer. This will put the encryption under the user's direct control, as well as making it easier for messages to be digitally signed, and checks to be made on the origin and authenticity of data received from other sources.

If cryptography is applied at the Physical Layer, it is common to find a 'black box' approach being taken. A self-contained encryption unit is plugged in at each end of the link. This can provide strong protection against eavesdropping and tampering, but only while the message is in transit across that particular link.

are directed at protecting the *integrity* and not the secrecy of data. They are useful for ensuring that business data is accurate and authentic, thus meeting some of the needs identified by Clark and Wilson (1987) (see Introduction).

The mechanics of cryptography do not actually need to be visible to those who are using it. Increasingly, suppliers are producing software packages which take care of all the technical details, and enable the user to apply cryptography by clicking on simple menus and icons. Nevertheless, there are certain dangers in using such facilities blindly, without some idea of the strengths and limitations of the protections which cryptography is providing.

Cryptography turns human-readable data into what seems to be a completely meaningless stream of data bits. But the result only *seems* to be meaningless: anyone who knows the cryptographic algorithm which has been used, and who has the correct cryptographic key, can reverse the process, and so make sense of the material, as shown in Figure 6.4.

In today's multi-media world, the 'plaintext' could actually be a voice recording, a photograph, a video-clip, or any other form of data which is

SOME DEFINITIONS RELATING TO CRYPTOGRAPHY

Cryptography originally denoted the art of keeping information secret by the use of codes and ciphers. However, as a US Academy of Sciences Report points out, 'Today, cryptography can be used for many applications that do not involve confidentiality' (Dam and Lin 1996). Cryptography is a constantly expanding field. It is increasingly concerned with methods of proving the origin or status of data, rather than simply keeping it secret.

Encryption is the actual process of encoding data into a 'scrambled' form; it usually refers to cases where cryptography is being used to protect secrecy. Decryption is the same process in reverse, i.e. the scrambled text is converted back into a meaningful form.

Cryptology is sometimes used to denote a more theoretical approach to the investigation and analysis of cryptographic methods, and the invention of new ones.

A **cryptographic key** is a string of digits, anything between forty and several thousand bits long, which is selected and used as part of the input to an encryption or decryption process.

A **cryptographic algorithm** is a series of mathematical operations, usually carried out by a computer, which facilitates the encryption or decryption process.

The original form of encrypted messages is known as **plaintext**; an encrypted message is sometimes known as a **cryptogram**.

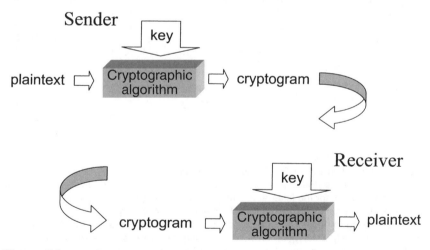

Figure 6.4

based on a stream of bits. Modern encryption methods can work on anything which is represented in digital form. Since business increasingly uses electronic documents which contain charts and diagrams, or computer-generated presentations incorporating sounds and video sequences, it is important that all such materials can, if required, be protected by putting them through the encryption process.

This marks a significant difference between modern encryption methods and those used in the past. Historically, encryption has relied on the *transposition* of individual letters (as in the Spartan example) or the *substitution* of one letter for another according to a prearranged scheme. An example of the latter approach is the cipher invented by Blaise de Viginere in the sixteenth century (see Figure 6.5).

A	B	C	D	E	F	G	H	I	J	K	L	M	N	O	P	Q	R	S	T	U	V	W	X	Y	Z
B	C	D	E	F	G	H	I	J	K	L	M	N	O	P	Q	R	S	T	U	V	W	X	Y	Z	A
C	D	E	F	G	H	I	J	K	L	M	N	O	P	Q	R	S	T	U	V	W	X	Y	Z	A	B
D	E	F	G	H	I	J	K	L	M	N	O	P	Q	R	S	T	U	V	W	X	Y	Z	A	B	C
E	F	G	H	I	J	K	L	M	N	O	P	Q	R	S	T	U	V	W	X	Y	Z	A	B	C	D
F	G	H	I	J	K	L	M	N	O	P	Q	R	S	T	U	V	W	X	Y	Z	A	B	C	D	E
G	H	I	J	K	L	M	N	O	P	Q	R	S	T	U	V	W	X	Y	Z	A	B	C	D	E	F
H	I	J	K	L	M	N	O	P	Q	R	S	T	U	V	W	X	Y	Z	A	B	C	D	E	F	G
I	J	K	L	M	N	O	P	Q	R	S	T	U	V	W	X	Y	Z	A	B	C	D	E	F	G	H
J	K	L	M	N	O	P	Q	R	S	T	U	V	W	X	Y	Z	A	B	C	D	E	F	G	H	I
K	L	M	N	O	P	Q	R	S	T	U	V	W	X	Y	Z	A	B	C	D	E	F	G	H	I	J
L	M	N	O	P	Q	R	S	T	U	V	W	X	Y	Z	A	B	C	D	E	F	G	H	I	J	K
M	N	O	P	Q	R	S	T	U	V	W	X	Y	Z	A	B	C	D	E	F	G	H	I	J	K	L
N	O	P	Q	R	S	T	U	V	W	X	Y	Z	A	B	C	D	E	F	G	H	I	J	K	L	M
O	P	Q	R	S	T	U	V	W	X	Y	Z	A	B	C	D	E	F	G	H	I	J	K	L	M	N
P	Q	R	S	T	U	V	W	X	Y	Z	A	B	C	D	E	F	G	H	I	J	K	L	M	N	O
Q	R	S	T	U	V	W	X	Y	Z	A	B	C	D	E	F	G	H	I	J	K	L	M	N	O	P
R	S	T	U	V	W	X	Y	Z	A	B	C	D	E	F	G	H	I	J	K	L	M	N	O	P	Q
S	T	U	V	W	X	Y	Z	A	B	C	D	E	F	G	H	I	J	K	L	M	N	O	P	Q	R
T	U	V	W	X	Y	Z	A	B	C	D	E	F	G	H	I	J	K	L	M	N	O	P	Q	R	S
U	V	W	X	Y	Z	A	B	C	D	E	F	G	H	I	J	K	L	M	N	O	P	Q	R	S	T
V	W	X	Y	Z	A	B	C	D	E	F	G	H	I	J	K	L	M	N	O	P	Q	R	S	T	U
W	X	Y	Z	A	B	C	D	E	F	G	H	I	J	K	L	M	N	O	P	Q	R	S	T	U	V
X	Y	Z	A	B	C	D	E	F	G	H	I	J	K	L	M	N	O	P	Q	R	S	T	U	V	W
Y	Z	A	B	C	D	E	F	G	H	I	J	K	L	M	N	O	P	Q	R	S	T	U	V	W	X
Z	A	B	C	D	E	F	G	H	I	J	K	L	M	N	O	P	Q	R	S	T	U	V	W	X	Y

To use the Viginere cipher:
Suppose that the plaintext is HELLO and the key is TOAST.
Read across the top to the first letter in the plaintext, and then down the side to the first letter in the key. Look for the letter at the intersection of the row and column (this should be A in this case). Repeat the process for each letter in turn. Your cryptogram will be ASLDH.

Someone trying to decrypt this message would need to know the key (TOAST) and the cryptogram (ASLDH). Decryption involves reversing the process. Look down the side for the letter in the key, go across the row until you find the corresponding letter in the cryptogram, and look at the top of that column to find the letter in plain text.

In order to send longer messages, the key would normally be repeated over and over again, as many times as necessary.

Figure 6.5 **Viginere Cipher**

One parallel between the Viginere cipher and modern encryption methods is its dependence on the use of a *key*. The key in the example shown is five characters long, and must be known to both the sender and the receiver of the message. As with passwords, the general principle is that the longer the key, the better. The process of looking up letters in rows and columns can be compared with using an *algorithm* in present-day encryption.

While keys remain an essential part of cryptography, encryption methods based on the transposition or substitution of individual letters have been largely abandoned in the computer age. Because every human language has its characteristic patterns, with certain letters and letter sequences occurring more frequently than others, it is relatively easy to design programs which can hunt through the encrypted letters looking for patterns as a first step in 'cracking the code'.

Instead, modern cryptography takes no notice of individual letters or symbols, and simply treats any digitised information as a stream of bits. **Stream ciphers** operate on the bits a few at a time, in a continuous flow. They are particularly well suited to the encryption of data which has to travel in 'real time', such as a telephone conversation being carried over a digital network. **Block ciphers** first of all divide the data up into blocks of fixed length, before applying the encryption logic to each block, and then gluing them all back together again (for an example, see Figure 6.6). An individual block could contain several letters, a small part of a picture, or a short burst of a digital sound recording.

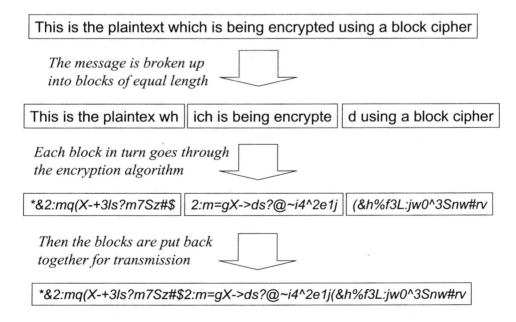

Figure 6.6 **The operation of a block cipher**

6.6 BUSINESS APPLICATIONS OF ENCRYPTION

The movement to electronic commerce has forced businesses to appreciate some of the built-in advantages which have always existed in paper-based systems. Paper, for example, can carry a signature to indicate that someone has checked or approved its contents, or a watermark to prevent anyone making a counterfeit copy. It can be produced as evidence that certain explicit assurances were given, or to prove that an order was placed on a specific date. It carries the authority which goes with having things 'put in writing'.

The search for equivalent ways of 'putting things in writing' in the electronic world has stimulated new ideas for applying cryptography. Two techniques have proved particularly useful: asymmetric cryptography and hashing.

1 *Asymmetric cryptography*. All the techniques described so far have assumed that the sender and receiver both use the same key. It is obviously essential that both the parties keep the key secret, in other words, they both regard it as a 'private key'. This is a 'symmetrical' arrangement, and indeed until quite recently this was the only kind of encryption available. However, in 1976 Diffie and Hellman suggested that encryption could be based on *pairs* of keys: one of the keys would be used to encrypt the message, and the other one to decrypt it. At first sight, this seems a quite unnecessary complication. However, it opens up a whole range of possibilities.

Let us suppose that Alice generates a pair of asymmetric keys on her computer. She keeps one of these secret, and this becomes her *private* key. The other key becomes her *public* key, which she gives to anyone who wants it. This makes no sense at all in terms of trying to keep messages secret. If you encrypt a message, and then give everyone a public key with which they can decrypt it, you might as well avoid all the effort involved, and just send everyone the plaintext.

However, the public key allows the recipient of a message to do something quite different. If the recipient decrypts the message with the public key, and this generates a meaningful plaintext, then this proves that the encryption *must have been carried out by Alice*. This is equivalent to Alice having 'signed' the message, and the process is sometimes described as applying a *digital signature*. Note that *anyone* who has a copy of Alice's public key can carry out this process of verifying that the message came from Alice. Meanwhile, so long as Alice keeps the private key securely hidden inside her computer, nobody can 'forge' her signature. The situation is illustrated in Figure 6.7.

The process of using asymmetric keys is reversible. This means that anyone can encrypt a message using Alice's public key, and send it back to Alice. Nobody except Alice will be able to decrypt it. Alice is now using her private key as the *decrypting* key. This is useful if a number of people want to send confidential information to one particular person.

Alice uses her private key (**K_pr**) to "sign" the message ...

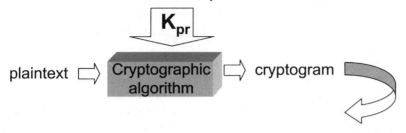

... Bob uses Alice's public key (**K_pu**) to decrypt the message, thereby confirming the identity of the sender.

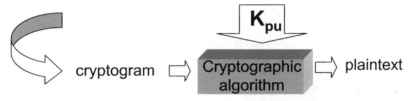

Figure 6.7 **A simple digital signature**

For example, all the doctors in a family practice could be given the public key of a hospital consultant. This would enable them to send messages about their patients to the consultant, knowing that the consultant was the only person with a key capable of decrypting them.

Signature with an asymmetric private key can also be useful in establishing *non-repudiation*. Circumstances sometimes arise where Alice may be tempted to deny that she sent a message. For example, she may have asked her stockbroker to buy some shares, only to see the value of them fall dramatically within the next few hours. If her instructions were sent encrypted with her private key, it is impossible for her to deny that she issued them. Non-repudiation may also be important in respect of the *receipt* of a message. For example, if the shares had actually risen sharply in value, the stockbroker might be tempted to hold on to them, and claim that Alice's order never reached him. This kind of problem can only be covered by an insistence that all messages must immediately be acknowledged, usually through the automatic generation of a return message. Clearly it will help resolve any subsequent disputes if this message, too, can be encrypted, in this case using the *receiver's* private key.

2 *Hash functions.* Hashing converts plaintext into a meaningless string of digits, and in this sense it works in much the same way as encryption. However, there are two important differences. The first is that the output from the hashing process is much *shorter* than the original

message: the hash function deliberately 'shrinks' it to a fraction of its former size. The second difference is that hashing is intended to be *irreversible*. The whole process works in one direction only, so that there is no way of working backwards from the hash, to find out what was in the original message.

Once again, hashing techniques are not particularly concerned with secrecy. The most common use of a hash is to add it on to the end of a message, which may well be sent quite openly as plaintext. What the hash provides is *evidence that the message has not been altered* since it left the sender. On receiving the message and the hash, the recipient re-applies the same hashing technique to the message contents. The results of this are compared with the hash provided by the sender. If the two are identical, the recipient can be assured that the message has not been tampered with somewhere along the way. The procedure is illustrated in Figure 6.8.

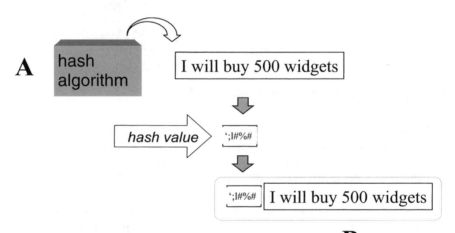

... if B can reproduce the hash value, this **B** means the text of the message has not been altered.

Figure 6.8

The hash is sometimes known as a *Message Digest*. It provides the same kind of verification for whole messages that a check digit can provide for an individual number (see section 5.2.2). A good hashing algorithm is designed to make life as difficult as possible for anyone trying to interfere with the message. It will ensure that even a minor change, such as adding a zero on the end of a number, will result in a significant change in the hash value.

Like all cryptographic techniques, hashing is open to various forms of attack. Because the hash is very short, it is inevitable that the same hash will be produced by several plaintexts (although it is unlikely that many of them will be in the form of words which make sense). If the hashing algorithm is a widely used one, however, there is a possibility that an attacker may be able to change the message and generate an authentic hash value to go with it. For this reason, some hash algorithms require the use of a secret key. Alternatively, a selected part of the message may be encrypted under a previously agreed key, and this is appended as a *Message Authentication Code.*

Between them, Asymmetric Cryptography and Hash Functions provide a powerful 'kit of tools' for controlling information (see Figure 6.9). Each technique has a parallel in the traditional world of paper. Equivalent measures are taken daily in respect of legal and other important documents, and were even enshrined in the Constitution of the United States, Article II, which laid down how votes were to be counted in presidential elections:

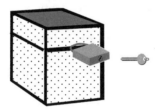

Protection of secrecy of communication (symmetric and asymmetric encryption)

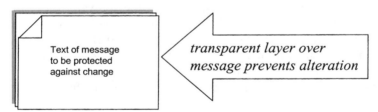

Protection against tampering (hash, message digest, and message authentication code)

Verification of identity of originator of message (digital signing with asymmetric private key)

Figure 6.9 **The cryptographic kit of tools**

And they shall make a List of all the Persons voted for, and of the Number of Votes for each; which list they shall sign and certify, and transmit sealed to the Seat of the Government of the United States, directed to the President of the Senate. The President of the Senate shall, in the Presence of the Senate and House of Representatives, open all the Certificates, and the Votes shall then be counted.

All these procedures *could* be carried out electronically. Indeed, the signing process would, if anything, be more reliable, since a digital signature is 'affixed' to the entire document, and not just the final page.

The techniques just described are frequently used in combination. For example, a hash function can be generated for a message, and then *both* the message and its hash can be fed into an encryption algorithm. This provides two forms of protection: one is aimed primarily at protecting the integrity of the message, and the other at ensuring that its contents are kept secret.

It is also possible to re-encrypt something which is already encrypted. For example, Alice could encrypt a message using her private key, and then encrypt the result using Bob's public key. This will ensure that nobody apart from Bob can unpick *both* the layers of decryption required in order to read the message. Assuming that Bob has Alice's public key, he can also check that she was indeed the person who sent it. The double layer of asymmetric encryption thus provides extra value: it protects the secrecy of the message, and identity checks both the parties.

Note that computer users should not have to deal with cryptographic keys and algorithms directly. Many vendors now offer products which are designed to simplify the business of securing and signing messages. Because the cryptographic keys themselves are a long, meaningless jumble of digits, these will be taken care of by the cryptographic software and kept out of sight. To use the facilities of the software, the user will use a more conventional password (which is sometimes known as a *passphrase* in this context). Similarly, most users will not actually compute hash results for messages, and then compare them. This will be done 'under the covers' of the computer, with messages being sent to the screen to indicate whether or not the hashing checks have been successful.

6.7   COSTS AND VULNERABILITIES OF CRYPTOGRAPHIC METHODS

As the use of cryptography has expanded, so has the level of interest in finding ways of attacking and subverting it. There have been a number of well publicised cases where attackers have succeeded in decrypting messages, even against quite sophisticated methods of encryption (see examples). These attacks usually involve an approach based on 'brute force'. Brute force involves trying each possible encryption key in turn, in the hope of finding the one which delivers intelligible results. This is by no means a trivial undertaking; for example, if a key is 40 bits long, it will be necessary to test over a million million combinations. Even a fast computer will need years to do this. The process can however be speeded up by harnessing a large number of computers to hunt for the answer in parallel, together with special software to speed up the analysis.

BRUTE FORCE AND OTHER ATTACKS ON ENCRYPTED MATERIAL

Cryptographers enjoy challenges, and over the years a number of them have been remarkably successful in beating them. In September 1995, a French student organised a brute force search for the 40-bit key used for secure links by the Netscape web browser. 120 workstations and a few larger computers were harnessed to carry out the task at the Ecole Polytechnique and two other institutions. The key was found after trying just over half the possible key combinations, in 8 days.

Later in the same year, a student at Berkeley, California, discovered weaknesses in the way Netscape generated keys, and was able to identify keys much more rapidly. In January 1997, RSA Security started a series of challenges, in the first instance to find a 40-bit key used with one of their own symmetric algorithms. The same student, Ian Goldberg, linked together 250 of the Berkeley university computers, and won the $1000 prize.

Since then, RSA Security has issued a series of challenges, and the techniques used to meet them have become more sophisticated. In July 1998, a collaborative project invested $250,000 in a Key Search Machine which was able to unravel a DES 56-bit key in less than three days. A subsequent 56-bit challenge, in January 1999, was solved in less than one day (RSA 2000).

Such attacks are unlikely to be levelled at messages unless they are perceived to have an extremely high value. In most of the reported cases, the attack has been intended to prove a point, or to respond to a challenge, rather than to retrieve any information of commercial value.

However, since it must be assumed that the amounts of computer power available to would-be attackers will increase with time, ways of making encryption stronger are continually being sought. This ongoing battle of wits between the cryptographers and the attackers is likely to continue for the foreseeable future (Schneier 1998). It revolves around the two main ingredients in the encryption process. On the one hand, cryptographers strive to create ever more sophisticated *algorithms*, designed to deny an attacker any clues, however trivial, about the relationship between the plaintext, the cryptogram, and the encryption key. They also try to anticipate all the different ways in which other people might try to launch counter-attacks against the encryption method. On the other hand, the *key length* can be a factor in making encryption more powerful. Longer keys mean that an attacker has more combinations of digits to work through. They offer better protection in much the same way as has been observed for longer passwords and PINs, in the context of system access controls (see section 4.2.2).

Another way of making life more difficult for attackers is to put layer upon layer of encryption. Having been encrypted with key-1, the encrypted output is then re-encrypted using key-2, and so on. This is rather like making a visitor to a building go through a series of doors, each one having been fitted with a different lock.

All these methods of increasing the strength of cryptography come at a cost. Some rules of thumb for the use of cryptography are that its overheads are likely to *increase* if:

- *the encryption is asymmetric rather than symmetric.* Asymmetric algorithms require more processing power than symmetric ones. This may not be important if messages are short, but it can be a significant factor when trying to send large quantities of text, or multimedia files. An asymmetric algorithm like RSA can require 1,000 times more processing time to encrypt a given message than a symmetric algorithm like DES (details of some of these algorithms are given below).
- *a longer encryption key is used.* The computer processing time increases for longer keys, and the increase may be disproportionate (for example, one benchmark showed that doubling the length of an RSA key from 512 bits to 1,024 bits caused the decrypt time to increase nearly six-fold (Schneier 1998)).
- *multiple layers of encryption are used.* In this case, the overheads will be roughly proportionate, i.e. triple-layer encryption will need approximately three times the processing power of single encryption.

Once a message has been encrypted, it will be the same length as the plaintext; it therefore creates no extra traffic load on the network. However, there is sometimes a requirement for 'instant' encryption, for

SOME ENCRYPTION ALGORITHMS USED IN COMMERCE

The *Data Encryption Standard* (DES) was published by the US Department of Commerce in 1977, based on an algorithm developed by IBM. It has since become one of the most widely used of all symmetric algorithms. It is a block cipher, based on 64-bit blocks with a 56-bit key.

The *International Data Encryption Algorithm* is licensed by Ascom Information Security, based in Switzerland (Ascom 2000). It was developed at the Swiss Federal Institute of Technology in Zürich. Like DES, it is symmetric and works with blocks of 64 bits, but has a longer key (128 bits) and a number of other extra features intended to protect it against attack.

Other symmetric ciphers include *RC2* (block) and *RC4* (stream), developed by RSA Data Security (RSA 2000). The algorithms are proprietary and have not been published by the owners, although Internet sites have carried what purport to be the specifications. Two other symmetric block ciphers are *Red Pike*, developed by GCHQ for the intelligence services in the UK, and *Blowfish*, developed by Bruce Schneier (author of a standard work on cryptography (Schneier 1996)).

Asymmetric encryption is dominated by *RSA*, named after Rivest, Shamir and Adelman who invented it at MIT in 1978. RSA Security Inc. has incorporated the algorithm into a number of security products. Key sizes are normally 512 or 1,024 bits.

example, for video conferencing or voice conversations. As mentioned in section 6.5, stream rather than block encryption can be advantageous here. Whatever encryption method is used, the processing power available must be sufficient to avoid any slow-down at peak loads. This may mean investing in a rather more powerful processor than might otherwise be necessary.

Two of the ways in which the overheads of encryption can be minimised for routine transactions are as follows.

- *Digital signing using a hash.* Using an asymmetric algorithm and her private key, Alice can encrypt, and thereby 'digitally sign', a whole message. However, she could equally well prepare a hash of the message, and sign that. Because the hash is much shorter than the original message, a much smaller encryption overhead is involved. Bob now has to decrypt the hash, and check it against the value he computes from the message he has received. If this all works satisfactorily, he can be assured that both the hash and the message came from Alice. This process is illustrated in Figure 6.10.
- *Asymmetric followed by symmetric encryption.* If Alice has Bob's public key, she can use this to send him another key of her choosing under conditions of secrecy. This key is now known only to Alice and Bob. They can then use this as a *one-time key* for their subsequent messages

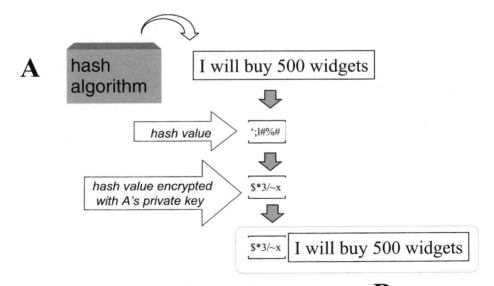

... if B decrypts the hash value, and **B**
re-calculating the hash value from the message text gives
the same result, the message must have originated with A.

Figure 6.10 **Digital signing using a hash**

(in either direction), using symmetric encryption. This enables them to switch from a brief burst of asymmetric encryption (with its high overheads) for the start-up, to symmetric encryption (with lower overheads) for the rest of the data traffic.

VULNERABILITY OF ENCRYPTION: THE CASE OF OPERATION GOLD

In 1954, Berlin was still a divided city, locked inside East Germany, with one of its sectors under American control. US intelligence knew that a number of landlines, carrying communications traffic for the Soviet military headquarters at Karlshost, were located about 500 metres across the border, inside what was then East Berlin. The British and US intelligence services decided to dig a tunnel under the border, with a view to tapping into the landlines. The project was given the name Operation Gold.

The whole venture came close to disaster when, in the depths of winter, it was noticed that there were tell-tale signs of snow melting above the path of the tunnel. Nevertheless, it was successfully completed, and for more than a year a stream of intercepts was taken from the landlines. The tunnel was then 'discovered' by the Soviet authorities, and closed down.

The CIA subsequently learned that the Soviets had known of the existence of the tunnel from the outset, thanks to reports provided by a British spy, George Blake. But because the messages on the landlines were encrypted, using an extremely secure method based on one-time pads, the Soviets were confident that the eavesdropping would be of no avail. By feigning ignorance of the tunnel, meanwhile, they avoided drawing attention to the possibility that a spy was at work in one of the intelligence services.

Unfortunately, the encryption machines used by the Soviets at the time sent faint traces of the plaintext along the line, as well as the encrypted signal. The plaintext signals were just strong enough to be picked up and recorded.

The moral, then as now, is that the protection provided by encryption should never be taken for granted. Although modern computer-based encryption methods should not create any 'ghost' signals, care is still needed to ensure that there are no 'back doors' into the system, which could enable a hacker to find some way of getting straight to the plaintext.

Based on Andrew 1996

6.8   SECURITY ON THE INTERNET

Connecting a business onto the Internet, whether as a web provider or just to browse and use email, immediately puts it in touch with millions of people across the planet, on a completely indiscriminate basis. The business can communicate with customers, suppliers, regulators, banks, and others who can be expected to have some joint interest in furthering its business aims. Meanwhile, it is also making itself accessible to dissidents, anarchists, fraudsters and many others whose interest could be a lot less welcome. Much the same universal connectivity is, of course, also found in other services, such as the mail and the telephone. However, the Internet alone is capable of delivering serious damage, quickly and directly, to computerised functions at the heart of the business.

The only assumption which can safely be made when considering the Internet as a communication medium is that it offers no security whatsoever. Worse still, it is operated as a loose federation of networks around the world, with supervision and regulation which is patchy and frequently non-existent. So if a remote user *does* carry out a successful attack against the business, the chances of obtaining redress will be negligible.

Not surprisingly, this situation has given rise to a thriving market in products and services designed to reassure business users. For example, there are suppliers who will build (and in some cases, also operate) a *Virtual Private Network* (VPN). This is a networking service which guarantees certain security facilities to all its users, even though the traffic may actually be passing over insecure links, such the Internet. (This creation of secure routes is also sometimes referred to as *tunnelling*). There is also a wide range of products called *firewalls*, which are intended to create a protective barrier between the business and the Internet. The firewall protects one particular site, whereas the protection of a VPN extends over several sites. A simplified picture of a firewall and a VPN is shown in Figure 6.11.

Suppliers package their products together in ways which they feel will appeal to the market. There is no agreed definition of what exactly should be provided in a VPN or a firewall. However, both types of product tend to work on the *lower* communication layers (as described in section 6.4). They concentrate on the control information which has been inserted into the data in order to route it around the network. Their aim is to detect anything which seems suspicious, for example, a request for a service function which seems unusual for the kind of traffic in question, or the use of an inappropriate network address. The assumption being made is that the packets of data arriving at the barrier may have been tampered with by skilled hackers, who are looking for a way of setting up a path for themselves into the computing facilities of the organisation.

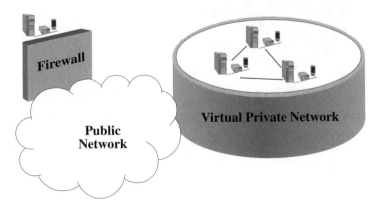

Figure 6.11

For such checking to be effective, the VPN or firewall software has to be told what it should regard as correct or normal activity. From time to time this situation will change (for example, when new computers are brought on to the network) and so the rules will need to be modified. As with access control tables and virus checkers, VPNs and firewalls have to be kept constantly under review, and updated as quickly as possible when changes occur.

Unfortunately, there are certain types of attack which cannot be detected in the lower communication layers. For checking to be really rigorous, it needs to be applied across *all* the layers. Some more expensive firewalls attempt to do this by acting as a *proxy* for selected activities in the upper layers. For example, a proxy firewall will intercept requests to log on to an application, and carry out the necessary checking of the user's credentials *before* the user gets anywhere near the real application. Such precautions are extremely expensive, as they will involve not just the provision of an extra machine for the firewall, but a re-working of application programs to ensure that the security elements can be divided up and handled separately. Proxy firewalls are also costly to maintain, since their software will need to be upgraded in step with any modifications to the application programs. A proxy firewall is shown in Figure 6.12.

In deciding whether a firewall or VPN will be helpful for a given organisation, it is useful first to take a look at how the Internet is going to be used. Not everyone connects to the Internet in the same way, or for the same reasons. The following are some key considerations.

Proxy Firewall

Anyone logging in interacts with the proxy, not the real system.

Public Network

Figure 6.12

- *Connectivity within the business.* If a solitary PC is linked to the Internet, the potential for damage is confined to that PC. However, if the PC is also connected to a LAN or Intranet operating within the business, intruders can potentially go anywhere and attack anything. For some electronic commerce applications, it may be essential to have this kind of linkage (for example, if the public are to be able to enter bookings on a web page, and these are to be transferred immediately onto a central reservation system). On the other hand, if all that is required is for office staff to make occasional inquiries onto the Internet, the cheapest and most effective barrier may be to use a standalone PC which contains a minimal set of software, including a web browser, but which has absolutely no other network connections, apart from its link to the Net.
- *Predictability of data traffic.* Communications may be more or less predictable in terms of their source, destination, or type of content. For example, an e-commerce trader may deal only with customers who have previously been registered on his system, and even then may confine their activities to a specified range of transactions. This makes the situation a great deal easier to control. A firm of lawyers or a social services department, on the other hand, may expect to send and receive a much more diverse collection of materials from all kinds of sources.
- *Skill and motivation of staff.* Very little time is needed to learn how to use the Internet, but this should not be taken to mean that staff training is unnecessary. It is desirable that all staff should be 'street-wise' with regard to the ruses which may be encountered on the Internet, whereby they may be encouraged to reveal confidential information, or to download programs which are intended to cause harm. If, on the other hand, it is not practicable to train staff in this way, it may be necessary to compensate by installing some extra preventive measures, for example, by disabling certain facilities altogether.
- *Requirements to filter and block traffic.* Besides blocking incoming messages which appear to have some devious or malicious intent, the organisation may also wish to limit the type of activities which employees are permitted to undertake on the Internet. For example, it may wish to discourage the downloading of computer games, or other uses of the Net for entertainment. It may also seek to prevent access to sites which offer computer viruses, pornography, terrorist skills, or other anti-social material. A firewall can be made to scrutinise traffic both into and out of the organisation, and to operate either a banned list of undesirable sites, or an approved list of sites required in the normal course of daily work. These issues are discussed further in section 8.6.

As with any security product, firewalls and VPNs should never be purchased on the assumption that simply having them is bound to do some good. Still less should it be assumed that an expensive product will achieve more than a cheaper one, or that the purchase cost of the equipment has any particular relationship to its lifetime cost, since the overheads of running it may be substantial if the facilities for updating are rudimentary, or require frequent intervention by the supplier.

6.9   QUESTIONS

1   True or false?
   (a) It is difficult to intercept messages sent along an optic fibre cable.
   (b) UNIX is a good operating system to use from a security point of view, because so many people understand its internal workings.
   (c) Cryptology is concerned with encrypting each word in turn in a message.
   (d) The best place to apply encryption is in the Link Layer.
   (e) Asymmetric encryption uses up more processing power than symmetric encryption.
   (f) A good firewall will never need any updating.
   (g) Substitution ciphers are an excellent way of protecting secret email messages.
   (h) A Message Digest is the same length as the message on which it is based.

2   Explain what is meant by a 'brute force attack'. What measures can be taken to make this kind of attack more difficult?

3   A hacker plans to eavesdrop on messages sent to and from the terminal of a senior manager. What would be the advantages and disadvantages, from the hacker's point of view, of trying to attack via (a) the application layer, and (b) the link layer?

4   If you are a spreadsheet user, you can experiment with creating a simple hash function for yourself. Type in a brief message, putting only one letter per cell in a row across the worksheet. Now find the spreadsheet function which converts a letter into its corresponding digital code (in Excel, this is the CODE command). Use this command to create a row of numbers corresponding to the letters (for example, if your first letter is in cell A1, you could create a row of numbers immediately underneath, by entering =CODE(A1) in cell A2, and then filling right). You can now use these numbers to create your hash. If you wanted your hash to be, say, five numbers in length, you could add together all the numbers in row B, and take the last five digits of the resulting total. To give your hash a more unpredictable result, you could multiply each letter by a different factor, and use a modulus function to give you a 'remainder' which has a fixed length.

   When you have designed your hash, try writing out a set of instructions which would enable someone else to use it. This will be your 'hash algorithm'.

chapter seven

MANAGING THE SECURITY OF NETWORKED FACILITIES

SOME TOPICS ADDRESSED IN THIS CHAPTER

- How arrangements need to be made for *distributing cryptographic keys* among network users
- Other aspects of key management, in particular ensuring that data can be retrieved even if the required cryptographic key cannot be found
- Measures which are appropriate for different types of *business-to-business* links
- The additional requirements created by the development of *on-line services direct to the public*
- Some *tools and techniques* which are available for monitoring and managing security on a network

SECURITY AND CONTROL OBJECTIVES

- Protect secrets
- Prevent tampering
- Prove authorship

7.1   INTRODUCTION

The simplest view of networks is that they are pipelines for information, based on cables which are part of the basic infrastructure in the same way as the electricity or water supplies. It is tempting to assume that any security issues will revolve around the communications hardware, and such matters as the route to be taken by cable ducts, or the type of connectors being used. However, as the previous chapter showed, this will result in some vital aspects of network security being overlooked altogether.

As with all security measures, network security needs to be based on a much broader view, and must involve people who understand the business priorities. For example, if a business is embarking on a new venture in electronic commerce, it must have some idea of which network-based threats might cause particular loss or embarrassment. If it is a public authority launching an on-line service to the public, it may need to review whether particular care needs to be taken with personal information in transit.

Only then will it be possible to begin to identify the best counter-measures. First, management will need to focus on the way access to the network is controlled. The methods of identifying users, and the creation and use of access control tables, will be essentially the same as those outlined earlier in Chapter 4. However, there are some additional complications in ensuring that employees distributed around a network are provided with all the necessary software, passwords and keys, in a secure fashion. Problem situations also have to be anticipated and planned for, such as an employee losing the key needed to decrypt an urgent message, or the collapse of part of the network through equipment failure.

Management involvement continues to be essential once the network facilities have been put in place. Few networks remain static, and (as was seen with firewalls and VPNs) it is dangerous to assume that counter-measures will remain effective indefinitely, and so updates must be made on a regular basis.

Notwithstanding the 'hi-tech' nature of many current developments in networking, much network security management still remains a matter of common sense and attention to detail. A new generation of control tools is appearing, based on cryptography, and at first sight these may seem incomprehensible except to boffins. However, the underlying principles are not difficult to grasp, and in future it is likely that networks will deploy them on a routine basis. It is therefore important for managers to have some idea of their functions, and their strengths and weaknesses.

Cryptography is particularly crucial for projects in electronic commerce. Unfortunately, some products are quite expensive to install and maintain, yet their effectiveness can quickly be compromised if they are not managed and administered properly. It is an area in which businesses can easily find themselves pouring money into solutions which turn out to be fragile and short-lived. At the same time, a management which fully understands the capabilities and benefits offered by these techniques can expect to protect its business interests *better* than it has ever been able to previously.

7.2   MAINTENANCE AND DISTRIBUTION OF CRYPTOGRAPHIC KEYS

An initial requirement for most cryptography applications is that every user will need a key (which may be either symmetric or asymmetric) which must be kept privately. It is essential that these keys are issued under carefully controlled conditions, otherwise their effectiveness will be compromised from the outset.

Private keys are like passwords in many respects, in that they 'belong' to users. However, there are important differences. Symmetric private keys need to be known to more than one person (i.e. one sender, and one or more receivers), but are kept secret within this select circle. For asymmetric encryption, a user must keep his or her private key absolutely secret (making it very much like a password), but it is also necessary to have a record of *other people's* public keys. Distributing keys is therefore more complicated than it is for passwords: it is not simply a matter of generating a key for each person, and sending it off to them.

Setting up keys for network users is further complicated by a 'Catch-22' type of problem, as pointed out by Meyer (1995). Meyer's paradox is this:

- to establish a secure channel requires the use of cryptography;
- to send people their cryptographic keys requires the use of a secure channel.

The only way to break out of this vicious circle is to find some quite independent, and secure, method of distributing the keys in the first instance. In theory, keys can be written down and sent in sealed envelopes, in the same way as passwords. However, if they are recorded on paper they will appear to the users as long streams of gibberish. People will not be very happy at having to type them in to their computers, and will probably commit errors in doing so.

Any distribution of keys is therefore best done via an electronic medium. For example, keys could be recorded on diskettes, sent out in personally addressed and tamper-proof envelopes. In practice, it will usually be easier to send all the keys for a number of users at one site to a trusted employee, who will then take charge of installing them directly on individual PCs.

Fully automated methods, capable of working across unsecured network links, have also been devised, but these have some limitations. One of the earliest examples was a sequence of exchanges devised by Diffie and Hellman, whereby Alice and Bob could, without any prior arrangement, agree on a symmetric key known only to themselves (Gove 1999). When using methods of this kind, a distribution centre must be certain that it is indeed communicating with the correct user at the other end, and that the user's software has not been compromised in any way. It is vital, therefore, that the procedure incorporates checks made via an independent line of communication, such as a phone call to a known extension number, or some other independent verification that all is what it appears to be.

If large numbers of keys are to be distributed, it should be assumed that this will attract the curiosity of hackers. For example, hackers could try to masquerade as authorised users, in order to acquire genuine keys, or to intercept keys in transit, in order to substitute fake ones. If such attacks are successful, they will give enormous scope for compromising the system later. It is worth investing time and effort in making any initial key distribution as foolproof as possible, as it is the foundation stone on which all subsequent cryptographic protection depends.

Let us assume that a distribution centre has successfully issued everyone with a symmetric private key. It now becomes possible to create a secure channel between each user and the centre, and to break out of the 'Catch-22' situation. However, at this point, only the centre knows *all* the keys. Users can therefore communicate securely with the centre, but not with each other. For every user to be able to send encrypted messages to every other user, potentially very long lists of keys will have to be distributed to every point in the network. The names and keys on the lists will change constantly. Such an arrangement is an administrative nightmare, and very difficult to keep secure.

To avoid some of these problems, larger organisations may opt to set up a *Key Distribution Centre* (KDC), which works as follows:

- A different private key is issued to each user, via a secure procedure of the kind indicated above. The KDC retains a record of each person's key.
- If Alice wants to communicate with Bob, she first sends a message to the KDC, encrypted under *her* private key, indicating what she wishes to do.
- The KDC generates a key which will be used just for the duration of the conversation between Alice and Bob (sometimes called a *session key*). This key is sent to Alice (encrypted under Alice's key) and to Bob (encrypted under Bob's key). Alice and Bob each decrypt the session key. They now have a key known only to them (and to the centre), which they can use to exchange messages with each other.

The procedure is illustrated in Figure 7.1. The actual implementation of it will all be taken care of by software, so that once Alice has made a menu selection or clicked an icon to say she wants to set up secure communication, the rest will be completely invisible to both her and Bob.

Note that once their conversation has finished, the session key is discarded. If Alice and Bob commence another conversation, they will need to be given a new key. This avoids the need for them to build up any lists of keys on their computers. There is also a security bonus, in that the temporary nature of each key creates an extra challenge for anyone who may try to intercept and decode the messages.

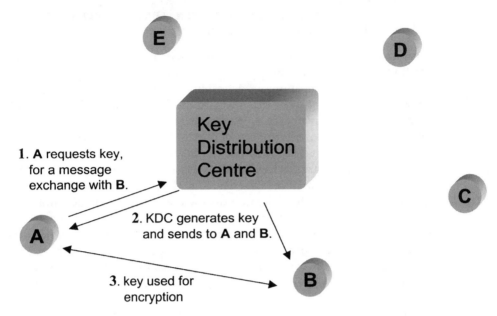

Figure 7.1 **Key Distribution Centre**

A KDC is a flexible and efficient way of managing cryptography to protect secrecy. Using symmetric keys as session keys means that the overheads of the encryption process can be kept low. If there are changes in staff, or the network is reconfigured, all the necessary updates can be sorted out centrally. However, Kaufman *et al* (1995) identify three drawbacks which should also be taken into consideration:

- *Single point of failure.* Since everyone depends on the KDC, if it goes off the air, secure communications will come to a halt. Duplicate equipment and software can be used to improve availability, but this will add significantly to the costs.
- *Performance bottlenecks.* Even if the KDC is running normally, it may slow down if large numbers of requests for session keys are being received at peak times, thus delaying the sending of messages.
- *All-or-nothing vulnerability.* The KDC eliminates risks which could otherwise arise from having lists of keys distributed around the network. However, if anyone *should* succeed in gaining unauthorised access to the lists of keys or the software inside the KDC, it would put them in a position to do much as they pleased on the entire network.

Given the crucial role played by a KDC, and the need for it to be extremely well protected, it should be made the direct responsibility of a very senior manager. If for any reason this is a function which is looked after under an outsourcing agreement, the strictest possible terms and conditions should apply.

7.3 PGP, CERTIFICATION AUTHORITIES, AND PUBLIC KEY INFRASTRUCTURES

Organising key distribution with a KDC offers a neat, centralised solution which fits in well with an 'institutional' network, such as might be used for the internal communications of a hospital or an accounting firm. At the opposite extreme, it is possible to distribute keys using a 'do-it-yourself' arrangement, to allow people to use cryptography on a more ad hoc basis. Perhaps the best known example of this is Pretty Good Privacy (PGP), invented and published in the public domain by Phil Zimmerman (1995).

The PGP shareware package enables a user to generate an asymmetric key pair. Let us assume that Alice has done this. She now sends her public key to Bob. Bob, having generated his own key pair, sends *his* public key to Alice. They can now set up a secure link between them, because messages encoded under each of the public keys can only be read by the owner of the correct private key. Once this secure link is established, a private session key is agreed, in the same way as for the KDC. Symmetric encryption, with its lower overheads, can then be used for the remaining messages.

The software also ensures that the private key is properly protected, and provides a facility for storing other people's public keys on 'key rings'. Collecting public keys is then left to the initiative and enterprise of the user.

PGP is ideal for small groups of people who want to communicate securely, but without the rigidity or bureaucracy of more formal schemes. Each person generates a key pair, and sets up a 'key ring' to store other people's public keys. Exactly how public keys are exchanged depends on the group. Among the group, consensus has to be reached about the conditions which are regarded as trustworthy. Thus, if two parties are well known to each other, they may be happy to send each other keys via email.

Once B has acquired A's public key under conditions which he feels are reliable, he may decide to pass it on to C, whom he also knows well. This mechanism is shown in Figure 7.2, and is sometimes referred to as a 'web of trust'. Such procedures are quick and informal. However, they are not particularly well suited to the needs of business, the two principal drawbacks being:

- Ultimately, no-one is taking responsibility for the *authenticity* of the keys. Keys may come from all kinds of sources, with each one being vouched for by the person who provides it. This is of little consequence if the aim is to achieve privacy of communication between friends. However, a business often has to deal with people or companies about which it knows very little. Taking the authenticity or provenance of keys 'on trust' could leave it open to all kinds of deception.
- Although web-of-trust software can be quite user-friendly, it runs as a *separate application*, and anyone using it needs to have a good under-

A sends
his public
key to **B**...

.. who sends
A's key to
his friend, **C** ...

..who sends
the key to
his father, **D**.

Figure 7.2 **Web of trust**

standing of what it is doing and how it operates. Again, this is fine if a hobbyist is using it on a truly 'personal' computer, but will cause problems if the PC in question is part of a wider corporate system. Employees who have to work under pressure, or who have limited computing skills, will not want to get involved in the 'nuts and bolts' of setting up cryptographic protection.

Most businesses require an approach to key distribution which lies somewhere between the rather rigid and centralised approach of the KDC, and the more free-association approach embodied in a web of trust. A solution can be found in another approach based on asymmetric keys, which employs more formalised methods of making the public keys available and vouching for their authenticity. An agency is appointed by the parties involved to carry out this role, and is known as a *Certification Authority* (CA). A CA may offer its services to the public at large, or to an alliance of companies, or it can operate just within one organisation. The single most important asset which a CA has to possess is the trust of everyone using it. This means making itself highly visible, and offering ways in which people can easily contact it (both electronically and otherwise). Some CA services, such as Verisign and Thawte, are new enterprises which have developed their business identity on the Internet. Existing institutions, such as banks, have seen the advantage of putting a strong, widely recognised brand behind a CA, and are also entering the field (Anon 1998a). In some countries, the respectability of CAs offering services to the public is enhanced by making them subject to government licensing.

Commercial CAs market their services in different ways, sometimes offering price tariffs which depend on the complexity of the certificate, or the depth of the background checks which are made. Certificates are sometimes given catchy names (such as 'digital passports'). However, all certificates perform basically the same function, and their generation involves a version of the following sequence.

The CA first generates a key pair, and follows the usual pattern of keeping the private key secret, and making its public key known as widely as possible. It then institutes a procedure whereby:

- Alice applies to the CA for a certificate, and provides them with a copy of her public key;
- the CA carries out checks to ensure that Alice is who she claims to be;
- the CA then generates a certificate, signed under the CA's private key.

The certificate which is created has four main components:

1 enough information to identify Alice reliably, by giving her full name and other personal details;
2 a copy of Alice's public key;
3 an expiry date, beyond which the certificate will cease to be valid;
4 a digital signature, created using the CA's private key.

In practice, the CA may choose to sign the certificate by hashing the contents of (1) to (3), and then signing the hash. This is just as secure as signing the whole certificate, and has the advantage of leaving all the important information in the certificate in plaintext. The CA might also undertake to generate Alice's key pair for her, but ideally Alice should do this independently, to ensure that she alone has a copy of her private key.

Alice can now pass on a copy of the signed certificate to anyone who wants it. For example, Bob, having obtained the CA's much-advertised public key, uses this to check out the signature on his copy of Alice's certificate. Once he knows that Alice's key has a CA 'seal of approval', Bob can feel more confident about using it to set up communications with Alice.

A good Certification Authority does more than just sign certificates. Indeed, if this is all that a CA provides, it is of limited value. It should also offer a number of ongoing services, including:

- *Revocation of certificates.* It may occasionally be necessary to cancel a certificate. This could arise, for example, because it has been issued to someone in connection with their employment, and the personal details include a reference to job status. A certificate cannot be 'handed in' in the same way as a physical card or token when the employee leaves the company. Instead, the CA must maintain a list of all certificates which have been cancelled, and make this available to anyone who wishes to check it. Ideally, this should be an online facility, perhaps accessible via the Internet.

- *Legal liability.* A certificate is intended to convey an assurance that a key and its user are linked, and are genuine. The CA should therefore accept some liability for the accuracy of the information which it has signed. This is by no means always the case. Some 'CAs' advertise certificates for which no checks whatsoever are made on the background of applicants. Certificates from such sources are completely worthless (rather like certificates for bogus university degrees, which can be ordered for 5 dollars through the mail). Even those CAs which *do* carry out reasonable checks often protect themselves with legal disclaimers, which can set strict limits on their liability.
- *Security within the CA.* It is imperative that the private key of the CA remains completely secure at all times. Anyone obtaining this key can forge new certificates, and undermine the credibility of all the certificates already in existence.

This range of requirements, of which the CA signing process is just a part, defines what should be included in a proper *Public Key Infrastructure.* A PKI embraces all the services and facilities needed for the dependable allocation and distribution of public keys. A good PKI will provide facilities which are well administered and convenient for users, and which can meet any special needs (such as providing for a mixture of keys which are issued to individuals, and 'corporate' keys for a whole department or organisation (Dam and Lin 1996)). More sophisticated PKIs make use of smart cards and other additional technology to help with the key distribution and management.

A summary of the three main methods of key distribution is given in Table 7.1. Many variations on these approaches have been devised. Some

Table 7.1

Method	Characteristics	Suitable for:
Key Distribution Centre	Centralised; sets up symmetric key for each session	Large bounded group
Web of trust	Dispersed and informal; distribution of public (asymmetric) keys	Small ad hoc group
Public Key Infrastructure	Dispersed and formal; distribution of public (asymmetric) keys	Large unbounded group

(like the *Kerberos* authentication system) extend the functions of a KDC, by generating 'tickets' to define the facilities on networked machines which are to be made accessible to each user (Kaufman *et al* 1995). It should be noted that *all* such authentication systems, however sophisticated, ultimately depend crucially on the quality of the checks which are made on users' identities at set-up time.

7.4   KEY STORAGE, ESCROW AND RECOVERY

A business making regular use of cryptography should consider what will happen if things, occasionally, go wrong. A common example of this is where text has been successfully encrypted, either by the business or one of its trading partners, but the key to carry out the decryption turns out to have been lost or corrupted.

This is particularly embarrassing if the business has sent out its public key to all its clients, and only then discovers that it has lost the all-important private key. It will now be unable to read incoming messages, and will have no means of signing messages digitally. The loss of a symmetric key will have similar devastating effects if it is being widely used within the business, and particularly if it has been used to encrypt data which has been archived.

All these situations call for some procedure for getting hold of a 'spare' key. There is no way in which the business can set about 're-creating' its key – if it could, this would make life far too easy for any would-be attackers. There are two basic approaches, which can be compared with the arrangements people might make for having a spare front-door or automobile key. The easiest solution is to make a copy of the key, and give it to someone else for safe keeping. Alternatively, the company which supplied the key in the first place may be able to re-create it, subject to appropriate safeguards (for example, the owner of the lost key might be required to provide a unique reference number associated with the key).

Any duplicate copy of the key should preferably be held somewhere well away from the original. If the copy is held in the same system, there is a danger it could suffer the same fate as the original key (for example, being wiped out by a virus attack). Putting it on a different system, or on a diskette locked in a strong box, will also make life particularly difficult for any hackers who might take an interest in it. By convention, any of these arrangements which are set up by the business on its own behalf are known as *key recovery*.

An outside body may be contracted to hold a copy of the key. If the key owner requests this, this amounts to no more than 'outsourcing' the key recovery. However, sometimes there is an element of compulsion. Where there is a legal obligation to furnish a copy of a key to an outside body – usually an agency concerned with regulation or law enforcement – this is referred to as *key escrow*. 'Escrow' is a term borrowed from the law, and simply means that an independent third party takes custody of an asset.

Why are authorities interested in key escrow? Around the world, governments are increasingly anxious about their ability to monitor communications, as more and more commerce is conducted electronically. Hitherto, official eavesdropping has been presented with few *technical* problems. In countries where the rule of law is well developed, it is normal to have legislation to limit the circumstances under which these interceptions are permitted. However, one consequence of modern developments in cryptography is that this situation is being turned upside down. As more and more traffic is encrypted, governments face huge technical problems in reading it, even when the law allows this. They have therefore been looking for ways of empowering themselves to obtain any cryptographic keys which they may need. The reasons they advance usually centre on the need to track the transfer of funds suspected of connections with drug trafficking or money laundering, and to investigate tax evasion and fraud. Some less charitable critics, on the other hand, have suggested that governments may also have developed a taste for carrying out commercial espionage on the businesses of other states (Anon 1999a).

The first major debate in this area began in 1994, when the United States government introduced an 'Escrowed Encryption Standard'. The standard was to be embodied in 'Clipper Chips'. These mass-produced logic chips were to be incorporated in all encryption products, and would give their owners highly secure encryption *but* with a so-called Law Enforcement Access Field. The LEAF would not reveal the encryption key directly, but officials would be able to work it out, by combining the LEAF with other government-held information. The LEAF therefore acted rather like the reference number on an automobile key (Dam and Lin 1996). Businesses and civil libertarians were united in their vociferous opposition to the proposals, which were eventually withdrawn (Diffie and Landau 1998). The Clipper approach would in any event have had several practical limitations, since the chip was designed primarily for devices carrying out encryption in the lower communications layers, which is not always the most effective place to use it (see section 6.5).

In 1997, a consultation paper from the UK government came up with a new approach to escrow (DTI 1997). Under the UK scheme, keys would have to be handed over on-line, within an hour of receiving a 'validated warrant request'. This scheme, like the American one, came in for widespread condemnation, as being both oppressive and impracticable.

Governments have also sought to prevent cryptographic software from falling into the 'wrong hands' by placing restrictions on its sale and distribution. In the United States, cryptographic products have been defined as 'munitions', and made subject to export controls in the same way as tanks and missiles. Much argument with the computer industry has ensued, since suppliers feel handicapped by the regulations in selling credible products to transnational companies and others who want to set up secure communications around the world. Some compromises have been agreed, but these have centred on exemptions for weaker cryptographic products (which it can be assumed that governments would be able to decrypt).

Elsewhere, many other countries have followed suit in placing restrictions on the transfer and use of cryptography (see section 14.1).

7.5 INTER-COMPANY TRANSACTIONS: EFT, EDI AND ELECTRONIC MAIL

Where a business exercises full control over its own internal network, it can use cryptography and other security measures exactly as it pleases. This is not the case if it wishes to exchange messages securely with other organisations. Here, it is likely to find that its options are restricted by the preferences or capabilities of the other parties. For example, they may be unable to handle certain methods of encryption, or may want to keep to the standards set by an outside provider such as a VAN.

Generally, business-to-business links can be divided into three categories:

1 *Electronic Funds Transfer.* EFT messages only need to contain a few basic details relating to amounts, account numbers, etc. The recipient of the message will usually be a bank (or, some would argue, an EFT message is involved in authorising an ATM to issue cash). The construction of EFT messages is fairly simple, but great attention has to be paid to ensuring that they cannot be altered en route and that they are fully authenticated.

The transfer of funds 'by wire' dates back to 1871, when the Western Union Company introduced this service in the United States. Security depended upon a system of authorisation codes used across the company. The potential weaknesses of wire transfer were exposed quite dramatically by the Security Pacific Bank fraud case in 1978, when a contractor working at the bank managed to observe staff using the funds transfer procedures on a number of occasions, and memorised the authorisation codes. He used this knowledge to transfer more than $10 million to an account in New York (Cornwall 1989).

Today's systems are much more sophisticated and computer-driven. An international service for sending financial instructions between banks is provided by the SWIFT organisation, based in La Hulpe, Belgium. (It is generally known by its acronym, but originally the initials denoted the Society for Worldwide Interbank Financial Telecommunication.) Membership of SWIFT comprises a select group of just over 6,500 financial institutions around the world. Access to the network is rigorously controlled, and members are required to use encryption, based on strict standards laid down by SWIFT.

For routine commercial payments, there are services in most countries for funds transfers involving relatively small amounts. Often these are 'batches' of payments, for example, to transfer the pay of all an organisation's employees into their bank accounts at the end of each week or month. In the UK, more than three quarters of the workforce is now paid in this way. Users of such services must register, and will be required to use identification codes and passwords. However, encryption is ruled out because of the overheads involved in administering it for the many thousands of businesses involved.

2 *Electronic Data Interchange.* EDI provides a set of standard formats for business-to-business messages. For example, formats are specified for the contents and lay-out of such items as sales invoices and booking confirmations. (Similar formats are used for the transfer of funds, and so EFT can be regarded as a specialised sub-set of EDI.)

EDI originated within several different business sectors in the 1980s, and originally each industry developed its own 'dialect' – for automobile manufacturing, shipping, construction, tourism, and so on. Differing standards also prevailed in Europe and the USA for a while. All these standards eventually coalesced into the UN/EDIFACT specification (Electronic Data Interchange for Administration, Commerce and Transport), which is now used around the world.

One of the efficiencies provided by EDI is that its messages are now recognised by many commercial computer packages. This means that, for example, details of an order can be passed straight into an order entry system, or a notice of despatch can be recorded directly onto a warehouse database. This absence of human intervention undoubtedly speeds up business processes and reduces costs, but it also removes a sometimes crucial chance for someone to notice there are improbable or suspicious elements in the message.

3 *Electronic Mail.* Mail messages are completely free-form. They can be used to convey business information and instructions, but this information will have to be interpreted by human readers (or perhaps an 'intelligent' computer program). The most commonly used format for electronic mail on the Internet is SMTP (Simple Mail Transport Protocol). The basic SMTP format is much more simple and general-purpose than EFT/EDI, and assumes that the messages it is carrying consist of text only. However, SMTP 'extensions' have since been invented to enable it to carry other kinds of data (see below).

Electronic mail can be used, in principle, to send anything from the company's secret production plans to the smallest piece of trivia. Unless businesses are willing to encrypt their emails on a routine basis, the only practicable policy is to issue edicts forbidding the use of email for anything which is at all sensitive. In this context, it should be remembered that different types of messages are often 'chained', as for example in the case illustrated in Figure 7.3. In this example a manager working at home sends an email to a clerk in the office, and her instructions result in an EDI message being sent to a bank. The bank in turn responds to *its* instructions by making an EFT payment to a supplier.

As the world relies more and more on electronic messaging, it becomes commonplace to find such chains, where one message triggers another. From a security perspective, it is important that all links in the chain should receive similar levels of protection. It may be, for example, that the

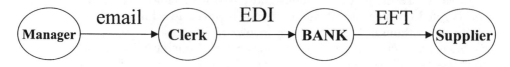

Figure 7.3

EFT message is subject to very tight controls because cash transfers are involved. Ultimately, these controls are wasted if an enterprising hacker is able to forge a convincing email which will set all the other events in motion. Email forgery is not particularly difficult, as the US software company Oracle found to its cost when an e-mail message, supposedly sent by an Oracle manager, was cited in a claim for unfair dismissal. The message turned out to have been forged by the ex-employee making the claim (Savarnejad 1997).

Businesses may find that security policy is also complicated by the growing practice of using the Internet to exchange EDI messages. This is an increasingly attractive option for small and medium-sized businesses who want a cheap point of entry to data networking (Tucker 1997). To ensure that the EDI message arrives with its special lay-out intact, it is 'wrapped up' inside an email message, using special MIME extensions to SMTP (where MIME stands for Multi-Purpose Internet Mail Extensions). This enables businesses to gain the benefits of EDI (for example, in avoiding the need to re-key the details into their accounting systems) while also exploiting the cheapness and connectivity of the Internet.

7.6 TRADING WITH THE PUBLIC: ELECTRONIC COMMERCE

EDI has now proved itself indispensable to many businesses, and has become an accepted part of the commercial landscape. Most EDI trading is between organisations which are well established, and know each other. As well as being able to identify each other from public registers and directories, the parties will usually have marked the start of the arrangement by signing some kind of formal agreement which determines their respective responsibilities and liabilities in the event that anything should go wrong with the EDI transactions.

The new wave of commercial development of the Internet, on the other hand, is centred on selling directly to consumers. In this case, a sales transaction may be the first (and possibly only) contact between the parties. The vendor is looking for two key advantages from the Internet. First, it is a cheap selling medium, which operates around the clock and reaches customers anywhere in the world. Second, customers can be enabled to move quickly in making and confirming a buying decision. Vendors are therefore wary of security measures which appear to threaten either of these advantages. For example, if extra steps are needed to check on the customer's credentials, or methods of payment are unduly cumbersome, much of the appeal of on-line shopping will start to disappear.

In fact, a number of factors need to combine favourably for Internet selling to be a commercial proposition, and the position varies in different parts of the world. For example, in Latin America, consumers are particularly distrustful of on-line payment systems. This is rooted in experiences of poor service levels, and a general lack of responsiveness on the part of businesses to enquiries and complaints. Credit card services are also not very highly regarded, because they have traditionally avoided giving customers any kind of indemnity if problems arise, such as the fraudulent use of cards or the non-delivery of goods. As well as facing an uphill struggle against this unhelpful climate of opinion, would-be web traders also have some technical obstacles to overcome, since telecommunications services are expensive and not always reliable, and Internet Service Providers have tended to charge high fees (Davis 1999). Meanwhile there are parts of South East Asia where substantial investments have been made in the telecommunications infrastructure, but developments in Internet service provision have not always kept pace. Thus in India, some companies have preferred to set up web sites in the United States, rather than in their own country (Chowdhary 1997).

So far as control and security is concerned, new consumer-oriented services appearing on the Internet give rise to three particular challenges:

- *Establishing the credentials of buyers and sellers.* There is a problem of trust in *both* directions. The minute a customer stops browsing through an on-line catalogue, and places an order, the vendor has to place trust in the customer's proposed method of payment. The customer, meanwhile, must have faith in the vendor's intention and ability to deliver whatever is being ordered. Neither party has much to go on, except what is being communicated across the Internet.
- *Reconciling speed with security.* The great attraction of dealing over the Internet is that it is immediate and responsive. To achieve this, security procedures have to take place in 'real time', while the transaction is still in progress. Any attempts to introduce additional checks, such as supplementary telephone calls or fax messages, will destroy this immediacy, and with it most of the Internet's appeal. Indeed, even some of the supposedly 'instant' methods of securing transactions are being resisted by vendors as being too slow (see the discussion of SET below).
- *Small value transactions.* In theory, the Internet should be an ideal medium for small purchases, particularly of 'digital' items, like the text of a short report or a track of recorded music. However, traditional electronic payment systems (such as debit and credit cards) are not geared up for the small amounts involved. Hence the search is on for ways of making it easy to spend money electronically, for the kind of small amounts which would be paid out of loose change by someone on a conventional shopping trip.

One of the first products aimed at addressing at least some of the above issues was the *Secure Socket Layer* (SSL) protocol, introduced as a feature of the Netscape web browser. SSL quickly established itself as a de facto standard, through being given away as part of a popular Internet browser. It has been developed further since its launch, and version 3 not only provides for encryption of messages, but enables the identity of both the sender and the receiver to be authenticated, using asymmetric cryptographic keys.

Subsequently Microsoft introduced its *Secure Channel Services* product, which claims to support a number of security protocols, including SSL. Meanwhile the *Secure Electronic Transaction* (SET) protocol was being launched, backed by an alliance of major business names, including IBM, VISA and Mastercard. All these products work close to the Application Layer, as shown in Figure 7.4.

All these products offer similar facilities. The extent to which any of them emerge as dominant standards will depend very much on commercial and political factors, as well as their technical merits. SET is the most specialised of the products, since it has been designed specifically with on-line credit card transactions in mind. At first sight, this would seem to give it a head start in the race to dominate electronic commerce. However, not everyone is keen to see credit cards become the dominant method of payment on the Internet. Some commercial interests would rather see alternative methods used, perhaps more independent of the existing banking systems. Furthermore, SET has had to fight a certain amount of resistance from the merchants and card issuers for whom it was designed. SET's first hurdle is that customers must all be persuaded to install software on their PCs which will create an 'electronic wallet' for them. Each

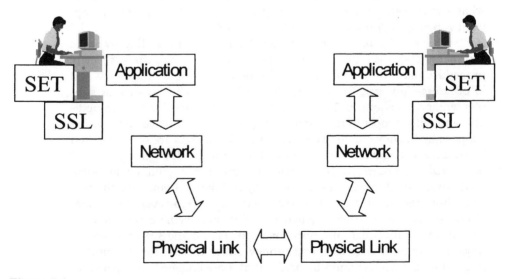

Figure 7.4

customer then uses the software to generate an asymmetric key pair, with the public key being vouched for by a Certification Authority (usually the bank issuing the credit card). This ensures proper authentication of the customer, but also adds to the marketing and start-up costs. Disquiet has also surfaced within the financial services industry because individual SET transactions, although secure, can take an unacceptably long time to process (Lambeth 1999).

There are a number of other schemes, besides SET, which use the idea of the electronic wallet. In some cases, such as eWallet, new features are added automatically from time to time by downloading code into the user's PC. A recurring problem with electronic wallets is that sensitive functions like generating and storing keys, or adding functional upgrades, have to be carried out on machines where control is informal or non-existent. The average home PC will be accessible to all the members of the family, as well as friends and visitors (including school friends), some of whom may be more computer literate than the residents. Designing software resilient enough to stay secure in this kind of environment is no mean task. Since access to the wallet will be password-controlled, there are also risks of security leaks within the household, at which point the whole arrangement starts to look extremely insecure.

It remains to be seen whether electronic wallets will take hold. This is a market with low entry costs, but where the ultimate survivors will only emerge after a series of bruising turf wars. Besides the problems of launching and branding electronic wallets, suppliers must also beware of technological changes which may render their products obsolete. In particular, it is probable that expansion of Internet services direct to consumers will be based on new forms of workstation, tied to television sets or mobile phones. Having a workstation which is purpose-built for the Internet, and which runs only browser functions, simplifies the control problems considerably.

Apart from the type of technology which is deployed in the home, several other factors will influence the development of Internet payment systems. Proposed payment systems generally fall into three categories.

1 *Extensions to the existing systems for debit and credit card payment.* Here the customer continues to have an account with the card issuer, and payment is authorised by transmitting the card number, ideally together with other corroborating details, such as the card expiry date. Processing card payments necessarily involves collaboration between different financial institutions. In the case of credit cards, one will have issued the card to the customer, while the other (usually known as a merchant acquirer) will have an agreement with the vendor to look after the processing of all the payments received. The merchant acquirer passes details of transactions back to the card issuer, who debits the customer's credit account. Debit cards work on a similar basis, but with charges entered directly onto the customer's personal bank account.

These settlement arrangements are already established and proven world-wide, and are already used regularly on the Internet. Two factors inhibit their wider use. First, the overheads associated with each transaction remain relatively high, and rule out the use of cards for the kind of high-volume, low-value sales which many Internet vendors would like to offer. Second, the public remains concerned about sending card numbers over the Internet. This anxiety tends to centre on the secrecy of communications between the customer and the vendor, although this is not necessarily the weak point. Problems are more likely to arise because banks and traders fail to enforce routine checks for incomplete or inconsistent card details. This is illustrated by a case described in the next section 7.7.

2 *The creation of systems based on 'electronic cash'.* In this case, instead of using a card number to authorise a debit against an account, the purchaser transmits a string of bits to the vendor. The bits have an intrinsic value. This means that settlement occurs immediately, and comes closest to a purely information-based equivalent to conventional money (as is emphasised by its alternative name of *digital cash*). The customer buys bit strings from an electronic cash provider, and pays for them using a conventional method such as cheque or credit card.

A scheme for electronic cash can only claim to emulate all the features of real money (as possessed by ordinary currency notes and coins) if the cash is:

(a) *independent and portable.* The cash issuer is not involved each time a transaction occurs.

(b) *non-reusable.* Once the cash has been 'spent', it leaves the possession of the spender for good.

(c) *easily transferred.* The process of handing over the cash is quick and uncomplicated.

(d) *payable in any amount.* It is possible to tender cash for the exact amount the customer has spent, or to hand over a larger amount and receive change.

(e) *visible.* It is easy for the customer to find out how much cash is currently held, or how much is being transferred in a transaction.

A number of digital cash schemes have been launched, but all have revealed shortcomings in one or more of the above areas. For example, since a bit string can easily be copied any number of times, it is very difficult to make electronic cash non-reusable. To defeat attempts at electronic counterfeiting, it is necessary to check on whether someone is trying to use the same bit string more than once. This conflicts with other aims, such as indicated by features (a) and (c). It is also cumbersome to issue and use large numbers of electronic coins in small denominations, which is necessary if feature (d) is to be achieved.

A survey of several embryonic schemes is provided by Lynch and Lundquist (1996). Most of these turn out to rely on ingenious updates to traditional methods, and rely on electronic equivalents of credit authorisation or payment by cheque. An early scheme to provide genuine electronic coins was launched by Digicash, which offered the added benefit of a guarantee of anonymity for the person making the payment. Digicash ran into financial difficulties in 1998, and subsequently sold the rights to the special encryption methods it was using to eCash Technologies Inc, of Seattle (ecash 2000).

3 *The creation of 'electronic purses'*. Unlike an electronic wallet, which can be loaded onto any PC, an electronic purse is based on a token (usually a smart card) which can be carried around. Security mechanisms are built into the purse so that, for example, money cannot be 'spent' unless a PIN is entered at the time of the sale. Building intelligence into the purse gives it great versatility. It can double as a conventional credit or debit card, and its value can be topped up by 're-charging' it at special terminals. Small portable devices are being developed to provide a read-out of the value of the card, and to enable recharging to be done by downloading over telecommunications links. With the aid of such devices, the electronic purse can provide all five features mentioned in connection with electronic cash. The Mondex card is probably the best established product, and has been the subject of trials in many parts of the world. Originally issued in 1994, this has been developed as a standard to the point where a number of manufacturers can offer 'Mondex-compatible' equipment (Mondex 2000). Trials to date have included the city of Guelph, Ontario (Campbell 1998), the fast-food outlets of McDonald's Deutschland (Essick 1998), and several university campuses. Success has tended to be greatest in small, enclosed communities, where a 'critical mass' of retailers can be persuaded to install the necessary card reading equipment at the point of sale.

To ensure security, standards for the software in the smart card need to be backed by agreed procedures whereby cash is to be loaded in to it, and special situations are to be handled (for example, if a customer is to be given a refund). The European Committee for Banking Standards has been investigating these issues on behalf of its members, and has drafted a number of standards (ECBS 1999).

7.7 MONITORING AND SURVEILLANCE OF NETWORKS

As they have been unable to rely on the widespread adoption of protection mechanisms such as SET, banks and merchants have had to turn to other ways of combating and detecting card fraud on the Internet. The dangers of assuming that existing arrangements for handling card transactions will suffice in the electronic age have been highlighted in a case estimated to have affected 900,000 victims in 22 countries. Investigations by the US Federal Trade Commission resulted in the press release in January 1999, reproduced here.

The FTC alleged that the defendants obtained consumer credit and debit card account numbers without consumers' knowledge or approval, and billed or debited consumers' accounts for services the consumers had not ordered, did not want, and in some cases, couldn't use because they had no computer. The charge item on the bill contained the name of one of the various businesses and an 800 phone number. Consumers who called the number to get the charge removed from their credit card got a busy signal, no answer, or a recording directing them to enter their credit card number to discuss charges. They often were unable to get through to a person to discuss the charges. Consumers, many of whom were billed repeatedly over successive months, appealed to credit card companies for help, but were told by them that they could not block future charges to the cards. Many consumers canceled their credit card accounts to avoid the charges, the FTC alleged.

FTC 2000

This scam appears to have been well organised, and the details have been pieced together by Dr John Faughnan of the University of Minnesota (Wallich 1999). Dr Faughnan identified five main ingredients in the fraud.

- *Acquisition of card numbers*. The perpetrators had no need to intercept messages or hack into files. Because the specifications for the formats and check digit calculations of VISA cards are well known, anyone can generate a list of valid VISA numbers. These will pass any input validity checks, which only look for conformance with the basic formatting rules.
- *Merchant status*. The fraud was operated through companies which applied for, and obtained, authorisation to accept credit card payments as vendors. In some cases, another company would be used as a front for the supposed source of the 'sales' – perhaps without even being aware of the scam. These sales companies would be involved in Internet trading in electronic materials, usually of a pornographic nature.
- *Transaction processing*. Details of the bogus transactions would be sent via the normal transaction sorting process to the bank responsible for the victim's account. Some of the card numbers might be bounced during the sorting process, others later on by the banks themselves. However, many of them got through, particularly in some countries (which obviously then became a favourite target for the scheme).
- *Setting up account charges*. Transactions would all be for small amounts (typically just under $20) to be paid on a recurring basis, each month. Those that made it through the screening process would now generate a regular revenue stream from the bank back to the merchant.
- *Victims' reactions*. Victims would be deterred from taking action by the fact that credit card transactions in the USA are normally only indemnified if they are for amounts over $50, and many banks do not entertain claims after 60 days. Attempts to seek redress through the 'vendor'

would meet the obstacles described by the FTC. Some nevertheless seem to have been particularly incensed by the implication that they had bought pornography, which may have helped to swell the number of complaints reaching the FTC.

This kind of scam could easily be carried out on a small scale by any dishonest merchant. However, by taking a systematic approach and coordinating the efforts of several participants it was possible to clear profits estimated to be in the region of $40 million. The risks of being detected were kept low by the inability of any of the major parties to obtain a complete and detailed picture of what was happening. The chances of such frauds might of course be reduced if there were only a very small number of dominant card providers, but when this was actually the case in the UK, such dominance was held to reduce competition and be contrary to the public interest (MMC 1989). Also, since the fraud was international in extent, it was difficult for one national regulator such as the FTC to put all the pieces together, and if the perpetrators had turned out to be based outside the USA, it would have lacked jurisdiction.

Given the large number of financial institutions involved in credit card processing, it is not too surprising if inconsistencies arise over exactly where checks are to be applied in the processing cycle. In theory, it is possible to exclude any 'invented' card numbers quite easily, by checking all numbers against lists of cards which have actually been issued. Requiring corroborative details such as the expiry date or card-holder's name will help, since these will have to be invented to accompany bogus card numbers, and may help to give the game away. Such details are captured automatically when the card is produced at a point of sale terminal in a store, but must be explicitly requested in dealings over the telephone or the Internet. As the FTC case shows, it has to be assumed that some of the vendors responsible for requesting such details may be actively involved in fraud.

Another weapon in the armoury of the financial institutions is software which embodies *artificial intelligence*. This can 'learn' about normal patterns of activity by monitoring transactions, and pick out suspicious events. Such software has proved successful in detecting misuse of cards, and is in use by banks and some of the national VISA organisations. The software will review a number of factors relating to a transaction, and give each one a weighting. If the total exceeds a certain threshold, the transaction is deemed to be unduly suspicious. Ideally, this should be done by the bank issuing the card, which has a record of the individual card-holder's normal buying habits, and can look for unlikely spending patterns at an individual level. Sifting through massive numbers of transactions at a national or international level is less likely to be productive, and certainly the fraudulent $20 charges in the case described earlier seem to have slipped 'under the radar'.

Organisations may need to bring monitoring and surveillance to bear on their own private networks; this is discussed further in section 13.4.

7.8 QUESTIONS

1 The research division of a pharmaceutical company employs 150 staff. Because most of the information exchanged by staff is commercially valuable, the company would like to make it mandatory for staff to encrypt all their internal communications. What approach would you recommend for key distribution in this situation, and why?

2 You have been asked to select a Certification Authority to look after the authentication of keys for your organisation. Choose *four* features or facilities which you would regard as being particularly important for a CA to provide, and write a brief note by way of explanation for each of them.

3 What different functions do EFT, EDI and email fulfil? Imagine that you work in an organisation which uses email extensively for communicating internally and with its suppliers and customers. Draft a one-page guidance document for employees, advising them of the main security risks associated with the use of email, and advising them on ways in which they could adopt best practice.

4 Explain what is meant by an 'electronic wallet' held on a PC used in the home. What are the main security issues associated with the setting up and operation of this facility?

chapter
eight

CONTROLS FOR LOCAL AREA NETWORKS AND SMALL SYSTEMS

SOME TOPICS ADDRESSED IN THIS CHAPTER

- How good security practice can be fostered in a *local work group* or *small business*
- Controls needed if the members of a work group *share their use of equipment, files or software,* and the allocation of responsibilities for administering and enforcing them
- Taking advantage of the *standard security facilities* in business software
- Setting up and administering *LANs*
- Countering common threats, such as virus infections and loss or corruption of files, *at the local level*

8.1 INTRODUCTION

Networking has opened up many new possibilities for 'virtual' working groups, whose members collaborate from different locations, and may never actually meet one another except over a videoconferencing circuit. Most people, however, still use their computers in a more traditional setting, seated at their desk, and surrounded by other people from their unit, department or small business. The computers may all be linked together by a local area network, but typically this will be small enough for most of its users it to know each other personally. It is at this localised, personal level that the roots of the organisation's data security practices are to be found.

The situations which arise in this level can provide a good test of management's wider commitment to security. For example, an employee may be worried that her password has been compromised, but she does not know how to change it. Or a virus checking program has come up with an enigmatic message, leaving a secretary completely baffled, and uncertain what to do about it. Or confidential figures from head office have just been found on a memorandum lying in the out-tray of the networked laser printer.

How should a manager respond to this kind of situation? Let us assume that the employees have shown a responsible attitude, in bringing the problem into the open. Their future conduct will be strongly influenced by the way their enquiries are received. It will obviously send entirely the wrong signals if they are told that they are wasting time over trivial matters, or they are treated to a heartfelt tirade about the stupidity of computers, or they are simply told to stop fussing and take the problem elsewhere.

Even if the reactions are more circumspect they may fail to conceal a certain amount of weariness or impatience. Where humanly possible, the reaction should be positive and appreciative, and the presentation of the problem should be welcomed as an opportunity to promote good practice. This does not mean that anyone should attempt to conceal the fact that resolving the problem is going to be irksome. However, if a manager shows determination to pursue the matter, and gives it some priority, this will send a more powerful message than any number of security briefings or lengthy office memoranda.

This chapter is concerned with all such issues which arise 'at the sharp end' – in the course of the daily work of the office or clinic or store – and suggests how security techniques should best be applied in this setting.

8.2 MANAGING COMPLIANCE WITHIN THE LOCAL WORK GROUP

Having accepted the normality of PCs on desks, most offices have now moved on to seeing it as natural that they should be connected by local area networks. So unobtrusive has this process been that it has led one consultant to observe: 'I've visited a lot of small companies that weren't even aware that they had LANs' (Alexander 1995).

This interconnectedness on the desk top opens up many possibilities for new ways of working. It should not be assumed that because the technology is much the same everywhere that it is always being used in the same way. At one extreme some (usually larger) organisations install software to determine the tasks presented to each member of the group, and track all their activities. This can be contrasted with more informal arrangements, where staff are able to communicate electronically and share facilities, but only if they want to. This latter style prevails in most organisations. Software which helps to support group working, particularly in a more formal sense, is generally referred to as 'groupware', and its use is known as Computer Supported Cooperative Work (CSCW).

Where CSCW is organised to allow scrutiny and intervention by management, it can lead to resentment on the part of staff, who will feel that they are being kept under surveillance. It may also lead to feelings of being devalued and de-skilled. This can result in a more inhibited and less committed style of working, with people anxious to follow the cues given by the software, and concerned about the way their performance is likely to be reflected in the records it is keeping (McCarthy 1994).

On the other hand, if collaboration is informal, it can lead to the formation of new, unofficial arrangements, which bypass the procedures which were previously in place. These may lead to feelings of insecurity on the part of managers, since they are no longer 'in the loop'. Electronic communications also have the effect of making people less aware of the status of others, in particular, in terms of their seniority or gender (Sproull and Kiesler 1992).

Within small businesses, as opposed to units within a larger organisation, group working is almost invariably on a more relaxed basis. This reflects the culture of small business entrepreneurs, who are motivated primarily by a desire to 'be their own boss', and who rate autonomy as more important than wealth or status (Gray 1992). Even large corporations may wish to 'empower' local work groups (perhaps as part of Business Process Re-engineering) and to take advantage of their adaptability. Autonomous small groups can, where necessary, respond quickly and inventively to unforeseen situations (Hutchins 1991), and can be expected to find ways of working round problems, rather than doing everything 'by the book'.

Whatever mode of working is adopted, one outcome is likely to be the emergence of new forms of dependence on IT. As Orlikowski (1966) observes:

> Inevitably, the more technologically mediated the work, and the more valuable and effective that mediation, the more dependent the work and the worker become on the technology. The dependence is apparent on two fronts: a physical dependence on the availability of the hardware, network, software and data quality, and a psychological dependence on the knowledge contained within the technology. The former is manageable with various backup mechanisms, tests and review procedures. The latter is more problematic to manage because it represents a state of mind. It is particularly problematic for users who have never performed the work without the use of technology.

CSCW does not only change the mechanics of the way people work: it changes their sense of how authority is being exercised, and creates new social pressures, especially within peer groups which are linked electronically. Securing compliance with information security measures has a number of implications for managers:

- *Levelling effects of IT*. If using email to issue instructions or notifications, bear in mind that your message will be one among many others, all of which look very much the same on the screen. It will be less impressive and less effective than, say, a pep talk or a personal letter.
- *IT dependency*. Well-managed IT is unobtrusive, and comes to be accepted as being 'just part of the furniture'. Staff come to rely on IT without realising it. Your efforts to make them security-aware, particularly with respect to possible loss or corruption of data, may strike them as pointless, and maybe just a little obsessive.
- *Surveillance through IT*. If staff have a feeling that CSCW software is controlling and monitoring their activities, they may conclude that security is being well taken care of, and no further participation is needed from them.

8.3   CONTROLS WITHIN OFFICE SOFTWARE (1): CLERICAL AND ADMINISTRATIVE APPLICATIONS

Security features are often mentioned as a selling point in promotional material for business software packages. However, making comparisons between the security claims of rival suppliers is more problematic than for other aspects of software. If a word-processing product is supposed to provide a workaday feature like spell checking, for example, this can quickly be tested and verified. Claims that the package also offers highly secure encryption facilities in its filing system, on the other hand, may be supported by all kinds of references to standards and named algorithms and other technical data, but these can only be properly checked out by a technical expert.

Suppliers can, in any event, provide no more than the means for putting security in place. However excellent they may be *potentially*, any security measures are quite useless unless and until they are properly configured and activated. While it may feel reassuring to buy a package which has five-star security features, there is little point in doing so if there is only a half-hearted commitment to using them. Indeed, such an investment could be a complete waste of money. To pursue the analogy, it is rather like booking into a five-star hotel, and then walking out to eat at the fast-food counter down the road.

Selecting and installing the security in office software has been further complicated by the way the software has come to be packaged and marketed. In the PC marketplace particularly, the market is dominated by one supplier (Microsoft) which is keen to sell everyone an integrated approach, based on its product range of office and network management software. Rival suppliers have similar ambitions. One result is that users find themselves under pressure to set up systems in which the work group and network activities are all inextricably knitted together. This suits the marketing strategies of suppliers, who want to 'own' as many activities as possible on the desk top, and extend them via their own proprietary standards. Security may not always benefit from this situation, especially if too much emphasis is placed on sharing resources, and making them 'user-friendly'.

1 *'Virtual' file storage*. Users are encouraged to suppose that there is no difference between files held on their own hard disk and those held in other machines, or on sites on the Internet. The mechanisms for retrieving files from all these different sources are deliberately made to look the same. This means that people do not have to learn any new procedures for dealing with remote files, and opens up new and exciting ways for them to work. At the same time, it creates a brand new range of security exposures.

The best solution to the security problem will often simply be to eliminate it altogether, by making it impossible for people to access files outside their own machine. However, software is increasingly designed to sell itself; users will find that it has built-in demonstrations of ways in which facilities can be expanded, and invitations to subscribe to new products and services. At the very least, this creates a demand for users to be allowed wider access. In the worst cases, the access is already available by default, and may even include pointers to web sites from which entirely new programs, and further marketing material, can be downloaded.

The problem for the business is that it cannot presume that setting up a new office package is necessarily 'fail-safe' from a security point of view. The dilemma is particularly acute where a PC supplier offers a 'ready-to-run' system, pre-loaded with office applications. This undoubtedly saves an enormous amount of time in set-up and configuration. However, those who pre-load the software are trying to make it fit all the possible needs of a broad range of customers. Since they want to have these customers making productive use of the PC in as short a time as possible, their emphasis will be on removing barriers, and making it as easy as possible to activate applications.

2 *Over-helpful software*. The conflict between security and convenience can surface in many other ways. For example, 'auto-completion' is a very user-friendly device but it can negate security, as has been pointed out by Schifreen (1999). Auto-completion steps in to complete a phrase or address which it thinks it recognises. This can be helpful if you are typing in a long web site address, and the auto-complete feature fills in the rest of the address for you after you have put in the first few characters. But what if it also volunteers the entries to go in a panel requesting your ID and password? An even more bizarre example is given by Alexander (1996). With one particularly 'helpful' function, if three unsuccessful attempts were made to enter a password, a prompt appeared asking if you would like to start afresh by setting up a new password which would be easier to remember.

3 *Do-it-yourself access control*. A problem for suppliers is that, having whipped up enthusiasm for the fully networked office, they must then provide a means of setting up authorisations to restrict what people can see and do. This means creating the kind of access control tables described in Chapter 4. On the old-fashioned mainframe computers, such tables were set up and managed by expensively paid systems

programmers. Suppliers are faced with simplifying this task to a level which can be handled by a moderately computer-literate office supervisor.

They have not entirely succeeded. It is possible to eliminate some of the technical jargon, and replace it with terms which sound more familiar in the office. So, for example, someone with read-only access to documents is styled a 'reviewer', while someone who 'owns' the file can do pretty well anything. Even so, when faced with terms such as 'Publishing Editor' versus 'Publishing Author' it is sometimes necessary to look at the small print to find out exactly what each set of rights does and does not permit.

Even if the access control administrator can work all this out, it then becomes necessary to ensure that everyone using the documents *also* understands how the restrictions work. In many cases, they will need this understanding so that they themselves can set up access limits on documents they create, and which they want others to update or review. The time and effort required to make this work satisfactorily should not be underestimated. Conversely, if access rights are badly managed, people will simply side-step them by giving each other unrestricted rights wherever they can. This then becomes a good example of a potentially 'five-star' facility being turned into a one-star service.

4 *Standard protection, standard counter-measures.* Office software now routinely offers methods of protecting documents and files, usually based on the entry of a password at the time the data is saved. The problem with such passwords, which may be chosen and entered on the spur of the moment, is that they are easily forgotten.

A conscientious user will follow the rules about choosing obscure, random passwords, and varying them on each occasion. This means that large amounts of business data may end up being locked away, protected by passwords which are kept privately – and perhaps not very systematically. The situation is similar to that of files protected by encryption (see section 7.4), for which there is the possibility of ensuring that, if an encryption key is lost, it can be retrieved via a scheme for Key Recovery.

It is not nearly so simple to devise a secure and practicable scheme for storing and recovering the passwords which have been used for individuals' file, perhaps over many years. It is therefore not surprising that a lively market has grown up for password cracking services; these offer either a program capable of finding passwords in popular products, or a per-item service where the file is sent away (usually by email) for its contents to be unravelled. Files from versions of Microsoft Word prior to Office 97, for example, could have their password protection removed by software available over the Internet for less than $100. Services have now appeared to deal with the stronger facilities introduced into later editions of Word, based on brute-force attacks.

5 *Deleted – or not?* A similar dilemma arises with files which have been 'deleted'. There are invariably some cases when the deletion turns out to have been a mistake. Most filing systems do not actually erase the

contents of a file, but simply pretend it is no longer there. This means that the original data will stay recorded on the disk surface, until the space is needed again and it is over-written by a new file. In practice, this means that the data is often still retrievable several months later.

Users of DOS who understood this principle could easily get their files back by using the UNDELETE command. In Windows, it is even easier to retrieve files which have been sent to the Recycle Bin. For most of the time, this is a useful and pragmatic solution, whereby users can throw away their files, knowing that they still have a good chance of recovering them in an emergency. However, this form of 'deletion' is not at all adequate if the aim is to remove all traces of the data, for example, because the PC is being passed on to a different owner.

6 *Clip boards and screen grabbers.* The ability to flip data from one application to another is another advantage of 'integrated' office software touted by the suppliers. This can speed up editing considerably, for example, in enabling charts from spreadsheets to be transferred directly into a word-processed report. Similarly, it may be useful to 'grab' images which appear on the screen while browsing the Internet. Unfortunately, there is a security down-side: once something has appeared on the PC screen, it must be assumed that it could find its way almost anywhere. It is just too easy to 'lift' a piece of text or an image and transfer it to an email, a disk file or a printer. All the different versions of electronic 'scissors and paste' – whether a part of the 'official' software used in the office, or acquired from shareware disks and web sites – make a mockery of one of the key rules in every classic security model, namely that there must be control over the way data is manipulated at all times.

Two further weaknesses to be found in many PC-based office systems sound rather esoteric, but are potentially more dangerous than anything mentioned above. First, it should be noted that if files are 'owned' by a particular application, this does not prevent them being read by other software as well. Special file search products, normally used by auditors, will look through any type of file, and will attempt to arrange the contents in some sort of meaningful lay-out on the screen. Even without such products, it is possible to get a good idea of what is contained in a file just by opening it as if it were a text file, in a notepad or word-processing facility. This enables anyone to browse through the file contents, even if they are not normally allowed to access the application which created them. Particular targets might be records created in an electronic diary system, or other people's email messages.

Ideally, all such sensitive files should be held in encrypted form. Encryption options are sometimes provided with office products, but they are of variable quality. In particular, encryption is likely to be of limited value if the package creates its own internal key, rather than requiring the user to provide a passphrase. Failing this, packages are available which will tighten up the access controls on the PC, making it more difficult for any unauthorised users to browse the hard drive.

The second major vulnerability concerns passwords. Every application will have its own cluster of files, usually in its own directory or subdirectory. Some of these will contain program code, while others record control information which the program needs to refer to. These files can be browsed like any others. Snoopers will be particularly interested in any which have been updated by the activities of the program, rather than the static files which have remained unchanged since the program was shipped. Finding updated files is easy, as the date and time of the last update is listed alongside each file name.

One of the updated files will contain the current passwords. Most suppliers disguise these in some way, but their efforts are sometimes a little half-hearted. This is because they know that sooner or later they will have to deal with an anguished call from a customer who has lost a master password, and thereby locked himself out of all kinds of data which is vital for running the business. The only pragmatic solution is to make password retrieval hard, but not *too* hard. This is good news for the really determined hacker.

Password protection *can* be made extremely secure. One approach is to not to store individuals' passwords on the hard drive in the clear, but to convert them into hashes. Hashing, it will be recalled, converts the text into meaningless bit strings, and works in one direction only, so that it is impossible to reverse the hashing process to get back to the password. When the software is processing a log-in, it requests the password from the user, and immediately hashes it. It then compares the result with the hash stored in the list in its control files. Only if the two hashes are the same is the user granted access.

This makes life difficult for the hacker, but the hashed list is still vulnerable to a determined attack. For example, if the application software in question is a package which is widely available, it is possible to experiment with it and generate a list of likely passwords, and their corresponding hashes. This will be a long list, but storing and searching it is not a major problem if the hacker puts it all on a portable computer. To frustrate this kind of attack, a further twist is added to the hash computation, by hashing the password together with a 'salt'. The salt is a random number hidden elsewhere in the software.

The security literature regularly features devious tricks which have been discovered to prise passwords out of software. One of the more surprising ones involved a back-up utility which, when first installed, saved the master password for the operating system in a file which would be easily accessed by anyone (Hancock 1999). Although a rather arcane subject, password protection is an issue which should always be raised with suppliers. Any weaknesses will leave the way open for an attacker to obtain a password with access rights at a senior level, and with it the power to roam widely, causing any amount of damage and confusion.

8.4 CONTROLS WITHIN OFFICE SOFTWARE (2): ACCOUNTING APPLICATIONS

Accounting information, in various forms, matters to a wide range of people, both inside and outside the organisation. Its credibility is derived from the accounting conventions by which its collection and processing are governed. These conventions are often seen as being directed against attempts to commit fraud, but they are just as much concerned with preventing records from being kept in ways which are careless or inconsistent. The aim is that the output of the accounting system should always present a 'true and fair' picture of all the financial transactions conducted by the organisation.

To achieve this, it is essential that access rights are assigned judiciously. Some users will need to be able to read certain ledger entries and little else, while at the other extreme the audit team must be able to home in on the fine detail of any transaction which has passed through the system. Accordingly, suppliers of accounting software will typically offer a rich set of security features. As with other software, these features cannot do the job just by being there: they must be evaluated, configured, and put to work in ways which are tailored to the needs of the organisation.

A common difficulty in setting up access control tables is that the first attempt has to be made when the system is new and unfamiliar, and no-one fully understands how all the facilities work. It is therefore difficult to know exactly which access rights to assign; there is a temptation not to exclude too many functions from too many people, just in case they are needed.

As time goes on, this problem is compounded by the fact that the more junior staff, who are using the software on a daily basis, come to understand many aspects of its operation better than their seniors. At this point, it may not occur to anyone to do anything fraudulent, but the opportunity may be taken to try out any functions which are accessible, if only out of curiosity. From here, the classic pattern of fraud may develop. A user sees a possible way of deceiving the system, and makes a few tentative experiments. If these go unnoticed, the way is open to develop the fraud on a more systematic basis.

The fact that everything seems to be running smoothly should not therefore be taken as a sign that the access rights are correctly set. The access control tables should be reviewed every few months, and it should be explained to staff that it is not intended as any reflection on their integrity if certain access rights are removed, simply because it has now been realised that they are not needed for their work.

At the same time, care should be taken not to become too preoccupied with the commonly perceived threat to accounting systems from greedy or disloyal employees, who find devious ways of siphoning off funds into their personal bank accounts, or arrange to send 'free' goods to an accomplice. Attention should also be given to threats such as the following.

- *Corporate fraud.* This is the reverse of fraud perpetrated by the individual employee. All the basic transactions may be entered correctly, but senior members of the organisation conspire to doctor the figures en route to the published accounts. Alternatively, staff may be deliberately kept in the dark about the real implications of transactions they are being asked to carry out, a technique which was much favoured by the late Robert Maxwell (Bower 1991). This presents particular problems for more junior staff who suspect something is amiss, because they have to balance being a 'whistle-blower' against the consequences they may face: (see also section 3.7).

- *Software faults and errors.* Programming calls for meticulous attention to detail, and sometimes the results bear out the truth of the industry saying, that 'a program does what you tell it to do, not what you *want* it to do'. A review of many, often bizarre, programming errors is given by Neumann (1995). The errors need not necessarily arise in the accounting system itself. A UK company introduced a computerised inventory management system, and found that the erroneous information it provided caused it to understate its sales costs by £800,000 (Anon 1994). Flaws of this kind, where the errors accumulate and go unnoticed over quite a long period of time, represent one of the most serious threats to the financial health of a business.

- *Human error.* Input controls can trap some, but not all, errors in entering figures. Errors can also occur in the course of setting up the system in the first place, particularly in respect of the chart of accounts, and the assignment of other codes to identify groups of products, personnel, etc. Entries which are generated automatically can also be a source of trouble. For example, asset values may be reduced each year to allow for depreciation, or recurring payments may be made to suppliers. The danger is that these automatic calculations may be set up to run for too long, or at the wrong times (for example, monthly rather than annually).

- *Tolerances in the system.* The aim of a good accounting system is to provide figures which balance exactly, with no margin for error. However, in some industries it is quite normal to find discrepancies, even when in theory two sets of figures ought to be exactly the same. A typical retail store provides a case in point. The goods recorded as having been received at the back of the store *ought* to match exactly with the goods recorded as passing through the check-out at the front. In practice, there will be some shrinkage, i.e. a small proportion of the items on the shelves will routinely 'disappear'. Only by monitoring and benchmarking these discrepancies can the management ascertain the extent to which they are due to normal errors in measurement (e.g. for goods sold loose by weight, or unrecorded instances of items being substandard or damaged), rather than deliberate theft by customers or staff.

In some cases, discrepancies may provide the key to uncovering an altogether more sinister problem, as the Lawrence Berkeley case illustrates.

ACCOUNTING FOR 75 CENTS

Clifford Stoll, an astronomer working at the Lawrence Berkeley Laboratory in California, suddenly found himself transferred to the laboratory's computer centre. He was to assist in operating the machines which carried out complex calculations for the scientists working at the laboratory. The centre had developed an elaborate system for charging the scientists for their use of computer time. On his second day in the centre, Stoll was asked to take a look into a small discrepancy (75 cents) in the way these charges had been calculated.

The discrepancy had arisen because two independent accounting systems were in place. The first was built in to the operating system of the computers themselves. The second system had been put together by vacation students over the years, and carried out more detailed analysis of the figures, and printed out the bills to be sent to the user departments. The totals produced by the two systems should have been exactly the same, and indeed this had always been the case up to now.

Such a small discrepancy was not easily explained: any errors in calculation were more likely to lead to results which diverged a lot more than this. Stoll began to investigate the cause of the mystery 75 cent shortfall. This quickly led him to the conclusion that hackers were gaining access to the computing service, and threatening the work of the laboratory. This led him into a battle of wits with the hackers, and onto a trail of detective work across the Internet in his efforts to identify the source of the attacks.

Based on Stoll, C. *The Cuckoo's Egg*, Pan, London 1991

If discrepancies are to be resolved in the accounts, it is important that this is done with proper transactions. For example, entries about which there is some uncertainty at the time may be put into a 'suspense' account. If the entry is subsequently found to belong elsewhere, it should be moved by an explicit transfer of the amount from one account to the other. Similarly, the writing off of debts or goods which are lost or damaged should always be done by means of additional transactions.

The corollary of this is that entries in the ledgers should never be 'corrected' by simply altering them directly. Packages will prevent this during normal operation, but may nevertheless contain facilities for direct editing of the ledgers, usually as a measure of last resort, in case some major problem develops which cannot be resolved in any other way. Such facilities should be barred to everyone except a select few. Even legitimate users can easily make a mistake which reduces the accounts to chaos, and absolutely no opportunity should be given to anyone who might have less honourable intentions.

Suppliers face similar problems of reconciling security and practicality in determining when and how to record material needed for the audit trail. (In accounting terms, the audit trail is not just the log of events kept by the computer. It comprises all the electronic and paper documentation needed to trace the financial aspects of a business process from start to finish.) The supplier has first to decide just how much trail information to keep on the computer (since detailed trails will eat up large amounts of storage space). The trail data must itself be protected (particularly from anyone browsing through the files in the way described in the previous section). In some instances, a printed report associated with a transaction may be desired as part of the audit trail. It is difficult to make this absolutely mandatory, since printers are prone to malfunction. On the other hand, if there is to be an over-ride facility this in its turn will need to be carefully controlled.

8.5   VIRUSES, DOWNLOADS, AND OTHER HAZARDS OF NETWORKED PERSONAL COMPUTING

Virus protection is a good example of an area where active participation by everyone at the 'grass roots' is essential. Many good anti-virus products are now available, but all of them involve a degree of inconvenience for users, in waiting while the software runs its checks, or responding to its warning messages. On no account should staff ever ignore a warning issued by the virus checking software. To do so invites disruption for themselves and everyone else in the organisation.

Computer viruses are miniature computer programs which have been designed to reproduce themselves, and to cause harm. They share many of the properties of biological viruses, but differ in one important respect, in that there is nothing 'natural' about them. They are dreamed up by programmers who, for the most part, remain unidentified. Their aim is to introduce a kind of 'germ warfare' into the world of business and personal computing.

Writing the code for a virus offers a technical challenge, like any programming. However, the added twist in this case is that the writer must produce something which can survive in systems where it is quite definitely not wanted, and still find ways of causing damage and propagating itself. There is no doubt that this represents an interesting challenge, albeit a rather warped and anti-social one.

The virus writer seeks to achieve four main aims.

- *The virus must be able to attach itself to programs in a popular format.* One of the prices paid by Microsoft for achieving dominance in the software products used on PCs around the world is that the company's products have become the main target for virus writers. There is no reason why, in theory, a virus could not be written for *any* software product. However, a virus will have no opportunity to spread if it affects software which is only used by a handful of people, especially if they never communicate with each other. Users of the MS-DOS, Windows and Office range of products are, on the other hand, constantly sending each other files on diskettes, and via attachments to emails. This makes it much easier to get a virus circulating in the user community, with a consequent 'epidemic' of infections.

- *The virus must be able to replicate itself.* Having arrived on System A, the virus will set about finding a way of getting itself transferred to Systems B and C. Network links are especially helpful for this purpose, and have been used very effectively by viruses such as Melissa and Explore.zip.
- *The virus should be difficult to detect.* For the early virus writers, this meant keeping the code as short as possible. Programs did not occupy nearly as much space as they do on today's machines, and a quick scan of the executable files could reveal any programs which had suddenly and mysteriously grown in size. The boot sector of a diskette, which has very limited space, was also a favourite place to put viruses to enable them to travel from one machine to another. Modern software has become much more extravagant in its storage requirements, and its components can be spread over several different directories, so it becomes much harder to spot a few hundred extra bytes here and there.

  Avoiding detection is part of the ongoing battle of wits between the virus writers and the providers of anti-virus software. The writers cannot avoid leaving tell-tale sequences in their code, which the anti-virus scanners hunt for. However, the writers can try to confuse things by making part of the code change slightly each time it replicates, or concealing it in obscure and inaccessible corners of the host software.
- *The virus should make itself noticed.* This may seem to contradict the previous requirement, but there is little point to the virus unless it carries some kind of 'payload'. If the victim is lucky, the virus will do no more than send a humorous or political message, or make some irritating but easily rectified changes to a document. More serious viruses destroy entire sets of files, or randomly alter the sequence of words in a text (which is tantamount to destroying it). It may interfere with the way software behaves so that, for example, a PC may suddenly be convinced that the diskette drive no longer exists. Very often the *uncertainty* surrounding the possible effects of a virus is damaging in itself. It is practically impossible to check through *all* the files held in a typical office PC to see whether anything appears to be amiss.

Protection against viruses should go further than simply installing some anti-virus software. Staff should, for one thing, be advised very firmly that the use of this software is compulsory, and that they will need to comply with other measures, including:

- *Bans on 'fun' software.* At the risk of being seen as kill-joys, managers must insist that no unauthorised software is loaded on to office machines. This includes apparently innocuous items such as screen-savers, fonts, collections of clip art, and 'helpful' additions to the operating system. The introduction of completely inappropriate programs, such as computer games or unauthorised web browsers, should be treated as a serious disciplinary matter.
- *Maintenance of back-up copies.* Back-up copies of files and some programs will be needed for disaster recovery (see section 9.4). Irrespective

of this requirement, locally held copies of all important files should be made on a regular basis, and there should always be a fall-back route for generating software (perhaps using the original disks from the supplier). Some viruses will destroy the entire contents of a hard drive within minutes, and there is no way of reversing such damage.

- *Use of central copies of software.* The file server on a LAN can be used to store 'clean' copies of commonly used software, and to keep these under especially strict protection. Users' machines are then set up so that they automatically refresh their copies from this central source on a regular basis, perhaps every time the machine is powered on. Even if a user's machine does become infected, the infection will be wiped out when it is over-written by the clean copy.

- *Restrictions on Internet activities.* A number of web sites act as distribution centres for viruses (usually claiming that this is for 'educational' reasons). Even if there is no intention to download viruses, this can happen by accident or from following mischievous instructions given on a web site. If staff need access to the Internet for their work, they should be instructed never to agree to the downloading of programs, and to put any downloaded files through a virus checker. This should apply for even the most reputable sites (the author once retrieved an infected file from an official site concerned with data security).

Viruses are the most common and widely experienced cause of data security incidents. In the majority of cases the damage caused is slight, but a combination of lax procedures and bad luck can leave a complete PC or LAN in complete disarray.

Because the concept of virus attacks is now familiar to most people, various ruses have been dreamed up to play on their fears. A common one is the email message which warns of the existence of a highly dangerous virus being circulated by electronic mail: if the user receives a message containing a particular header message, it should on no account be opened because the PC's hard drive will immediately be seriously damaged, etc, etc. The warnings are usually presented as having originated from some authoritative source, such as IBM or Microsoft or an official agency. The recipient is urged to pass the warning on to others. Most of these messages are hoaxes, devised in the hope of worrying a lot of people, and generating large amounts of pointless email traffic. Staff should be advised never to forward such messages, except perhaps to someone in the IT department who is competent to assess whether the message is genuine.

Other hazards are constantly appearing on the Internet. Some of these are malicious programs of some size and sophistication, making the original DOS viruses look very primitive. Some examples are described here.

EXAMPLES OF WORMS AND VIRUSES

Computer viruses began to appear in the mid-1980s, at the same time that sales of PCs took off in a big way. The early viruses were transmitted by diskette, and attacked the DOS operating system, which was the standard on PCs at that time. Having a widely used standard was important for the virus writers, since it created a wide user base, with people keen to exchange software. Computer games and handy DOS extensions for the office were favourite 'carriers' for viruses.

Virus-hunters face problems in cataloguing viruses, since the writers are not keen to reveal their identities. Some viruses take their name from a key characteristic, such as the 'Michaelangelo' virus, programmed to wipe out the contents of a hard disk on 6 March, Michaelangelo's birthday. A growing problem is that slightly different variants of the same virus may be found, as virus writers seek to improve on the work of others.

In 1988 the first serious attack by a network virus, or *worm*, was launched by Robert Morris. This propagated itself between UNIX systems, and quickly brought several sites in the USA to a standstill. Morris had not anticipated the extent to which a comparatively simple program could cause such havoc (the damage was estimated to be in the region of several million dollars). The incident was perhaps even more embarrassing for his father, who was a senior scientist with the National Security Agency (Hafner and Markoff 1993: 338).

By 1995, yet another new form of virus was beginning to appear. This took advantage of the *macro* facilities built into word-processing and spreadsheet products, normally intended for users to automate routine procedures for themselves. In fact, as demonstrated by Bontchev (1996), Microsoft relied heavily on macros in the basic construction of their Word product, and this meant that almost any function could be infected. Bontchev succeeded in introducing a 'benign' virus into nearly a hundred Word functions. Macro viruses were easy to spread, as they could be carried by ordinary reports and documents, which people were now routinely sending to each other by email. (The only certain defence is still to avoid the Word format altogether, and use a less 'clever' format such as Rich Text Format, which retains the typeface and layout of the original, and can be read into most word-processing packages).

In the late 1990s, virus writers developed ever more ingenious methods of attack. In particular, the Melissa virus, which appeared early in 1999, travelled as a Word macro. On arrival on the user's machine, it sent a document containing addresses of pornographic sites to the first 50 names in the user's Microsoft Outlook address book (Hancock 1999). In this case, the writer (unusually) was tracked down and prosecuted. The Bubbleboy virus works in a similar way. More devious still is the 'Back Orifice' program, which is sometimes described innocently as a 'remote administration system' – views about this depend very much on who is doing the remote administering. Once the program has been installed, it allows someone elsewhere on the Internet to send instructions to the user's PC, and activate functions by remote control. Various ruses may be employed to encourage people to download the program, perhaps the most ingenious being claims that they will be acquiring code to *protect* against Back Orifice.

Even more devious schemes for propagating malicious code can be expected in the future. *It is essential that users realise that nothing can ever be taken for granted about documents or programs taken from an outside source*, especially over the Internet.

8.6   REGULATING USAGE OF THE INTERNET

Installing a connection to the Internet, whether via a gateway which is part of the organisation's network, or through a telephone line connected directly to the PC, is now a relatively trivial task, which can be completed in a few minutes. Before authorising such a connection, management should be convinced that it is going to be useful and necessary. Otherwise it will be creating a great many hazards, to little purpose.

One available control option is the use of filtering mechanisms, which restrict the activities which can be carried out by the PC users. Initiatives in this area have come mainly from schools and parents' organisations concerned about children's ability to retrieve 'adult' material from the Internet. An example is Internet 4 Families (see Figure 8.1).

Businesses may wish to use a similar kind of screening, as a way of preventing employees from browsing inappropriate sites via the office facilities. Screening can work in a number of different ways.

- Checking can be based on category codes included in the web page headers. Standards have been suggested for such codes (the 'Platform for Internet Content Selection', or PICS). This however depends on widespread co-operation from the page providers in including the codes, which is not always forthcoming.
- Reliance can be placed on a 'filter list' provided on a commercial basis. This is a list of web addresses, which is constantly updated to include all web sites whose material the provider feels should be *excluded*. This can be compared to setting up a list of 'barred' telephone numbers in a private telephone exchange.
- Suppliers are developing 'intelligent' filters which examine incoming images and look for suspicious characteristics, such as a high proportion of flesh tones. This may trap more obvious forms of pornography, but there is always a risk that it may also object to the digitised portraits

Figure 8.1

of the board of directors urgently needed for inclusion in the annual report. Such programs must also be able to deal with the many different formats in which images can be transmitted (including video, and various forms of image compression).

- If the legitimate use of the Internet is expected to be limited to only a small number of sites, these can be specified as the only ones to be *included*.

- Filtering can also be applied to messages which are *outgoing* from the PC. Generally, the user generates a tiny amount of traffic out on to the Internet, compared with the megabytes of screen images and bits of Java code which are sent in reply. This outgoing traffic can be screened for key words in web site addresses or sent to search engines. The difficulty with this approach is in identifying 'offending' key words. Many sites use very oblique and euphemistic references to sex and violence.

Protection may additionally be sought in connection with incoming email, where unsolicited 'junk' messages can easily exceed the number of legitimate messages being received. Screening can again be based either on allowing all messages through, unless they originate from addresses in a proscribed list, or only accepting messages from addresses on an approved list. For many organisations, the latter approach is not very practicable, particularly if they rely on email enquiries from previously unknown addresses as a source of new business.

Suppliers are now also offering software which can scan emails 'intelligently'. This can avoid some of the problems of list maintenance, but its use can also raise difficult ethical questions, which are discussed further in section 13.6.

8.7 QUESTIONS

1 You are the office manager for a group of twenty secretaries and administrators. Your staff have network connections via a LAN, through which they can use the company's electronic mail services. They have no access to the Internet. Write a memorandum (approximately 500 words) setting out advice for staff on the ways they should guard against infections from viruses. Include reference to the action which should be taken in the event that a virus is detected.

2 Explain how the introduction of Computer Supported Cooperative Work may change the relationship between staff and management, with particular reference to issues of compliance and control.

3 An accounting package advertises that it contains 'all the controls which a modern business is ever likely to need', and goes on to say that 'setting up controls is fast and simple, and can be done in a few minutes by someone with no previous experience of the system'. Explain why you might have suspicions about the truth of these claims.

Illustrate your answer by describing one type of control where the product might have difficulty in living up to its claims.

4 You have just installed a new software package to support the activities of your small business, which is a small travel agency based in a city's business quarter. What restrictions might you wish to place on the following facilities in the software, and why?

- The software manual advises that regular upgrades for the package can be downloaded from an Internet web site. The address of the site is provided.
- The manual also explains how, if a customer cancels a booking, there is a command which will instantly remove all details of the customer, and the booking, from the system.

Part 4

BUSINESS CONTINUITY AND ARCHIVING

INTRODUCTION TO PART 4

Reference was made earlier in this book (in Chapter 2) to the problems of dealing with risks where potential damage is extremely serious, but probability is very low. Calculating an Annual Loss Expectancy in such cases will always yield a modest figure, which is, in itself, not too alarming. However, at the back of everyone's mind will be the thought that if the damage *were* to materialise, the effects could be devastating – perhaps even resulting in the collapse of the business.

Part 4 looks more closely at two particular instances where this arises. First, there is always a small but real possibility that something drastic will happen to the information systems, leaving the organisation unable to function. If this is a glitch which only lasts for an hour or two, it may be possible to catch up quickly on any backlog of work, and to restore customer goodwill with a simple apology. On the other hand, if the disruption looks likely to last for days, the company could soon be fighting for survival.

Business Continuity Planning (BCP) is concerned with 'thinking the unthinkable' about catastrophes which could destroy the business. BCP is not concerned solely with information systems, but they are usually high on the agenda. Efforts will need to be directed at trying to mitigate the damage from disasters, and enabling alternative facilities to be brought in to play. In the latter case, it is vital to have a Disaster Recovery Plan, which has been fully tested, and which can be activated at a moment's notice.

The second example of risks which combine high impact with low probability is found in the field of electronic archiving. A Record Retention policy should determine how long records are retained. However, if records are being stored on optical or magnetic media, it cannot be assumed that they will be readable indefinitely. It may also be difficult, after the passage of years, to prove that a record was actually originated by a particular department or individual. Perhaps only a few records will ever need to be retrieved, but if they are, they may have a crucial role in a lawsuit or a regulatory hearing. If their authenticity can easily be invalidated, the effort and expense involved in keeping them will have been wasted.

The probabilities of these eventualities is very small; but ignoring them will not make them go away. For most organisations, and particularly those with a high dependence on their information systems, BCP and electronic archiving should both be regarded as significant strategic issues.

chapter
nine

BUSINESS
CONTINUITY

SOME TOPICS ADDRESSED IN THIS CHAPTER

- How continuity planning for IT services relates to *other aspects* of BCP
- The kind of *threats* which put the entire business operation in jeopardy, and the justification of investment in counter-measures
- The cases in which it is possible to take *preventive* measures
- The desirability of having *recovery plans*, in case the worst happens. The contents and purpose of the plan
- Some particular BCP issues associated with *distributed and dispersed* systems

SECURITY AND CONTROL OBJECTIVES

- Ensure survival
- Protect secrets

9.1 INTRODUCTION

In September 1989, Hurricane Hugo devastated much of South Carolina. 18 people died, and the damage to the region was estimated at around $5 billion. A subsequent study of 41 companies in the area revealed that 23 of them had been caught without any contingency plans for their computing facilities. Of these, 20 reported that they had lost computer services for between 1 and 16 days, and the rest had longer downtimes, the longest being 4 months (Cerullo and McDuffie 1991).

In more recent years, the importance of 'disaster recovery' for IT services has been widely recognised, and it has become part of a wider preoccupation about the ability of a business to survive major setbacks of every kind. The general area is known as 'Business Continuity Planning', or 'Business Continuity Management'. It is now accepted that this needs to involve almost every aspect of the business. According to one official guide:

> Policy for BCM will almost certainly overlap with that in other areas, and care should be taken to ensure that BCM policy is compatible with other business and technical policies.
>
> CCTA 1995: 16

However, this chapter is concerned solely with the measures which can be taken to assure the continuity of IT services. These of course have to be set alongside all the many other assessments and activities which are required in planning for business continuity. At the same time, the IT elements of BCP do present some particular challenges which are not likely to arise in other areas; for example:

- It is all too easy to end up in a situation where operational and management data is lost, and completely irreplaceable. The same can happen in respect of any software which has been specially commissioned or adapted by the organisation. Few other major assets can be destroyed quite so quickly and conclusively.
- With the growth of 'direct' services to the public, the loss of IT facilities can be extremely visible, and hence very embarrassing. This in turn can quickly translate into a wave of negative publicity, and a serious loss of customer confidence.
- Even if it possible to put IT services 'back on the air', it is difficult to do this while maintaining all the checks and controls which are described elsewhere in this book. In the aftermath of a failure, management has to be concerned just as much with keeping control, as with restoring service.
- Putting BCP in place not only increases the overheads of running the IT services, but also, in some cases, comes into direct conflict with other security requirements. For example, taking regular back-up copies of data creates multiple copies of data, and so increases the problems of access control.

Undertaking BCP for every IT service is by no means a trivial exercise, and cannot be done without the wholehearted support of senior management. This does not mean that many of the ideas cannot equally well be applied at a local or personal level. Even if the organisation has BCP well in hand, it may be worth looking at individual systems in the office, and considering whether there are further measures which could be taken to minimise any disruption which might result from a more localised disaster.

9.2   THREATS TO BUSINESS CONTINUITY

BCP entails two quite distinct types of preparation. First, there is the identification of those threats which can be *averted*. For example, it makes sense not to locate a computer centre below ground level near a river which is prone to flooding. Similarly, vital electronic records can be protected by putting them on a read-only medium, so no-one can over-write them by accident. Second, there are the more intransigent threats which can never be entirely eliminated. In this case, the only available option is to assume the worst, and set about deciding what can be done to *expedite recovery* if and when the threat materialises.

In either case, the first step is to draw up as comprehensive a list of threats as possible. At this stage, nothing should be discarded as being too outlandish or trivial. Life has a habit of throwing up situations which most people would be reluctant to imagine, as in the examples given here:

SOME UNFORESEEN THREATS

- The air conditioning in a computer room consistently over-heated, and generated an excessive amount of static electricity. This caused the computer to malfunction. The problem was eventually traced to a cat which lived in the building (supposedly to catch mice). It had found a comfortable place to sleep over the hot air vent, and its hairs had fallen into the vent, partly blocking it and increasing the levels of static.
- During a police siege of the Libyan embassy in London in 1985, the entire area around the embassy was cordoned off for 10 days. Executives of a firm based in the area were unable to get to their offices, and therefore their computer files, throughout this time.
- A boiler, weighing more than a ton, blew up and projected itself like a rocket through the computer room immediately above it. The main computer and some of its peripheral equipment slid down into the resulting 20 foot square hole.
- A storekeeper was bitten by an insect while unloading a consignment of shoes from Brazil. Five days later, he suddenly attacked a computer terminal in the warehouse with a crowbar, and had to be restrained by his colleagues. He was taken to a hospital isolation unit, suspected of having been infected with an unknown illness by the insect bite.

BIS 1987

The initial exercise in 'lateral' thinking about all the possibilities needs to be accompanied by painstaking research into the location and function of the IT equipment used in the business. This will include probing some of the inter-dependencies between different parts of the IT infrastructure, particularly where networked facilities are concerned. It will be necessary to pursue questions such as: will server X be able to continue working if server Y is destroyed? Will remote access be feasible if the main PABX is out of action? From this should emerge a comprehensive list of threats, which should cover every location where IT equipment plays a significant role in processing or storing data, or routing telecommunications.

At this point it is useful to make some preliminary decisions about what can be done about each of the threats. For example, if the perceived threat is one of *loss of electrical power* to a computer, the response could be one of the following:

- Route an extra power supply to the computer via an entirely different route. This ensures that power will still be available, even if one of the supplies is damaged, perhaps by a contractor digging a hole in the road nearby.
- Install an emergency power supply, which can take over immediately if the normal power fails.
- Have an arrangement whereby the computing work can quickly be transferred to another computer in a different building.

These three options are illustrated in Figure 9.1.

Generally, the most difficult option will be to eliminate threats at their source. Unfortunately there will often be factors at work which are completely outside the organisation's control. This happened in the case of power supplies in Auckland, New Zealand (as described on page 203). Other examples would be a tanker spilling toxic chemicals on an adjoining highway, an aeroplane falling out of the sky, or a fire starting in another part of a shared building.

If a threat cannot actually be prevented, it may be possible to eliminate its effects, or at least to minimise them. Examples would include the pro-

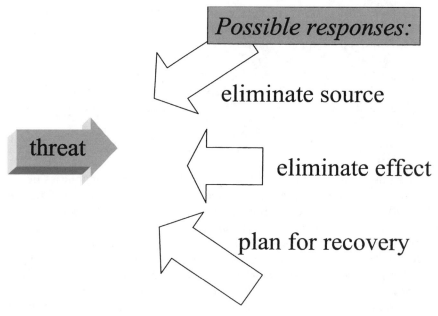

Figure 9.1

POWER CRISIS IN AUCKLAND, NEW ZEALAND

The city of Auckland is home to approximately one third of the population of New Zealand. At the beginning of 1998, electrical power was brought in to the city through five different heavy-duty transmission cables.

During January and February 1998, four out of the five cables failed. This was attributed to the effects of exceptionally hot and dry ground conditions. As a result, Auckland experienced severe power outages over a period of 6 weeks.

A subsequent Ministerial Inquiry concluded that a contributing factor was that the power company had not implemented adequate risk management and contingency planning, and that these were below industry standards.

Based on A. Carlisle in Survive! Magazine, August 1998

vision of some alternative IT equipment which can be activated immediately, or the automatic release of an inert gas to extinguish a fire.

However, if all else fails, the organisation will have to recreate its IT services, perhaps in an entirely different location. In the worst-case scenario, it could face such devastation of its premises that no other option is available. Even if the damage were only partial, the quickest way to get services back to normal might still be to make a completely fresh start. All these kind of decisions will have to be anticipated in the Disaster Recovery Plan, which is described further in section 9.5.

9.3 PHYSICAL PROTECTION OF PROCESSORS, NODES AND TERMINALS

Physical protection is preoccupied with eliminating or protecting against *sources* of possible damage. Originally, these were perceived to centre on extreme weather conditions, accidental explosions, and other infrequent but calamitous events which insurers classify as 'Acts of God'. Over the years, experience has caused businesses to add malicious attacks by humans to the list. Although it is hard to imagine in today's climate, at the time when computers were new and comparatively rare, companies frequently showed off their prestigious acquisitions by installing them where they could be seen from the street, or setting up special viewing areas for their visitors. Such an approach today would be considered extremely naïve. A primary rule for protecting any type of computer installation is that there should be nothing which advertises its existence in any way, and it should generally be as unobtrusive as possible.

Other, more explicit, steps can be taken to protect against wilful damage. Access to any major IT or telecommunications complex should be controlled by the usual methods, such as swipe cards, biometrics, or key pads beside all the entrances. Compromises will sometimes be necessary, as although the restricted areas must be difficult to get into, they must be easy to escape from in the event of a fire or a bomb alert.

Access to dispersed items of IT equipment can be more difficult to control, and is easily overlooked. This can be because computer equipment has been added as an afterthought in office space which was originally laid out for other purposes. Thus the main server for an office LAN may end up next to the stationery cupboard, just because this was the only place which could be found for it. However, this will make it vulnerable to physical damage, and to various kinds of hacker attack: note that it is irrelevant if the server's visual display unit is in a different room, since an attacker can easily plug in another one, or attach other monitoring equipment via the sockets at the back of the machine. Even if it is not feasible to make the room secure, it should be possible to surround the server with some kind of lockable enclosure.

Equipment also needs to be properly protected against 'natural' disasters. Within the office building, the most common threats are from fire and flood. Fire damage can take a number of different forms:

- The equipment itself can catch fire. This is particularly likely if wiring is carried out inexpertly, or rubbish is allowed to gather inside or beneath cabinets in which the equipment is housed.
- Storage media can be inflammable. Sherwood (1992) describes an experiment at the UK Atomic Energy Authority, where a rack of magnetic tapes was deliberately set ablaze. No other equipment was in the room. The experiment was supposed to run for 20 minutes, but had to be abandoned after 12, when the heat generated by the fire began to cause structural damage to the building.
- Heat from fire which breaks out on a floor below, or even in an adjacent building, can be enough to melt or deform magnetic media, or cause serious damage to logic chips.
- Smoke sucked into IT equipment can cause damage, particularly if it is deposited on the surface of magnetic or optical disks.
- Even normally fire-proof equipment can be damaged by an arson attack, if the attacker pours combustible materials on it, or deliberately short-circuits electrical connections.

Fire can also cause havoc indirectly, if attempts are made to douse it with foam, sprinklers or hoses. Water-based extinguishers ought never be used on electrical equipment, but in the event of a panic in an office crammed full of IT equipment this rule may be forgotten. Nor can the risk be ruled out that water will seep through following the activation of *someone else's* sprinkler system higher up in a shared building.

Floods are normally pictured as featuring huge quantities of water flowing from overloaded rivers, or other effects of heavy rainfall. However, a building can suffer just as badly from leaks from water mains, drains and sewers nearby. Internal water pipes turn up in almost any part of a building, as they route their way along walls and across ceilings to supply sinks, toilets, central heating radiators, and sprinkler systems. Unfortunately, it is often difficult to ascertain exactly where all this pipework is located. In any case, a slow leak can work its way down a building through all kinds of unexpected routes, and can accumulate to create quite serious flooding, especially if it occurs unobserved over a weekend or other holiday period.

Other natural hazards will vary with local circumstances. For example, earthquakes present a threat in many parts of the world. Many leading US computer companies have plants in 'Silicon Valley', which lies over the San Andreas fault in California. Several of them suffered disruption, together with businesses in San Francisco, when a major earthquake struck the area in October 1989 (Foremski 1989). One UK facility which is based in a coal mining area has included ground subsidence in its list of possible dangers. The possibility of exceptional weather conditions must be considered, including lightning strikes and freak conditions such as tornadoes. Even snowfall, in unusual quantities, can have disastrous effects (see account of snow damage at EDS on page 214). Ideally, all these environmental factors will be taken into account in determining the building location and design. If tremors and subsidence are serious threats, it will be helpful to build in ways of fixing equipment securely to floors and walls. However, in most cases businesses will be limited to doing the best they can with their existing premises, which will inevitably mean some compromises.

Ultimately, physical protection of IT equipment differs little from that for most other types of asset. Planning in this area should always be in close cooperation with those responsible for physical security in the organisation as a whole.

9.4 PRE-EMPTING DISASTERS

The second line of defence for IT systems is to consider whether, especially if the damage is limited, it is possible to continue running the system without any ill effects. Elimination or avoidance of the effects of damage calls for some form of 'safety net'. Extra equipment and error management software are installed, which cut in when trouble occurs. Ideally, this will happen seamlessly, so that users will not even realise that anything is amiss. In practice, it may not always be possible to achieve 'instant' recovery, or there may be a noticeable degradation in the quality of the service.

Failures can of course occur in software as well as hardware. Most PC users have had direct experience of system 'crashes', where the screen freezes, leaving the user to figure out what best to do on the basis of an enigmatic message about pointers and memory limits. Various software products are available which claim to make systems 'crash-proof'. In fact, as Halfhill (1998) points out, a better solution is often to minimise the amount of software which is installed or which is running at any one time, and to follow a few other basic rules of good system housekeeping. Achieving 100% availability is rarely, in any case, a priority for the average office PC.

For larger systems the position may be quite different. If the system is crucial to the enterprise, error recovery from whatever cause will be taken very seriously: a case in point is the UK National Lottery. On Wednesday and Saturday afternoons, prior to the main prize draws, queues form at the 27,000 terminals around the country. To lose service to any of these terminals will result in a substantial loss of revenue, and upset a great many customers and retailers. The lottery has therefore invested heavily in extra equipment to enable it to survive as many as possible of the failures which might affect its system, including power losses, crashes of processors or disks, and telecommunications failures (Partridge 1994).

To be assured of instant recovery generally requires three key ingredients.

- *A duplicate facility.* This could be a processor, a disk drive containing up-to-date copies of files, a power supply, or a communications line. The facility may be invoked very rarely, so it is vital to make sure that it will work if and when it is needed. It is like carrying a spare wheel in the back of the car: if a motorist has a puncture late at night on a deserted highway, this is not a good time to find that the spare is unusable.

  Checking can either be carried out through regular tests of the equipment, or can be built in to the way the system works. For example, dual-processor systems (which are commonly used in computerised telephone exchanges and for supermarket check-outs) can take it in turns to be the 'master' processor for a day at a time. During this time the 'slave' machine mimics every activity, so that it is always ready to take over immediately. The following day, the roles are reversed. If one component is 'shadowing' another in this way, each must be as independent of the other as possible. There is little purpose in having two processors if they share, for example, the use of a crucial and fault-prone component, such as a power unit or network interface card.

- *Integrity following the cut-over.* No procedure is truly 'instant', and so there is always a risk that when a duplicate facility takes over, it will not be in exactly the same state as the original. This can mean that some data will be lost 'falling through the cracks', or the system is left with transactions which cannot be completed properly. Addressing these problems calls for some sophistication in the design of software which is, after all, being activated in less than ideal circumstances; for example, it may have to run on a failing processor which does not 'die' suddenly, but suffers a series of intermittent faults. Software designers have two basic options: one is to retrace the steps taken by the software, until a point is reached where everything should be in order. The software is then re-started. This is known as *backward recovery*, and can be compared to the facilities used by human operators of some word-processing packages, whereby it is possible to 'undo' commands and keystrokes. The alternative is *forward recovery*, which involves clearing the decks and starting again. In terms of the word-processing analogy, this is like restarting the word-processing package, and reloading the last saved copy of the work in progress. Generally, it is extremely difficult to design software capable of preserving integrity under every possible set of circumstances. In order to help in sorting out any discrepancies which do emerge, it is essential that the system should provide good diagnostics at all times, and keep a detailed log of all faults, and the exact time when they occur.

• *Feasibility of repairs.* If the system is closed down for maintenance on a routine basis, any faulty items can be repaired or replaced at the next available opportunity. For systems which operate round the clock, the situation is not so simple. Instant recovery only makes sense if it is feasible to make repairs 'on the fly'. Otherwise, users will still be inconvenienced, although there may be some choice about the timing of the disruption, and they can be given some advance warning.

Running repairs will only be possible if this has been allowed for in the design of the equipment. For example, technicians must be able to gain safe access to all parts of the assembly, without disturbing any of the equipment which is unaffected, or having to switch off common power supplies.

It pays to look closely at what *exactly* is expected to happen if and when a failure strikes, and this can be illustrated by looking at two particular instances (power supplies and disk drives) in more detail.

9.4.1 Power supplies

The arrangements which might be made by a business trying to cover every eventuality are shown in Figure 9.2. In normal operation, power is fed in through from the top left, via Normal Power Supply (1). If this source fails, but the electricity utility is still sending power over the public grid, the equipment draws its power from Normal Power Supply (2).

The Uninterruptible Power Supply (UPS) unit (on the right) is constantly monitoring these external supplies, and if they have *both* failed it cuts in immediately. However, the UPS depends on a bank of batteries, which will be rated to maintain the power for perhaps 15 or 30 minutes. The UPS therefore provides no more than a breathing space, during which the back-up generator is started, and takes over for as long as necessary until the normal power is restored.

The objective is that the computing equipment should receive a steady supply at all times. The UPS must be in a position to cope with all kinds of unpredictability in the external supply. For example, during severe storms in the west of England in 1990, companies suffered from supplies which kept cutting out and coming back for short periods (Collins 1990). A good UPS will smooth out all the fluctuations, even if they turn out to be extremely short-lived. Since computer equipment often monitors the power situation for itself, and its response to transient power drops will usually be to shut itself down, it is vital that the UPS is ahead of it, by being even more sensitive to changes and quick to react.

Normal Power Supply (1)

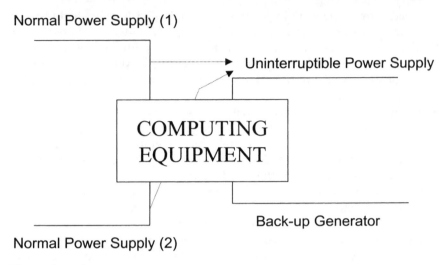

Uninterruptible Power Supply

COMPUTING
EQUIPMENT

Back-up Generator

Normal Power Supply (2)

Figure 9.2

Regular checks will be required on every aspect of the stand-by power system, for example, to ensure that the UPS batteries are holding their charge, and that the generator is capable of working properly and has fuel in the tank. Larger UPS systems generate a good deal of heat from the batteries, and so some special cooling arrangements may be needed. The capacity of the back-up supply should also be included among the matters to be reviewed if new computing equipment is installed, to ensure that it will be able to cope with any increased demand which may be placed on it.

9.4.2   Disks: mirrors and shadows

PCs typically depend on a single disk drive with a capacity of a few gigabytes. Larger systems use multiple drives, not all of which may be the same; for example, data which is being archived may be written to slower and cheaper devices, such as WORMs ('write-once, read-many' optical drives).

Protection against component failures is only likely to be considered for data which is regularly in demand. There are three different ways of approaching this, which are illustrated in Figure 9.3. This shows a considerably simplified picture, where a processor can store data on any one of three disks. There are two files, A and B, each of which is assumed, again for simplicity, to contain just two records.

The simplest method of duplicating file A will be to write it in its entirety to *both* of the disks in the same unit (unit 1, at the top of the diagram). Alternatively, a copy might be sent to an entirely different disk unit (unit 2), which could be in a completely different location. The first option will be easier and cheaper to implement, but the use of a separate unit in the second option makes the arrangement much more resilient.

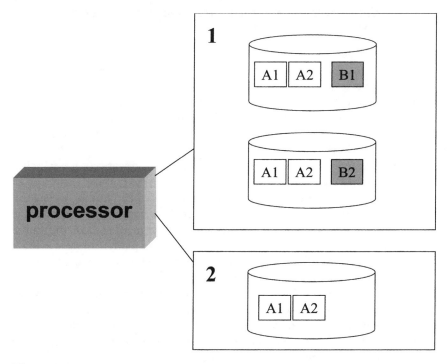

Figure 9.3

Creating copies, especially if they are kept at a remote site, is known as *mirroring* or *shadowing*.

A third possibility is shown, using file B. Again, the file has just two records, but this time the records are split across two drives. This is known as *striping* the data. Striping makes little sense when applied to just two records, but it is an integral feature of RAID storage systems, where RAID stands for Redundant Array of Independent (or Inexpensive) Disks. RAID systems contain large numbers of disk drives, with data being striped across all of them (not necessarily as individual records, but in whatever way the RAID unit's control system chooses). RAID suppliers have devised sophisticated ways of managing the data, to help ensure access even if failures occur in individual drives.

RAID has become popular not just for its resilience, but because it can deliver extremely good response times for writing and retrieving records. Suppliers have developed a wide range of systems, many of which combine the benefits of *both* striping and shadowing (Brackenridge 1993). It is therefore possible to have the best of both worlds – performance and resilience – though usually at a premium price. Users should bear in mind that in the event of a serious disaster, the contents of the individual disks will be largely meaningless, and the data can only be pieced together again with the help of the proprietary RAID software, and the tables which it maintains.

9.5   CREATING AND IMPLEMENTING THE DISASTER RECOVERY PLAN

Schweitzer (1996: 112) quotes an information system manager who was asked to produce a copy of the Disaster Recovery Plan as part of a site inspection. He responded by saying: 'We don't have an emergency plan *because we have never had a disaster.*' This perhaps sums up the private view of many managers. Why bother with the trouble and expense of a DRP? There has never been a need for it in the past, and there is every chance that it will never be needed in the future.

There is a small, and dwindling, number of organisations for which a DRP is unnecessary; the members of this rare breed make little use of information systems, and work on long sales and production cycles. All organisations should at least review whether they need a DRP. Once the case for a plan has been made, senior management must take the initial steps by resourcing the work needed to develop the plan, and approving a definition of those services to be covered by the plan, as being absolutely essential for the organisation's survival.

If some or all of the IT systems are outsourced, recovery procedures must be covered by the outsourcing agreement. Even then, the actual process of recovering from a disaster will need the collaboration of *both* parties, and the DRP should set out which responsibilities belong to the organisation, and which to the outsourcer.

A DRP needs to contain the six key ingredients shown in Figure 9.4. The first two entries are underlined because they refer to assets which, once lost, may be impossible to replace. Everything else on the list can be bought, begged or borrowed from elsewhere. What the organisation will find itself unable to buy on the open market (and indeed, would not wish to) are the details of last month's sales, and the experience and expertise of its staff.

Figure 9.4

The DRP is a plan for action, and so it should concentrate on practical issues such as how people are expected to make contact, what they should do, and where they will find things. At the height of an emergency, staff will not be interested in reading the finer points of policy. The structure should be modelled on the best examples of guides issued to owners of a new car or computer, providing all the essential reference material with good indexing, and giving simple explanations of the procedures to be followed.

Copies of the plan should be issued to everyone who is likely to play an important role in implementing it. Staff should be encouraged to take copies home, so that they will be available even if their offices are rendered inaccessible. This implies maintaining a circulation list and a systematic issuing of any updates; otherwise, confusion will result from people trying to implement different versions of the plan.

Some measures will need to be put in place on an ongoing basis. For example, regular back-up copies will have to be taken, and stand-by facilities will need to be tested.

Let us consider each of the ingredients of the plan in turn.

1 *People.* There are strong reasons for insisting that the person who draws up the plan should *not* be the person who takes charge if and when it is put into effect. First, the author of the plan should assume that it will be necessary to spell out *all* the roles and responsibilities of staff, including those of the person who is going to be running the recovery operation. This ensures that nothing in the plan depends on information known only to the author, thus avoiding problems which could arise at the crucial time if it turns out that the author has left the company, or taken a holiday. Second, it is likely that if a disaster threatens the entire future of the business, the chief executive will want to take direct control anyway.

   Similarly, the procedures defined in the plan should not assume that named individuals will be available. In the event, they may prove to be uncontactable, or could have suffered injury or even death from the effects of the disaster. This does not mean that names should be avoided in the plan – indeed, names and home telephone numbers will be an important part of it; but, wherever possible, stand-ins and deputies should be identified.

2 *Data and software.* It should be assumed that the disaster will destroy all copies of data and software which are held on the organisation's premises. This raises numerous questions about where back-up copies should be held, and how they should be kept up to date.

   The simplest approach to keeping back-up copies of data is based on 'generations', as illustrated in Figure 9.5. On 1 January, a back-up copy of data is made onto tape A. A week later the back-up is made on tape B, and a week later tape C is used. At this point, the installation has three back-ups. Only one of these is up to date, but in the event that anything should happen to it, the other two are available as 'long-stops'. At

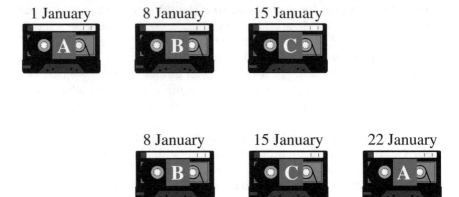

Figure 9.5

this point, the tapes start to rotate, so that on 22 January tape A is re-used, and becomes the most current copy. This ensures that at any given time there will always be three generations of tape: an elderly 'grandparent', a younger 'parent' and a new 'child'. To improve the chances that at least one copy will always survive, the tapes are all stored in different locations. This could mean using other buildings belonging to the organisation, or a commercially operated secure vault service.

In practice, data back-up strategies need to be a little more sophisticated than this, for a number of reasons.

• Since full back-ups often involve huge amounts of data, it can be easier to work with *incremental* back-ups. These contain only the *changes* to data which have been made since a previous back-up. To re-create the data in its entirety, it is necessary to start with one full back-up, and add back all the incremental back-ups which have been made since.

• Other copying procedures may be in place for other purposes; for example, records may be regularly removed from the 'live' files on the main computer disks, and put into some form of archive. It may be assumed (perhaps quite wrongly) that the archiving provides protection against disaster. If the archives are not protected, they too must be included in the back-up plans, since they may be needed for legal reasons, or to assist with audit, or for long-term analysis required for management decisions.

• When data is live on the system it will be subject to the kind of access controls described in Chapter 4. The data must continue to be protected once it is on the back-up tape (which will usually mean placing strict restrictions on the situations in which the tape can be used), and it must be possible to re-create the data in an exactly equivalent form on another system, so that the access controls will continue to work. Particular care must be taken to transfer files complete and intact, if they have been subjected to controls based on hashing or encryption.

In some cases the backing up of data seems pointless; for example, reference data used in planning or design work may have been obtained from external sources, making it easy to replace. Duplicate copies of some datasets may be held on the system, to serve different groups of users, or to improve system performance, and making duplicate back-ups of these seems excessive.

In a large installation, it may be worth the effort of sifting out such data. One way of doing this is by ranking it by 'criticality'. Toigo (1996: 167) defines data with high criticality as that which supports vital business functions, or is required for legal or audit purposes, or which comprises proprietary information and trade secrets. Low criticality data, which occupies a lot of storage space in some organisations, can then be ignored.

Software usually accounts for much less storage space, and so there should be no problems in backing it up in its entirety. Particular attention must be paid to critical software, i.e. that which is unique to the business, and which handles core activities like inventory management and accounting. Nevertheless, it pays to make software back-up as comprehensive as possible, to avoid being caught out by inter-dependencies between programs, which are not always obvious. For example, a package may need to make use of data-compression utilities, without which it will be unable to open its files.

3 *Premises.* If the existing computer facilities are a mass of rubble, where do you go? This question should have been considered long before, and the answers incorporated into the DRP. To ensure availability, the alternative premises should be a long way away, increasing the chances that they will be unaffected by any wider disaster which may have engulfed the original site. However, this will slow down the recovery, as it will take longer to transfer staff, and any materials which have been salvaged.

4 *Processors.* Decisions about processors are closely linked with decisions about premises. Generally, stand-by sites can be grouped in three categories.

(a) *Mutual.* Agreement is reached with another site that space and computing power will be set aside, and will always be available in the event of a disaster. The idea is that the two parties each operate similar systems, but always allow for a certain amount of spare capacity, so they can, if necessary, provide back up for each other. This is an attractive option for two sites within the same organisation, especially if they are run as part of a single IT department. The situation can be more complicated if separate organisations are involved. Each party has, after all, to fund spare capacity for the other's benefit, and it may be difficult to agree exactly how this should be paid for. Tensions may also arise because the installations, even if they were very similar initially, may need to develop in different directions in terms of their equipment or software.

(b) *Warm or hot stand-by.* A hot stand-by site offers facilities which closely match those available in the organisation's own installation. This includes all the necessary power, cabling, telecommunications, air conditioning, and a complete set of computer equipment.

A site which offers more basic facilities may be known as a 'warm' site. Here the expectation is that not everything will be immediately available, but plans will have been put in place to bring in and activate whatever is needed within a matter of hours. Very few organisations can afford the luxury of either a hot or a warm stand-by site of their own, and this is a field for a few specialist commercial providers, who cover their costs by charging annual fees to subscribers. Even then, the small print of the agreement may state that there is no guarantee that the site will be available when needed, as in the case of snow damage at EDS.

SNOWSTORM DAMAGE AT EDS, 1993

In 1993, Electronic Data Services (EDS) had a computer centre in Clifton, New Jersey, which supported a network of more than 5,000 Automated Teller Machines. During blizzard conditions in March of that year, so much snow accumulated on the roof of the building that it caved in, putting the computer centre out of action.

EDS had an agreement for 'hot' stand-by with a commercial disaster recovery company nearby. However, the contract stipulated that facilities would be provided on a first-come first-served basis, and they were already being used by a firm affected by a bomb attack in New York some weeks earlier.

EDS was therefore obliged to purchase space in another building, and organise the transfer of the equipment from its Clifton site. The equipment had to be dug out of piles of snow and debris, and cleaned and checked over before being re-installed. The process of setting up the new site and attaching the necessary telecommunications lines took 2 weeks.

Unofficial estimates put the costs to the affected banks at around $50 million. Apart from the adverse publicity, processing fees had to be paid to competing financial institutions for cash withdrawals made through rival ATMs while the computer centre was inactive.

Based on Menkus 1994

(c) *Cold stand-by.* A cold stand-by site (sometimes called a 'shell' site) offers no more than space in which the computer service can be rebuilt from scratch. It will have adequate power supplies and some rudimentary telecommunications links, but little else. It will be up to the client to borrow or buy in processors, disks, and printers, and to arrange for any extra telecommunications links which are required.

Variations on this theme described by Barnes (1999) include a retail bank which ran extra power and telephone cables into the staff canteen, so that this could be their cold site, and a scheme devised by a London publishing company, whereby a property agent undertook, for an annual fee, always to identify three vacant sites on his books which would make suitable cold sites, and which would be instantly available on a six-month lease.

5 *Telecommunications.* Provision will need to be made for ordinary telephone lines (including any needed for use with telephone-based order entry or enquiry services which are being relocated). The DRP should also specify the numbers and types of connections which will be needed for data links to other parts of the organisation, for example to sub-offices or warehouses, as well as for external services, such as links for EDI and email via VANs or the Internet. If the organisation operates its own web site, it may find the best solution is to arrange that a mirror copy of the site can quickly be activated using the services of a commercial Internet web site provider.

6 *Supplies.* Sometimes the simplest things are the easiest to overlook. However, no computer system can run without basic supplies such as ink cartridges, paper for continuous and sheet-feed printers, and plenty of blank tapes and diskettes. Foresight in this area may play a big part in maintaining the confidence of customers and suppliers, for example, if the organisation can continue to send out letters and cheques on its own preprinted stationery.

The exact form the plan takes will depend on factors such as the size of the organisation, and its priorities. Useful check-lists and templates to help with the development of a plan are provided in CCTA (1995) and Toigo (1996).

When a disaster strikes, it will be difficult to predict what will happen in the first hour or two, since so much will depend on the time and the circumstances. However, the recovery plan should be activated as quickly as possible, following the sequence shown in Figure 9.6. When an IRA bomb devastated several buildings in London's financial centre in 1992, the managing director of one of the worst affected companies, Commercial Union, convened a crisis meeting at his home within 40 minutes. The damage was so extreme that CU had no option but to activate its DRP immediately.

If the damage is only partial, the disaster assessment stage may be more difficult. Clearly, there is no point in directing everyone's energies into moving to a stand-by site, if there is a reasonable possibility that the original site can be brought back into service. However, once it has been decided to implement the plan, there should be as little doubt as possible as to which part each person is expected to play.

The only way to be confident that the plan will work is to have subjected it to testing. Effective testing will probably be unpopular. One Californian company instituted tests which were held randomly at weekends. Employees were required to respond as if the test were the real thing, even if this meant abandoning a much-cherished visit to the ski slopes or the beach. Only by introducing this degree of realism can the gaps and glitches in the plan be discovered; for example, staff telephone numbers may be found to have changed; or technical problems may emerge when

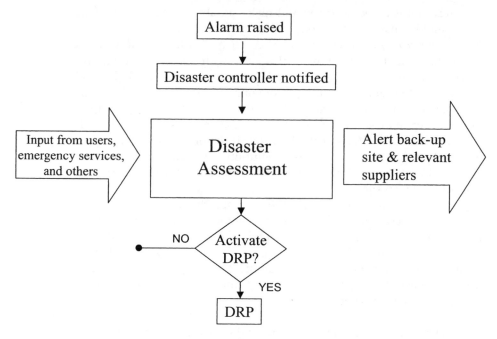

Based on Computer Disasters and Contingency Planning, Amdahl Executive Institute, 1990

Figure 9.6

software which runs perfectly on the 'home' machine does not do so when transferred to another, apparently identical, one. This may be due to license protection checks which have been built into it, or access controls which apply to the data it uses. The test will also reveal any items which have been forgotten about; for example, contractors' telephone numbers or email addresses which turn out to be needed, or simple tools to carry out running adjustments and repairs.

Where possible, equipment and software suppliers should be involved in the testing, also without advance warning. If a cold stand-by site is to be used, it may not be feasible to check out much of the actual rebuilding of the system. It should nevertheless be possible to check whether all the relevant suppliers are contactable, and whether they hold stocks of the items which would be required.

9.6   IMPLICATIONS OF THE PROLIFERATION OF IT

The procedures laid down in the Disaster Recovery Plan will cover all the programs and files which are kept at the heart of the organisation. Ideally, these will contain everything of significance which has been captured or generated in remote offices. In practice, there will always be some locally held materials which have not been absorbed into the central information systems in this way.

In some ways, the existence of local files in electronic form is an advantage. Previously, documents might be lost through the destruction of a filing cabinet in an explosion or fire, and the only possible protection would be through massive amounts of precautionary photocopying. Electronic records can, in contrast, be backed up in a few seconds, and stored away on a single disk. A local office does not need to draw up a full Disaster Recovery Plan, but it should put some basic measures in place, using the following principles.

- *Ease of compliance.* The simplest option is to take copies of absolutely everything. It is quite feasible to take full copies of every disk of every PC on a regular basis, using a tape streamer or high-capacity diskette drives. But, as in the case of virus checking, this will only be effective if everyone's compliance is assured. There may be a reluctance to bother with back-ups if it involves procedures such as plugging equipment into the back of the machine, and searching for the right screen icons to activate it.

  The process of saving files should be automated, to the extent that it is reduced to selecting a menu option just before shutting down the machine, or is even triggered automatically on a daily basis. If the PC is attached to a LAN, the back-up copy can be sent to the LAN server, and the servers' files can then be backed up en masse. If the PC is portable, it may need to have its own back-up storage device. Increasingly, back-up services for PC files are becoming available on the Internet, although in this case care will need to be taken to ensure that any sensitive files are properly protected.

- *Text and voice messages.* As well as files which are directly under users' control in the office PCs, there may be copies of incoming and outgoing messages which are important to the work of the department. These may comprise EDI messages, electronic mail and voice mail. It will be useful to check which, if any, of these are actually held on the office server. If they are kept elsewhere, it will be worth enquiring what provision has been made for these to be recovered in the event of a disaster.

- *Availability of tools.* Occasionally employees may be required to work with sensitive information. In a traditional office, they might be required to ensure that all the relevant papers were kept in a specially secure cabinet. It is important that equivalent facilities are easily available to people carrying out such work electronically. For example, the organisation should make it easy to acquire and install extra access controls and back-up facilities for individual PCs, particularly if these are portable.

9.7 JUSTIFYING INVESTMENT IN MEASURES FOR BUSINESS CONTINUITY PROTECTION

The selection of measures to protect business continuity (BCP) should be based on an appraisal of all the risks, costs and benefits, using methods such as those outlined earlier in this book (see Chapter 2). These methods will not be applied in quite the same way, however, as for many other types of security risk. Generally, the risks being considered in BCP have less to do with technology, and more to do with wider issues. Some of the differences which set BCP apart from other aspects of information security are as follows.

- *Many of the threats under consideration are not specific to IT.* This means that there is often a wealth of experience from people working in other fields, and that there may be relevant statistics going back long before IT was invented. Examples are natural phenomena, such as patterns of severe weather and the effects resulting from it.
- *BCP covers the whole enterprise, not just IT.* This means that IT assets may need to be considered alongside other entirely different types of assets, and that the methodologies being used for analysis will have to conform with those chosen by the BCP project team.
- *BCP will be looking beyond the organisation.* If disaster strikes a whole region or community, recovery will be impeded by a lack of public services and competition between companies for facilities which are in short supply. It may be difficult to obtain reliable information about what is happening, or to establish who is in charge. Reflecting on experience in Canada, Newton and Pattison (1998: I12, 1) note: 'Actions on the part of elected officials or response agencies can shift the locus of control away from senior corporate executives to the myriad of organisations responsible for emergency management in your area. Simply put, your management no longer "calls the shots" for the recovery of your business at that location.'
- *Countermeasures relevant to BCP can often be tested.* As has been seen in previous chapters, it is almost impossible to verify whether, in the event, an electronic wallet or an Internet firewall is going to be sufficiently resistant to attack. However, BCP issues often centre on more mundane questions, such as whether a wall is fire-proof, or a roof is strong enough to take a given load. The Disaster Recovery Plan, too, can be thoroughly tested simply by pretending that a building is unusable. This contrasts with the uncertainties associated with other forms of security testing, where it is necessary to guess how talented hackers might launch their attacks: this depends on an assumption that resident experts or a 'tiger team' of tame hackers can identify all the possible threats.
- *BCP is concerned with the preservation of assets*, and so it is not too difficult to reduce the estimates of possible damage to a cash figure. In contrast, with issues such as privacy or the integrity of messages, which are every bit as important, it is difficult to quantify the benefits which are being provided by security measures.

Most of the factors listed above have the effect of making calculations for BCP feel more 'mainstream' and familiar (at least to accountants). However, the very large scale of potential losses, and the very low probabilities which are often associated with them, take calculations into problematic areas which have been discussed earlier (see section 2.4).

In considering the impact of a major failure, the possible consequences can be classified under two headings: *direct* and *indirect* losses.

DIRECT LOSSES

Destruction of buildings, equipment and furnishings
Loss of revenue from services
Additional payments to employees and contractors

Direct losses are usually insurable. Payments from the insurance company will undoubtedly help to soften the impact of a disaster, but they should never be regarded as a substitute for recovery planning. Insurers are understandably reluctant to underwrite any losses which cannot be defined clearly in advance. They will provide cover for the replacement of equipment, or for compensation to be made in defined circumstances, but beyond that the exclusion clauses start to become very extensive, or dramatically higher premiums will be demanded. Restitution for direct losses will anyway be of little importance, except perhaps to the company's creditors, if the net result of the disaster has been that the company could not continue trading and has been forced into receivership.

The most important losses to be considered are therefore those which are *consequential* or *indirect*.

INDIRECT LOSSES

Loss of confidence by customers, employees and shareholders
Loss of market reputation and market share
Breaches of regulations or legal requirements
Penalties payable for late or non-delivery
Loss of data leading to loss of management control

Indirect losses tend to be intangible and difficult to quantify. They will often exceed the direct losses by a wide margin, and will continue to be felt for a long time after the disaster is over. For example, a study of the share prices of 15 firms which survived disasters showed that it took an average of around 50 days for the share prices to get back to the level they had been prior to the event (Knight and Pretty 1997). A low share price may seem to be a rather distant problem for a company to have, but it could have a very real effect on the company's efforts to recover, for example, by making it more difficult to secure lines of credit.

The quantification of possible losses may be based on a *business impact analysis*, in which direct losses are categorised as having a *hard* impact and indirect losses a *soft* impact (CCTA 1995). Soft or indirect impacts will

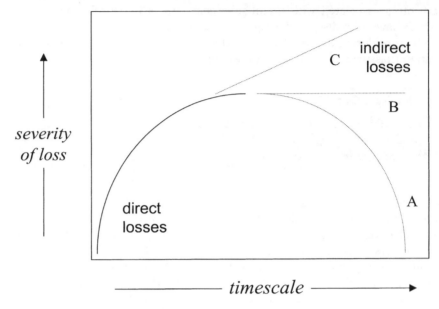

severity of loss

timescale

Figure 9.7 Possible patterns of loss following a disaster

tend to take longer to develop, and will have a longer lasting effect. An initial assessment may show impacts in one of the forms suggested in Figure 9.7. In all cases, initial direct losses will be severe, but compensation can be sought through insurance.

It is what happens later which will really determine the fate of the organisation. If the disaster has destroyed the only copies of vital records, the losses may escalate, as shown in line C. If records can be recreated, but only by laborious processes such as keying them back in from other sources, the organisation will face a protracted period of high overheads, as shown by line B. The aim should clearly be that costs return quickly to their normal level (line A) through the implementation of an effective recovery plan.

9.8   QUESTIONS

1 Identify an important computer installation in your place of work or study. Identify five *physical* threats to the installation, and rank them in order of seriousness. In each case, decide whether any counter-measures would be feasible, and if so, select *one* which could be implemented at reasonable cost.

2 Read the following memorandum carefully. What illogicalities and inconsistencies does it contain?

To all staff from the Chief Executive Officer

Ashley Towers: Disaster Recovery Plan

I am pleased to announce that the bank has reviewed its procedures in the event of a computer disaster, and these have been documented in our Disaster Recovery Plan.

The documentation will be kept in my office (on the fourth floor of Ashley Towers, above the main computer room). The plan will also be available on-line on the employees' electronic noticeboard.

In the event of a disaster, back-up facilities will be provided by arrangement with Cadle & Co, on the seventh floor of Ashley Towers, who use computer equipment which we believe to be similar to our own. We shall be asking for volunteers to assist in testing these arrangements, by simulating the conditions of a disaster at 10.00 a.m. next Saturday morning. All our main suppliers have been contacted and have agreed to help with this exercise.

You are reminded that if you hold crucial data on your desk top computer, you should take regular diskette copies, and keep these in a place where they can easily be found.

Should a disaster affect the Ashley Building out of working hours, may I remind computer staff that they should ring the number of the computer room help desk right away.

3 Draw up an outline of a Disaster Recovery Plan to cover the loss or destruction of your own personal computer. Make a very rough estimate of the costs you would incur if you were to make all the preparations required by the plan, including the equipment and materials you would require, and the cost of your time.

4 'Business Continuity Planning is of interest only to pessimists and bureaucrats'. Discuss this proposition in a short essay (600–800 words), indicating whether you agree or disagree.

5 Explain why, in some circumstances, the creation of back-up copies may make it more difficult to achieve the objective of keeping commercially valuable information secret.

chapter
ten

CONTROLS FOR
ARCHIVED DATA

SOME TOPICS ADDRESSED IN THIS CHAPTER

- The implications for organisations of increased dependence on *electronic archives*
- Reasons why electronic records created today could prove unreadable in the not-too-distant future
- Steps which can be taken to ensure the *integrity and authenticity* of records, with the passage of time
- The definition and implementation of a *record retention policy*

SECURITY AND CONTROL OBJECTIVES

- Authenticate over time
- Ensure survival
- Prove authorship
- Prevent tampering

10.1   INTRODUCTION

Computer systems encourage the hoarding of data. An inspection of the hard drive of a typical personal computer will reveal hundreds of files, many of which will remain there for the lifetime of the machine. Disk space is now so cheap that there is little incentive to weed out the material which is no longer wanted. All the immediate preoccupations of daily work also divert attention from the kind of planning and housekeeping which is needed to keep files in order. As a result, the files slowly become disorganised, and the process of finding a document becomes a matter for much head-scratching and hunting around with key word searches.

All this wastes time for the business, although the impact is rarely very serious; nor is this a particularly new phenomenon – hunting for 'lost' documents is, after all, a time-honoured activity in connection with box files and filing cabinets. Electronic media may encourage a proliferation of files, but this is compensated for by the availability of powerful search tools. The problems of congestion and proliferation of files are not, ultimately, a reason for worrying about reliance on electronic media for the long-term storage of records.

The more serious problems associated with computer-generated records are more fundamental, and are likely to become more apparent over the next few years. There are some uncomfortable parallels with the way the world initially welcomed the advent of nuclear energy. It was seen as a clean and inexpensive power source. Only when the costs of reprocessing spent fuel and decommissioning reactors became clear did questions began to surface about the *overall* economic viability of nuclear technology.

Today, cost cases for computer systems tend to concentrate on the way the technology will affect the day-to-day operations and working practices of the business. Extra revenues from improved order processing, or cost savings from reduced paperwork, are duly balanced against the investment costs for new equipment and software. The economic and other consequences of having to retain records over long periods are rarely considered. This overlooks some major advantages of the old-fashioned paper systems: that paper files, once filed away, comprised a record which would not fade away, and which anyone could read and understand. In many cases, the record also contained evidence of authentication, since people had signed or initialed the document, or had made notes in their own handwriting. Paper provided all these features automatically, at low cost.

These simple and obvious properties are not available in many forms of electronic file, so becomes necessary to find ways of building them back in. Unfortunately, it is not obvious how far this process needs to be taken. Computer storage media are based on technologies which have all been invented quite recently. No-one can be quite sure how long the magnetic and optical patterns recorded on them are going to last. There has to be some uncertainty as to whether equipment to read today's disk formats will be available in the future. The data can of course always be copied to new media, but how will disputes about the authenticity of the copy be settled? Indeed, how will those interrogating any digital data in the future be able to check if it is authentic?

Failure to preserve and authenticate records adequately could result in substantial costs later, since the records may be needed for the business to prove its case in response to a law suit or the attentions of a regulatory body. Apart from all the commercial implications of records proving unreadable or unreliable, many researchers and public archivists are also concerned at the way information about the functioning of business could become lost to future generations.

10.2   OBSOLESCENCE OF SOFTWARE AND MEDIA

The diaries of Samuel Pepys, with their vivid description of life in London in the seventeenth century, are held in six leather-bound volumes in a college library in Cambridge, England. Providing that they are not exposed to extreme conditions of heat or damp, paper records of this kind can provide a record which will survive for many hundreds of years. Indeed, Pepys's diaries are young compared with many other historic books and documents, paper-making having been established early in the previous millennium, and commercial paper-making having been established throughout Europe over 200 years earlier (Guild 1999).

One interesting feature of Pepys's writing is that, although the text survives, it is not at all easy to interpret. Pepys used a contemporary version of short-hand invented by Thomas Shelton. Needless to say, this has little in common with short-hand in use today, and so the interpreter of Pepys's writing also needs to have access to a copy of Shelton's guide to his short-hand method, published in 1642 (Latham 1987).

A similar problem could confront a researcher of the future, trying to read a magnetic or optical disk. As Rothenberg (1995) has pointed out, there is nothing self-evident about what is contained on a digital storage device such as a CD-ROM. Every disk contains a long stream of bits, and before being able to interpret them it is essential to find out some additional information: for example, how files on the disk are indexed, and whether they are encoded as text or images.

This may seem to be of little practical concern in today's world of almost-identical PCs, when an IBM-compatible CD-ROM can be read by any suitably configured machine. However, that is a temporary situation. Let us suppose that archive data is committed to a CD. Someone who is trying to read the CD in 10 or 20 years' time could face three basic problems.

1   *Software conventions and standards.* Software is constantly developing, as suppliers upgrade their products, and persuade their customers to discard the older versions. Suppliers have a vested interest in ensuring that any files created by an older version continue to be readable by the new one, to avoid costly file conversions and to keep their customers 'locked in' to the same product range. So, for example, every market-leader word processing product is able to read back-level files. Depending on the company's marketing strategy, it may also provide a facility for reading files which have been produced on the software packages of its rivals.

This flexibility in reading files is, however, provided for just as long as the supplier regards it as expedient. No supplier can afford to keep supporting all file formats indefinitely, even in generic packages which sell in their millions. For more specialised packages, such as those used in accounting or medicine, the cost constraints are much stronger, and it is rare for support to go back beyond the immediately preceding version.

The net result is that the chances of being able to read an out-of-date file correctly are constantly diminishing. In order to understand a file, we must have a program which can interpret it (the equivalent of Thomas Shelton's guide to short-hand). The trouble is that the program in question may have long since been withdrawn from the market. Indeed, so may the machines for which it was written. The problem is compounded by the fact that not everyone uses market-leader products, and anyway the market leaders change over the years. Thus companies such as Apple and Amstrad have, in the past, shipped successful ranges of office machines running their own proprietary software, using diskettes formatted in ways incompatible with the dominant IBM standard. Software companies, too, have fluctuated in their ability to set the standards used in PC software. For example, back in the era when PC software was driven through the keyboard rather than by mouse, Lotus dominated the spreadsheet market, word-processing was predominantly WordPerfect, and database was pioneered by dBase IV.

Although less visible to the average user of the office PC, exactly the same situations have occurred in respect of larger systems. Suppliers of mainframes, for example, regularly give notice that support for certain older versions of their software will be withdrawn on a certain date. After that point, the software may continue to run quite happily, but it is living on borrowed time. If problems arise, perhaps because of conflicts between the old software and some new facilities the supplier is introducing, the purchaser is left to sort them out as best he can.

2 *Obsolescence of hardware.* New generations of hardware appear every few years, and the pace of change shows no sign of slackening. The changes affect both the computers themselves and the storage devices they rely on. The ability to keep on using a processor is closely tied to the operating system which it depends on. The DOS operating system, which was introduced with the first IBM PC, has survived through several generations of chip technology, so that most DOS programs can still be run today. However, other operating systems have not lasted so well. For example, DOS originally vied with another operating system called CP/M (Steffens 1994). CP/M has long since vanished from the scene, along with other proprietary operating systems used on business-oriented machines such as the Commodore Amiga. In the early 1990s, IBM attempted to take the PC market along a route based on its OS/2 operating system, tied to processors using a feature called Micro Channel Architecture. This battle was eventually lost to more conventional PCs running Microsoft Windows.

Diskettes have also changed in design and format. The early standard was based on a $5\frac{1}{4}$ inch diameter diskette in a floppy casing, which could store 360 KB of data. The $5\frac{1}{4}$ inch diskette became widely used, and remained a standard throughout the 1980s. Yet anyone coming across one of these diskettes today would have a hard time finding a machine capable of reading it.

Again, parallel changes have been observed in the world of mainframe computing. Magnetic tape has long been the traditional medium for archiving, but formats and designs have changed radically over the years. Better magnetic coatings have been developed, so that it has been possible to pack more data onto a given surface area. Large 10-inch reels have given way to more compact cassette systems, and similar problems have arisen: the tape and its data may be in perfect order, but a machine capable of reading it may only be available in a science museum.

3 *Deterioration of media.* The final set of doubts about optical and magnetic media concerns their ability to retain information accurately over the years. The main attraction of these media (their ability to hold data at very high densities) also proves to be one of their weaknesses. Damage to just a small area of a surface can render quite a large amount of data unreadable. Recording techniques try to compensate for this, by adding extra coding to detect and correct errors. Unfortunately, these cannot cope with serious damage, for example where a disk or tape has been exposed to a strong magnetic field, weakening the signals stored on its surface, or a sharp object has pierced the fragile plate of an optical disk, which is little more than a millimetre thick.

Additionally, these media are apt to deteriorate over time. It is difficult to make accurate predictions, since manufacturers are improving the quality of their products all the time. In the 1980s, the US National Bureau of Standards suggested that magnetic tapes should be regarded as having a life of 20 years (Saffady 1993). The music industry has already experienced problems with tape recordings made in the 1960s, some of which are now unreadable (Beacham 1996). Optical disks have not been in existence very long, and most figures for their longevity are based on extrapolations from stress testing in laboratories. Manufacturers clearly expect that optical disks should last for 100 years or more, but are more cautious when it comes to giving warranties (Arps 1993).

10.3   REQUIREMENTS FOR ARCHIVING OF BUSINESS DATA

Public archivists seek to preserve records so that historians of the future will be able to build up a complete and balanced view of events. Commercial organisations preserve records out of enlightened self-interest – either because of some requirement imposed upon them by law, or because they want to be sure they will have the evidence to hand if arguments should ever develop over questions of fact. Organisations in the public sector can find themselves caught by all these requirements, as they undertake many of the functions of business, but will also be expected to contribute records to the public archives.

Most countries require organisations to retain records of their business activities for specified periods of time. A common example is records relating to tax liability. Minimum time periods for retention are set down in legislation and tax codes, which are usually linked to the time allowed for either party to challenge the tax assessments which have been made. This has the advantage that after the set period of time has expired, the information can no longer be used in proceedings, and so it loses its importance.

A tax regime will specify different time periods for different situations. Thus the US federal tax system requires that accounting records should be held for 3 years after the date of the relevant tax return, but this is extended to 6 years if the taxpayer has seriously understated income or the return is in any way fraudulent (Williamson and Marcum 1998). In the UK the Inland Revenue is barred from raising its assessments after 6 years have elapsed, although if fraud or negligent conduct has occurred this increases to 20 years (Taxes Management Act 1970). Different rules apply for different forms of taxation, so the company may have to develop quite a complex retention policy to ensure compliance.

Many organisations will want to keep accounting and administrative records for much longer periods, because of the nature of their activities. In some cases, this will mean keeping records over the lifetime of a client. This is particularly evident in health care, where patients accumulate records 'from cradle to grave'. These records can have legal implications many years after the event, as one Health Authority found when a patient was permitted to sue for wrongful diagnosis of a spinal tumour, some fifty years later (Anon 1998b). Other examples of businesses keeping long-term records include those dealing in mortgages, life assurance, pensions, property, equipment leasing, or products where there are long-term health and safety issues, such as aircraft and pharmaceuticals. It is also prudent for organisations of all kinds to retain records in certain areas, such as records about past and present employees, and those who have worked for them as contractors. However, retention of people's personal details may be covered by data protection legislation requiring that any information no longer relevant to the organisation's needs be deleted. Specific guidance on just how such judgements should be made is not always very forthcoming (see section 14.4).

Companies may find that they have, perhaps unwittingly, incorporated assumptions about paper-based documentation into their articles of association. For example, in 1996 Rolls Royce plc adopted a number of changes to reflect the introduction of the CREST paperless share trading system in London. The company articles previously allowed the destruction of any transfer instrument 6 years after its registration. This was extended 'to enable the Company to destroy any *electronically generated or stored* information arising from the transfer of uncertificated securities' after a 6 year period (Rolls Royce 1996).

10.4 AUTHENTICATION OF ARCHIVED FILES AND DOCUMENTS

If Alice wants to send Bob an authenticated document over a data network, she will put the document through a hashing algorithm and add a digital signature, using her private asymmetric key (see section 6.6). Authentication of archive material works on exactly the same principles. In authenticating an archive record, however, Alice is not communicating with Bob over a network, but sends the message on a journey through time. Bob will not be checking the credentials of the message within the next hour or day, but at some future date (maybe many years from now). The two situations are illustrated in Figure 10.1.

An example of a case where authentication of archive records is important can be found in the research laboratories of a pharmaceutical company. Traditionally, researchers would collect their notes and reports at the end of the week, and have a witness sign and date them. Authentication of the records in this way has to be company policy, in case it ever needs to prove to the US Food and Drug Administration exactly how its research has been conducted (Wayner 1999). If researchers are generating the research data electronically, it makes little sense to print it all out simply to enable someone to sign a paper copy. Instead, the company can use an electronic approach to authenticating the data.

The method is based on 'time stamping', which works as follows. Suppose that a company wishes to be able to prove that an electronic document was produced on or before a certain date, say 1 June 2001. It puts the electronic record through a hash algorithm (exactly as if this were a network message to be protected against tampering); however, in this case

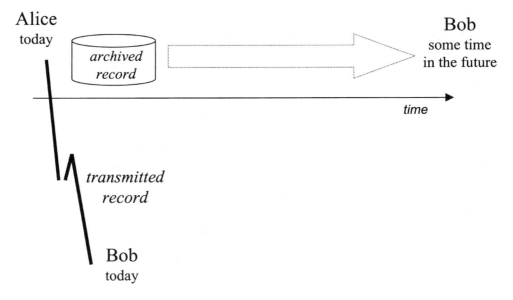

Figure 10.1

the hash is used differently. It is put 'on the record' in a way which links it directly with 1 June 2001; for example, it is printed in the personal columns of that day's edition of a newspaper, or included in some other document circulated widely at the time. Alternatively, it can be given to an independent third party, who makes a record of the hash and the date of its receipt. Companies prepared to offer this service for 'notarising' hashes are already in existence. If further security is required, the archived records can be encrypted and/or digitally signed, just as for network messages.

In the event of any dispute concerning the dating of the record, the processes can be reversed, with the evidence being linked back together to show that the contents were as claimed on that particular date. The procedure is illustrated in Figure 10.2. Time stamping is simple and effective for individual records and files. Using it on larger collections of data is technically feasible, but a great deal more difficult to administer. Problems arise from the need to keep the data in exactly the same form as it was when it was hashed. This means that no parts of it can be deleted, and if it is copied onto a different recording medium, there must be no incidental changes in the way the data is structured or encoded. The removal or alteration of just one bit will change the hash dramatically (this being the way the hash algorithm is intended to work) and invalidate the whole exercise.

An alternative approach is to maintain an electronic log of everything which happens to the files. If the log is kept entirely separately, it can be used as part of an audit trail to check whether all the data has been

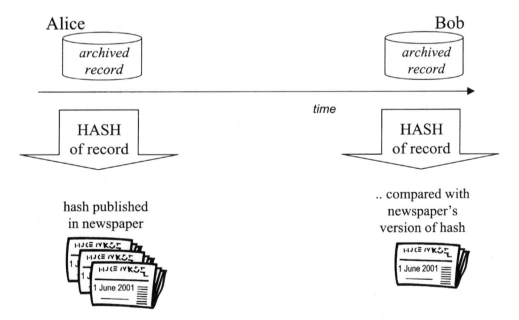

Figure 10.2 **Digital time stamp**

created in ways which are properly authorised. Unfortunately, a closer look at the implications of this reveals that this, too, can quickly become an administrative nightmare. This issue has been extensively debated in respect of medical records. A patient may typically be treated by a number of physicians, and each of them will want to be sure that the record is correct – even if a long period elapses between one clinical consultation and the next. It is also useful to be able to check back to see who was responsible for a particular test or diagnosis.

In the UK, a draft standard for patient records in primary care included the requirements shown here.

AUDIT AND ACCOUNTABILITY

Each patient medical record file shall be supported by an audit trail which records details of all additions, updates, deletions and viewings of those records;

The use of audit trail records shall allow a means of viewing or reconstructing any individual patient medical record throughout a day as it was on any previous day.

NHS Draft Requirement for Accreditation v 5, 1999

Here again, the problem is not so much whether suppliers would be able to deliver a system with these features, as whether users would be able to maintain it. The audit trail records, for example, will include user IDs which will be meaningless without supplementary tables to connect them with real people: to show, for example, that 'DR05' is actually Dr Raj Singh. Furthermore, the table must give full details and be *exactly as it was at the time*: otherwise it could be that Dr Singh has since moved on to another surgery. Since then, it may even be that the same ID of 'DR05' has been assigned to his successor. Without extensive corroborative evidence (which will need to be stored alongside the audit trail) any attempts to 'reconstruct' records will quickly fall apart. All these problems may be compounded by the fact that, as mentioned earlier in the chapter, the version of the software which was used to create the records has since been superseded, and is no longer available.

There is one final challenge facing anyone who tries to lay down an archive which can be authenticated over long periods of time. Protection has to be based on the hashing and cryptographic techniques available today, but it is inevitable that these will appear primitive to the cryptographers (and hackers) of the future. It must further be expected that anyone in, say, 2025 who wishes to falsify a record from 2001 will have access to computers which are staggeringly fast by today's standards. The problems of trying to anticipate what form attacks on encryption may take some years hence are reviewed by Schneier (1998), who concludes that 'like it or not, cryptographers have to be futurists'. Unfortunately, this is another area in which there can be no firm or reassuring answers. Wrapping up data in a lot of apparently secure cryptography is like putting papers into an iron box, in the knowledge that there is every chance that eventually the box is going to rust away.

10.5 RECORD RETENTION POLICIES

In the electronic era, organisations will have to decide which records to save, *and* what kind of technology should be used to save them. Even if they already have a well defined retention policy based on paper records, they will not anticipate many of the situations which can arise with electronic storage – particularly if many of the core business records are being *originated* electronically, as often happens as a result of exercises to 're-engineer' business processes.

Electronic records are much more malleable than paper ones. They are easily edited, copied, and exchanged over networks. A text may go through a series of revisions by several authors from different departments, maybe working thousands of miles apart. The 'final' version may be printed out to be sent to others outside the organisation, but ironically the paper version is the one thing that nobody wants to preserve.

If the company is making use of EDI or email, then it will also be processing perhaps hundreds of messages a day. Each of them is equivalent to a piece of paper – an order form, an acknowledgement of receipt, the agenda for a meeting – which would normally be stored, at least for a time. Some of these messages will need to be retained, in connection with accounts, contracts and compliance with regulations. Others, such as emails advising everyone of a new staff appointment or the revised opening hours of the canteen, can be treated as disposable.

Emails can be written and widely circulated on the spur of the moment, which opens the way for all kinds of pitfalls. The problem has been summed up by Skupsky:

> When individuals communicate via electronic mail, they often utilize 'loose' language that may be appropriate for internal conversations but would be totally inappropriate for formal written documents. Some people use verbiage that reflects personal opinions or biases, believing that electronic mail is personal and private. Court cases have now confirmed that electronic mail is neither personal nor private.
> Skupsky D. S. 'Establishing Retention Periods for Electronic Records',
> *Records Management Quarterly*, April 1993: 40–9

Emails have featured in a number of legal proceedings, particularly in the United States. In June 1999, for example, Microsoft was obliged to release a number of internal emails in anti-trust proceedings concerning the marketing of its web browser software. The emails revealed how Microsoft staff discussed ways of rebutting some of the allegations which had been made against the company (Anon 1999b). It has also been held that electronic mails can be a 'public record', and should not be destroyed (as in the case of emails circulated in the White House). In the UK, emails making unfavourable comments about a rival company were circulated by the employees of a health insurance company. The emails formed the basis of a libel suit, which was settled out of court, with the payment of substantial damages (Nelms 1999).

The case of electronic mail highlights the difficulty of defining the 'documents' to be covered by a document retention policy. As business applications make greater use of voice and video technologies, the diversity of document types will increase. It will no longer be enough to specify what the documents are about; account must also be taken of the precise form in which they are stored.

A retention policy should therefore cover three main areas.

- *Definitions of documents covered by the policy.* This may be by reference to their subject-matter, or authorship, or to the nature of possible future requirements (e.g. papers which may be relevant to litigation). Definitions should use precise terms wherever possible (e.g. 'records of children under 17 years old' rather than just 'records of children').
- *Rules covering the time periods for retention.* These should indicate both the period of time, and the date from which the period runs. For example, is it the date on which a record was created, or the date on which it was last updated? The rules should also make clear whether records *may* be destroyed after this time, or whether they *must* be (as required by some data protection legislation).
- *The medium on which the record is stored.* In current policies, this is presumed to be sheets of paper. Some policies will refer specifically to binders or cards, or other human-readable media like microfilm. In future, a great deal more will have to be included under this heading, to specify how magnetic and optical files are to be held, with allied procedures for making authenticated copies onto new media as and when necessary.

An example of policies suggested for the UK National Health Service is shown here. A comprehensive guide to UK legal requirements for the retention of business records is published by the Institute of Chartered Secretaries and Administrators in London, and is updated periodically (most recently in 1997) (ICSA 1997).

RECORD RETENTION IN THE UK NATIONAL HEALTH SERVICE

The following indicates the outline of general advice issued to managers in health authorities in the UK. The authorities all have similar requirements, making it easy to adapt the advice to each one's individual needs. The kind of issues covered by the advice are described briefly below, as they are likely to be relevant in almost any retention policy.

1 *A review of relevant areas of legislation.* In this case, most of the requirements flow from obligations imposed on all government bodies under the Public Records Acts. The advice draws attention to instances where there are exceptions to the general rules (for example, in respect of some patient records) and indicates where the law allows discretion to be exercised.

2 *Guidance on how records are to be selected for retention.* In some cases this is quite precise (e.g. one set of the annual accounts and statements, as submitted to the Secretary of State). In others, the advice is more general, for example, 'key records' relating to building and engineering works. In several instances, the advice includes an explanation of why the records may be required, perhaps for research purposes, or for possible use in legal proceedings. Some advice is quite categorical, such as 'records which are evidence of title must never be destroyed'.

3 *Guidelines on lengths of time for retention.* This reviews cases where the definition of records and their associated retention periods requires some explanation, often because the time period may vary with circumstances. For example, certain records have to be retained for 20 years after an illness has ceased, but only for 8 years if the patient has died. Notes are also provided on computerised records, including: 'the question of re-recording may have to be considered as equipment becomes obsolete.'

4 *A detailed list of requirements for retention over specified lengths of time.* The final section lists the retention period for each type of record, grouping them under three main headings (financial; stores, equipment and buildings; and health).

Based on Preservation, Retention and Destruction of Records, Responsibilities of Health Authorities under the Public Records Acts, HC (89) 20 Department of Health, London, 1989

10.6 QUESTIONS

1 You have been given a tape cassette which you are told contains a copy of the text of the instruction manual for a new piece of equipment which has just been installed in your factory. You have no other information. What else would you need to know in order to be able to read and interpret the information on the tape?

2 Activate the word-processing package on a PC, and take a look at the options which it provides for (a) reading in files created by back-level versions of the software, and by software from other suppliers, and (b) creating files which can be read by *other* word processing software. (Hint: a look at the Help screens concerned with converting files may be a good place to get started). Make an assessment of *why* you think the supplier has provided this particular mix of conversion capabilities.

3 A company has generated a diagram on its computer system, which it intends to use as part of a patent application. It wishes to be able to prove that it was created by Professor Baffle on a particular date, and would like to be able to store it electronically in a form which will be unintelligible to hackers. How should it set about achieving these aims?

4 Devise and document a simple record retention policy for a computer system with which you are familiar (for example, your own PC, or the office accounting system). Pay particular attention to records which might be needed as evidence, or for reference, some years from now.

When you have drafted the policy, make an honest appraisal of the extent to which you think you would be able to motivate yourself to adhere to it. From this, identify two or three key disincentives which are likely to impede the implementation of well organised record retention in a typical organisation.

5 A Life Assurance company has a file listing all the details of its customers' accounts, including the premiums they have paid in the current year. This file is held in electronic form on a disk drive.

The company wishes to make an archive copy of the file, with a view to using it as evidence of the state of the customers' accounts, if there are any queries or challenges at some future date. What steps would you recommend in order to ensure that the company will be able to prove that the file was created on the date claimed, without being changed or added to since?

Part 5

COMPUTER
AUDIT

INTRODUCTION TO PART 5

Auditors, like many other professionals, easily fall prey to the idea that they are being misunderstood by the rest of the world. They are seen variously as financial detectives, whose main mission is to sniff out fraud, or zealous control freaks, obsessed with the enforcement of rules and regulations. Appointments with the auditors may be looked forward to with the same enthusiasm as a trip to the dentist.

Part 5 is mainly concerned with the role of Computer Auditors. They may sometimes have a slightly different job title, such as IS Auditor, or Internal Auditor (Computer Systems). However, the idea of having a 'Computer Auditor' has taken root in many organisations, and this designation is used throughout Part 5. The description provided of computer auditing aims to lay to rest some of the lingering suspicions which surround it (for example, that it is a magnet for geeks with autocratic tendencies). In fact, a skilled and enthusiastic computer auditor can pre-empt many types of problems, and help deliver cost savings from improvements in systems' stability and control.

Strictly speaking, auditors only advise and comment. If action is required, this should be taken by management in the normal way. In theory, the recommendations of a Computer Auditor will be implemented by someone with specific responsibilities, perhaps an IS Security Officer. However, it is not always feasible to allocate responsibilities in such a clear-cut way, and Part 5 looks at some of the relationships and compromises which develop in practice.

A further chapter is then devoted to the emerging field of Computer Forensics. This is concerned with ensuring that evidence gathered from information systems is accurate, and valid as evidence. This can require a great deal of painstaking effort, especially if no hint of the investigation is to be given to the person suspected of wrongdoing. Such investigations may seem, in the popular mind, to be the bread and butter of audit work, but in practice they are relatively rare. Overall, it is hoped that Part 5 will provide a useful guide as to what computer auditors *really* do.

chapter
eleven

COMPUTER AUDIT: THE INTRODUCTION OF NEW SYSTEMS

SOME TOPICS ADDRESSED IN THIS CHAPTER

- Defining the *role and status* of a computer auditor
- The part played by a computer auditor in *selecting and developing* systems
- The extent to which the computer auditor should play an active part in *coding* and *design* work
- Aspects of systems *testing* and the *cut-over* to a new system which should be of particular concern to a computer auditor

SECURITY AND CONTROL OBJECTIVES

- Maximise auditability

11.1   THE ROLE OF THE COMPUTER AUDITOR

When companies first began to move their core accounting systems onto computers it quickly became apparent that some traditional approaches to auditing simply would not work. Processes that previously relied on forms and memos were now being hidden 'under the covers' of the computers. In order to check on exactly what was happening, it was now necessary to consider the logic of the programs running inside them. Conventional auditors were unsure about how they should deal with the new technology, which lacked any of the user-friendly features taken for granted today, and which could be quite baffling for the non-technician. In response, a new type of specialist emerged, known originally as an EDP auditor (for 'Electronic Data Processing'). EDP was a term associated with early mainframe systems, and as computing spread and diversified it became more appropriate to change the name to 'computer auditor'. The term 'IS auditor' is also sometimes used.

True 'audit' should be carried out by someone who is completely independent of those who are responsible for installing or running the systems, and this status is assumed in the chapters which follow. It is not uncommon for people to describe themselves as doing 'audit' work when undertaking various kinds of checks and surveys; or technical staff may be assigned to do 'computer audit' work on behalf of the internal audit department, even if their usual reporting line is elsewhere. If the audit department is small or under-resourced, this may indeed be the only option available.

Ideally, corporate governance will be best served if computer auditing is made an integral part of the internal audit function, and carried out under its direction. This sets it firmly within a wider framework of internal controls, which will in turn be subject to review by the external auditors.

In practice, those who take up the role of computer auditor have usually moved across from jobs in programming and systems design. They have often started out with only a rudimentary knowledge of the rules and methods of audit, but by working within the audit team they have acquired these skills through practical experience. Meanwhile, they will have helped to develop the tools and procedures needed to deal with the audit of systems based on new technology.

The field of computer audit has continued to develop apace, but much uncertainty remains as to whether computer audit can actually be regarded as a career or profession in its own right. For it does not make much sense in the information age to have *any* kind of auditor who feels unable to deal with at least the basic aspects of computing. This has been recognised by the professional accounting bodies around the world, who have steadily introduced more IT-related elements into their curricula. However, it is still extremely difficult to be thoroughly proficient in *both* audit and IT, particularly when it comes to keeping abreast of constant innovations on the technological side. It is therefore likely that audit teams will still need to co-opt and train people whose expertise is primarily technical.

IT has had a big impact on the work of both internal and external auditors, but the designation of 'computer auditor' is usually reserved for those working in the internal audit team. Firms providing external auditing services have taken to hiring and training large numbers of IT experts, partly to help in developing their thriving sidelines in consultancy. Because external audit is a very competitive business, it has also come to depend heavily on computer-based tools, which help to improve the efficiency with which the audit can be planned and its results analysed and presented. Auditors working in these areas may nevertheless not see themselves as being *computer* auditors in any particular way. This is partly because they take it for granted that nowadays that they will have to deal with computer systems for the great majority of their clients, and partly because the law and the accounting profession define very clearly what must be achieved in a public audit – having a purely 'computer' version of it does not make much sense.

External audit can be traced back to the closing years of the nineteenth century, when accountancy professional bodies were founded in several countries, and governments began to make audits compulsory, as a way of protecting the interests of shareholders. The focus of external auditing remains the publication of the report and accounts at the end of each financial year. The emphasis is on providing reassurance for shareholders that their resources are being used efficiently, and confirming that the information in the published accounts is untainted by fraud or error (Sherer and Kent 1983). This requires that the workings of the client's accounting systems are fully understood, but at the same time the external auditor will often have to rely on checks and controls which have been set up and vouched for by the internal auditor. Pressure of time and resources make it difficult for external auditors to investigate security and control mechanisms in any real depth.

Internal audit is, by comparison, a much younger profession. The Institute of Internal Auditors in the USA, for example, was founded in 1941. The role of the internal auditor has evolved in a pragmatic way, responding to the need felt by organisations, particularly the larger ones, that they should have some way of checking that rules and procedures were being properly followed. This could best be done by making it the responsibility of a person or department who worked slightly apart from everyone else, and who could provide an independent view. This independence might be reinforced by having the auditors report directly to an audit committee (although the efficacy of this has been questioned (Wolnizer 1995)). Alternatively, internal audit may have a more conventional reporting line, usually to the director of finance. In the worst cases it may be little more than a token presence, based on a barely visible and very part-time responsibility assigned to some unfortunate person in the accounts department.

Internal audit is predominantly concerned with financial transactions, but can extend to other areas of administration. Its role is not defined by legislation, and so organisations are free to set it up with whatever remit they prefer. They may, for example, decide that the auditors should be involved at the very earliest stages in the selection and design of new systems, and expect them to contribute to all the subsequent stages, right through to final implementation. In other cases, they may wish the auditors to be more self-effacing, and give advice only as and when requested. It is not essential that auditors should be involved in all systems projects, only that they are involved in the *appropriate* way in the *relevant* projects. The implications of this are discussed in the sections which follow.

Internal auditors have long been viewed with some suspicion by other employees, being assumed to have a 'policing' role, particularly in respect of sniffing out fraud. However, one leading textbook (Venables and Impey 1991) suggests they should have at least four other responsibilities:

- the prevention and detection of errors;
- eliminating waste (from causes such as poor planning and control, and lack of care of assets);
- ensuring that management reports are based on accurate and reliable information;
- checking on compliance with relevant legislation.

Internal auditors cannot expect to operate in all these areas without encroaching on other people's territory. For example, management accountants are concerned with generating reports, and most managers see it as their responsibility to attack waste, particularly if they are involved in fields such as operations management or quality assurance. Good internal auditing is based on a sense of collaboration between all the various parties, with the auditor resorting to a more confrontational line only when things go seriously adrift. An interesting feature of the responsibilities in the list above is that they all involve some requirement to check up on the integrity and security of information systems. Hence the *computer* auditor role fits here quite naturally.

The way computing features in internal and external audit is summarised in Figure 11.1. As Figure 11.1 implies, the Computer Auditor will be a useful point of contact with IS experts in the external audit firm. She

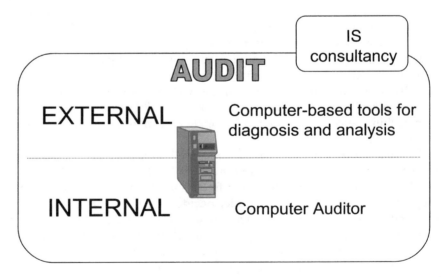

Figure 11.1

will be able to assist in extracting data from systems, in running tests on the external auditors' behalf, and finding any technical documentation (such as program flowcharts) which they require. If the organisation is running systems which operate internationally, she should also be able to provide a co-ordinated view of the network, and of any automated controls which apply across national boundaries. Many external audit firms also have a consulting arm, which will be eager to help in implementing new controls and countermeasures. This can raise delicate ethical questions as to whether the audit is being used as a 'fishing trip' for consultancy business. Again, the expertise of the auditor may be useful in deciding whether such consultancy will be useful.

11.2   AUDITING OF SYSTEMS DEVELOPMENT

The demise of custom-built or 'bespoke' software has been predicted from time to time, particularly by suppliers of packaged solutions, but there continue to be many situations where businesses prefer to take this route. For example, a government department may have to implement a system in accordance with the rules and legislation which apply uniquely in that country, or a business may have set itself an objective of creating a unique service to outclass its competitors. Custom-built software is often large in scale, and crucial to one or more of the core activities of the organisation. It is therefore desirable that questions concerning its auditability, and the control mechanisms to be designed in to it, should be debated at an early stage.

Two different views can be taken as to whether the computer auditor should be involved in these early stages. On the one hand, early involvement should ensure that all the appropriate controls are incorporated as part of the basic design, and do not have to be 'bolted on' later as an afterthought. Since any additions and changes tend to get progressively more expensive as a software project proceeds to its later stages, this suggests that early intervention by the computer auditor should help to keep the development costs down. On the other hand, if the auditor becomes very closely involved with the project, it may be difficult for her to preserve her independence and impartiality. She may find that attitudes within the development team are rubbing off on her: for example, the team may set great store on meeting deadlines, bringing about an atmosphere in which risks are more likely to be accepted and short cuts taken.

A study of internal auditors in a leading US company suggests giving them a 'participative' role in projects significantly increased their job satisfaction (Allen 1996). This enjoyment of a 'hands-on' role is just as likely to apply for computer auditors. In the process of contributing actively to design and development, however, there is a real danger that they will lose objectivity when it comes to probing system weaknesses at a later stage, particularly if the quality or suitability of the built-in controls is being called into question.

Whatever the involvement of the computer auditor is to be, it is important that its scope is defined at the outset, and agreed by everyone

Table 11.1　Computer auditor responsibilities during System Development Life Cycle (SDLC)

SDLC stage	Areas of involvement for computer auditor
Initiation	Review security needs, investigate alternatives, and prepare proposals for preferred alternative
Requirement specification	Provide definition of security requirements, determine how quality assurance is to be applied to the development of security features
Design	Specify security features in more detail, and suggest methods for testing their effectiveness
Construction	Assist in developing software features, oversee initial testing, and ensure that features are properly integrated with the rest of the software
Implementation and testing	Carry out final tests on security features in individual modules and in the integrated system. Ensure that all security and control measures are fully documented

Adapted from Hayam and Oz (1993).

concerned. Mitchell (1995) suggests that projects should be put in one of four grades, where the lowest grade denotes projects of little sensitivity, with little or no input from auditors being required, and the highest grade implies regular and continuing involvement. In the latter case, decisions should be made about which meetings the computer auditor should attend, which circulation lists to include her on, and so on.

Agreement should also be reached on which aspects of the development are to fall within the computer auditor's terms of reference. A list of possible areas of responsibilities is given in Table 11.1.

11.3　NON-TRADITIONAL APPROACHES: PACKAGES AND END-USER COMPUTING

With in-house software development, the computer auditor at least has an option of taking part in the design and coding decisions which could affect security. However, most of the recent developments in the software industry have conspired to take this option away. Instead, the computer auditor is faced with having to make evaluations from some distance away, and not always from a very good vantage point.

At one extreme, there is the 'take-it-or-leave-it' nature of commercially produced packages. These may claim to include facilities for access control, back-up generation, encryption of files and messages, and so on.

Verifying these claims is extremely difficult, because most suppliers regard the innermost details of their products as proprietary. The computer auditor will not be able to examine the source code, as originally written by the programmers, because the product will be shipped in the form of 'object' code which is ready to run on the machine. Similarly, there will be no program flowcharts to refer to, except perhaps a few at a very superficial level produced for marketing purposes.

At the other extreme there are the 'do-it-yourself' programming tools which can be used to create simple applications on a PC, such as Visual Basic and Java. There are also numerous options for 'customisation' built in to packages such as word-processors and spreadsheets. This hotch-potch of activity is sometimes categorised as *end-user* computing. This option can prove particularly tempting for departments who are frustrated by delays in central programming services, and who want to put together some simple tailored facilities. The risks are particularly high if the end-user approach is applied in sensitive areas, such as adding front-end facilities to a database of personal information, or setting up web sites accessible to the public. Unless they take steps to control the situation, businesses are wide open to the hazards of dependence on programming created by enthusiastic amateurs. The computer auditor's ability to control these developments will be minimal because, in the majority of cases, she will be blissfully unaware of them.

Between the two extremes are a number of other options, most of which raise just as many problems of control. Software packages may come with some modules which are standard and others which are 'tailorable' to meet the needs of the customer. Additions or extensions to existing software may be commissioned from outside programming contractors (who might be teleworking in another location altogether, maybe on a different continent) or from students doing work experience. There are also countless pieces of code in circulation via Internet sites and the give-away CD-ROMs on magazines, which claim to provide useful business functions. Much of the rigour which could be enforced quite naturally through centralised programming departments has all but disappeared. Computer auditors now have to develop strategies for ensuring that all information systems developments, even those which at first appear to be of very little consequence, are brought within their jurisdiction.

Some of the other issues which can confront the computer auditor include the following:

1 *Requirements creep.* This happens when those who are commissioning the software start to change their minds about what they want it to do. It is a common problem in in-house software development, but in that case the consequences, though expensive, can be resolved by revisions to the software specification. Attempts to alter an off-the-shelf package are likely to be even more expensive, besides undermining most of the advantages which will have been used to justify taking the package

route in the first place. An example is the ill-fated TAURUS project, which began in 1988 with the aim of computerising the London Stock Exchange. Having decided to base the system on a package from Vista Corporation, the project team started to realise that substantial changes would be needed to adapt it to reflect UK rather than US trading practice. Drummond (1996: 102) describes the problems thus:

> The alterations were a problem. The Vista Corporation was not a software house but an enterprise with one ready-made product. Accustomed to making minor alterations only, they were ill-equipped to perform the wholesale rewriting now required by the Stock Exchange.

From the point of view of integrity and security, modifications to packages give rise to a no-win situation. If the vendor is operating in a small niche market, the resources to make major changes are unlikely to be available (as in the case of Vista). If the product serves a much larger market (for example, small business accounting or EDI messaging) the selling price will have been reduced considerably by economies of scale, and faults and errors should have been shaken out by the early users. Even if the supplier is willing to provide modifications, this will now be at higher charging rates normally associated with bespoke systems, and with every possibility that new errors will be introduced.

2 *Kite marks and standards.* Suppliers may cite various standards in respect of the quality or security of their products. An example is the ISO 7498 series of standards relating to data security. (Details of some of these standards are given in chapter 14). Two considerations should be borne in mind before placing reliance on these. First, some standards may not be particularly relevant. For example, a number of types of security feature can be rated on scales from A1 (excellent) through C2 (minimal), as laid down in the 'Orange Book' (see section 14.3). However these are ratings which are mainly relevant to secrecy protection in centralised systems. They do not provide any guarantee, for example, that the system will be able to resist virus attacks, check messages for tampering, or carry out other functions which may be wanted in a commercial environment. Second, the rating can only give some idea of the *potential* capabilities of the product. If the security features are not actually implemented in a competent way, any quality ratings the product may have will quickly prove irrelevant.

3 *Facilities for security administration.* Once installed, security administrators will need to update user authorisations from time to time, and computer auditors will want to consult audit trail information. If interaction with the system proves awkward, or the documentation is obscure, the use of these facilities will be inhibited. It may also be indicative of weaknesses in the overall design. With a package, it should at least be possible to see a demonstration of the facilities concerned on a live system, and to ask other sites whether any problems have been

encountered. With end-user computing, it is unlikely that the authors will have given much thought to the security or audit implications of their programming efforts, which may even turn out to undermine controls previously in place.

4 *Integration with existing software.* This is an issue which will concern those who will have to install the software, but it also has implications for internal control. Packages will have their own conventions in respect of features such as the maximum permitted password length, the timing out of inactive users, or the taking of incremental back-ups. End-user programs may have no such conventions, or rely on those of standard products. This is a particular problem if users are accustomed to high levels of integration, for example because the system provides single sign-on, or a unified approach to taking back-up copies.

11.4 AUDITING SYSTEMS TESTING AND IMPLEMENTATION

There are plenty of well documented cases of IT projects which have gone completely 'off the rails', and there is a growing literature examining the factors which lead to this kind of project escalation (Beynon-Davies 1995, Drummond 1996, Keil 1995, Margetts and Willcocks 1993). If, as sometimes happens, the project goes so badly adrift that it is cancelled, the result may seriously impact on the organisation's finances and the credibility of its senior management. If the old system has continued to operate throughout the disaster, however, there will not necessarily have been any security exposures.

A clear sign of danger is a project becoming beset with problems while the old system is being replaced by a new one, and it becomes clear the new system is going to fail to live up to expectations. An example of what can happen is provided by the experience of the Foreign and Commonwealth Office (FCO) in London in 1990. The FCO had commissioned a new accounting system, and over a period of 2 years the conversion project had struggled from crisis to crisis. Eventually the FCO was obliged to adopt the new system, even though it was far from acceptable, because the old system broke down and was beyond repair.

The FCO had planned the implementation of its new system according to all the right principles. There was provision for testing out the new system before it went live, using dummy accounting information. There would be a period of parallel running, during which time the old system would still be there as back-up in case the new one failed. However, so horrendous were the problems with the new system that during the period allowed for parallel running, staff tried to compensate for known errors in the software by transferring entries into special 'dump accounts'. The contents of the dump accounts were never properly unravelled. Initial attempts to reconcile the figures from the new system with those derived from the old one revealed a discrepancy of some £46 million (UK Accounts 1991). There was no reason to suppose that this money had disappeared, and some rough and ready balancing of the accounts was eventually achieved. However, for a period of several months the FCO depended on an accounting system which lacked all internal controls, and was completely unauditable.

Disarray in a project can of course arise because every effort has been made to exclude the attentions of auditors from the outset. In 1993, the Department of Motor Vehicles in California was finally obliged to cancel a project to upgrade its databases holding details of driving licences. In the course of investing around $50 million in the project, various ruses were adopted to conceal the way the project was being funded, and over-optimistic reports were constantly being provided about the state of the work in progress. Collins (1997: 228) notes that: 'deception over the tests would have been detected if there had been a regular independent verification or audit, whereby the auditors would report not to the computer department but to the chief executive or equivalent'. The case gives a good illustration of the need for *all* audit to be directed by the internal audit function, with a direct line of communication to the head of the organisation.

The prospect of having to 'blow the whistle' about the technical viability of a project puts a computer auditor in a position which undoubtedly feels very uncomfortable. It provides an ultimate test of whether her loyalty is to the application development team, or the organisation at large. However, if an auditor is not willing to take such action, there is little point in creating the audit role in the first place.

In the majority of cases, where projects reach some kind of successful conclusion, the objectives of the computer auditor will be:

- *To verify that preventive and feedback controls specified in the design are operational and effective.* This may mean pressing the case for these to be given priority, when the emphasis is on getting the more productive features of the software 'through the door'. Controls can easily be seen as an option or an overhead, which can be kept for later if there is pressure on time and resources. Testing of controls may also be resented because some of them (especially access controls) cannot be fully tested until all the elements of the software are brought together, and it is close to being ready to ship.
- *To ensure that any required concurrent controls are in place.* Concurrent controls enable the computer auditor to check on processes within the software while it is in everyday use. They are discussed further in section 12.3.
- *To ensure that controls are fully documented.* There should be no mystery about the purpose of controls, where they are built into the software, or how they are supposed to be used. All this should be explained in documentation.
- *To check that provision has been made for change management.* Inevitably there will be modifications and upgrades to the software after it has been put into production. Some of these changes will have security

implications. The change management system should ensure that the computer auditor is notified if such changes are being contemplated.

11.5   QUESTIONS

1   Should a computer auditor be an active participant in a software development project? Explore the case for and against having the computer auditor contribute to the different stages of the system development life cycle.

2   Describe some of the difficulties likely to be faced by a computer auditor in evaluating and implementing controls in:
   (a) a software package serving a specialised market, and
   (b) a JAVA program written by an administrative assistant in the payroll department.

3   You are in charge of an internal audit department, and you are trying to appoint someone in a computer audit role. What drawbacks might you envisage for each of the following possibilities?
   (a) An offer from a company marketing security software to let you have the services of an 'audit consultant' free for a month.
   (b) Appointing a systems programmer from IT Services, who has been in this job ever since the first mainframe was installed, 30 years ago.
   (c) Appointing someone aged 25 who describes himself as a 'professionally qualified' computer auditor. He has 3 years' experience as a computer auditor in a company which uses computer systems very different from your own.

4   You are a junior manager, and you have just been given access to a brand new human resources application developed by your employer. When you log in to the new system, you are surprised to find that you can browse the personal files of the most senior managers, and employees in various other parts of the company. What reasons might there be for such a lapse? In which instances would you regard the computer auditor as having been at fault?

chapter
twelve

COMPUTER
AUDIT: CONTROL
OF EXISTING
SYSTEMS

SOME TOPICS ADDRESSED IN THIS CHAPTER

- How auditors can institute *checks* on systems which are in active use
- Methods of controlling *changes and upgrades* to systems
- The *skills and qualities* required of a computer auditor
- Ensuring that computer audit work *reinforces and complements* the work of others in the organisation

12.1   INTRODUCTION

In 1973, a massive fraud was exposed in the Equity Funding Corporation of America. It was heavily dependent on the use of computers, which were used to invent fictitious insurance customers on a grand scale. At one point, a program was written to create many thousands of records for non-existent insurance policies, totalling $430 million in value. Many of the company's employees actively colluded in the fraud. The case provided a graphic example of the power of the computer to generate a lot of authentic-looking data very quickly, in the complete absence of any effective internal controls.

Such things could not happen today. Or could they? One auditor has suggested that many of the factors which led to the failures of control at Equity Funding (which were in turn compounded by serious incompetence on the part of external auditors) could easily resurface in a modern setting (Hancox 1997). Technically, it is not difficult to spot a computer program which is inventing phoney records, and ideally this would be challenged before it went anywhere near being part of a production system, using the procedures outlined in the previous chapter. However, there are many other ways in which rogue programs, and other unauthorised modifications, can be introduced into a production system. The challenge for the computer auditor is to make this as difficult as possible, and to be in a position to detect it quickly if and when it does occur.

Today's computer auditor has access to a much more impressive range of tools with which to monitor and investigate systems, compared with the position in 1973. Additionally, the status of computer auditors has improved, and there are many more of them. At the same time, the temptations evident in the Equity Funding case have not gone away. The computer auditor may still be put under pressure not to 'make waves' or ask indelicate questions. The value of computer audit may be questioned, especially at times of financial stringency, and it may feel obliged to look for ways of justifying its existence. This can prompt efforts to market itself and its services within the organisation. One consultant has summed this up by urging auditors to 'create value – be political' (Krull 1995). Computer audit *can* easily be perceived as a non-productive drain on everyone's time and resources, and there will be occasions when it is appropriate to 'bang the drum' about the benefits it brings. However, the process of winning friends should never go as far as creating a sense of obligation, however vaguely felt or expressed, which could bring the auditor's independence and integrity into question.

What is the kind of regime in which a computer auditor should seek to operate? This chapter concentrates on three factors which will assist in the successful audit of systems on an ongoing basis.

- It must be possible to establish exactly what has been installed in every part of the system, and to identify all the changes and modifications which have been made.
- The internal control mechanisms built into the systems must be subject to regular checks, to see that they are working properly.
- Those carrying out the computer audit function must have an appropriate mix of technical and audit skills.

12.2 CHANGE MANAGEMENT AND CONTROL

Successful businesses thrive on constant change, and this tends to be reflected in the demands made of their computer systems. The pressures for change come from all quarters, as people seek to make systems run more efficiently, or exploit new developments in technology, or improve the services available to users. If the changes are not properly managed, the systems will begin to show unwanted side effects, usually in the form of unexplained problems and faults. As one expert has noted wryly: 'If no software ever changed, most installations would soon achieve a substantially improved production service level – production problems would diminish and all but disappear' (Williams 1994). The writer could well have added that stability of this kind would also wipe out much of the work of computer auditors.

Since the installation does not have the option of standing still, it needs procedures in place to keep track of all the changes as they occur. The need for sophisticated change tracking was recognised on early mainframes, where a constant flow of upgrades and fixes had to be applied to the software. It quickly became apparent that the best way to organise this was to use the power of the computer itself, through products such as IBM's System Modification Program. Such programs would keep a record of everything running on the machine, and accumulate knowledge of all the changes which had been added. Meanwhile, in the applications development department, similar techniques were being developed to help programmers keep track of the modules of code being written in large software development projects. Such techniques were generally referred to as *change management*. A change management database could end up holding considerable quantities of data, but most of this originated on a single site. It was therefore not too difficult to ascertain who had provided the data, or to locate and identify the particular software and equipment it described.

As IT began to be dispersed across the whole organisation, the business of collecting information about what was happening became extremely difficult. PC users, in particular, started to 'do their own' thing by adding equipment and software, often out of their own budgets, and neglecting to notify anyone. Attempts were made to apply ideas from change management, to bring some kind of order into the situation. The result was a new set of techniques, which were again often incorporated into special supporting software, known as *configuration management*.

Configuration management is complicated by the fact that several different parties may want to initiate changes, and there is little to stop any of them doing exactly as they please unless appropriate administrative controls are put in place. The position is illustrated in Figure 12.1.

Examples of the possible types of changes wanted include the following.

- *Management* may wish to introduce new facilities to help with the running of the business, such as on-line diaries or electronic noticeboards. Or they may be under pressure imposed from outside by legislation, for example, to bring in a new type of visual display screen which complies with health and safety requirements.
- *Users* may be discontented with the services they are receiving, perhaps because response times are slow, or they feel that the menu screens are badly designed.

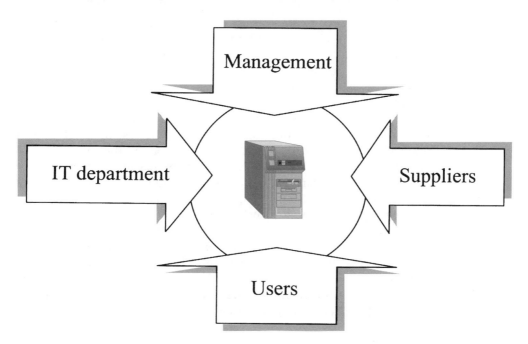

Figure 12.1 **Configuration management: the pressures for change**

- *Suppliers* will have fixes and upgrades which they would like to see applied, particularly with a view to eliminating errors in software.
- The *IT department* will be constantly reviewing the reliability and capacity of the infrastructure, and may want to take actions such as installing new LAN cables or upgrading the network management software.

Computer auditors, too, may occasionally wish to put forward a case for changes, but for the most part their aim in life will be to ensure that all the changes being requested by everyone *else* are being properly managed. This is not a job that computer audit will normally undertake itself. It is more usual for the administration of configuration management to be taken on by the IT department, for whom a comprehensive register of equipment is essential in planning much of its work. Many commercial software products are now available to help with maintaining a register of equipment and any software installed on it. More advanced versions are capable of acquiring much of this information by retrieving it directly from PCs over a network.

From the computer auditor's point of view, registers for change and configuration management are helpful.

- If a change is introduced and it causes problems, it is still possible to find out exactly what the situation was immediately beforehand. If necessary, the change can be 'backed out', and the system can be returned to a previous state which was known to be stable. If required, a whole series of changes can be reversed in this way. This avoids the kind of uncertainty and disagreement which can lead to people trying to resolve the problem on the basis of inspired guesswork, which in turn causes security exposures.

- Because all changes have to be approved, and cannot be made spontaneously, there is an opportunity to check them out in advance. This again contributes to stability and control in the system, since known conflicts can be avoided, for example, by avoiding the installation of two programs which both use the same resources in the computer, or an upgrade to software package A which cannot work unless a corresponding upgrade is also made to software package B.
- The register can be used to help in checking that policy is being followed in areas such as compliance with licensing agreements, the installation of virus protection software, and the installation of hardware for access control based on tokens or biometric scanners.
- There is a definitive list of what *should* be in place, which can occasionally be useful in detecting whether extra equipment has been added without approval, and for purposes which are unauthorised.

Configuration management helped many organisations in their programmes for tracking down and testing equipment for Year 2000 compliance. A search by processor type, for example, could reveal all those which were likely to have problems, and eliminate many which were not. Such searches can be used to address other strategic questions; for example, if it is proposed to give every PC user a new version of some software, it is possible to find out how many machines have enough memory to cope with it.

A register therefore has many possible uses. Like many useful resources, it is very time-consuming to create, particularly if there are no existing electronic records which can be used as a starting point. It has to have a number of key features. The register will be made up of a large number of *configuration items*, which must be specified consistently across the organisation. To be useful, a configuration item needs to be defined at quite a low level. It must be possible to pick out all the possible variations which exist around the organisation. Thus if every PC in the organisation is identical and runs exactly the same software, the PC itself *could* be a configuration item. However, since few, if any, organisations ever achieve this level of uniformity, it will be necessary to record details such as the type and version of word-processing software used, the memory size, type of network card, and so on.

Once the register is functioning, any changes to the items must be subject to *control procedures*, which again are applied uniformly to all equipment and staff. There must be methods of retrieving and analysing the data in the register, sometimes known as *status accounting*. Finally, there will need to be *verification* of the entries through regular and ad hoc checks, a process in which the computer and other auditors will usually wish to be involved (Jacobs 1999).

12.3 ROUTINE CHECKS AND INVESTIGATIONS

There is no shortage of ways in which the computer auditor can set about checking what is happening on systems around the organisation. However, unless some thought and purpose lies behind what is attempted, the checks will not achieve a great deal. A feeling of aimlessness may also be detected by those whose work is affected, and become a cause of resentment.

The computer auditor's objectives in this area are broadly the same as for internal audit in general. The emphasis will be on technical issues, but it is rare for these to stand in isolation. All testing activity should therefore be arranged in collaboration with others in the internal audit function, thus avoiding potential overlap and enabling all the parties to benefit from each other's investigations.

The targeting of audit checks has been developed to a fine art by external auditors, who want to find out as much as possible during the relatively short time at their disposal. Many of these ideas can be borrowed and adapted by the computer auditor. The aim should *not* be to arrange a 'practice run' for the external audit, which implies a rather defensive attitude, but to take a fresh look at the systems, in the same way as an outsider would. This will mean running tests even where one's first instinct would be to think that nothing untoward could possible emerge from them.

Before embarking on tests, computer auditors should also perhaps bear in mind the sobering message provided in two separate surveys from the UK Audit Commission, which showed that just over half the incidents reported in the surveys had come to light not through the operation of checks and controls, but by accident (Audit Commission 1998). This is not an indictment of auditing, which can never hope to track down every security exposure, but suggests that avoidance of relying on well-trodden paths, and a certain amount of alertness and lateral thinking, will occasionally pay dividends.

Auditors regard tests as falling into two main categories:

- *Substantive tests.* These are used to discover whether the system is generating results which are incorrect, or not in the form expected. The cause could lie almost anywhere, including faults in equipment, misjudgements and mistakes by staff, or even fraud. For example, a clerk could have made a mistake when entering cash amounts, or figures may have been misinterpreted by an optical character reader, or software may contain a flaw or 'bug'. Substantive testing involves making independent calculations of what certain output values *ought* to be, perhaps by working out totals by hand, or cross-checking related entries from different files. This is not particularly the province of the computer auditor, although he or she may need to be involved if errors are found and some kind of system malfunction is suspected to be the cause.

- *Tests of controls.* Here the auditor is interested in whether the controls in the system really work. This falls very much in the province of computer auditing, particularly where the controls are automated. Controls can be checked out from first principles (ultimately, by examining the code in the programs which are used to apply them) or by more practical tests, such as seeing whether out-of-range values are indeed rejected by input controls, or if the audit log has actually recorded all the appropriate data relating to a transaction.

Practical testing is particularly useful for determining whether access control tables have been set up correctly. For example, the auditor can log on as a junior employee, and verify whether there are any loopholes allowing access to inappropriate areas of the software. If PCs are supposed to be password-protected, it will be important for the auditor to turn up unannounced occasionally to run spot checks, to ensure that the protection is active.

The different types of test are directed at reducing different forms of risk. Tests of controls are aimed at reducing the *control risk*. Control risk embraces only those risks which controls *ought* to eliminate; in other words, if all the controls worked perfectly, the control risk would be reduced to zero. Substantive tests are aimed at *inherent risk*. Inherent risk arises from the presence of errors and circumstances which everyone realises may happen, and which cannot readily be controlled, perhaps because they originate outside the organisation. The auditor tries to identify all such risks, with a view to concentrating on areas where they are thought to occur. A third category of risk is sometimes added, namely *detection risk*. This is a little more abstruse, because it is intended to cover all the risks which the auditor has failed to recognise. It follows that detection risk can never actually be measured, but it provides a useful target for the auditor, who is constantly trying to reduce it.

Auditors' objectives in analysing risks are much the same as those outlined more generally for risk appraisal in Chapter 2. They aim to use objective and quantifiable measurements, and they expect that new and unfamiliar risks will constantly be arising, which they must try and anticipate. However, the categories of risk mentioned above are defined by auditors for auditors, and do not necessarily match those used by other professionals.

Any check which the auditor contemplates making is directed specifically at one or more of the risk categories, and this provides a useful framework for the audit. Some individual areas of risk analysis have also been particularly well developed by auditors, for example in respect of sampling of records, to ensure that they are an appropriate cross-section of the whole file. In general, computer auditors face more detection risks than would be expected in traditional audit, and will not rely so much on formal techniques. For example, if PCs are being acquired in an uncontrolled fashion, or if there is no change management in place, it will not require in-depth analysis to see that the risks are high.

Particularly in larger and more complex systems, checking may be based on facilities which have been deliberately 'implanted' especially for the purpose. These are known as *concurrent* auditing techniques. Two examples of concurrent techniques are:

- *Integrated Test Facility* (ITF). This allows fictitious or 'dummy' transactions to be entered into a system. These will be chosen to be as awkward as possible, to stretch the capabilities of the processes involved. Afterwards the results will be checked against independent calculations (as in substantive testing, above). The problem with using an ITF is that transactions must not be allowed to show up in any of the 'real' accounts, inventory, etc. This can be solved in one of two ways. The first possibility is to devise a way of labelling the dummy transactions so that they are processed normally, but all the results are diverted to a special test file. This avoids making updates to the real-life records, but introduces additional complexity (and maybe new errors) into the application code. The second option is to follow the original transaction with an exactly opposite one, designed to return the files to the position they would be in if nothing had happened. This too carries some slight dangers, for example, if the reversal is done incorrectly, or someone bases a decision on information in a file, before the reversal takes effect.
- *Snapshot techniques.* This again requires the addition of extra software, this time to trace what happens at each step of a transaction. 'Snapshots' are taken by having a tracing program which stores away such things as the contents of fields which have been read in from disk drives, and the intermediate stages of calculations. It can be compared to a physician injecting radio-opaque dye into a patient in order to follow its progress on X-ray pictures. The auditor can subsequently put all the information from the snapshots together, and compare what has been happening with what *ought* to happen, according to the logic laid down in the program documentation and elsewhere.

Other concurrent techniques are based on embedding audit modules which detect and record details of certain types of situation (for example, all transactions involving cash payments over a certain amount), or specific audit 'hooks' which give the alert if unexpected activities occur, such as attempts to withdraw money from an account which has been designated as dormant (Spiram and Sumners 1992).

12.4 COMPETENCIES REQUIRED OF COMPUTER AUDITORS

If computer auditors are to use techniques such as concurrent testing, with all that this implies in terms of meddling with the internal code of live systems, it would seem prudent to make sure that they have the necessary technical competence. It is also important for computer auditors to have good personal qualities, including diplomacy (something which does not always come naturally to those of a seriously technical disposition), together with a certain amount of tenacity and initiative.

Not surprisingly, there has been much debate about the way in which computer auditors should be trained and examined. One of the longest-standing schemes is run by the US-based Information Systems Audit and Control Association (ISACA 2000). To become a Certified Information Systems Auditor (CISA) under this scheme, candidates must have practical experience in systems auditing, and pass a 4-hour multiple-choice test (available in nine different languages). Just over a third of the test is concerned with information security, and the rest covers wider issues of systems development and management. Those who qualify are expected to follow a code of ethics, and undertake continuing education. Some other qualification schemes are described in section 14.1.

The main ingredients of schemes such as CISA are familiar from other well established professional areas such as law and accountancy. However, computer auditing has made limited headway in establishing itself as a profession in its own right. There are two main reasons for suspecting that progress in this area will continue to be slow.

First, it is difficult to define a core set of technical skills. Some of the techniques cited in section 12.3, for example, imply an ability to understand program source code and flow charts, and the use of traces based on code extensions buried deep inside the operating system. Computer auditors can also expect to be drawn into evaluating the risks associated with any new 'cutting-edge' technologies which the organisation is thinking of adopting. This all implies levels of technical competence of quite a high order. One job specification drawn up for a UK retailer includes knowledge of systems development methodologies and practices, and project management techniques, and states that these practical skills should be combined with 'specific knowledge of systems and processes in this company and its industry' (Blackburn 1997). This suggests that the organisation would do best to 'grow' its own computer auditors. In many cases it is likely to be easier to take someone who works in the IT department, and train them up in audit techniques, rather than go hunting for a suitably experienced 'professional' computer auditor from outside.

This, second, raises questions about just how transferable the skills of computer audit are ever likely to become. Qualifications such as CISA can guarantee that someone understands the basic elements of a typical computer system, and the principles by which they should be managed. They may also insist on substantial auditing experience. Nevertheless, employers may put a still higher priority on in-depth knowledge of the equipment, operating systems, and applications which are actually used in their business. They would prefer to employ a poacher turned gamekeeper. This is particularly evident in sectors where computer audit has become well established, for example, financial services and some branches of public service.

Computer auditors therefore have some difficulty in meeting the

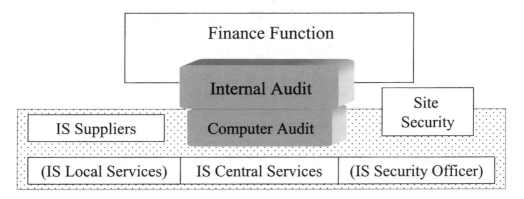

Figure 12.2

criteria usually laid down for a 'profession'. The schemes for accreditation are still fairly embryonic, and they lack other characteristics such as regulation at the point of intake or some form of licensing (Freidson 1986). Instead they rely on less formal recognition, which is nevertheless real and forthcoming because of the demand for their specialist services. In practice, however, this means that computer auditors sink or swim by their technical skills. Publications concerned with computer audit, unlike those relating to more established professions, are predominantly concerned with technical matters. In view of this technical emphasis, it is unsurprising to find computer auditors often networking extensively with other people in the organisation who share their interests in information systems. At the same time, they have to rely for their status and independence on their association with more established functions in internal audit and accounting. Figure 12.2 gives a simplified view of this position. The shaded area depicts a zone within which concerns about IT provide a common bond. Maintaining appropriate working relationships in this zone will not always be straightforward, and there are various areas of potential conflicts.

- *Site security.* Measures to protect the organisation's staff and physical assets increasingly rely on the use of technology. On occasions, there can be useful collaboration, for example if the computer auditor needs to know whether an employee has been on site at particular times, or if there is an opportunity to integrate information system controls with those enforcing physical access. In military or government bodies where secrecy of information is a prime concern, this security function will be quite powerful, with strong links with those running the information systems.
- *IS security officer* (ISSO). Many organisations, particularly smaller ones, do not have a formally appointed ISSO. Generally, however, someone in IS Central Services will have oversight of security. The responsibility

may be combined with that of administering passwords and access control tables, making the role very technical. One advantage of having an ISSO is that someone can be appointed who has wider insights into how the business operates (Kovacich 1997).

- *IS central services.* Members of this department will have the task of administering access controls, and will be responsible for enforcing and applying many of the measures described elsewhere in this book. Ideally, they will work closely with the computer auditor, but the roles of enforcement and audit should be kept apart. Security administration is concerned with delivering measures and enforcing compliance. The auditor is there to act as a watchdog, and provide objective reviews and recommendations. Whether this makes for a productive relationship will depend on the climate of opinion in the organisation. One study of more than 300 information system managers in the USA revealed that, in general, they did not have a very high opinion of the technical skills of IS auditors, and felt that anyway they were not given enough resources to implement the auditors' findings. They nevertheless felt under strong pressure to act on these findings. A large majority (85%) rejected the idea that auditors worked in partnership or simply as consultants, and took a more traditional view that the auditors had an adversarial 'policing' role (Hunton and Wright 1995).

- *IS local services.* Whether administration of services is devolved to local level will depend very much on the structure of the organisation (see section 3.3). At this level, the computer auditor may also find a somewhat adversarial atmosphere, particularly if the culture is one which is distrustful of 'head office' functions in general. This can make it difficult to motivate staff in securing compliance. Consider an incident cited by Gordon, in dealing with her bank. Ms Gordon wished to change one of the conditions applying to her account, and produced a cancelled cheque to indicate the account number. The account details were duly modified by an officer of the bank, and Ms Gordon was invited to choose a new PIN code for telephone access. Ms Gordon (1999) notes:

> . . . at no point in time was I required to produce a photo ID. I had never met this officer before in my life, and she did not know who I was. I took out my passport, which has a different name on it than my bank account, and said, 'You forgot to ask for this'. She glanced at it, and said, 'Okay, thanks!'. That was it.

Perhaps the officer encountered by Ms Gordon did not know the rules. More probably, she knew them but did not particularly see the point of them. Turning such attitudes around requires a constant drip-feed of observations and explanations. One approach which the computer auditor can take is to ensure that technical staff are fully briefed on security measures, in the hope that they will make a point of explaining and justifying them to the other staff working around them.

- *IS suppliers.* Suppliers generally sell to the managers who make purchasing decisions, but if security is regarded as a strong features of a product, the computer auditor will become a target. In addition, the computer auditor is likely to be asked to field exploratory approaches from vendors offering IS security products and services. This is a useful way of gathering information, but the auditor must beware of appearing to be aligned with any one supplier, which will not fit well with claims of auditor independence.

Although operating in this predominantly technical domain, the computer auditor also needs to be alert to some of the seismic shifts occurring in the world of audit in general. For example, in 1992 the nature and purpose of internal controls was reviewed by accounting's Committee of Sponsoring Organisations (COSO) in the United States. It recommended that more attention should be paid to factors such as the general integrity, ethical values and competence levels of people in the organisation, the so-called 'soft' factors. This in turn triggered new debates about the proper role between internal and external auditors. Another US body (the Institute of Internal Auditors Research Foundation) has sponsored research more recently which suggests that businesses around the world are beginning to bring together previously separate functions dealing with risk management, including internal audit, quality assurance, and health and safety. The project director has predicted that 'risk management and assurance will be considered a dimension of management. Under these circumstances, internal audit disappears into the management process' (IIA 1998). It remains to be seen whether internal audit will indeed be absorbed in this way, and computer audit along with it.

12.5 QUESTIONS

1 All the staff in your department have just received a letter from the Chief Executive. This states that a new analysis package has been installed which can identify all the programs installed on any PC which is connected to the company's network. The letter complains that use of this package has revealed that everyone in your department has games installed on their machines. The letter goes on to adopt a threatening tone, pointing out that this is a very serious infringement of company rules, which could give rise to disciplinary action.

  On making enquiries, you find that the games in question are those supplied as standard on the Windows software, which was installed by central IT services in the first place. Draw up a short statement (1–2 pages) setting out the policies and procedures which you feel it would be prudent to adopt, governing the future use of the new analysis package and its findings.

2 What sound business reasons may there be for wanting to change the hardware or software components of a desktop PC in an office? Give

three reasons why it is important that all such changes are tracked and recorded in a systematic way.

3 You work for a financial services company which is heavily dependent on its information systems for delivering customer service. Following a series of lapses in controls in these systems, it has been decided to appoint a computer auditor.

Identify *five* important competencies which you feel this person should have, and list them in order of importance.

4 The Mega Corporation has a central Information Services Department, in which a senior member of the staff acts as the Security Administrator. Within the Corporation's Internal Audit Department, there is a small group of computer auditors, one of whom is assigned to issues connected with accounting on the central mainframes.

Describe at least two ways in which these two employees would have something in common in their work, and at least two ways in which their work would differ.

chapter thirteen

COMPUTER FORENSICS

SOME TOPICS ADDRESSED IN THIS CHAPTER

- The *circumstances* in which it may be necessary to carry out an in-depth investigation of computer files
- The *tools* which are available to help the investigators
- The *procedures* which should be followed, to avoid the possibility that any evidence obtained can subsequently be discredited
- The limits which apply as to what is *ethical or legitimate* in investigating the activities of employees

13.1   INTRODUCTION

Managers often have to act on the basis of hunches or suspicions. If there are warning signs that computing facilities are being misused, the instinctive response will usually be to take some pre-emptive action. For example, the access control regime may be tightened up, or staff responsibilities re-assigned; if this is done discreetly, no accusations need be levelled at any one, and no damage is done to good working relations. At the same time, management sends a clear message that it will not tolerate the misuse.

However, these 'softly, softly' approaches are not always appropriate, and then it becomes necessary to obtain hard evidence and confront the culprits. To do this successfully requires a good understanding of **computer forensics.** Computer forensics may be used where:

- the misuse is so flagrant and serious that it is felt to be important to identify and punish the perpetrator;
- management wish to know exactly how the misuse was being accomplished, so that they can be sure that their counter-measures will be effective;
- the organisation faces legal proceedings from other parties arising from the misuse. Examples would be claims from software suppliers for breach of the terms of licensing agreements, or allegations that materials circulating in the computer system are defamatory.

In such cases, investigations are called for which go much further than merely establishing that misuse has taken place. These investigations can be regarded as 'forensic', by analogy with police detective work. They aim to provide evidence strong enough to resist any challenges which may be made by those who are implicated.

Since computer-based evidence can be very quickly destroyed, it is vital to gather it without alerting any of those who are under suspicion. The evidence must also be comprehensive enough to rule out any alternative explanation of events. Even if the organisation has no intention of taking the evidence into court, it has to assume that it could end up being forced in this direction, and therefore must always collect evidence with this possibility in mind. Once it has made accusations against an employee, the employee may seek to press for some kind of formal review, particularly if there is the prospect of punitive action. This opens up the possibility that evidence will eventually have to be presented in the context of full-scale litigation, where it can be expected that every effort will be made to discredit it.

In an ideal world, forensic investigations would be made on a routine basis, and not just when trouble is suspected (as in Case A, on page 264). Unfortunately, such investigations are invariably expensive, and at the outset it is rarely possible to predict exactly *how* expensive any particular investigation will be. Once started, the investigation could last for a few days, or several months. Investigators' time is costly, since they must be highly skilled in finding their way around systems, using sophisticated search and analysis tools. Care must be taken in protecting and documenting evidence, adding considerably to the overhead costs. Organisations are bound to be reluctant to invest in such resource-hungry exercises unless there is a serious loss or crime which seems to warrant it. Still less will they want to fund them if there is no evidence that anything is particularly wrong in the first place.

At first sight, forensic investigation would seem to be an ideal task for the organisation's own computer auditors, but consultants in this field advise strongly against this, and not entirely from self-interest. Wilding (1997), for example, points out that those who have worked closely on a system for some time are not in the best position to spot its weaknesses. If failings are discovered, they may react defensively, feeling that they are in some way responsible. Furthermore, they may not know enough about legal requirements relating to the collection and storage of evidence.

Whether or not computer auditors actually instigate forensic investigations, their input and assistance will be essential at various points in the process. This chapter outlines some of the approaches and tools which are available to today's 'computer detectives'.

13.2 TECHNIQUES AND PROCEDURES TO OBTAIN VALID COMPUTER EVIDENCE

Whether investigators are faced with two or three PCs on a LAN, or a huge corporate system based on a mainframe, the first problem they face is much the same. Where to start looking? An expert on larger systems has summed up the problem: 'Evidence of fraud is usually buried beneath hundreds of thousands of valid records held on a computer' (Iyer 1996: 396). The first and most important tool which the investigator needs to have to hand is software which can help to burrow into all this data.

In mainframe-based systems, such tools may be an integral part of the application software or the operating system. This is particularly likely if the organisation has set up a corporate database or data warehouse, or uses application software covering several major departments, as in Enterprise Resource Planning. Suitable tools may also be available in an Executive Information System (EIS), which enables senior managers to 'drill down' into corporate data in order to investigate how individual units are performing.

Planners and forecasters may also have similar facilities in a Decision Support System, which also aims to retrieve data from all parts of the organisation, though with a different purpose in mind. DSS users are interested in pulling together information so that they can build financial models and make forecasts. For most of the time, they are looking at aggregated figures and trying to spot significant trends in them.

If the target system is based on smaller machines, such as PCs, it is less likely that any suitable analysis software will already be in place. Some small companies or departments may include a high-powered research group which is used to extracting and monitoring figures, for example, a firm of specialised bond traders, or a quality assurance department. However, it is far more common to find little more than the normal database and spreadsheet packages. These have quite powerful capabilities for analysis, but they are not well suited to ad hoc investigations. Data will often need to be converted into different formats, and the lay-out of each individual field will have to be defined to the package. At this point, some of the more esoteric features of generic packages have to be used, and they are not always particularly appropriate.

Whether the data comes from a PC or a mainframe, professional investigators will much prefer to use their own specialised search and analysis tools. They will have acquired skill and experience in using them, and know the kind of results they can hope to obtain. Using their own tools also means that they are free to direct the spotlight at *any* data which may be important, and not just the data which happens to be accessible in a facility which has been designed for some other purpose, such as an EIS.

If the data to be analysed is confined to one source, such as the hard drive of a PC, the best option will be to copy it in order to analyse it at leisure on another system altogether. Investigators may favour the taking of copies for other reasons. First, one copy can be taken for analysis, and another copy can be taken and stored under controlled conditions. This is important if it is suspected that legal arguments may arise later about what exactly was on the disk at the time. Use can be made of proprietary copying systems which add integrity checks at the time the copy is made, for example, by taking and recording a hash value for each block of data, and encrypting the copy. The recording media containing the data and all the associated hashes will be sealed in tamper-proof bags, and full documentation prepared giving every relevant detail of when and where the copy was taken, and by whom.

A second reason for working with copies is that this can be done quickly and, if necessary, by physically removing the hard disk for the copy to be taken. The PC does not even have to be powered on. If the aim is to avoid alerting the PC's owner, this can all be done secretively at dead of night, leaving no indications that the PC has been touched. Care will of course have to be taken that no tell-tale traces are left from moving the PC or items around it. This requires a well organised operation, with great attention to detail. One member of the team, for example, may be charged with taking Polaroid or digital photographs of the desk area before any activity starts, so that everything can be put back exactly as it was found.

Finally, even if there is no need to make the copies in conditions of secrecy, there are numerous advantages in being able to analyse data as and when required, without any risk of interfering with live applications.

WHOSE PORNOGRAPHIC FILES WERE THESE?

Case A

As part of its planned audit activities, a company investigated a small system which had been set up to handle customer contacts out of normal office hours, when the mainframe systems were not running. The checks were made without notifying the IT department responsible for the system.

The first step was to apply password-cracking software to enable the investigators to find the top-level password. This enabled them to take control of the system server and browse through its contents. Among the files, they were surprised to find 70 MB of very explicit pornographic material. This was in a folder containing Internet web site addresses, and high-quality image, sound and video files which had clearly been down-loaded intentionally.

The finance director and chief legal officer were alerted, and efforts were made to identify the user responsible. This involved combing through records of telephone calls, and the times that individual employees were on site. Suspicion fell on one individual in the IT department, and at this point a manager from the department was brought into the picture. He recalled that the suspect had put his laptop computer in for repair, and as a precaution all the files on it had been copied on to the server before the work was begun. This explained how the files had come to be in the folder.

When confronted with the findings of the investigation, the suspect denied having ever accessed any of the Internet sites in question. However, he had used the laptop to work at home. It subsequently emerged that his son had been using the laptop to surf the Internet without his father's knowledge.

The use of the laptop from home had side-stepped all the measures which the company had in place to prevent employees from visiting inappropriate sites on the Internet. Also, since no guidelines had been issued about use of equipment at home, no disciplinary action could reasonably be taken against the employee.

Based on Foggon, F. *Internal Audit Case Study*, 1999, www.itaudit.org

Case B

Dr Bill Hancock, a well-known figure in computer security, was asked to review a case in which an information systems manager was accused of using his office computer to frequent pornographic sites. The allegations were made by an employee who looked after the network servers, and had high levels of access authorisation. Relations between the employee and the manager were generally poor, and the employee had since been dismissed.

Examination of the manager's PC revealed folders containing 200 pornographic images. There were some puzzling aspects to the folders, since the images all appeared to have been downloaded at the same moment, via a browser the manager did not use. Examination of the machine used by the sacked employee revealed that all its data files had been deleted. However, after 'undeleting' them, Dr Hancock was able to verify that some of the same pornography images had also been held on that machine.

The question was: who planted the files on whose system? By studying logs of employee access to the building, and logs from the telephone system, it was possible to build up a picture of how the disgruntled employee *might* have gained access to the manager's office to tamper with his PC. Since the employee had left the company, evidence was not needed in any formal proceedings, but the findings did offer some vindication of the manager's version of events.

Based on Hancock B., Editorial, *Computers and Security*, 17, 278–9, 1998

13.3 CORRELATION OF DATA FROM MULTIPLE SOURCES

When looking at a set of computer records, the investigator is presented with a 'virtual world', which may or may not correspond with the real one. In the Equity Funding case (see section 12.1), thousands of fictitious insurance policies were created. Since an insurance policy is a financial asset which exists only in an abstract form, it is not that easy to check whether it 'really' exists.

Assets can be fictitious and anything but abstract, however, as US disk manufacturer Miniscribe showed in a series of frauds in the late 1980s. The company began to shift obsolete spare parts, faulty equipment and even building bricks around its warehouses and distribution points, all the time claiming that these were sellable products, with correspondingly high book values. The secret was to keep the flow of junk items on the move. This made it difficult for anyone to verify whether the company's records reflected what was actually being held in store at any given point in time (Foremski 1989a).

A golden rule for any auditor is to take 'reality checks' from time to time and to do so, if possible, without warning. This may involve anything, from turning up unannounced at a warehouse to check the inventory levels, to asking to see whether the office on the third floor has indeed been painted, as per the details in the decorator's contract. The importance of taking an outward-looking view has been emphasised by a senior official in the UK's Serious Fraud Office. He suggests that auditors frequently fail to detect fraud because, among other things, they do not make adequate enquiries, they allow management to restrict the scope of their work, and they fail to identify the relationships involved in transactions (Knox 1994).

The situations facing the auditor can take three main forms:

1 *Misrepresentation, but with internal consistency.* The records do not match up with reality, but the fraud has been accomplished with such skill that there are no inconsistencies to be found just by looking at the computer files. This usually requires some collusion at a high level in the organisation, as in the Equity Funding and Miniscribe cases. However, this state of affairs *can* be engineered by people of much lowlier status, as is shown by the vintage computer fraud case involving Jerry Schneider, a Los Angeles high school student. In 1971 young Jerry had acquired a complete library of guides to the computerised inventory system used by the local telephone company. Acting on the information in these guides, he acquired an ex-telephone company truck (at auction), a pass key to the company's warehouse gates (by bribing a friend), and a touch-tone telephone. He used the telephone's keypad to requisition materials from the automated warehouse system, as though from one of the telephone company's construction sites. He then drove to the warehouse in his 'company' truck to collect the items, and sold them on the open market.

Later, he discovered that he could dispense with finding buyers for the goods. Using his knowledge of the computer system, he would dial up and make a requisition to lower the number in stock of an item to just below its reorder point. He would then telephone the company, asking whether by any chance they were looking for supplies of that item. On checking the computer files, the company found that, not surprisingly, they were, and arranged to buy their own goods back again. The net result of all these transactions was that no inconsistencies ever appeared in the warehouse records, even though goods and payments were being sent to improper destinations at an alarming rate. The whistle was eventually blown on the scam by a disaffected friend of Jerry's. The company then found itself, such was their dependence on the computerised system, in the embarrassing position of being unable to work out just how much of their inventory had actually been stolen (Moscove and Simkin 1987).

With hindsight, it is easy to suggest that some simple auditing would have discovered whether the outflow of goods from the warehouse matched up with other records relating to activities at its construction sites; or there could have been a programme of random checks on individual transactions. In a modern system, one would expect to find a log of activities on the system being kept, which would help to reveal if data entries were being fixed. When investigating a UK criminal case involving multiple murders of his patients by a family doctor, detectives examining such logs found that the accused had entered backdated histories for his victims, inventing serious medical problems for them, with all these details actually being entered just *after* the patient had died (News 2000).

The moral is that when looking at an apparently perfect set of records, any investigator or auditor should always consider how aspects of them could be verified from independent sources. In companies which adopt highly integrated systems such as Enterprise Resource Planning, or which work as part of a value chain which relies on EDI and other completely electronic communications, finding corroborative information from genuinely independent sources outside the system is not always easy.

2 *Buried patterns and discrepancies.* Reference was made in section 5.2.1 to the railroad clerk who entered his own employee number alongside other people's names, in order to route extra payments to himself without attracting attention. This was not picked up by preventive controls. Uncovering such frauds by retrospective analysis of the records is inevitably a much more laborious and expensive process, and of course the business will have suffered financial losses from the fraud in the meantime.

Once a fraud has really taken root, the problem for the auditor is to know where to start digging. Consider the case of a fraud which a pensions clerk ran successfully for 15 years, involving more than £500,000 of misappropriated funds. The clerk set up a number of building society accounts under false names. He authorised regular payments to these accounts, always adhering to the following rules: the payments were for small amounts using older pension schemes which he surmised (correctly) would be less likely to come under review, and the payments never involved any questions of tax liability. Local controls were evaded by always submitting the requests in 'urgent' batches of forms, and judiciously removing any documents which might later form the basis of an audit trail (Essinger 1991). Given the number of times the procedure was repeated, a regular pattern must have been discernible in the clerk's activities. However, it was a pattern which was extremely difficult for the auditors to spot.

3 *Ghosts and dual personalities.* Anyone who creates fictitious customers or suppliers for use in a fraud still faces the problem that payments or goods will need to be sent to a real destination. This problem can be solved by renting accommodation or using an address serviced by an agent, but fraudsters are often tempted to save money by using their own address details, and simply using a false name for the 'client'.

Such ruses can be discovered fairly rapidly by running checks on whether, for example, any customers or suppliers have the same telephone number as employees. It may also be informative to see if anyone is using an address which belongs to an accommodation agent. Wilding (1997) suggests that it may be worth extending such cross-checking to include other details which may be on file, such as the name and address of next of kin. Other suggestions made by Wilding would have to be used with a careful eye on data protection laws: for example, checking whether two employees have regularly taken holidays at the same time, in case there is some close relationship which is incompatible with the division of duties between the employees concerned. Data protection is also inevitably an issue if data is correlated from sources outside the organisation. For example, the Finance Director of a London council has described the problems of detecting fraudulent claims for housing benefits. Claimants were known to be making multiple applications for benefits to 33 different local authorities in the London area. (One, showing an enterprising use of IT, kept a database on his PC to ensure he wore the right clothes each day, to match each of his many different identities.) Correlation of data about claimants was a powerful weapon in attacking fraud, but could only be used after ensuring that it was legal (Leeming 1995).

13.4   MISUSE OF TELECOMMUNICATIONS SERVICES

Telephone services have traditionally been an independent domain within a business. Even though most private exchanges are now computerised, their security is not always well integrated with the security of information systems generally. Such integration is growing in importance, as telecommunications become more digitally based, and more data traffic is routed via private exchanges.

Computerised exchanges can log a huge amount of detail about the traffic passing through them. The logs are a valuable source of information about the time and duration of connections, both incoming and outgoing. Logs will also indicate the source and destination of a call, although this may be complicated by the use of advanced features such as re-routing, conference calls, or voice mail.

Information from the logs can be correlated with records obtained from other systems, or used on its own to find suspicious patterns of activity that indicate unauthorised use of services by employees. The logs can be a vital source of evidence in detecting attacks from outside, for example by *phreakers*. Phreakers are the telephone equivalent of computer hackers, and although they sometimes set out to cause damage, their main aim is usually to make calls without paying for them. This is achieved by routing calls through the private exchange in such a way that they appear to have originated there. The unsuspecting business will then be billed for the calls. In some exchanges phreakers will be assisted by the presence of facilities which are actually *intended* to work in this way. These facilities are meant to allow authorised users to make a cheap or toll-free call to the exchange, and from there to dial out to another number. The investigations manager for one telephone utility has noted (Mulhall 1995: 298) that, although most exchanges have facilities for password protection, many organisations do not bother to use them. 'Various reasons have been given for this lapse in basic security, for example: "You cannot expect out senior executives to remember a 3/4 digit PIN." This is a ridiculous situation, bearing in mind the salaries paid to such people.' More sophisticated versions of this scam involve setting up dial-through calls to numbers which charge a premium rate. Needless to say the premium rate number in question will have been set up as part of the fraud, so that payments can subsequently be claimed, under normal revenue-sharing arrangements, from the telephone utility.

In countries with liberal regimes for telecommunications, telephone bills can now be used to levy charges for a wide variety of services, some of which might previously have been paid for via a credit card company. This has led to the emergence of a practice known as *cramming*, defined as 'the practice of including charges on telephone bills for goods or service that the consumer did not order' (Valentine 1998: para. 14).

Even a small organisation will generate copious amounts of data in its telephone logs, and so a file interrogation package is essential for carrying out analysis. Williams (1996) suggests how such a package can be used to pick out cases of irresponsible or unauthorised usage, for example, by listing calls which are excessively long, or which involve premium rate numbers. Williams cites as an example the discovery of calls being made from a UK company to Nigeria at around six o'clock in the morning. It was eventually found that a cleaner was responsible. Clearly, it is helpful if the analysis is done by someone close to the business who knows, for example, that clients are not based in Nigeria, and that staff do not need to make calls outside normal office hours. However, for organisations which do not want to invest in the time and software to do the analysis for themselves, outside contractors will undertake it, sometimes on a 'no savings – no fee' basis.

13.5 PROOF OF OWNERSHIP: ELECTRONIC WATERMARKS

The methods of establishing the source and authenticity of information discussed previously (in Chapter 6) all assumed some degree of cooperation between the sender and the receiver. For these methods to work, both parties must decide on appropriate algorithms for encryption and hashing, and provide each other with cryptographic keys.

Sometimes, however, cooperation from the receiver is the last thing which can be expected. Someone who has acquired information illicitly will not be inclined to assist in proving where that information was sourced. Investigators will therefore need to be able to prove that it could only have originated from the rightful owner. Such instances usually revolve around breach of copyright, where the material may have been stolen, or perhaps used in ways which contravene a licensing agreement.

Techniques of *electronic watermarking* have been developed, largely in response to the requirement of new information-based industries to be able to protect their products. With music, films and software all easily transmittable over the Internet, copyright has become difficult to enforce. Attempts have been made to outlaw equipment likely to be used in order to make illegal copies, but these face huge problems of feasibility and enforcement (Simons 1998).

The potential uses for electronic watermarks are not confined to the protection of copyright. For example, a company may be concerned that internal documents are being 'leaked' to outsiders. By applying a different watermark to each copy of a document, it would be possible to trace the origins of any copy found outside the organisation.

The requirements for a successful electronic watermark are that:

- it should be embedded in the digital material in a way which cannot be detected, except by those who know the watermarking process;
- even if it is detected, it should be as difficult as possible to corrupt or remove;
- it should survive intact if the material is transmitted across a network, or undergoes certain commonly used transformations, for example, if a picture is converted to a different bitmap standard, or is trimmed at the edges.

It can be seen that the parallels with a traditional watermark, as seen in bank notes or certificates, are not exact. Electronic watermarks are generally invisible (although a visible symbol may be included to act as a deterrent). Paper watermarks, on the other hand, can be inspected by anyone. Electronic watermarks are designed to survive copying, whereas paper watermarks cannot be reproduced by even the best photocopier. Electronic watermarking is actually an application of a more general set of techniques for hiding information, known as *steganography*. As with cryptography, some steganography techniques are quite simple, but this makes them vulnerable to attack. For example, a message can be hidden in ordinary text by moving selected letters up or down very slightly, or by using the gaps between words as a code (a single space might represent a digital '0', and a double space a digital '1'). Most readers are unlikely to notice the small irregularities which this will create. However, once the method has been spotted it is very easy to decode, and create a forgery. The message can also be very easily lost through quite ordinary activities with the text. For example, if the margins are changed on a word processor, a different pattern of word gaps will result, because all the spaces at the end of a line are ignored.

Techniques more suited to the digital age are described by Bender *et al* (1996). These techniques work best with digital objects which contain a large number of bits, such as high-definition images, or passages of music. The aim of the steganographer is to replace bits which occur randomly in the original with 'pseudo-random' bit sequences containing the hidden message. This will result in subtle changes to the settings of brightness or colour for parts of an image, or in the tones heard in a piece of music. However, the art of successful steganography is to make these changes completely unnoticeable. For best results, the steganographer will ensure that the bit changes are spread across the entire picture or sound sequence, so that they are difficult to edit out, and there will be checking mechanisms to indicate whether the message has been changed or corrupted.

Many steganography systems are still at the experimental stage, but some packages are being marketed commercially. These products enable the owner of valuable digital materials, such as copyright sounds and images, to apply a unique watermark. A watermark 'reader' can be used to examine copies of materials, to check whether a watermark is present. The supplier may also maintain a central registry, so that if the reader reveals the presence of someone else's watermark, it is possible to find out who the watermark belongs to.

Like encrypted messages, electronic watermarks are vulnerable to attack by skilled hackers. They can use a watermark reader to detect the existence of a watermark, and then set about removing or distorting it. Their aim will be to eliminate the watermark, thereby making it ineffective, or perhaps to undermine it in more subtle ways. As Berghel (1997) points out, in some cases it may be possible for a forger to create an *alternative* version of the watermark which will still be accepted as authentic by the software which is used to check it. This will have the effect of casting doubts on the reliability of genuine watermarks.

One way in which copyright owners may seek to track down infringements on Internet sites is to launch 'sniffer' programs which roam the net, looking for images displayed on web sites, and checking through them to see if they contain a watermark. Such programs, too, can all too easily be thwarted at present, for example by breaking up the image into several smaller parts. These can be put back together as a single image on the screen, with no discernible change so far as the human eye is concerned. The effect will be to break up the watermark and spread it across all the sub-images, making it much more difficult for the sniffer program to detect.

13.6   THE ETHICS OF INVESTIGATIONS

In setting out to prove that some kind of misconduct has taken place, it is likely that ethical questions will arise along the way. For example, it may be necessary to check up on matters which in normal circumstances would be considered private. There is also a danger that blame may be steered towards one particular person, as others try to distance themselves, leaving that person isolated as the scapegoat. Inquiries must also be based on principles of fairness and consistency. For example, if a practice has been quietly condoned for several years, it is hardly reasonable to bring in an instant policy of 'zero tolerance', and initiate a surprise crackdown on offenders.

The ethical judgements are made especially difficult because no rule book can cover all the twists and turns which might occur in the course of an investigation. They are given an additional edge because the stakes for both management and employees may be high. The company could stand to lose valuable information assets, the employee could end up being fired. These are ethical decisions for which, in the words of Sir Adrian Cadbury, managers will need to 'make their own rules'. By this, he does not mean that they should simply regard themselves as free to do as they please; his point is that ethical, commercial and other considerations frequently come into conflict, and anyway managers may find that 'ethical signposts do not always point in the same direction' (Andrews 1989: 70).

So how should a manager set about 'making the rules'? One widely accepted general rule in ethics is that one should always begin by seeking out a complete and accurate version of the facts. However, in the case of enquiries involving an information system, there are usually strong feelings that certain facts ought *not* to be accessible to the investigators. Respect for privacy will require that some aspects of a person's background or activities should be allowed to remain secret. There are circumstances in which similar protection may be claimed by other legal entities, such as a partnership or company.

Three main strands of argument are advanced for respecting privacy, even where this may hamper the progress of an investigation. The first emphasises a requirement to make judgements without being influenced by information which, although it may arouse prejudices of one kind or another, actually has nothing to do with the matter in hand. Here it is useful to borrow the idea of a 'veil of ignorance', used by the legal theorist John Rawls in developing his concepts of a well-ordered society. It will be helpful in arriving at rules which are fair, Rawls argues, if decisions are not influenced by 'certain morally irrelevant information' about the parties concerned (Rawls 1999: 236). A common aim of data protection rules is to specify how and where veils of ignorance should be imposed: for example, a Directive on which much European data protection law is now based specifies that data should always be collected for a specified purpose, and not revealed in any way which is inconsistent with that purpose (EC 1995; see section 14.4). However, such rules cannot be made absolute, and exceptions have to be permitted in the wider public interest. So, for example, if an employee deliberately enters false information into the system, she can hardly demand that it be kept secret, on the grounds that this is a purely private matter. At the same time, investigators would not be justified in trawling through *all* records relating to an employee. In this area it is hard to define hard and fast ethical or legal rules, especially in investigative work; there are inevitably times when it is impossible to know what you may stumble across while hunting for evidence.

The second line of argument focuses on the rights of the data subject. This starts from an assumption that an individual can assert rights over personal information which are akin to ownership. If information is revealed, it should therefore always be with the individual's consent. This again creates problems in the context of an investigation, since it may be crucial that the suspect is kept unaware that the investigation is in progress. In such circumstances, asking for consent will simply give the game away. It can, in any case, be difficult to decide on the 'ownership' of personal information, which is frequently ambiguous: for example, if A is married to B, or if A has already given the information to a large number of people. Some writers therefore prefer to explore the extent to which an individual should be able to assert his or her *autonomy* through control over the way personal information is used (Gross 1971).

Finally, a more pragmatic argument is often advanced by professionals who receive information in confidence from their clients. Their concern is that clients will only give them intimate and personal details if they can be assured that these will be treated in complete confidence. This has emerged as a major issue in many countries in respect of the records held by family physicians. Donaldson and Lohr (1994) point out that various investigative agencies may seek access to such records, in pursuing possible irregularities in claims or payments for health care, details of children at risk of abuse, and so on. Doctors can therefore no longer give categorical assurances that information will go no further than the filing cabinet in the consulting room, and there are fears that patients will be more reticent as a result.

The three views of privacy are by no means mutually exclusive, and may all prove to be equally important in any particular situation. For example, it could be that in the course of efforts to track down a fraudulent health insurance claim by X, medical details emerge about Y, which Y would have preferred to keep private. Assuming that Y is an innocent third party, this could be seen as being variously an unfair release of irrelevant information, a violation of Y's privacy rights, and a breach of doctor-patient confidentiality.

Dilemmas about intrusion into employee privacy may also be thrown up by the use of programs which carry out routine scanning of electronic communications. The use of information extracted from monitoring systems can of course be to the benefit of employees. For example, the circulation of offensive electronic mail messages is bound to upset staff, and indeed the organisation could find itself facing legal proceedings if it took no action to pursue offenders. Total privacy of movement and communication at work is neither practical nor desirable. However, it is easy to stray into unacceptable territory if the use of the information is not used judiciously, for example, if an employee is 'picked on' for minor infringements of company rules. Interception and intervention must always be carried out in a way which is sensitive to the ethical issues involved.

SOFTWARE TO MONITOR ELECTRONIC MAIL

Products to monitor electronic mail are usually sold with external communications in mind, but they can equally well be used on internal messages. The software filters out what appears to be 'junk' mail, and searches for potentially damaging viruses in attached documents. It can also check the language used in the message, with a view to screening out words or phrases which are likely to cause offence.

Problems can arise with 'false negatives', if the software screens out legitimate messages. Assentor from SRA attempts to get round this problem by putting suspect messages into 'quarantine'. Quarantined messages are passed to a compliance officer, who decides whether the contents are acceptable.

In a review of another product, it was noted that it was capable of detecting offensive words the moment they were typed in via the keyboard; the user would immediately be locked out from the document or message in question. This over-reaction to the entry of banned words through 'finger trouble' would be likely to cause considerable annoyance to employees.

13.7 QUESTIONS

1 The same data may be searched and analysed with different purposes in mind by (a) a forensic investigator, and (b) a department concerned with planning and forecasting.

Identify the key differences you would expect to find between the two approaches, with particular reference to:
- the objectives of the search and analysis;
- the manner in which the investigations are carried out;
- the skills required by those carrying out the work.

What kind of software tools might be used in *both* types of investigation?

2 You have reason to suspect that a group of employees is defrauding the company by setting up false customer details in the accounting system. The accounting is done using a standard package on the office PC server. The system is normally only run in normal office hours, but it is customary for staff to work at other hours, especially towards the end of each accounting period.

You would like to find out whether your suspicions are correct and, if so, to establish who is involved in the fraud. Identify the types of data records you would seek access to in order to further your investigations, and give some examples of the kind of analysis to which you would subject them.

3 Give *three* reasons why it can be preferable *not* to carry out forensic analysis on a 'live' system, but to copy the data and take it away for analysis elsewhere.

4 Explain how an 'electronic watermark' works. What are the main differences between this and a more conventional watermark, as applied, for example, to a bank note?

Part 6

REGULATION AND STANDARDS

INTRODUCTION TO PART 6

If I am trying to sell you a door lock, I can take a demonstration model to pieces while you watch, and try to convince you that its innermost workings are so sophisticated and well engineered that it will defeat even the most determined burglar. Alternatively, I could have asked an expert to make a thorough inspection of the product beforehand. If the expert concluded that the lock met certain standards, and you were willing to accept these conclusions, we would both save much time.

Testing for compliance with standards is well established in connection with consumer products. Many bear seals of approval or 'kite marks', which indicate that they have passed through some kind of certification process. Numerous efforts have been made to bring the same approach to bear on IS security and control. Standards have been defined for security features in IS products, for security products themselves, and even for the overall security management in an installation.

The criteria for security in firewalls or operating systems are, of course, much more complicated than those for a door lock. Furthermore, the principles of secure door locks are well understood and generally known. If you wished, it would not be too difficult to dismantle the lock and take a look for yourself. In the realm of IS security, the opposite situation applies. Experts do not always agree on how security features should be built, and there is little chance that the average person will be able to evaluate products which consist of circuit boards and lines of code.

In Part 6, some of the schemes which have been developed for setting and measuring standards are described. In most cases, these schemes are backed by a regulatory body, and the status of some of these bodies is described. Attention is also given to questions of Data Protection, where regulation is now in force in many parts of the world. The Part concludes with a few pointers to the way things may change in the future.

chapter fourteen

STANDARDS, CODES OF PRACTICE AND REGULATORY BODIES

SOME TOPICS ADDRESSED IN THIS CHAPTER

- Ways in which standards are applied to *products* and *security practitioners*
- Examples of certification schemes, particularly *WebTrust* and *BS 7799*
- How *Data Protection* legislation operates in different parts of the world
- Some implications for electronic commerce, and its development in the future

SECURITY AND CONTROL OBJECTIVES

All of the objectives, but particularly:

- Protect secrets
- Promote accuracy
- Prevent tampering
- Prove authorship

14.1   FRAMEWORKS FOR REGULATION

With so much at stake over the integrity and security of information systems, one might expect to find public authorities eager to encourage supervision and regulation. Initiatives have indeed been launched by many governments and international agencies. However, the situation has become confused by a proliferation of would-be regulators, each with their own standards, rules, benchmarks and codes of conduct. Some are sponsored by governments, others by industry alliances, and others by professional and consumer groups. Overall, the results have not proved to be very coherent. On the one hand, there are well-resourced bodies which can enforce their standards using rigorous procedures, and on the other are bodies which, even though they have titles which sound imposing, lack any real substance or authority.

This makes life difficult for anyone looking for 'official' guidance or reassurance. There is also much potential for confusion about who is entitled to jurisdiction in any particular instance, and on what basis. There are several reasons for this less than ideal situation, the main ones being as follows.

- Technology continues to advance rapidly, setting a moving target for those who are trying to establish rules and regulations.
- Networked trading is increasingly carried out on a global basis, so regulatory regimes must be world-wide to be effective. This invariably generates intense pressures, as countries press for what they see as being in their national interests.
- Because information systems permeate so many aspects of business, their regulation does not fit neatly into the remit of any one profession, industry sector or government agency.
- At the technical level, there is a huge range of business software and hardware products to choose from. Each organisation sets up its own permutation of products in its own particular way. It is very difficult to predict what kind of vulnerabilities will emerge when all these products are put together in a system, and start to interact.
- Even where there is a desire to set up regulatory regimes, there are severe shortages of people with the appropriate skills and know-how who can put them into practice.

In the face of these obstacles to progress, it is perhaps remarkable that there are many useful and worthwhile measures which have in fact been implemented. Efforts to introduce some degree of orderliness and reassurance can be seen as coming from three different directions, as illustrated in Figure 14.1.

In the case of *products*, there are two quite different ways in which 'standards' can be relevant. First, standards may be applied in the sense of detailed specifications, which indicate exactly how a product should work. These are vital if, for example, a connection is to be set up between two

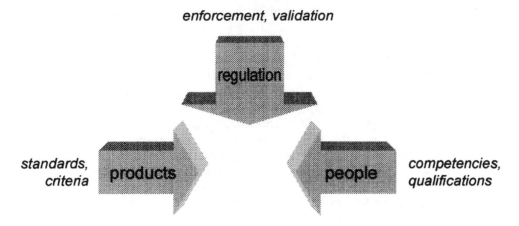

Figure 14.1

computers across a network. The messages travelling to and fro must be handled in exactly the same way at both ends. This depends on *standardisation*, which will be necessary both for the basic communications protocols, and for any security functions applied to the messages (such as encryption, or message authentication codes).

There is also the more everyday meaning for 'setting standards', where the aim is to ensure that products achieve certain levels of *quality*. It is possible, for example, to write a program which faithfully follows a security protocol such as SET or SSL, but which contains coding flaws making the program vulnerable to attack by an unscrupulous person. For security-related products, it is vital that implementations meet standards in *both* senses. Of the two, it is generally much more difficult to prove that the product is of good quality and free from flaws. For this to be tested, the design and coding of the product must be subjected to rigorous scrutiny, and it should be subjected to various kinds of problem situations or malicious attacks, under controlled conditions. The importance of such checks has been demonstrated in a number of studies by Anderson, who has found weaknesses in the implementations of several commercial security systems, including smart cards and teller machines (Anderson 1994).

Compliance with *standardisation*, on the other hand, is often easier to check, because an incorrect implementation will give rise to obvious errors, or may not even work at all. For example, my not-quite-correct implementation of a standard encryption algorithm is likely to produce output which will defeat the attempts of everyone else to decrypt it, even with the correct algorithm and key.

Even when it is successful, product standardisation is often a two-edged sword. Simply by becoming familiar and popular, the products attract the attentions of hackers and virus writers. The problems are compounded when users install a 'family' of products from one supplier, something which suppliers are naturally keen to encourage. This ensures that the products work smoothly together, thanks to their compliance with the supplier's proprietary standards. Recent innovations in virus writing have exploited this, as for example in the case of the 'Bubbleboy' strain of viruses launched against electronic mail processed by Microsoft Outlook (Hancock 1999a). Further description of the security aspects of product standards, and the bodies which sponsor and monitor them, is given in 14.3.

Attempts to specify competencies and qualifications for *people* are usually made with a job specification in mind. In the majority of cases, this means that there is a strong emphasis on information systems auditing. Table 14.1 shows some of the qualifications which are available. Such qualifications play a valuable role in providing an incentive for people to advance their expertise. However, they also raise some wider questions, so far as their relevance to the average business is concerned.

First, some suppositions have to be made about the range of matters for which IS security and control 'professionals' are going to be made responsible. If their role is *purely* one of audit and advice, then this will raise few problems of jurisdiction. Those who actually take the decisions will always, ultimately, have the option of ignoring any advice which is offered to them, and will not feel that they have to give up any of their authority.

However, many organisations, particularly smaller ones, are reluctant to employ people just for their specialist advice. Nor are they keen to pay the high charges associated with bringing in consultants. Instead, they will try to ensure that the necessary expertise is, as far as possible, distributed among staff in various different parts of the company. This will include functions such as site security, quality control, emergency planning, and human resources, as well as those who are managing the information systems themselves. In these circumstances, it begins to look preferable for appropriate

Table 14.1 **Some organisations offering qualifications in IS audit and security**

Organisation	Qualification	Notes
Information Systems Audit and Control Association (ISACA)	Certified Information Systems Auditor (CISA)	ISACA was formerly the EDP Auditors Association
International Information Systems Security Certification Consortium Inc (ISC)[2]	Certified Information System Security Professional (CISSP)	CISSP is supported by the Computer Security Institute (CSI) and Information Systems Security Association (ISSA)
Institute of Internal Auditors (IIA)	Certified Internal Auditor	Includes IS technical skills.
Institute of Internal Auditors – United Kingdom (IIA-UK)	Qualification in Computer Auditing (QiCA)	Also offers a more general Internal Audit qualification

For relevant web site addresses, see Appendix 2.

subsets of knowledge about IS security and control to be included in the qualifications of *all* the relevant professional and management groups.

A second set of questions arises from the way skills are tested. It is always going to be easier to set examinations which deal with matters of technical fact or theory, particularly if the tests (as with CISA and CISSP) use multiple-choice questions. It is more difficult to test softer skills, such as carrying out a major risk analysis, or persuading staff to comply with a new security regime. Qualifications attempt to address this by requiring practical experience in a relevant role, but it is always difficult for anyone to judge what the candidate may or may not have learned from this. Indeed, without extensive supervision, there is always the risk that the experience will simply reinforce and perpetuate bad practice.

Those promoting qualifications also have to make sure that they can sell their product. If there are no job prospects to inspire candidates, few will be interested in investing the time to study. If the criteria for qualifying are not made objective and transparent, the qualification will lack credibility. Hence, it is not surprising to find repeated emphasis on the one role which has been widely recognised (the computer auditor), and a strongly technocentric emphasis in the examinations. Some of the knowledge required in two particular cases is outlined here.

EXAMPLES OF TOPICS COVERED BY CERTIFICATION EXAMINATIONS

The ten domains in the *Common Body of Knowledge* defined by (ISC)^2:

Access Control Systems and Methodology
Computer Operations Security
Cryptography
Application and Systems Development
Business Continuity and Disaster Recovery Planning
Telecommunications and Network Security
Security Architecture and Models
Physical Security
Security Management Practices
Law, Investigations and Ethics

Job Content Areas defined by ISACA:
Information Systems Audit Standards and Practices, and Information Systems Security and Control Practices
Information Systems Organisation and Management *(with an emphasis on topics such as quality management, planning and purchasing)*
The Information Systems Process *(covering a variety of topics, including hardware and software selection, configuration management, and system monitoring)*
Information Systems Integrity, Confidentiality and Availability
Information Systems Development, Acquisition and Maintenance

Sources: ISACA and (ISC)^2 web sites

Rather than trying to set standards for products or professions, it can be argued that it is preferable to adopt a 'top-down' approach through regimes of *regulation* specifying the security and control outcomes which organisations must achieve. It can then be left to the management concerned to figure out how they are going to comply. The regulation may be imposed directly through legislation, or be administered indirectly by bodies which are given oversight of particular business sectors or activities.

In creating new regulations, governments have tended to concentrate on areas where public interest is high (for example, where issues of individual privacy or freedom of information are at stake) or where government itself has a vested interest (for example, in connection with law enforcement and taxation). This has not always produced results which are logical or coherent. For example, an American court has been asked to rule on how a cable company offering Internet services to its customers can comply with both the Cable Communications Policy Act, *and* the Electronic Communications Privacy Act. Both these Acts specify conditions under which messages may be intercepted if a customer is suspected of criminal activity. Unfortunately the Acts disagree on significant details, such as whether the customer must first be notified. It has been argued that even the most law-abiding cable operator will be unable to comply with both pieces of legislation (Massachusetts 1999).

For many years, governments throughout the world have sought to regulate the use of cryptography, by banning the export of any really effective algorithms. Probably the best known example has been the use by the US government of its International Traffic in Arms Regulations. Cryptographic products were placed on the US Munitions List, and it became an offence to export anything (whether in the form of designs, code or hardware) which would enable someone to create strong cryptographic facilities. Many other countries imposed similar restrictions (a list can be found in Garfinkel and Spafford (1997) and a web site of current restrictions is maintained at Koops (2000)). Over the years, complaints from system suppliers and civil liberties groups have caused more and more exceptions to be made, but many restrictions remain (Dam and Lin 1996: Ch. 4).

In Europe, efforts have been made to harmonise laws relating to the conduct of electronic commerce. In 1999, after much consultation and amendment, a framework was agreed for regulating certification authorities, and giving digital signatures equivalence with conventional ones (EC 1999). Appropriate measures have now to be incorporated in national legislation, such as the Electronic Communications Bill brought before the UK Parliament in late 1999.

Meanwhile, European proposals to regularise the position of Internet customers who are in dispute with vendors have run into strong opposition. The proposals would give jurisdiction to the courts in the customer's country of residence. Vendors are understandably hostile to the idea that they might have to defend lawsuits in any one of 15 countries (Europa 2000).

The situation for the average business, in trying to choose tested products, obtain reliable advice, and comply with every relevant regulation is, to say the least, daunting. The three arrows in Figure 14.1 will often converge on the organisation in ways which are haphazard, and even contradictory. One probable outcome is that service providers, particularly in electronic commerce, will increasingly offer outsourcing arrangements, whereby they take over all responsibility for control and compliance issues. One other line of development is schemes which provide certification based on a comprehensive 'health check' of all or part of the organisation's IS system. Section 14.2 describes two such schemes.

14.2 CERTIFICATION SCHEMES: BS 7799 AND WEBTRUST

BS 7799 and WebTrust are both schemes for certifying the security of information systems. BS 7799 applies to the entire system and its working environment. WebTrust applies only to web sites.

The schemes have the following in common:

- A thorough process of testing and inspection is applied to all applicants.
- This has to be carried out by people who have undergone special training and appraisal.
- Certification is for a fixed period of time, and must be renewed periodically.
- The scheme is backed by well established public bodies.
- Users can easily check whether an organisation's claims to have been awarded certification are true.
- There is an ambition to have the standard apply internationally.

In return for submitting itself to the certification process, an organisation gains the right to advertise that it has met the standard, with all that this implies in terms of the quality of its security and controls. Both schemes have required considerable investment by their sponsors, in defining the criteria for certification, documenting and advertising the details of the scheme, and persuading companies and individuals to undergo training prior to carrying out certification.

BS 7799 was originally published in 1995, as a set of standards against which companies could measure themselves. In 1997–8 the standard was reviewed, and machinery was put in place to make the award of BS 7799 subject to an external auditing process. The scheme to do this was named c:cure, and was to be administered by BSI-DISC. (BSI is the British Standards Institution, and DISC is its IT section, with initials which stand for Delivering Information Solutions to Customers).

To meet the requirements of BS 7799, an organisation must be able to demonstrate its competence in ten main areas:

Security policy
Security organisation
Assets classification and control

Personnel security
Physical and environmental security
Computer and network management
Access Control
System Development and Maintenance
Business Continuity Planning
Compliance, with respect to internal policies, and the law

Clearly these different areas will need to be given differing weight, according to the nature of the organisation. For example, not all businesses develop their own systems, and some may make only limited use of networks. As a rule of thumb, the scheme organisers suggest that certification should take about 6 days' work for a typical business employing 100 people, and around 25 days for a business of 1000 employees. Once awarded, certification is valid for 3 years.

The Australian/New Zealand scheme for certification of information security management, AS/NZS 4444, has similar objectives to BS 7799, and there is the possibility of some harmonisation between the schemes. Wider adoption of BS 7799 is also being promoted through French and German translations of its documentation, and there are moves to have it adopted as an ISO standard. However, some criticisms have been levelled at the scheme for being too 'standalone' in its approach, and not being linked sufficiently to the internal control processes which may already be in place in the organisation. Also, while it requires that security policies should be in place, it is not very specific about checking that appropriate members of the management team have been charged with implementing and enforcing them.

The WebTrust scheme was developed jointly by the American Institute of Certified Public Accountants and the Canadian Institute of Chartered Accountants in 1998, in association with Verisign. Since accountants have long held exclusive rights to conduct external audit, and many accounting firms also have thriving IS consultancies, the audit of web sites would seen to be a logical progression. The scheme has moved quickly from its North American base to a more international footing, thanks to the global reach of the major accounting firms, and endorsement of the scheme by other bodies, including the accounting institutes in the UK and Ireland.

The WebTrust certification focuses on three main areas:

- *Business practice disclosure.* The site must make clear to customers exactly how their orders and enquiries will be handled.
- *Transaction integrity.* An investigation is made of the accuracy, completeness and timeliness with which transactions via the web page are processed. An examination is also made of the accounting records which are generated as a result of the transactions.
- *Information protection.* An assessment is made of the protection afforded to client details while they are in transit, and while they are stored in the client's system.

On completing the certification process, the site is permitted to display the WebTrust seal of approval for 90 days. The WebTrust emblem which is displayed on the screen should be 'live', so that it is possible to click on the emblem and be routed immediately to a copy of the relevant auditor's report. In practice, this report may turn out to contain significant caveats. For example, in one instance the following appears:

> Because of inherent limitations in controls, errors or fraud may occur and not be detected. Furthermore, the projection of any conclusions, based on our findings, to future periods is subject to the risk that (1) changes made to the system or controls, (2) changes in processing requirements, or (3) changes required because of the passage of time . . . may alter the validity of such conclusions.

Such clauses illustrate the difficulties of applying certification, in an environment where the goal posts can be moved very quickly. If consumers wish to make further checks, they can consult a list of all currently certified sites, which is maintained independently by Verisign.

The main problem facing schemes such as BS 7799 and WebTrust lies in marketing them against much cheaper, if less rigorous, schemes which award 'seals of approval'. For example, the UK Consumers' Association has a scheme whereby sites can use the Which? Web Trader emblem if they undertake to abide by a code of good practice. Many of the requirements in the code are similar to those laid down by WebTrust. However, in this case no external audit is applied. Online consumer sites such as Epinions (2000) invite customers themselves to provide a form of audit, by registering their impressions and experiences of sites via *reputation managers*. These make it possible to see what previous customers have thought of the quality of service, although of course there is no guarantee that all the views will be reasonable or impartial.

14.3　TECHNICAL STANDARDS FOR IS PRODUCTS

The definition and adoption of technical standards involves numerous official and semi-official bodies around the world. Most of them are inter-linked by collaborative agreements and cross-representation. They generally fall into three categories:

- *Industry-led.* The membership may be drawn from suppliers of IS goods and services, as with ETSI (European Telecommunications Standards Institute), or comprise representatives of an industry sector which is heavily reliant on IS, for example ECBS (European Committee for Banking Standards).
- *Professional.* Some associations of professionals who work in the field of IS have developed a standards-making role. One of the most long-established is the Institute of Electrical and Electronic Engineers (IEEE), based in the USA.

- *'Official' standards-making bodies.* Some of these are funded by governments, but many are independent and non-profit-making. Perhaps the best known is ISO, which is a federation of 130 national standards organisations. (ISO's name is not based on its initials (it is actually called the International Organization for Standardization) but on the Greek word for 'equal').

Some bodies work in ways which involve a mixture of the above. The American National Standards Institute, for example, is a not-for-profit body whose declared aim is to improve the competitiveness of US industry through standards. It has members drawn from a wide cross-section of private sector companies and government agencies.

For comprehensive, if now slightly dated, overviews of IT standards-making the reader is referred to Judge (1991) and Cargill (1989). Today, it is quite impossible for any IS purchaser to keep track of all the standards-related activity around the world, but most standards bodies now have well organised web sites, and it will often be worth checking up on any references to standards which are discovered in marketing materials. (It may also be interesting to follow this up with one or two salient questions to the vendor. It should never be taken for granted that sales teams are any more *au fait* with IS standards terminology than their customers).

Details of the web sites of some of the leading standards bodies are provided in Appendix 2. The following two examples show how standards may be encountered in product specifications, and why they may be significant.

Example 1

The following is taken from an actual specification of an electronic mail product.

> Message signatures are generated using the National Institute of Standards & Technology's (NIST) Digital Signature Algorithm (DSA) and Secure Hash Algorithm (SHA-1); messages are encrypted using the cryptographic coprocessor on the FORTEZZA PC Card
>
> LJL 2000

This statement is one of the better ones, in that it at least explains what all the acronyms stand for. However, for the uninitiated, the names may still not mean a great deal.

NIST is not a national standards body in the usual sense, but an agency of the US Department of Commerce. NIST issues its standards as FIPS (Federal Information Processing Standards), which anyone is free to adopt. All US government bodies, however, are expected to abide by FIPS where possible. The Digital Signature Algorithm is one of two algorithms which are authorised for use in the Digital Signature Standard, published as FIPS 186–1 (1998). The Secure Hash Algorithm is defined in FIPS Publication 180–1 (1995). All this can be gleaned from the NIST web site at www.nist.gov.

The FORTEZZA encryption card is a standard promoted by the US National Security Agency. Compliance with the standard can be certified, using tests developed by the NSA, of which details are given at www.fortezza-support.com.

The would-be purchaser can therefore conclude that the facilities for encryption, signing and hashing which are mentioned in this particular product specification are all based on standards developed by official agencies of the US government. Furthermore, the standards should have been tested out through widespread use within the US government itself. Some will find this reassuring. There are others who take a more negative view of the US government's involvement: for example, some accuse it of deliberately leaving 'trap doors' in products it has developed, to allow the surreptitious decryption of messages. This is where the *openness* of the standard specification becomes important, since if it can be implemented and tested quite independently of government, it is unlikely that any underhand facilities can be built into it.

The vagaries of the standards scene can perhaps be illustrated by reference to another series of standards for hash algorithms. Ronald Rivest (of RSA encryption fame) invented a series of hash (or Message Digest) algorithms called MD2, MD4 and MD5. Details of these standards can be found on the web site of RSA Security Inc, or on several other sites which hold catalogues of RFCs. An RFC (Request for Comment) is a way of publishing specifications relevant to products used on the Internet, for people to use as a standard, if they so wish. Such standards derive their authority through widespread adoption and testing, rather than from official government endorsement.

Example 2

Some marketing material relates to software which enforces access controls or protects against hacker attacks, and claims that the product has been certified to a certain level of security. Assurances are given such as: 'The X operating system has been rated at TCSEC level C2', or 'This firewall meets the ITSEC E3 standard'.

Again, the average customer may wonder about the relevance or otherwise of this gobbledegook in making the purchasing decision. In the two instances just cited:

- TCSEC stands for Trusted Computer Security Evaluation Criteria. This is one of the oldest security standards, originally developed by the US Department of Defense in 1983, and known as the 'Orange Book'. It concentrates on the 'trusted computing base', i.e. the software which enforces security controls in a system.

   TCSEC has always reflected its military origins, by being mainly concerned with the preservation of secrecy. Systems can be rated from A to D. D is the lowest category, offering little or no security, and A is the highest possible. Some categories are subdivided, so for example C2 is actually lower than C1.

- ITSEC stands for the IT Security Evaluation and Certification Scheme. It is promoted by the European Commission, and administered in the UK by the government security and communications body (CESG) in Cheltenham, UK. Efforts are being made to align ITSEC with TCSEC and other national schemes, under what is known as the Common Criteria project.

    ITSEC grades software products from E0 to E6. E0 offers no protection, while E6 offers extensive protection, together with appropriate management tools. The higher the level of certification, the greater the amount of documentation and testing that will have been required to check out its security claims.

Categories awarded under these schemes should always be seen as indicating no more than the *potential* security of the product. If the product is not installed and administered properly, security will be compromised, and the investment in a quality product will have been wasted. Close attention should also be paid to the nature of the criteria set by the scheme. If, as in the case of TCSEC, the emphasis is on securing secrecy, this may not actually be of the highest priority for a business organisation.

As well as officially-sponsored 'kite marks', there are a number of schemes which operate commercially, such as the Checkmark from West Coast Labs, and the ICSA Labs certification scheme. The focus here tends to be on product areas where a large number of suppliers are in competition, such as firewalls, virus checkers, and uninterruptible power supplies. The assessments sometimes include ratings of individual features, which can provide useful points of comparison between the rival products.

14.4   ISSUES OF DATA PROTECTION IN BUSINESS SYSTEMS

Privacy has been the subject of some of the most extensive and heated debates associated with computerisation. Not only can information systems store away vast numbers of details of every aspect of people's lives, they can retrieve them instantly, broadcast them over networks, and correlate records from different sources to find implications which are incriminating or embarrassing. Such facilities are seen as putting unhealthy temptations in the way of both private companies and government agencies. In the latter case, suspicion has been directed especially at those concerned with law enforcement and national security. Even where personal information is being stored for reasons which are entirely reputable, people worry that it will be more vulnerable to intrusion than would be the case with paper records.

This debate found its first real focus when it was realised that computerisation would be applied extensively to the national censuses due to be held in the USA in 1970, and in the UK in 1971. (Even now, governments appear to be particularly sensitive about the census. The UK government took the precaution of issuing its plans for the 2001 census more than 2 years in advance (Census 1999)). During the 1970s much debate ensued about computers and civil liberties, and in the case of the UK, two lengthy official reports were commissioned. Much of the analysis in these reports has stood the test of time, and still makes relevant reading today. (Lindop 1978; Younger 1972). Meanwhile, both lawyers and computer professionals were painting a bleak picture of the future, and demanding that individuals should be given greater legal protection (Miller 1971; Sieghart 1976; Warner and Stone 1970).

In the years which followed, many countries responded to these public concerns by introducing Data Protection laws. Despite the fact that these initiatives all began in different ways, and within many different legal systems, the end results all tended to converge towards a similar basic set of measures. This process of convergence has been described by Bennett (1992). Within Europe, moves began to carry this harmonisation further, with a draft directive published by the European Community in 1990 (Michael 1994). It took a further 5 years for the directive to emerge in its final form (EC 1995).

The Directive has since formed the basis for legislation in all the countries within the European Union. Two justifications for action are given in the opening paragraphs of the Directive. First, it asserts that 'data-processing systems' (to use its terminology) must respect people's rights and freedoms, 'notably the right to privacy'. Second, it offers a justification which is a lot more commercial at heart: that the free movement of goods, persons, services and capital require that 'personal data should be able to flow freely from one Member State to another' without risk to individuals' freedoms.

The Directive sets out several of the principles on which data protection is to be based in Article 6, reproduced here.

FROM ARTICLE 6 OF DIRECTIVE 95/46/EC

Member States shall provide that personal data must be:

(a) processed fairly and lawfully;
(b) collected for specified, explicit and legitimate purposes and not further processed in a way incompatible with those purposes. Further processing of data for historical, statistical or scientific purposes shall not be considered as incompatible provided that Member States provide appropriate safeguards;
(c) adequate, relevant and not excessive in relation to the purposes for which they are collected and/or further processed;
(d) accurate and, where necessary, kept up to date; every reasonable step must be taken to ensure that data which are inaccurate or incomplete, having regard to the purposes for which they were collected or for which they are further processed, are erased or rectified;
(e) kept in a form which permits identification of data subjects for no longer than is necessary for the purposes for which the data were collected or for which they are further processed. Member States shall lay down appropriate safeguards for personal data stored for longer periods for historical, statistical or scientific use.

The convoluted wording and careful use of terminology found in Article 6 reflect the difficulties of defining *exactly* where data protection is to apply. Elsewhere in the Directive, precise definitions are provided for terms such as 'personal data' and 'processing'. Procedures are laid down for enabling people to inspect records which refer to them, and certain categories of permissible exemptions, in fields such as law enforcement and national security, are defined. The Directive covers all types of filing system (whether computerised or not) and all kinds of media (including images as well as records). Holder of personal information are required to implement 'appropriate' security measures. It is left to those in charge of systems to judge what may or may not be 'appropriate', since the Directive gives only the most general guidance. Article 17 states:

> Having regard to the state of the art and the cost of their implementation, such measures shall ensure a level of security appropriate to the risks represented by the processing and the nature of the data to be protected.

In the UK, the provisions of the Directive have been transferred more or less completely into the Data Protection Act, 1998.

Like most Data Protection measures, the European Directive is by no means concerned only with privacy. It governs at least two other major aspects of information handling. As Article 6 shows, much emphasis is placed on the need for information to be *accurate*. The Directive is also concerned about the *fairness* with which personal information is handled, both in Article 6 and elsewhere. For example, Article 15 outlaws certain forms of automated decision-making (aimed particularly at techniques like credit-scoring), unless they are backed up by some kind of human review or mediation.

Privacy is the right to be let alone, to conceal personal information from others, and to be free from intrusive investigations. There are occasions when privacy, accuracy, and fairness fit uneasily together. For example, if you create a right of inspection, with a view to ensuring that records are accurate, the inspection procedure could be abused by someone who managed to impersonate the data subject. Equally, if you want to make fair decisions, a first priority is to find out as much as possible about the situation, a requirement which may conflict with requirements for privacy. It is the existence of these and other conflicts which can make Data Protection such a minefield. There are other, equally worthy, legislative requirements which may conspire to make life difficult for those who have to make day-to-day decisions. For example, administrators in the public sector may find there are conflicts between individual privacy and freedom of information. Many countries have specific legislation on matters such as health or credit records which must be considered. Alternatively, there may be relevant general provisions enshrined in the law, such as those on unreasonable search and seizure in the Fourth Amendment to the US Constitution (Diffie and Landau 1998).

Where data protection laws have been introduced, their enforcement depends on having someone (usually a Privacy Commissioner) who is responsible for keeping a register of personal databases, and taking action against those who flout the law. Privacy Commissioners of one kind or another now exist in most European countries, as well as Australia, Canada, Israel, New Zealand and Taiwan. Hong Kong had a Commissioner under an ordinance passed in 1995, but this office does not seem to have survived the transition to mainland rule.

Commissioners face an uphill struggle to enforce laws which, inevitably, cover ever-increasing swathes of business activity. They also have to fight the constant danger that the processes of registering and demonstrating compliance will degenerate into bureaucratic rituals. An early example of this was the registration form used under the first UK Data Protection Act of 1984. This had four pages for details of the organisation, plus an eight page set for each separate use of data. Realising that several thousand family doctors would have to register under the Act, all of them using personal data for much the same purposes, the British Medical Association duly published a 'crib sheet' showing which boxes to tick (BMA 1988).

In the United States, federal laws govern the use of personal information by credit agencies (US Law 1971) and by government (US Law 1974), but there are some areas where the law is weak (notably in relation to health records). A voluntary compliance scheme for web sites, Truste, has gathered momentum, and now has around a thousand subscribers (Truste 2000). Members agree to abide by general principles of data protection, and Truste administers what it calls an 'oversight and complaint resolution procedure'. The scheme has some advantages in that it can respond quickly to public concerns and to changes in technology, but ultimately it lacks any real teeth.

As with so many regulatory issues on the Internet, the problems arise from deciding exactly where personal information is being 'held' and 'used'. Modern technology makes it easy to hold information about citizens of country X in country Y, and to access the information in order to make decisions about them in country Z. Even if legislation purports to encompass all these situations, enforcement can be formidably difficult. Privacy Commissioners are already exploring ways of collaborating more actively. Since compliance adds to business overheads, a consistent approach around the world would have its benefits, in at least creating a level playing field.

14.5 INFORMATION SYSTEMS IN THE FUTURE: SOME ISSUES OF CONTROL AND REGULATION

In 1972, twenty industry experts were invited to speculate on how they imagined computers being used in the year 2000, and to point out the implications, if any, for public policy (Avebury *et al* 1972). Some 30 years later, the results make interesting reading. Although several writers had glimpses of the scale of the changes which lay ahead, for the most part they were preoccupied with the agenda of their own time. Computer networks might make services more widely accessible, but at their heart there would still be the lumbering mainframes which dominated computing in the 1970s. Serious job losses were to be feared through automation, and information systems would remain cumbersome to use, since everyone would still have to approach them in the spirit of computer programmers. No-one imagined the tidal wave of industries which would result from personal computers, graphical user interfaces, and the Internet. Indeed one wonders whether, even if anyone *had* described their visions of such things, the editors might have dismissed them as being altogether too fanciful.

Two lessons can be learned from the efforts of the writers who accepted the challenge in 1972. First, it is impossible to anticipate the amazing inventiveness with which people will employ new technologies, and the knock-on effects on businesses, which are forced to function and compete in new ways. Second, there are some causes for concern which have remained remarkably constant, security and control being among them. Among the authors in 1972 there were those who were anxious about the effects of computer databases on individual freedom, about the way governments might need to intervene in computer-related industries, and the effects of information systems on management and control in business. At the start of the twenty-first century, all these debates continue, even though the systems themselves have now advanced through several generations of technology.

To make predictions today seems particularly hazardous, as electronic commerce is moving forward at such a frantic pace. However, four predictions will be ventured here (which may in their turn provide some entertainment for readers in 2030). The aim in doing this is the same as that described by Meek in introducing the 1972 study:

> To try to identify places where problems may arise, in particular where important choices with potentially significant choices will be open . . . What worries us most is that decisions may be made by default.
>
> Avebury *et al* 1972: 19

The four predictions are as follows.

* **Information systems constantly change perceptions and expectations about time-frames. IS control and security will struggle to keep up.**

For example, customers will come to expect *all* services to operate interactively and instantaneously, and to see this as the norm. Systems which cannot respond immediately will come to be regarded as substandard. Such shifts in perception are easy to observe, but sometimes the consequences are not. Unfortunately, it is probable that ideas about controls will not move fast enough to keep pace.

The continued shift to 'instant' trading of all kinds will raise the stakes considerably. Businesses will have to make sure that their controls can cut in rapidly, and that they will operate in a 'fail-safe' way if unusual situations arise, or the system comes under attack. Such tactics are of course already used in many preventive controls, particularly in firewalls. However, they will need to be applied far more extensively, particularly in situations where information passes rapidly along value chains which are based on electronic links. Eventually, a point will be reached where it will be impracticable to place reliance on feedback controls.

Meanwhile, any business or public agency which is providing interactive services will continue to amass tremendous quantities of data. Most of this will be a by-product from all the everyday transactions. The simplest and most attractive option will be simply to keep dumping all this data onto mass storage devices (which will be continue to become larger, and cheaper). Given that the first priority is to get the transactions up and running, it will always be tempting to leave matters of record retention and archiving to be sorted out later.

Unfortunately, this is another area in which the time frames are constantly shortening. After only a few years, the data may be unreadable or unusable, for a variety of reasons. Unless data is properly filtered and annotated it may be difficult to track down. If the media and software happen to become obsolete it will be impossible to interpret. But above all, if it is not protected and authenticated, it will have no evidential value, and the organisation will be in an exposed position, because it will have no other copy of the record to rely on.

- **New forms of power struggle and competitive gaming will dominate the world of electronic commerce over the next few years.**

In the electronic goldfish bowl created by the Internet, it will be easy to monitor the activities of customers, competitors, and even those who seek to police the Net's activities. It is inevitable that we shall see new forms of spoiling operations and 'dirty tricks'. These may prove to be particularly effective and vicious because, like the Net transactions themselves, they can work in real time. Already, numerous instances have arisen of businesses being swamped with bogus messages, or finding that hostile material is being posted on a web site which has an address deceptively similar to their own, or suffering from cleverly planted Internet rumours.

Such tactics will be developed at a rapid pace, and may come from quite unexpected quarters. Even reputable businesses will be tempted to join the fray, if the technique involved is somewhere on the fringes of legality. Regulatory bodies will be desperately short of flexibility and jurisdiction, and will be powerless to do very much about it. International cross-border disputes will be a particular problem. Even if the majority of countries agree to enforce regulations, there will always be those who are tempted to profit from providing havens, where a blind eye is turned to sharp practice. Such countries will be the Internet's equivalent of those which set up lax licensing regimes for shipping, and offer 'flags of convenience'.

Most governments will find themselves possessed of fewer and fewer effective powers with respect to the businesses they seek to regulate. Since businesses will not want to operate under conditions of anarchy, it can expected that the impetus for imposing order will come from within, via strong commercial alliances. In order to reassure consumers, Internet service providers and traders will collaborate to provide them with 'comfort zones'. This will be accompanied by moves to take much greater control over what happens on the home workstation. Service providers will not be able to tolerate the anarchy which prevails on the average home PC, and will seek to install solutions based on smart cards and black boxes, whose innermost workings they can control at all times.

- **State controls over Internet-based activities will gravitate towards being minimal or total.**

It will be difficult to arrive at a compromise somewhere in between. In most democratic countries, there are strong business and civil liberties lobbies, which frequently find themselves in agreement in opposing state control. For example, the Broadcasting Services Amendment (Online Services) Act in Australia, requiring Internet Service Providers to block access to indecent and offensive web sites, ran into a storm of criticism from both lobbies. The result in most cases is weak legislation which is almost impossible to enforce. Speaking to a US Department of Energy committee, the director of the Office of Declassification commented:

> What I am suggesting is that the Internet is completely disestablishing the philosophy of a management in which Congress passes laws and we bureaucrats carry them out.
>
> Siebert 1996

Concerns that the Internet will undermine the authority of government have also been expressed in connection with the ability to collect taxes, prevent the burgeoning of underground economies, and enforce laws on the licensing of goods such as liquor or prescription drugs. In the United States, many of these issues were put on hold in 1998, when a 3-year moratorium on any Internet-based tax changes was introduced, under the Internet Tax Freedom Act.

Some have carried the argument to its ultimate conclusion, and predict the collapse of the nation-state (Angell 1995). Meanwhile, some countries, notably China, have expressed a determination to keep all activity on the Internet under state control. If a state wishes to invest heavily in the technology of control, and is prepared to back this up with draconian punishments for those who step out of line, it will probably succeed. There is no reason why the Internet cannot deliver totalitarianism, just as effectively as it can deliver anarchy.

- **Consumers will be drawn to online shopping by its cheapness and convenience, but will also discover significant drawbacks.**

There are two problems in particular:

1 *The inaccessibility of vendors if things go wrong.* Web sites only present an illusion of accessibility. They can deliver rapid responses just as long as the vendor so wishes, but they can also present a stony exterior if the customer tries to complain. There is no equivalent of storming into the local store or travel agents, and demanding to speak to the manager.

   Web vendors may not indicate where they are located. Even if they do, the unreal nature of cyberspace may beguile the user into thinking this is a local enterprise, when its offices and distribution points are actually hundreds of miles away (perhaps even in another country). Vendors doing the electronic equivalent of a 'moonlight flit' do not even have to go to the inconvenience of moving premises. They can simply close down one web site, and open another under a completely different trading name.

2 *Better protection will generally come at the price of lost autonomy.* For example, the introduction of more purpose-built 'black box' Internet terminals will prevent users from undermining security, but will also prevent them from checking up on what the terminal is doing. A case in point is provided by the 'cookies' and other records on the user's own workstation which are created by web browsers. These can be written to by remote web sites, enabling them to keep track of the user's subsequent visits. At present, the user has the option of disabling the facility, and deleting the records.

   It is likely that vendors and service providers will increasingly offer their clients inducements in return for consent. For example, the black box could be offered free of charge, in return for permission to collect data about the user's activities, which would otherwise constitute an invasion of privacy.

Back in the 1970s, the 'silicon chip' was seen as a portent of change, rather as the Internet is today. The chip was seen as paving the way to massive unemployment, and new forms of totalitarianism. The fear was that computers would 'take over' in one way or another. Today, when most people have tried their hand with a PC, computers have acquired a more cuddly image, and are not seen as being quite so threatening. The greater friendliness evident in modern systems is not, however, without some problems of its own.

At least one research laboratory is dedicated to 'couch potato technology': the design and testing of devices which can be used from the armchair, and which will interact with the new audio-visual world being opened by hybrid services linking the Internet and television. Relaxed among the cushions, people will be able to browse through a wealth of product information. The quantity of information will be immense, but whether it will be wholly reliable, and enable valid comparisons and sound decisions to be made, remains to be seen. Even with good information, we may find that being able to make key decisions at any time (and with the growth of mobile data services, almost anywhere) is a mixed blessing. We can certainly expect Internet-based marketing to take full advantage of interaction with customers, and to offer all kinds of deals requiring rapid response. What we cannot perhaps be quite so confident about is our ability to resist new forms of manipulation, particularly if we are browsing late at night, or sitting, tired and bored, on a long-distance flight.

Much has been made of the way the Internet will make people 'information-rich'. Yet this richness will be illusory if the information itself is of poor quality, and cannot be trusted. No-one is made better off by being able to sift effortlessly through huge amounts of dross.

For businesses, just as for individuals, the value of having easy access to information will fall drastically if there are constant doubts about its accuracy and integrity. One hopeful prospect is that employees will gain new insights into this problem, through their personal experience of the Internet. If they find it frustrating to try and find reliable information on the Web, they may be more sympathetic towards efforts to provide them with well-controlled information in their working lives.

On the other hand, it is also possible that new forms of 'cyber-scepticism' will set in, and people will simply shrug off the problems, because they are seen as being outside their control. Whatever changes take place in the popular mood, there is one certainty: business managers will need to monitor it closely. The security and control of their information systems will rest, ultimately, not in the hardware or software, but in the hands of everyone using them.

appendix
one

TWELVE RULES
OF THUMB FOR
MANAGERS

1 However inadequate you feel about information systems, never hand over responsibilities to someone else simply because they seem more enthusiastic or knowledgeable than you are.

2 Listen to what your staff tell you about their difficulties with systems. Assume that, to get round their problems, they may be ignoring or evading controls (for example, by taking short cuts).

3 Wherever possible, use preventive controls in preference to feedback controls.

4 Never assume that people's attitudes to life, work, risk or discipline will improve just because they are sitting in front of a computer screen.

5 Make an issue of failures to follow basic rules on security matters, such as secrecy of passwords, but be consistent and don't go overboard. Always keep something in reserve for the person who is about to do something which is outrageously stupid.

6 Never take it for granted that security products, however impressive, are the only remedy. Always assume that there may be a simpler, low-tech alternative.

7 If you are considering buying a security product, make sure that you

(not the vendor) can give a precise description of the threat(s) it will protect against.

8 Always treat check lists as a starting point for your thought processes, and never as a way of reassuring yourself that you have covered every possible eventuality.

9 If you have no computer auditors in your organisation, persuade someone to take on the role as an amateur from time to time. Get them to cast a fresh eye over the systems you use, and tell you of any apparent weaknesses which concern them.

10 Always assume that files and programs obtained from unknown sources are contaminated with the equivalent of anthrax, botulism and bubonic plague.

11 Even if you have a first-rate record retention policy, never take it for granted that people are doing what it says. Ask for the occasional historical record at random. Ask yourself whether it would stand up as evidence, should this be required.

12 Never assume 'it will turn out alright on the night' for any aspect of your Disaster Recovery Plan. It won't.

appendix two

USEFUL INTERNET ADDRESSES

Up-to-date information on products, standards and legislation can be found on a variety of sites on the Internet. A selection of site addresses (URLs) is given below. Only the basic address is given, since individual page addresses are often changed at the discretion of the site. In most cases, further searching or navigation within the site will be needed to find material relevant to security and control. Many of the sites provide useful pointers to other related sites.

For convenience in reading the list, the standard prefix **http://** has been omitted from all the addresses.

SUPERVISORY AND STANDARDS ORGANISATIONS

ANSI. American National Standards Institute. **www.ansi.org**
Audit Commission (UK). **www.audit-commission.gov.uk**
BSI. British Standards Institution – DISC. **www.bsi.org.uk/disc**
CEN. European Committee for Standardization (Comité Européen de
    Normalisation). **www.cenorm.be**
ECBS. European Committee for Banking Standards. **www.ecbs.org**
Epinions (reputation manager). **www.epinions.com**
FTC. Federal Trade Commission (USA). **www.ftc.gov**
IAB. Internet Architecture Board. **www.iab.org**
ISO. International Organization for Standardization. **www.iso.ch**
ITSCJ. Information Technology Standards Commission of Japan.
    www.itscj.ipsj.or.jp
ITSEC. IT Security Evaluation and Certification Scheme. **www.itsec.gov.uk**

Korea Information Security Agency. **www.kisa.or.kr**
NIST. National Institute of Standards and Technology (USA).
  www.itl.nist.gov
PICS. Platform for Internet Content Selection. See World Wide Web
  Consortium site. **www.w3.org/PICS**
Singapore Productivity and Standards Board. **www.psb.gov.sg**
Standards Australia. **www.standards.com.au**
Truste (USA). **www.truste.org**
UNCITRAL (UN Commission on International Trade Law).
  www.un.or.at/uncitral
WebTrust. **www.cpawebtrust.org**

PROFESSIONAL AND TRADE ASSOCIATIONS

AICPA. American Institute of Certified Public Accountants.
  www.aicpa.org
British Computer Society (has Security and Computer Audit Specialist
  Groups). **www.bcs.org.uk**
ICAEW. Institute of Chartered Accountants in England and Wales.
  www.icaew.co.uk
IIA. Institute of Internal Auditors, USA. **www.theiia.org**
IIA-UK. Institute of Internal Auditors, UK. **www.iia.org.uk**
ISACA. International Systems Audit and Control Association.
  www.isaca.org
(ISC)^2. International Information Systems Security Certification
  Consortium, Inc. **www.isc2.org**
ISSA. Information Systems Security Association. **www.issa–intl.org**
ITU. International Telecommunication Union. **www.itu.int**
Survive, Business Continuity Group. **www.survive.com**

FINANCIAL SERVICES

APACS. Association for Payment Clearing Services (UK).
  www.apacs.org.uk
eCash Technologies, Inc. **www.ecashtechnologies.com**
Mastercard International. **www.mastercard.com**
Mondex (electronic purse system). **www.mondex.com**
NACHA: Electronic Payments Association (USA). **www.nacha.org**
SWIFT (international banking network services). **www.swift.com**
Visa International. **www.visa.com**

SECURITY AND CONTROL: PRODUCTS AND SERVICES

Note: These sites often provide useful background information about
information security, but no endorsement is being made here of the
products on offer.

Ascom AG. **www.ascom.com** (Swiss site, in German, **www.ascom.ch**)

Baltimore Technologies. **www.baltimore.com**
Gamma Secure Systems Ltd. **www.gammassl.co.uk**
ICSA.net. International Computer Security Association. **www.icsa.net**
Livermore Software Laboratories Intl. **www.lsli.com**
RSA Security. **www.rsa.com**
West Coast Labs/West Coast Publishing. **www.check-mark.com**
Major IS suppliers (such as Microsoft and IBM) also have pages on their
sites devoted to security issues and products.

ON-LINE PUBLICATIONS AND UNIVERSITY SITES

Byte.com. **www.byte.com**
Computerworld. **www.computerworld.com/**
Datamation. **www.datamation.com**
Disaster Recovery Information Exchange (Canada). **www.drie.org**
Disaster Recovery Journal. **www.drj.com**
Infoworld. **www.infoworld.com**
London School of Economics. **www.csrc.lse.ac.uk**
Purdue University (CERIAS and COAST projects)
   www.cerias.purdue.edu
Ross Anderson's home page. **www.cl.cam.ac.uk/~rja14**
Silicon.com, IT news service. **www.silicon.com**

PRIVACY AND DATA PROTECTION

Australian Privacy Commissioner. **www.privacy.gov.au**
Data Inspectorate, Norway. **www.datatilsynet.no**
Data Protection Commissioner (UK). **www.dataprotection.gov.uk**
Electronic Frontier Foundation. **www.eff.org**
Global Internet Liberty Campaign. **www.gilc.org**
Office of the Privacy Commissioner, New Zealand. **www.privacy.org.nz**
Privacy Commissioner of Canada. **www.privcom.gc.ca**
Privacy Exchange. **www.privacyexchange.org**
Registratiekramer (Dutch Privacy Commissioner).
   www.registratiekramer.nl

HACKING AND VIRUSES

Sites in this category obviously need to be viewed with some caution. Sites
run by and for hackers can provide interesting information, but are best
visited using a PC which contains nothing you value.

   The leading suppliers of anti-virus software maintain reference sites
which are good sources of current information. Hoax viruses are tracked
on a number of sites, including:

www.urbanmyths.com
urbanlegends.miningco.com
www.symantec.com/avcenter

Glossary

Access Control   A means of recognising the authorised users of an information system, and determining which facilities within the system they are allowed to use.

Access Control Table   A table listing everyone who is authorised to have access to an information system, or one of the applications within it. Against each user identifier, the table specifies what that user is or is not permitted to do.

ALE (Annual (or Annualised) Loss Expectancy)   A simple method for comparing risks. The possible damage from a given threat is estimated as a cash sum, which is then multiplied by the probability that the threat will materialise in any one year.

Algorithm   In cryptography, a set of instructions (usually in the form of a computer program) which determines how plaintext is to be transformed into an encrypted message, and vice versa.

Application Control   A control whose scope is limited to one particular application. An application is a single program, or a suite of programs, dedicated to serving one particular function within the organisation, such as accounting or computer-aided design.

Asymmetric Cryptography   A set of cryptographic techniques based on the use of specially generated *pairs* of keys. One key is used to encrypt a message and the other key is used to decrypt it. If the sender keeps one key secret and makes the other key public, it is possible to create a **digital signature** (qv).

Audit   A review made by an independent assessor. The concept of audit was developed by accountants, who undertake periodical *external* audits, to reassure stakeholders that the financial affairs of an organisation are being run properly. *Internal* audit is carried out by staff within the organisation, usually on a more ongoing basis.

Audit Trail   A collection of evidence which enables an auditor to trace what has happened at every stage of a business process. The trail may comprise a mixture of computer records and paper documents.

Authentication   The provision, usually by automated means, of proof of identity by one of the parties to an electronic transaction.

Biometrics   Physical attributes or characteristics of a person which can be used as a basis for automated identification, for example, the distinctive pattern of a voice or a fingerprint.

Block cipher   A method of encryption in which the data is first divided up into blocks of fixed length (usually 64 bits or more). Each block in turn is then transformed by the cryptographic algorithm. This introduces some 'choppiness' into the data, which can make the technique unsuitable for 'live' sound or video transmissions. See also **stream cipher**.

Business Continuity Planning   An enterprise-wide exercise which identifies threats which could seriously impair the ability of the business to function. Planning is then directed at eliminating such threats, or minimising their impact if prevention is not possible.

CEN (Comité Européen de Normalisation)   Also known as the European Committee for Standardisation. Promotes technical standards in Europe.

Certification Authority   A reputable body which issues electronic certificates to prove the authenticity of public keys. Each certificate should show, as a minimum, the identity of the key owner (whether an individual or an organisation), a copy of the key, and an expiry date. The certificate should be **digitally signed** by the CA.

Check Digit   One or two extra numbers are added on at the end of a reference number (such as a number for VAT registration or a credit card). These extra digits are recalculated whenever the number is being re-entered into a system, as a way of checking that the number is a valid one.

Chinese Walls   An arrangement whereby people within the same organisation keep certain information (usually relating to a client) secret from one another.

CISA (Certified Information Systems Auditor)   Qualification administered by **ISACA** (qv).

COBIT (Control Objectives for Information and related Technologies)   A set of standards for implementing security and control, developed by **ISACA** (qv).

Cold Stand-by   A back-up site to which computer services can be transferred in the event of a disaster. The site has only basic facilities, and it may take a day or two to get services up and running.

Concurrency   A term applied to computer audit facilities which are built in to a system, and which can be activated while the system is actually in use.

Control Total   If a batch of entries is being made into an application, or a series of calculations is being performed, the system calculates an appropriate total by number or by value. This total is then recalculated independently, and the two results are compared.

CRAMM (CCTA Risk Analysis and Management Method)   A risk analysis methodology devised by the UK Government Central Computer and Telecommunications Agency.

CRL (Certificate Revocation List)   A list issued by a Certification Authority, which identifies certificates it has issued and which have not reached their expiry date, but which the CA wishes to cancel. The list should be digitally signed by the CA, to indicate its authenticity.

Countermeasure   For each threat to an information system, there will be one or more possible countermeasures. These will either prevent the threat from materialising, or substantially reduce its impact.

Cryptography The transformation of data, using algorithms and keys, in ways which can be reproduced or reversed by others. Originally used mainly to provide secrecy in communications, cryptography now has a much expanded role in providing functions such as tamper-proofing, signing and date-stamping.

Data Encryption Standard A technique of symmetric encryption based on 64-bit blocks, which was first issued as a standard in 1977.

Decryption The de-coding of an encrypted message, to reveal the (meaningful) plaintext. Also sometimes referred to as the **deciphering** of a message.

Diffie-Hellman exchange An early method of establishing a private key, when two people are faced with trying to do this over an insecure communications link. Named after its inventors, Whitfield Diffie and Martin Hellman.

Digital Signature Any digital material can be 'signed', using asymmetric encryption with the signer's private key. It is essential that the signer keeps this key absolutely secret. Anyone who knows the signer's *public* key can then decrypt the material. Being able to decrypt successfully confirms that the material must indeed have come from the signer.

Disaster Recovery Plan A detailed plan specifying what is to happen in the event that the organisation's information systems suffer serious degradation or damage. The plan should be tested on a regular basis.

Discretionary Access Control Systems which allow users to 'own' certain data or facilities, and to make decisions about whether other users are to be given access to them. Such arrangements were regarded as quite advanced in early time-sharing systems, based on mainframes. With the advent of personal computers, it is commonplace for users to control 'their' resources, and for these to be shared on a discretionary basis.

EDI (Electronic Data Interchange) The exchange of business messages, using standard electronic formats.

EDIFACT (Electronic Data Interchange for Administration, Commerce and Transport) An internationally adopted standard for EDI messages. It contains some optional provisions for authentication and security.

Electronic Purse A smart card into which a cash value can be loaded. The cash can be 'spent' with retailers who have appropriate card reading equipment.

Electronic Wallet A program installed on a user's personal computer, which takes control when financial transactions take place over the Internet.

Electronic Watermark A method of proving authorship or ownership of electronic (digital) material. See also **Steganography**.

Encryption The encoding of a piece of plaintext, to produce an (unintelligible) encrypted message. Also sometimes referred to as **enciphering**.

ETSI (European Telecommunications Standards Institute) A forum for setting European standards, with several hundred members, mainly from within the telecommunications industry.

EU (Expected Utility) A method of quantifying risk. It is obtained by multiplying the size of the outcome (usually in terms of monetary gain or loss) by the probability that the outcome will occur.

Escrow An arrangement whereby a copy of electronic material is lodged with an independent party. Stipulations may be made about the circumstances under which the material may be released, and to whom. There is usually a small amount of material of high value, e.g. a cryptographic key.

False Negative A failure of user identification, in which a genuine, authorised user is wrongly rejected by the system.

False Positive   A failure of user identification, in which an imposter (pretending to be an authorised user) is wrongly accepted by the system.

Feedback Control   A control which depends on remedial action being taken *after* the event. (For example, detecting unauthorised telephone calls by examining a log generated in the telephone exchange).

Firewall   A protective device installed at the boundary between the organisation's internal data network and an outside network (usually the Internet). The firewall will screen out certain forms of unwanted traffic and attempts to launch malicious attacks.

Fraud   The misappropriation of assets, or the creation of a misleading impression of a financial state of affairs, where the perpetrator attempts to conceal the fact that anything improper is going on.

General Control   A term applied to any type of control which applies to the system as a whole. The concept was easier to apply to systems based around one or more central mainframes, since 'the system' could be found almost entirely in one computer room. However, general controls are still needed in more complex distributed systems, especially in providing an 'outer perimeter' of access controls.

Generation Data Sets   A technique for using the media on which back-ups are held in rotation. Typically, there are three 'generations' of copies. Whenever a new back-up copy is made, the *oldest* version is over-written and so becomes the 'youngest' generation.

Groupware   Software which is designed to enable a working group to share files, programs, and incoming electronic documents, usually with facilities for monitoring and control by a manager.

GSM (Groupe Spéciale Mondiale)   An international standard for mobile telephony, sometimes anglicised to Global System for Mobile Communications. User identification is provided by a SIM (Subscriber Identification Module).

Hacker   In newspaper parlance, a person who undertakes malicious attacks on an information system, particularly across a data network. Originally, 'hacker' denoted anyone with an obsessive interest in the internals of computers.

Hoax Virus   An electronic mail message which purports to give warning of a virus at large on the Internet, or some other danger. The recipient is urged to pass the warning on. In fact, no danger exists, and the purpose of the message is to generate alarm, and a lot of unnecessary emails.

Hot stand-by   A back-up facility for providing computer services which can be activated very quickly in the event of a disaster.

IAB (Internet Architecture Board) (previously Internet Activities Board)   A body which coordinates Internet development, and promotes technical standards.

ISACA (Information Systems Audit and Control Association)   A long-established body promoting good practice and professional standards in IS security. It is based in the USA, with Chapters in other parts of the world. Originally the EDP Auditors Association.

IIA (Institute of Internal Auditors)   A USA-based organisation, whose members work in internal auditing, computer audit, and governance and internal control.

IIA-UK (Institute of Internal Auditors – United Kingdom)   Has a similar role to the US body of the same name, with which it is linked.

(ISC)² (International Information Systems Security Certification Consortium Inc)   A non-profit corporation offering certification for IS security practitioners.

ISDN (Integrated Services Digital Network) A standard for digital telecommunications lines, which can be connected by 'dialling' them as and when needed, in the same way as ordinary business or domestic telephone lines.

ITAR (International Traffic in Arms Regulations) United States regulations relating to the export of munitions. The definition of 'munitions' includes cryptographic products and algorithms.

ITSEC (Information Technology Security Evaluation & Certification Scheme) A scheme promoted by the European Commission, to set standards for evaluating the security of IT products and systems.

KDC (Key Distribution Centre) A method of storing and issuing cryptographic keys, based on one central computer. The keys are usually symmetric, and the user group is 'closed' (e.g. limited to the employees in one organisation).

Kerberos An extension of the functions of a KDC, originally developed at the Massachusetts Institute of Technology, which enables users to be authorised to use a variety of facilities on an internal network, by issuing them with electronic 'tickets'. Kerberos has evolved through several versions, and has been incorporated in commercial products.

LEAF (Law Enforcement Access Field) A controversial feature of the 'Clipper' encryption chip which was heavily promoted by the US government in the early 1990s. The LEAF provided a 'back door' method of determining the cryptographic key, and thus de-coding messages.

MAC (Mandatory Access Control) A system of control which aims to set constraints on the facilities and data available to each user, these being determined by a central System Administrator. Individual users are *not* empowered to pass on or share any of their privileges (compare **Discretionary Access Control**).

MAC (Message Authentication Code) A short code added to a message, which enables the receiver to check whether the message has been tampered with. (Notwithstanding the reference to 'authentication', the MAC will not necessarily provide evidence of the sender's identity).

Message Digest A form of **Message Authentication Code** (qv). Message digest algorithms, for which a number of standards have been defined, use a hash function to produce a value which has a short, fixed length (typically 128 bits).

MIC (Message Integrity Check) Another term sometimes used for a **Message Authentication Code** (qv).

Non-repudiation An arrangement aimed at preventing the sender of a message from denying subsequently that he or she actually sent it. This may be done by requiring the use of a digital signature, or by including extra steps in the communication sequence.

One-time pad A method of encryption where both sender and receiver have a copy of an identical string of randomly selected digits or letters. The string must be at least as long as the message to be encrypted. The string and the message are then combined using a simple set of rules. An extremely secure method, but very cumbersome to set up and maintain.

Orange Book A set of security standards issued by the US Department of Defense (Trusted Computer System Evaluation Criteria).

Passphrase A term sometimes used to distinguish a password which is entered to activate the use of a stored cryptographic key (as opposed to logging on to IS facilities).

Password   A string of characters which must be entered by a user before access is granted to facilities in an information system.

PGP (Pretty Good Privacy)   A shareware cryptography product released on the Internet by Phil Zimmerman. Asymmetric keys are used to establish each communication. Users pass public keys to one another on an informal basis.

Phreaker   A term used to describe those who use technical trickery to obtain free telephone calls, and commit other types of fraud on telecommunication networks.

PICS (Platform for Internet Content Selection)   A general-purpose system for labelling the content of documents accessible on the World Wide Web.

PIN (Personal Identification Number)   A form of password. It uses numerical values only, so it can be entered through key pads such as those found on smart cards and automated teller machines.

PKI (Public Key Infrastructure)   A service which ensures that public (asymmetric) keys for cryptography are distributed and maintained securely.

Preventive Control   A control which detects a potential security or integrity problem and take protective action immediately. (For example, preventing employees from dialling certain telephone numbers by setting up a barring list in the exchange).

Privacy Enhancing Technologies   A term applied to a collection of techniques for ensuring that details of individuals cannot be retrieved from data which has been aggregated, e.g. to provide statistics for management or planning purposes.

Private Key   A cryptographic key which is effective only as long as it is kept secret. An *asymmetric* private key should be known to only one person. A *symmetric* private key will need to be known to at least two people, because the same key is used for both encryption and decryption.

Process   In the context of information systems, a sequence of tasks or transactions which must be completed in order to deliver a particular service, usually for an individual customer.

Public Key   When a pair of keys is generated in asymmetric cryptography, one of the keys may be revealed to all and sundry and becomes the 'public' key. This can then be used to check on a digital signature (qv).

RAID (Redundant Array of Independent Drives (or disks))   A large number of small disk drives are combined into one unit. Compared with a single large disk drive of equivalent capacity, RAID storage offers quicker retrieval times, and less vulnerability to failure by one drive.

RSA   A method of asymmetric encryption, introduced in 1978 and named after its inventors (Ronald Rivest, Adi Shamir, and Leonard Adleman).

SDLC (System Development Life Cycle)   A series of steps for implementing a new information system, from its initial inception, through to evaluation after the system has gone into service.

SET (Secure Electronic Transaction)   A standard for authenticating the parties, and providing secrecy of communication, for Internet transactions based on payment by credit card.

Smart Card   A plastic card which has the same dimensions as an ordinary credit card, but which has a computer chip embedded in it. The chip can be programmed to help in security checking, or to hold cash values if the card is intended for use as an electronic purse.

Social Engineering   The use of confidence tricks and other devious methods to persuade people to divulge sensitive information, such as passwords or individuals' personal records.

SSL (Secure Socket Layer) A method of securing Internet communications between a user's web browser and a remote site, which includes facilities for secrecy and authentication.

Steganography A group of techniques for concealing messages within an electronic file (which could contain text, sound or images). The concealed message can be used to convey secret information, or to provide evidence of ownership of the material in the file.

Stream cipher An encryption algorithm which works on very short 'slices' of data (for example, eight bits at a time). This means that the cryptography does not upset the smooth flow of data. However, stream ciphers tend to be weaker than block ciphers (qv).

TCSEC (Trusted Computer System Evaluation Criteria) A set of security standards issued by the US Department of Defense, often referred to as the Orange Book.

Threat A source of danger to the integrity or security of an information system.

Time Stamp A method of proving that electronic (digital) material was originally stored on a particular date, and has not been altered since.

Token Something a person possesses, which is required in order to gain access to an information system. Examples are plastic cards with a magnetic stripe, and key fobs which respond to a radio signal.

Transaction In the context of information systems, transactions are the everyday routine tasks which form the bulk of the activity on the system – for example, creating a new customer record, or placing an order via a web page.

Trap door A weak point in software, which may have been left deliberately or inadvertently, whereby someone can change the functions or settings in the software while it is running, without being subject to any access controls.

Trojan Horse A program installed in an information system which has (or appears to have) a legitimate function, but which contains malicious code. This will usually have been set up by an 'insider' (e.g. a programmer updating part of the system).

UMTS (Universal Mobile Telecommunications System) A global standard for mobile telephones, which includes provision for data transmissions.

UPS (Uninterruptible Power Supply) A battery-driven power supply which cuts in immediately in the event of a power failure. It is usually intended to provide a short-term source of power, while alternative arrangements are made (e.g. to use a generator).

VAN (Value Added Network) An arrangement in which responsibility for the set-up and management of telecommunications services is handed over to an outside contractor, and the contractor 'adds value' in various ways (for example, assistance with EDI).

Virus A program which is designed to spread itself from one computer to another. Every virus need a 'carrier', which is often 'fun' material which people will be tempted to pass on, such as a computer game or a screen saver. The effects of a virus can vary in severity, from e.g. displaying irritating messages, to wiping all the data from a disk.

Worm A virus which is designed specifically to perpetuate itself across network links (usually causing some kind of harm to the network connections in the process).

References

Adams, J. (1995) *Risk*, London, UCL Press.

AICPA (1999) *Service Description for Electronic Commerce Assurance*; www.aicpa.org

Alexander, M. (1996) *The Underground Guide to Data Security*, Reading, Mass., Addison-Wesley.

Allen, B. (1996) 'Can the participative audit approach improve job satisfaction?', in Chambers, A. (ed.), *Internal Auditing*, Dartmouth.

Anderson, R. (1994) 'Why cryptosystems fail', *Communications of the ACM* Vol. 37, No. 11 November: 32–40; other papers on related subjects can be found at Ross Anderson's web page, http://www.cl.cam.ac.uk/users/rja14

Andrew, C. (1996) *For the President's Eyes Only*, London, HarperCollins.

Andrews, K. (ed.) (1989) *Ethics in Practice*, Boston, Mass., Harvard Business School Press.

Angell, I. (1995) Winners and Losers in the Information Age; www.csrc.lse.ac.uk

Anon (1994) Computing, 29 September: 1.

Anon (1996) Wireless Local Loop Goes Global, *Telecommunications*, July: 20.

Anon (1998) Dual Modem Routers Double Your Bandwidth, *Byte*, March: 32.

Anon (1998a) 'Several big banks see CA status', *Bank Systems Technology*, March: 11.

Anon (1998b) *Health Service Journal*, London, 12 February: 6.

Anon (1999) Builders of the New Economy, *Business Week*, 21 June: 49–52.

Anon (1999a) US spy satellites 'raiding German firms' secrets. *Sunday Telegraph*, 11 April p. 23.

Anon (1999b) CNET News.com, 4 June.

Arps, M. (1993) 'CD-ROM: Archival considerations', in Mohlenrich, J. (ed.), *Preservation of Electronic Formats and Electronic Formats for Preservation*, Society of American Archivists/Highsmith Press.

Ascom (2000) www.ascom.ch/infosec

Audit Commission (1987) *Survey of Computer Fraud and Abuse*, London, HMSO.

Audit Commission (1998) *Ghost in the Machine: An Analysis of IT Fraud and Abuse*, London, Audit Commission Publications.

Avebury, Lord, Coverson, R., Humphries, J. and Meek, B. (eds) (1972) *Computers and the Year 2000*, Manchester, NCC.

Backhouse, J. and Dhillon, G. (1996) 'Structures of responsibility and security of information systems', *European Journal of Information Systems*, 5: 2–9.

Barnes, P. (1999) 'Work area recovery – the lateral view', *Journal of Business Continuity*, 8 April.

Beacham, F. (1996) 'Archivists warn: Don't depend on digital tape', *Pro Audio Review*, April.

Bell, D. and La Padula, L. (1973) *Secure Computer Systems: Mathematical Foundations and Model*, MITRE Report, MTR 2547 2: Nov. 1973.

Bender, W., Gruhl, D., Morimoto, N. and Lu, A. (1996) 'Techniques for data hiding', *IBM Systems Journal*, 35, 3: 313–36.

Bennett, C. (1992) *Regulating Privacy*, Ithaca, NY, Cornell University Press.

Berghel, H. (1997) 'Watermarking cyberspace', *Communications of the ACM*, 40, 11: 19–24.

Beutelspacher, A. (1994) *Cryptology*, Washington DC, Mathematical Association of America.

Beynon-Davies, P. (1995) 'Information systems "failure": the case of the London Ambulance Service's Computer Aided Despatch project', *European Journal of Information Systems*, 4: 171–84.

BIS (1987) *Computer Disaster Casebook*, BIS Applied Systems, 1987 and 1988 editions, London.

Black, G. (1999) 'Fixed–mobile convergence', *Financial Times*, 18 March, Survey: 8.

Blackburn, S. (1997) 'The competencies of the excellent information systems auditor', *BCS Computer Audit Specialist Group Journal*, 8, 1: 5–13.

BMA (1988) *Guidance to General Medical Practitioners on Data Protection Registration*, London, General Medical Services Committee, BMA.

Board of Inquiry (1995) *Report of the Board of Banking Supervision Inquiry into the Circumstances of the Collapse of Barings*, London, HMSO.

Boisot, M. (1998) *Knowledge Assets: Securing Competitive Advantage in the Information Economy*, Oxford, Oxford University Press.

Bontchev, V. (1996) 'Possible macro virus attacks and how to prevent them', *Computers and Security*, 15, 7: 595–626.

Bower, T. (1991) *Maxwell: The Outsider*, London, Mandarin.

Bowie, N. (1993) 'The ethics of bluffing and poker', in White, T. (ed.), *Business Ethics: A Philosophical Reader*, New York, Macmillan, 338–46.

Brackenridge, G. (1993) 'Implementing RAID on the VAX', UK Computer Measurement Group Annual Conference, 501–8.

Bridge, S. (1999) 'Streamlining the organisation', *e.business*, November: 64–9.

Broadbent, M. and Weill, P. (1993) 'Improving business and information strategy alignment: Learning from the banking industry', *IBM Systems Journal*, Vol. 32, 1: 162–79.

Burn, J. (1996) 'IS innovation and organizational alignment – A professional juggling act', *Journal of Information Technology*, 11: 3–12.

Cairncross, F. (1997) *The Death of Distance*, London, Orion.

Caldwell, B. (1998) 'New problems, new solutions', *Informationweek*, issue 700, 149–56.

Campbell, M. (1998) 'Thoroughly modern Mondex', *Canadian Banker*, 105, 1: 30–3.

Cargill, C. (1989) *Information Technology Standardization*, Bedford, Mass., Digital Press.

Carr, A. (1993) 'Is business bluffing ethical?', in White, T. (ed.), *Business Ethics: A Philosophical Reader*, New York, Macmillan, 328–37.

CCTA (1995) *A Guide to Business Continuity Management*, London, HMSO.

Census (1999) *The 2001 Census of Population*, Cm 4253, London, HMSO.

Cerullo, M. and McDuffie, R. (1991) 'Anticipating accounting's natural disasters', *Financial and Accounting Systems*, 7, 3: 32–5.

Chowdhary, T. (1997) 'The Internet Divide', *Telecommunications*, September: 96.

Clark, D. and Wilson, D. (1987) *A Comparison of Commercial and Military Computer Security Policies*, Proceedings of 1987 Symposium on Security and Privacy, IEEE Computer Society, 184–95.

Collins, T. (1990) 'Gone with the wind', *Computer Weekly*, 1 February.

Collins, T. (1997) *Crash, Ten Easy Ways to Avoid a Computer Disaster*, London, Simon & Schuster.

Cornwall, H. (1989) *Data Theft*, London, Mandarin.

Dam, K. and Lin, H. (eds) (1996) *Cryptography's Role in Securing the Information Society*, National Research Council, Washington, DC, National Academy Press.

Data Protection Registrar (1997) *Information Security: A Consultation Paper*, Office of the Data Protection Registrar, Wilmslow, November.

Davenport, T. (1993) *Process Innovation*, Boston, Mass., HBR Press.

Davenport, T. (1994) 'Saving IT's soul: Human-centred information management', *Harvard Business Review*, March/April, 72, 10: 119–31.

Davis, C. (1999) *Emergence of Electronic Commerce in Spanish-Speaking Latin America*, Canada, University of New Brunswick.

DERA (1997) Ively Road, Farnborough, Hampshire GU14 0LX.

Dhillon, G. (1997) *Managing Information System Security*, Basingstoke, England, Macmillan.

Diffie, W. and Hellman, M. (1976) 'New Directions in Cryptography', *IEEE Transactions in Information Theory*, November, 644–54.

Diffie, W. and Landau, S. (1998) *Privacy on the Line: The Politics of Wiretapping and Encryption*, Cambridge, Mass., MIT Press.

Dixon, G. and John, D. (1989) 'Technology issues facing corporate management in the 1990's', *MIS Quarterly*, 13, September: 247–55.

Donaldson, M. and Lohr, K. (1994) *Health Data in the Information Age*, Washington, National Academy Press.

Donovan, J. (1991) 'Singapore, Wiring Up a Dream', *Asian Business* 27, 10: 45; www.s-one.gov.sg

DP Registrar (1994) *Tenth Report of the Data Protection Registrar*, London, HMSO.

Drummond, H. (1996) *Escalation in Decision-Making*, Oxford, Oxford University Press.

DTI (1997) Public Consultation Paper, 'Legislation for Licensing of Trusted Third Parties for the Provision of Encryption Services', March, Department of Trade and Industry, London.

ecash (2000) www.ecash.net

EC (1995) Directive 95/46/EC of the European Parliament on the protection of individuals with regard to the processing of data and the free movement of such data.

EC (1999) Directive of the European Parliament and of the Council on a Community framework for electronic signatures; www.ispo.cec.be/eif

ECBS (1999) European Committee for Banking Standards, 'The Interoperable Financial Sector Electronic Purse'; www.ecbs.org

Emmerson, B. (1998) 'Getting closer to a world mobile phone', *Byte*, May: 15.

Epinions (2000) www.epinions.com

Essick, K. (1998) 'Put a Big Mac on my smart card please', *Computerworld*, 32, 34: 45–6.

Essinger, J. (1991) 'Prevention is the priority', *Accountancy*, September: 64.

Europa (2000) europa.eu.int/comm/scic

FAO (1999) www.fao.org/ag/ags/agsm/microbnk.htm

Farr, R. (1977) *The Electronic Criminals*, Glasgow, Collins.

FASB (1999) *Exposure Draft, Business Combinations and Intangible Assets*, US Financial Accounting Standards Board, September 1999.

Fay, S. (1996) *The Collapse of Barings*, London, Richard Cohen Books.

Feynman, R. (1985) *Surely you're joking, Mr Feynman*, London, Vintage.

Fischhoff, B. and MacGregor D. (1983) 'Judged lethality: How much people seem to know depends on how they are asked'. *Risk Analysis* 3: 229–336.

Foremski, T. (1989) 'Silicon Valley picks up the pieces', *Computing*, 26 October.

Foremski, T. (1989a) 'US View', *Computing*, 12 October.

Freidson, E. (1986) *Professional Powers*, Chicago, University of Chicago Press.

FTC (2000) www.ftc.gov

Fukuyama, F. (1995) *Trust*, Penguin.

Garfinkel, S. and Spafford, G. (1997) *Web Security and Commerce*, Sebastopol, Ca., O'Reilly.

Gladney, H., Worley, E. and Myers, J. (1975) 'An access control system for computing resources', *IBM Systems Journal*, 14, 3: 212–28.

Gordon, S. (1995) 'Social engineering: Techniques and prevention', Compsec Conference on Security, Audit and Control, London, Elsevier, 445–50.

Gordon, S. (1998) 'Breaking the chain', *Computers and Security*, 17, 7: 586–8.

Gordon, S. (1999) 'Telephone tales', *Computers and Security*, 18, 2: 120–3.

Gove, R. (1999) 'Fundamentals of Cryptography and Encryption', in Krause, M. and Tipton, H. (eds), *Handbook of Information Security Management*, Boca Raton, Fla., Auerbach.

Gray, C. (1992) 'Growth-orientation and the small firm', in Caley, K., Chell, E. and Mason, C. (eds) (1992), *Small Enterprise Development*, London, Chapman, 59–71.

Gross, H. (1971) 'Privacy and Autonomy', in Pennock, J. and Chapman, J. (eds), *Privacy*, New York, Atherton Press.

Guild (1999) *History of printing*, Canadian Bookbinders and Book Artists Guild; www.cbbag.ca

Hafner, K. and Lyon, M. (1998) *Where Wizards Stay Up Late*, New York, Simon & Schuster.

Hafner, K. and Markoff, J. (1993) *Cyberpunk*, London, Corgi.

Halfhill, T. R. (1998) 'Crash-proof computing', *Byte*, April: 60–74.

Hall, G., Rosenthal, J. and Wade, J. (1993) 'How to make reengineering really work', *Harvard Business Review*, November: 119–31.

Halsall, F. (1996) *Data Communications, Computer Networks and Open Systems*, Reading, Mass., Addison Wesley.

Hammer, M. (1990) 'Reengineering work: Don't automate, obliterate', *Harvard Business Review*, July, reprint 90406.

Hammer, M. and Champy, J. (1993) *Reeingineering the Corporation: A Manifesto for Business Revolution*, London, Brearley.

Hancock, B. (1999) 'NT Passwords for Sale', *Computers and Security* 18, 2: 92.

Hancock, B. (1999a) 'BubbleBoy virus – First of a nasty new strain', *Computers and Security*, 18, 8: 646.

Hancox, D. (1997) 'Could the Equity Funding Scandal happen again?', *Internal Auditor*, October: 28–34.

Hardy, G. (1996) 'The truth behind single sign-on', 13th Compsec Conference on Computer Security, Audit and Control (London), Oxford, Elsevier.

Hares, J. and Royle, D. (1994) *Measuring the Value of Information Technology*, Chichester, England, Wiley.

Hawker, A. (1993) 'A few ethics at BA would go a long way', *Computing*, 28 January: 14.

Hawker, A. (1996) 'Hidden costs of computing: some evidence from general practice', *Current Perspectives in Health Care*, BJHC Ltd, 507–12.

Hayam, A. and Oz, E. (1993) 'Integrating data security into the systems development life cycle', *Journal of Systems Management*, August: 16–20.

Hinke, T. *et al.* (1997) 'Protecting databases from inference attacks', *Computers and Security*, 16, 8: 687–708.

Hoffman, L. and Miller, W. (1970) 'Getting a personal dossier from a statistical database', *Datamation*, May, 74–5.

Hoffman, W. and Frederick, R. (1995) *Business ethics: Reading and Cases in Corporate Morality*, New York, McGraw-Hill: chapter 7.

Holley, K. and Costello, T. (1998) 'The Evolution of GSM data towards UMTS', 1998 GSM World Congress; www.gsmdata.com

Hood, K. and Yang, J. (1998) 'Impact of banking information systems security on banking in China', *Journal of Global Information Management*, Vol. 6, No. 3: 5–15.

Huber, R. (1993) 'How Continental Bank outsourced its "Crown Jewels"', *Harvard Business Review*, January: 121–9.

Hunton, J. and Wright, G. (1995) 'How information systems managers view internal auditors', *Internal Auditing*, 11, 2: 33–43.

Hutchins, E. (1991) 'Organizing work by adaptation', *Organization Science*, 2: 14–39.

ICSA (1997) *A Guide to the Retention of Documents*, Institute of Chartered Secretaries and Administrators, 16 Park Crescent, London W1N 4AH, 0171 580 4741; www.icsa.org.uk/icsa

IIA (1998) IIA Today, June 1998; www.mrsciacfe.cjb.net

Impeachment Report (1974) *The Impeachment Report*, New York, Signet.

ISACA (2000) www.isaca.org

ITU (1999) Statistics published by the International Telecommunication Union, for 1998; www.itu.int

Iyer, N. (1996) 'SAP – Control and fraud prevention strategies', Compsec Conference on Computer Security, Audit and Control (London), Oxford, Elsevier, 393–9.

Jacob, R. (1999) 'Asian Centres jostle for supremacy in e-commerce battle', *Financial Times*, 23 March: 6.

Jacobs, A. (1999) 'Configuration Management', Technical Briefing of the BCS Computer Audit Specialist Group, London, January.

Jacobs, J. (1992) *Systems of Survival*, London, Hodder & Stoughton.

Judge, P. (1988) 'Open Systems', *Computer Weekly Publications*.

Judge, P. (1991) *Guide to IT Standards Makers*, Isleworth, England, Technology Appraisals.

Kaufman, C., Perlman, R. and Speciner, M. (1995) *Network Security*, Englewood Cliffs, NJ, Prentice Hall.

Keen, P. (1991) *Shaping the Future: Business Design through Information Technology*, Boston, Mass., Harvard Business School Press.

Keen, P. (1993) 'Information technology and the management difference: A fusion map', *IBM Systems Journal*, Vol. 32, 1: 17–37.

Keeney, R. and Raiffa, H. (1976) *Decisions with multiple objects: Preferences and value tradeoffs*, Chichester, England, Wiley.

Keil, M. (1995) 'Pulling the plug: Software project management and the problem of project escalation', *MIS Quarterly*, 19, 4, December: 421–48.

Kelly, A. (1984) 'Italian bank mores', in Donaldson, T. (ed.), *Case Studies in Business Ethics*, Englewood Cliffs, NJ, Prentice-Hall.

Kelman, S. (1995) 'Cost-benefit analysis: An ethical critique', in Hoffman, W. and Frederick, R. (eds) (1995) *Business Ethics*, New York, McGraw-Hill.

Knight, R. and Pretty, D. (1997) 'The Impact of Catastrophes on Shareholder Value', Oxford Executive Research Briefing, Templeton College, Oxford.

Knox, J. (1994) 'Why Auditors don't find fraud', *Accountancy*, February: 28.

Koops, B-J, (2000) cwis.kub.nl/~frw/people/koops/bertjaap.htm

Kovacich, G. (1997) 'The ISSO must understand the business and management environment', *Computers and Security*, 16: 321–6.

Krull, A. (1995) 'Marketing information systems audit', Compsec Computer Security Audit and Control Conference (London), Oxford, Elsevier, 417–20.

Lacity, M. and Hirschheim, R. (1993) *Information Systems Outsourcing*, Wiley.

Lacity, M. and Hirschheim, R. (1995) *Beyond the Information Systems Outsourcing Bandwagon*, Chichester, England, Wiley.

Lambeth, J. (1999) 'SET still too problematic for general Net uptake', *Network News*, 27 October: 12.

Latham, R. (ed) (1987) *The Shorter Pepys*, London, Penguin Books.

Law Commission (1999) Consultation Paper No. 155, 'Fraud and Deception', London.

Leeming, P. (1995) Paper at: A Question of Confidence (conference organised by the Data Protection Registrar), Manchester, UMIST.

Leveson, N. (1995) *Safeware: System Safety and Computers*, Reading, Mass., Addison-Wesley: Appendix A.

Lindop, N. (1978) *Report of the Committee on Data Protection* (chaired by Sir Norman Lindop), Cmnd 7341, London, HMSO.

LJL (2000) LJL Enterprises Inc.; www.ljl.com

Lynch, D. and Lundquist, L. (1996) *Digital Money*, New York, Wiley.

Marakas, G. and Hornik, S. (1996) 'Passive resistance misuse: overt support and covert recalcitrance in IS implementation', *European Journal of Information Systems*, 5: 208–19.

Marcella, A. (1995) *Outsourcing, Downsizing and Reengineering: Internal Control Implications*. Institute of Internal Auditors, Florida.

Margetts, H. and Willcocks, L. (1993) 'Information technology in public services: disaster faster?' *Public Money and Management*, 13, 2: 49–56.

Marschak, J. (1968) 'Economics of inquiring, communicating, deciding', *American Economic Review*, 58, 2: 1–18.

Massachusetts (1999) Civil Action 99-10015-MBD, District of Massachusetts, February 1999; www.bna.com/e-law

Mayer, C. (1995) 'The regulation of financial services', in Bishop, M., Kay, J. and Mayer, C. (eds), *The Regulatory Challenge*, Oxford, Oxford University Press.

McCarthy, J. (1994) 'The state-of-the-art of CSCW: CSCW systems, cooperative work and organization', *Journal of Information Technology*, 9, 2: 73–83.

McGothlin, W. (1956) 'Stability of choices among uncertain alternatives', *American Journal of Psychology*, 69: 604–15.

McKersie, R. and Walton, R. (1991) 'Organisational Change', in Scott Morton, M. (ed.), *The Corporation of the 1990s*, Oxford, Oxford University Press.

McKinnon, S. and Bruns, W. (1992) *The Information Mosaic*, Boston, Mass., Harvard Business School Press.

Meiklejohn, I. (1989) 'CIO's search for a role', *Management Today*, London, September: 137–8.

Menkus, B. (1994) 'The New Importance of "Business Continuity" in Data Processing Disaster Recovery Planning', *Computers and Security*, 13, 2: 115–18.

Meyer, C. (1995) 'Crypto System Initialisation: Simplifying the Distribution of Initial Keys', Compsec 95, Elsevier: 140–66.

Michael, J. (1994) *Privacy and Human Rights: An International and Comparative Study*, with special reference to developments in Information Technology, Aldershot, England, UNESCO.

Middlemiss, J. (1998) 'Canadian Mergers claim massive customer base', *Wall Street and Technology*, July, 16, 7: 74–8.

Miller, A. (1971) *The Assault on Privacy: Computers, Data Banks, and Dossiers*, Ann Arbor, Mich., University of Michigan Press.

Mitchell, J. (1995) 'Value Added System Development Auditing', Compsec Conference on Computer Security, Audit and Control (London), Oxford, Elsevier, 205–23.

MMC (1989) *Monopolies & Mergers Commission, Credit Card Services*, London, HMSO.

Moizer, P. (1991) 'Performance appraisal and rewards', in Ashton, D. *et al.* (eds), *Issues in Management Accounting*, Englewood Cliffs, NJ, Prentice Hall.

Mondex (2000) www.mondex.com

Monk, P. (1993) 'The economic significance of infrastructural IT systems', *Journal of Information Technology*, 8: 14–21.

Moscove, S. and Simkin, M. (1987) *Accounting Information Systems*, New York, Wiley.

Moses, R. (1992) 'Risk analysis and management', in Jackson, K. and Hruska, J. (eds) *Computer Security Reference Book*, Oxford, Butterworth-Heinemann, 227–63.

Mulhall, T. (1995) 'Dial-Thru fraud: the ramification for a business', Compsec Conference on Computer Security, Audit and Control (London), Oxford, Elsevier, 296–302.

Mumford, E. (1995) 'Review of Hammer and Champy, *Reengineering the Corporation: A Manifesto for Business Revolution*', *European Journal of Information Systems*, 4: 116–17.

NASA (1993) *Automated Information Security Program, Security Risk Management Guideline, 101(e)*; www.nasirc.nasa.gov

Nelms, C. (1999) 'Internet e-mail risks and concerns', *Computers and Security*, 18: 409–18.

Neumann, P. (1995) *Computer-Related Risks*, Reading, Mass., Addison-Wesley.

News (2000) News report of the conviction of Dr H Shipman, *Daily Telegraph*, 1 February: 3.

Newton, J. and Pattison, R. (1998) 'The business implications of wide-spread disasters', *Journal of Business Continuity*, July.

Orlikowski, W. (1996) Organizational Change around Groupware Technology, in Ciborra, C. (ed.), *Groupware and Teamwork*, Wiley: 55.

Parker, D. (1992) 'Computer crime', in Jackson and Hruska (eds), *Computer Security Reference Book*, Oxford, Butterworth-Heinemann.

Partridge, C. (1994) 'The dream machine', *Computing*, 24 November: 30; see also www.national-lottery.co.uk

Picard, M. (1994) 'Working under an electronic thumb', *Training*, February: 47–51.

Power, M. (1997) *The Audit Society*, Oxford, Oxford University Press.

Purcell, L. (1993) 'Exploring IT's cultural ties', *Insurance and Technology*, 18, 7.

Rawls, J. (1999) (ed. Freeman), *John Rawls: Collected Papers*, Cambridge, Mass., Harvard University Press.

Raymond, L., Pare, G. and Bergeron, F. (1995) 'Matching information technology and organizational structure: an empirical study with implications for performance', *European Journal of Information Systems*, 4: 3–16.

Rolls Royce (1996) 'Notice of Annual General Meeting', Rolls Royce plc.

Rothenberg, J. (1995) 'Ensuring the longevity of digital documents', *Scientific American*, January 24–9.

RSA (2000) www.rsa.com/rsalabs

Russell, D. and Gangemi, G. (1991) Computer Security Basics, Sebastopol, Ca., O'Reilly, chapter 10.

Saffady, W. (1993) 'Electronic Document Imaging Systems', Meckler, London, p. 118.

Sambamurthy, V. and Zmud, R. (1999) 'Arrangements for information technology governance: a theory of multiple contingencies', *MIS Quarterly*, Vol. 23, 2, June: 261–90.

Savarnejad, A. (1997) 'How secure are your messages?', *Communications International*, June: 78.

Schifreen, R. (1999) 'IE5 – A Necessary Evil', *Secure Computing*, West Coast Publishing, May: 24.

Schneier, B. (1996) *Applied Cryptography*, Chichester, England, Wiley.

Schneier, B. (1998) 'The Crypto Bomb is ticking', *Byte*, May: 97–102.

Schweitzer, J. (1996) *Protecting Business Information*, Boston, Mass., Butterworth-Heinemann.

Scott Morton, M. (ed.) (1991) *The Corporation of the 1990's*, Oxford, Oxford University Press.

Sherer, M. and Kent, D. (1983) Auditing and Accountability, London, Paul Chapman Publishing, 1983, p. 16.

Sherwood, J. (1992) 'Contingency planning', in Jackson, K. and Hruska, J. (eds), *Computer Security Reference Book*, Oxford, Butterworth-Heinemann.

Sia, S. and Boon, N. (1996) 'The impacts of business process re-engineering on organizational controls', *International Journal of Project Management*, 14, 6: 341–8.

Siebert, B. (1996) Presentation to the Openness Advisory Panel of the US Secretary of Energy Advisory Board, July 24; www.osti.gov/html/osti/opennet/document/oap1.html

Sieghart, P. (1976) *Privacy and Computers*, London, Latimer Press.

Silicon (1999) 'Alibris admits to spying on Amazon emails', www.silicon.com, 25 November.

Simons, B. (1998) 'Outlawing technology', *Communications of the ACM*, 41, 10: 17–8.

Spiram, R. S. and Sumners, G. E. (1992) 'Understanding concurrent audit techniques', *EDP Audit, Control, and Security Newsletter*, 20, 1, July 1992.

Sproull, L. and Kiesler, S. (1992) *Connections, New Ways of Working in the Networked Organization*, Cambridge, Mass., MIT Press.

State of California (1995) *Automated Risk Analysis Tool Evaluation* (Employment Development Department), October.

Stebbins, M., Sena, J. and Shani, A. (1995) 'Information technology and organization design', *Journal of Information Technology*, 10: 101–13.

Steffens, J. (1994) *Newgames: Strategic Competition in the PC Revolution*, Oxford, Pergamon.

Sullivan, J. *et al.* (1985) *Montgomery's Auditing*, 10th edition, Chichester, England, Wiley.

Taxes Management Act 1970, UK, section 36.

Thoreau, H. (1910) *Walden*, London, Dent, 45.

Toigo, J. (1996) *Disaster Recovery Planning*, New York, Wiley.

Truste (2000) www.truste.org

Tucker, M. (1997) 'EDI and the Net: A profitable partnering', *Datamation*, April.

UK Accounts, 1991, *Appropriation Accounts 1989–90*, Vol. 2 Class 2, London, HMSO.

US Law (1971) Fair Credit Reporting Act (amended in 1996, 1997 and 1998).

US Law (1974) Privacy Act.

Valentine, D. (1998) 'About Privacy: Protecting the Consumer on the Global Information Infrastructure', Yale Symposium on Law and Technology.

Venables, J. and Impey, K. (1991) *Internal Audit*, London, Butterworths.

Wallich, P. (1991) 'How to steal millions in chump change', *Scientific American*, August: 21; www.labmed.umn.edu/~john

Walton, R. (1989) *Up and running: Integrating information technology and the organisation*, Boston, Mass., Harvard Business School Press.

Ward, M. (1998) 'The light programme', *New Scientist*, 30 May: 4.

Warner, M. and Stone, M. (1970) *The Data Bank Society*, London, Allen & Unwin.

Watergate Hearings (1973) Bantam (see: Memorandum on the IRS, page 770), New York.

Wayner, P. (1999) 'Digital timestamps: Punching and electronic clock', *New York Times*, 10 January.

Westcott, B. and Hawker, A. (1994) *Under New Management*, London, Foundation for IT in Local Government.

Wilding, E. (1997) *Computer Evidence: A Forensic Investigations Handbook*, London, Sweet & Maxwell.

Williams, D. (1994) 'Automated Change Control across Multi-platform', UK Computer Measurement Group 9th Annual Conference: 229–34.

Williams, T. (1996) 'The Audit of Telephone Logs', *Journal of the British Computer Society Computer Audit Specialist Group*, 6, 5: 5–7.

Williamson, D. T. and Marcum, S. (1998) 'Taxpayer record retention requirements', *The Woman CPA*, April.

Wolnizer, P. (1995) 'Are audit committees red herrings?', *ABACUS*, Vol. 31, No. 1: 45–66.

Younger, K. (1972) Report of the Committee on Privacy, (chaired by Kenneth Younger), Cmnd 5012, London, HMSO.

Zimmerman, P. (1995) *The Official PGP User's Guide*, MIT Press, Cambridge, Mass.; www.nai.com

Index